Risk and Crisis Communication in Europe

AF872621

This timely volume offers an international and cross-disciplinary examination of risk and crisis communication theory and practice in Europe.

Placing the rapidly developing field of risk and crisis communication within the context of a Europe in flux – experiencing the amplification of the refugee crisis, Brexit, increasing terrorist attacks, a heightened awareness of the climate crisis, and the COVID-19 pandemic – a cross-continental team of experts explore these developments from a theoretical and practical standpoint. Drawing connections between culture, digital technology, identity, public health, politics, and industry, the analysis offers a multitude of perspectives from across the continent and provides ways ahead for the field of risk and crisis communication.

This exciting and innovative volume will interest scholars and students of risk and crisis communication, media studies, political communication, public relations, political studies, and international relations.

Audra Diers-Lawson is a Professor of Risk and Crisis Communication and Director of the PhD in Communication and Leadership at Kristiania University College. She wrote *Crisis Communication: Managing Stakeholder Relationships* and co-edited *Pandemic Communication.* She has collaborated with colleagues with the Asia Europe Foundation, WHO, and EU and currently serves as a member of the WHO Europe's Technical Advisory Group for Risk Communication, Community Engagement, and Infodemic Management.

Andreas Schwarz (PhD, TU Ilmenau, 2009) is senior researcher in risk and crisis communication at Technische Universität Ilmenau, Germany, is co-director of the International Research Group on Crisis Communication, and founding chair of the Crisis Communication Section of the European Communication Research and Education Association (ECREA), 2011–2018. Schwarz has received research grants to study risk communication of COVID-19, crisis communication of child protective services and nonprofit organizations, and perceptions of artificial intelligence or automated mobility. He is co-editor of the *Handbook of International Crisis Communication Research.*

Florian Meissner is Professor for Media Management and Journalism at Macromedia University of Applied Sciences. He serves as Chair of the Crisis Communication Section of ECREA. His research focuses on crisis and risk communication in both journalistic and social media. As one of the Principal Investigators in the research consortium "DigiFit", funded by the German Federal Government, he currently focuses on communication about digital security. He has practical work experience as a journalist for public broadcasters in Germany.

Silvia Ravazzani, PhD, is Associate Professor in Management at the Department of Business, Law, Economics and Consumer Behaviour at Università IULM in Italy. Her main research interests include crisis communication, social media, and employee communication. Other research areas relate to diversity management and inclusion, sustainability, and related discursive practices.

Routledge Research in Communication Studies

Internationalizing the Communication Curriculum
Edited by Paaige K Turner, Soumia Bardhan, Tracey Quigley Holden and Eddah M. Mutua

Innovation in Advertising and Branding Communication
Edited by Lluís Mas-Manchón

Free Speech and Hate Speech in the United States
The Limits of Toleration
Chris Demaske

Global Perspectives on NGO Communication for Social Change
Edited by Giuliana Source

Friendship and Technology
A Philosophical Approach to Computer Mediated Communication
Tiffany A. Petricini

Narratives in Public Communication
Edited by Fuyuan Shen & Heidi Hatfield Edwards

Organizing Eating
Communicating for Equity Across U.S. Food Systems
Edited by Sarah E. Dempsey

Risk and Crisis Communication During the COVID-19 Pandemic
Muddled Messages
Martin N. Ndlela

Risk and Crisis Communication in Europe
Towards Integrating Theory and Practice in Unstable and Turbulent Times
Edited by Audra Diers-Lawson, Andreas Schwarz, Florian Meissner and Silvia Ravazzani

Risk and Crisis Communication in Europe

Towards Integrating Theory and Practice in Unstable and Turbulent Times

Edited by
Audra Diers-Lawson, Andreas Schwarz, Florian Meissner and Silvia Ravazzani

Routledge
Taylor & Francis Group
NEW YORK AND LONDON

First published 2024
by Routledge
605 Third Avenue, New York, NY 10158

and by Routledge
4 Park Square, Milton Park, Abingdon, Oxon, OX14 4RN

Routledge is an imprint of the Taylor & Francis Group, an informa business

© 2024 selection and editorial matter, Audra Diers-Lawson, Andreas Schwarz, Florian Meissner, and Silvia Ravazzani; individual chapters, the contributors

The right of Audra Diers-Lawson, Andreas Schwarz, Florian Meissner, and Silvia Ravazzani to be identified as the authors of the editorial material, and of the authors for their individual chapters, has been asserted in accordance with sections 77 and 78 of the Copyright, Designs and Patents Act 1988.

With the exception of Chapter 5, no part of this book may be reprinted or reproduced or utilised in any form or by any electronic, mechanical, or other means, now known or hereafter invented, including photocopying and recording, or in any information storage or retrieval system, without permission in writing from the publishers.

Chapter 5 of this book is freely available as a downloadable Open Access PDF at http://www.taylorfrancis.com under a Creative Commons Attribution (CC-BY) 4.0 license.

Any third party material in this book is not included in the OA Creative Commons license, unless indicated otherwise in a credit line to the material. Please direct any permissions enquiries to the original rightsholder.

Trademark notice: Product or corporate names may be trademarks or registered trademarks, and are used only for identification and explanation without intent to infringe.

ISBN: 978-1-032-43713-2 (hbk)
ISBN: 978-1-032-45080-3 (pbk)
ISBN: 978-1-003-37529-6 (ebk)

DOI: 10.4324/ 9781003375296

Typeset in Times New Roman
by codeMantra

Contents

Contributors

Gregory Asmolov is a Lecturer at the Department of Digital Humanities, King's College London. His research interests include crisis-related digital innovation, digital disconnection, digital sovereignty, and participatory warfare. His recent publications include "The transformation of participatory warfare: The role of narratives in connective mobilization in the Russia–Ukraine war" in *Digital War Journal* (2022), and "Internet regulation and crisis-related resilience: From Covid-19 to existential risks" in *The Communication Review* (2022). He holds a PhD from the Media and Communications Department at the LSE.

Mark Badham, PhD, is Senior Lecturer in Public Relations at Leeds Business School. His research interests focus broadly around digital corporate communication and public relations, including issue and crisis communication in digital media-arenas and news media roles in mass communication processes. Prior to joining academia, Mark worked as a public relations professional for governments, politicians, corporations, and NGOs in Australia.

Monica Bîră is currently a senior lecturer at SNSPA, Romania teaching social media listening methods and techniques. Recently she has worked closely with agencies and companies developing media monitoring and social media listening tools and techniques in an approach that aims to bridge academic research and practices in the field of social media listening. Monica Bîră conducts research in areas of monitoring image in online environments and communication in cultural and creative industries.

Albena Björck is Associate Professor at the School of Management and Law, Zurich University of Applied Sciences (ZHAW). Her research activities lie in the areas of strategic management and communication in times of organizational transformation, crisis, and renewal in international firms and draw from cross-disciplinary and human-centered perspectives. She is member of the expert board of the Swiss Innovation Agency and a Program Chair of the Strategic Management Division at the European Academy of Management.

Prior to academia, Björck spent around 20 years in business practice and is currently a consultant and executive coach. She holds a PhD from the University of St. Gallen (Switzerland).

Christine Buse is a project researcher at Macromedia University of Applied Sciences. She studied Social Sciences and Political Communication at Heinrich Heine University Düsseldorf. Alongside her studies, she gained practical experience as a research assistant at the Institute for Communication and Media Studies at Heinrich Heine University Düsseldorf and at the Center for Advanced Internet Studies (CAIS) in Bochum.

Alfonsa Butera is Adjunct Professor in Corporate Communication at Università IULM in Italy and Head of Coordination and Researcher at the Centre for Employee Relations and Communication at the same institution. She is a freelance consultant in the field of corporate communication.

Corina Buzoianu is currently an associate professor at SNSPA, Romania, teaching crisis communication and qualitative research in the field of communication. In the last 11 years, Corina Buzoianu has been working in activities in the field of qualitative research in communication and crisis communication with both national and international teams. Her work includes research grants, publications, and international conferences. Before joining academia, Corina Buzoianu worked as a PR consultant and in-house brand and communication specialist.

Audra Diers-Lawson is a Professor of Risk and Crisis Communication, Director of the PhD in Communication and Leadership at Kristiania University College. She wrote Crisis Communication: Managing Stakeholder Relationships and co-edited Pandemic Communication. She has collaborated with colleagues with the Asia Europe Foundation, WHO, and EU and currently serves as a member of the WHO Europe's Technical Advisory Group for Risk Communication, Community Engagement, and Infodemic Management.

Ben Duncan (LLM, 1989, University of Edinburgh) is a senior risk communication and community engagement (RCCE) practitioner who worked on pandemic communication preparedness for nearly 18 years before COVID. His career has included working for the European Union as well as assignments for WHO across Europe, Asia, Africa, and the Americas. He was lead researcher and author of a compendium of case studies on good practice and lessons learned from across Europe and central Asia published by WHO in October 2022.

Mats Eriksson, PhD, is associate professor of media and communication studies and research leader for the Center for Crisis Communication (CCC) at Örebro University, Sweden. Eriksson's research mainly concerns strategic communication, as well as crisis, risk, and emergency communication. He is currently leading the ongoing Swedish research project Digital Urban Risk Communication (DURCOM) funded by the Swedish Civil Contingencies Agency (MSB).

Jesper Falkheimer is Professor at the Department of Strategic Communication in Lund University, Sweden, Honorary Professor at Hong Kong Polytechnic University and Adjunct Professor at Kristiania University College, Oslo. He is Editor-in-Chief for the *Journal of Communication Management*, has had management roles at Lund University for over a decade, and is also a senior advisor in practice. His research includes crisis and conflict communication, communication management, place branding, and social theories of communication.

Fabienne Farner is an accomplished BSc International Management alumna who dedicated her thesis to exploring the strategic crisis communication of the Swiss authorities. Currently, she is a strategic communication consultant and applies her knowledge to assist organizations in navigating challenging situations.

Maya Gadgil is a senior research associate at the ZHAW, School of Management and Law, Switzerland. She earned her master's degree in law at the University of Zurich. She is a regional Board Member of the national Swiss Marketing Association. Gadgil's research interests address challenges in business practice, and are focused around marketing, (crisis) communication, purpose, customer-centric ecosystems, and management of customer experiences, including intercultural and intergenerational aspects.

Marina Ghersetti is a Professor (retired) at the Department of Journalism, Media and Communication at the Department of JMG, University of Gothenburg, Sweden. She has conducted and participated in several research projects about news reporting of major events, crisis communication, and digital media. Her present research focuses on comparative studies of crisis communication in European countries, and studies of attitudes to, and use of, social media and online journalism among Swedish authorities, journalists, and the public when crises occur.

Gisela Gonçalves has a PhD in communication sciences and is an associate professor at the University of Beira Interior, where she directs the Master in Strategic Communication: Advertising and Public Relations. She is an integrated researcher in LabCom – Communication and Arts. Her current research interests are communication ethics, political public relations, political, and governmental communication. She is the vice president of the Portuguese Communication Sciences Association (Sopcom).

Stanisław Jędrzejewski is Professor in the Department of Social Science at Kozminski University in Warsaw and Graduate of Institute of Sociology and MBA at the University of Warsaw. He is also a former member and vice-chairman of European Broadcasters Union Radio Committee, Geneva (1995-2007). He has been a member of the board of the radio public broadcaster Polish Radio (1994-98), Polish Radio 1 Controller (2003–2005), Ex member of National Broadcasting Council – 2005, and Chairman of Supervisory Board of Polish Radio (2011–2014). He has worked in Communication and Society Research Centre at University of Minho, Braga, Portugal 2009–2011.

Bengt Johansson is a Professor in Journalism and Mass Communication at the Department of JMG, University of Gothenburg, Sweden. His research and teaching mainly focus on risk/crisis communication, with a special interest in citizen reactions during crises and is currently involved in three research projects on crisis communication and COVID-19. Another research area is political communication, where Johansson's work deals with political advertising, news media coverage of election campaigns, media effects, and political scandals.

Sofia Johansson is a PhD candidate at the Department of JMG, University of Gothenburg, Sweden. She holds a master's degree in Strategic Communication and a bachelor's degree in Development Studies, both from Lund University. Her research focuses on crisis communication from a citizen perspective. More specifically, she is interested in how individuals combine sources during a crisis and how that relates to various belief outcomes, such as belief in conspiracy theories and false information.

Sophie Johnson is a Principal Lecturer in Marketing at Nottingham Business School and a Course Leader for the BA Joint Honours Business Management and Marketing. Johnson's research focuses on the tipping point between value co-creation and co-destruction.

Janina Klingelhöfer holds a bachelor's degree in Media and Communication from the University of Passau and a master's degree in Corporate Communication from Aarhus University. In addition to her doctoral thesis on the scientific field of crisis communication, she works at the Bavarian Ministry of Health in the area of strategic communication and scientific dialog.

Carolin Köppel holds a bachelor's degree in Communication and Economics and a master's degree in International Public Relations from LMU Munich. In addition to her doctoral thesis on corporate crises and scandalization, she works as a strategic communications consultant at FGS Global with a focus on leadership positioning, corporate transactions, and transformations.

Krzysztof Kuźmicz is a media expert, journalist, media educator, researcher, university teacher, and a certified tutor. She is a research and teaching associate (assistant professor) in the Department of Social Sciences at Kozminski

University in Warsaw. She is also the Head of Studies in management and sociology in business and media, member of the Polish Society for Social Communication, the Polish Society for Educational Media and Technology, and President of the Board of the Quantum Institute for Social Analysis. Kuźmicz is expert, researcher, trainer in grants and projects of the National Research and Development Center.

Matias Lievonen, DSc (Econ.), works as a Senior Lecturer at the Jyväskylä University School of Business and Economics (JSBE), Finland. His research focuses on a broad spectrum of topics in the fields of digital corporate communication, public relations, strategic communication, and marketing. Dr. Lievonen has published research in peer-reviewed journals and books on various phenomena including negative engagement, stakeholder trust, and strategic ambiguity.

Carmen Daniela Maier, PhD, is Associate Professor at the School of Communication and Culture at Aarhus University in Denmark. Her research areas include organizational communication, CSR communication, knowledge communication, and multimodality. Her main research goal is the theoretical and methodological development of the multimodal discourse perspective upon organizational and CSR communication.

Alessandra Mazzei is Associate Professor in Management at the Department of Business, Law, Economics and Consumer Behaviour at Università IULM in Italy and Director of the Centre for Employee Relations and Communication. Her research interests include employee communication, engagement, voice; internal crisis communication; organizational communication.

Florian Meissner is Professor for Media Management and Journalism at Macromedia University of Applied Sciences. He serves as Chair of the Crisis Communication Section of ECREA. His research focuses on crisis and risk communication in both journalistic and social media. As one of the Principal Investigators in the research consortium "DigiFit", funded by the German Federal Government, he currently focuses on communication about digital security. He has practical work experience as a journalist for public broadcasters in Germany.

Valeriano Piñeiro-Naval has PhD in audiovisual communication, technological revolution, and cultural change from the University of Salamanca and a post-doctorate in communication sciences from the University of Beira Interior. He is currently an assistant professor at the Department of Sociology and Communication at the University of Salamanca, where he is also part of the Observatory for Audiovisual Contents. His main research lines are related to the study of culture, heritage, and tourism in the digital society and meta-research in communication.

Irene Pollach, PhD, is a Professor in the Department of Management at Aarhus University in Denmark. Her research focuses on organizational communication, particularly CSR communication, corporate financial communication, and communication after corporate failures. Another area of inquiry is the discursive interplay between news media and organizations.

Gavin Rae is the head of the Department of Social Sciences at Kozminski University in Warsaw. He has written extensively on Polish society and economy, as well as on topics related to Central and Eastern Europe. His main areas of interest include the welfare state, commodification, post-socialist transition, and the transformation of human capital. He has published two books: *Poland's Return to Capitalism. From the Socialist Bloc to the European Union* and *Public Capital. The Commodification of Poland's Return to Capitalism.*

Silvia Ravazzani, PhD, is Associate Professor in Management at the Department of Business, Law, Economics and Consumer Behaviour at Università IULM in Italy. Her main research interests include crisis communication, social media, and employee communication. Other research areas relate to diversity management and inclusion, sustainability, and related discursive practices.

Helge Renå is a postdoctoral researcher at the University of Bergen, Norway. He is currently working on a project on the Legal History of the Norwegian Police and Policing 1686 – 2016. Renå's doctoral dissertation (2019) concerned the police's response to the terrorist attacks in Oslo in 2011. Renå has published widely on related issues, such as crisis coordination in first responder organizations and the role of inquiry commission in crisis learning. In 2022, Renå published a highly acclaimed book in Norwegian about crisis management in organizations. The terrorist attacks in Oslo on July 22 are his core empirical examples.

Hogne Lerøy Sataøen is an Associate Professor in media and communication studies at Örebro University, and he holds a PhD in Sociology from the University of Bergen (2011). Sataøen is specialized in the field of strategic communication and public sector organizations. In recent years, he has been particularly interested in risk and crisis communication, as well as public organizations and branding. Sataøen has published in journals such as *International Journal of Strategic Communication*, *Corporate Communication: An International Journal*, *British Journal of Management*, *Public Management Review*, *Scandinavian Journal of Management*, and *Sociological Research Online*.

Andreas Schwarz (PhD, TU Ilmenau, 2009) is senior researcher in risk and crisis communication at Technische Universität Ilmenau, Germany, co-director of the International Research Group on Crisis Communication, and founding chair of the Crisis Communication Section of the European Communication Research and Education Association (ECREA), 2011-2018. Schwarz has received research grants to study risk communication of COVID-19, crisis communication of child protective services and nonprofit organizations, and perceptions of artificial intelligence or automated mobility. He is co-editor of the *Handbook of International Crisis Communication Research.*

Holger Sievert is Professor for Communication Management at Macromedia University of Applied Sciences. He also heads the Cologne Faculty for Culture, Media, Psychology as well as the National Research Committee of his institution. In addition to teaching, he has always been active in communication management functions including Roland Berger Strategy Consultants, the Bertelsmann Foundation, and a leading German communication agency. In research, he focuses on interactive, international, and internal communication. His studies at the Macromedia University were conducted for partners such as the German Foreign Office, The Federal Press Office, major agencies, several established protestant churches, and renowned companies like HUK Insurances, Payback, Porsche, TUI, UPS, or Vodafone.

Bianca Persici Toniolo is a PhD student in communication sciences at Lab-Com – Communication and Arts with a project funded (2020.05702.BD) by the Foundation for Science and Technology. Her research is focused on governmental crisis communication, supervised by professor Gisela Gonçalves.

Amalia Triantafillidou is an Associate Professor at the Department of Communication and Digital Media at the University of Western Macedonia, Greece. She holds a PhD in Marketing from Athens University of Economics and Business. She is the holder of Jean Monnet Chair on Risk and Crisis Communication in the EU (2022-2025). Her research interests focus on public relations, crisis communication, e-campaigning, e-government, crisis leadership. She has published in referred journals such as the *Journal of Contingencies and Crisis Management*, *Computers in Human Behavior*, *Public Relations Review*, etc. She teaches courses related to Public Relations, Crisis Communication, Integrated Corporate Communications, Corporate Branding, and Consumer Behaviour.

Chiara Valentini is Professor and Head of Corporate Communication, at Jyväskylä University School of Business and Economics (JSBE), Finland, and Adjunct Professor of Strategic Communication, at IULM University, Italy. Dr. Valentini is currently the Head of Scientific Committee at EUPRERA and is an advisory board of the Research Center in Strategic Communication, Italy. Former Chair of the Public Relations Division at the International Communication Association (ICA), she is a reviewer and editorial board member of several international journals and is active with several international professional organizations.

Prodromos Yannas is Professor of International Relations and Communication-Publicity in the Department of Business Administration at the University of West Attica, Greece. His research interests lie at the intersection of three areas: International Relations, Public Relations, and Political and Crisis Communication. His publications have appeared in refereed journals, books chapters, and international conference proceedings.

Hui Zhao (PhD) is postdoctoral researcher at the Department of Strategic Communication in Lund University, Sweden. Her research includes crisis communication, digital media, and social change. Her current project focuses on the problem of stigma and discrimination as challenges to social resilience in the context of public health crises.

Introduction

Silvia Ravazzani, Florian Meissner, Andreas Schwarz and Audra Diers-Lawson

Improving risk and crisis communication theory and practice matters more than ever. Global crises such as the COVID-19 pandemic, climate change, international conflict, and emerging technological risks related to, for instance, artificial intelligence and cybersecurity, mandate joint efforts to enhance how we manage crises and risks and how we communicate them. However, real progress cannot be made by looking at these issues from a singular national perspective. Instead, to tackle global challenges, an international outlook and cross-border collaboration are required (Beck, 2009). In the same vein, it is necessary for both scholars and practitioners of risk and crisis communication to share knowledge and join forces to help answer the many unanswered questions arising from the often interconnected, cross-border, and cascading crises of our time, with the goal of increasing the resilience of communities around the world.

This book seeks to contribute to the body of knowledge on risk and crisis communication at this crucial moment. It has two main goals: First, it addresses the ongoing challenge of translating academic work for practitioners, educators, and students to ensure that innovative theory and research is accessible to those who most need it. This way, the editors – and of course the authors who have graciously contributed to this book – aim to make a practical impact on risk and crisis communication and foster the dialog between researchers and practitioners. Second, the book honors the fact that Europe has emerged as a critical hub for the global development of theory and practice in risk and crisis communication. It provides case studies from across Europe to support teaching and practice and adds value by developing pan-European perspectives on risk and crisis communication to facilitate knowledge sharing across borders.

The European Context for Risk and Crisis Communication

While Europe is a relatively small continent, it consists of very diverse regions, countries, cultures, and historical experiences, making it a very interesting subject for comparative research. This is especially true if we look at the various crisis types the continent has been exposed to in recent years. For instance,

DOI: 10.4324/9781003375296-1

European countries have experienced the financial crisis and the Euro crisis, an amplification of the refugee crisis, political unrest and the rise of populism and disinformation, Brexit, increasing terrorist and cyber-attacks, a heightened awareness of the climate crisis including a variety of extreme weather events, environmental disasters, the COVID-19 pandemic, and, most recently, Russia's full-scale invasion of Ukraine. Each of these has not only impacted scholarship and practice but has also changed the contexts for considering risk and crisis communication in Europe across a variety of sectors (e.g., political, economic, social, environmental, public health, critical infrastructures, etc.).

In fact, the recent crises have created unique opportunities of providing new insights because many scholars from different countries and cultures have been able to study the same crisis simultaneously and comparatively. A key example for this is the COVID-19 pandemic (see, for instance, Croucher & Diers-Lawson, 2023; Schwarz et al., 2023), which is therefore also one of the key crisis themes of this book. This allowed for very diverse perspectives, illustrating different approaches to crisis management and communication in comparison and moreover showed how crisis responses play out under varying circumstances and over time. It also confirmed once again that how we perceive and deal with risks and crises is highly dependent on the cultural and political context that shapes our view of the world (Meissner, 2019). This is why the analysis of cross-border risk and crisis provides many opportunities to question our existing epistemologies and create progress in both theory and practice. The current era of global crises also means that scholars and practitioners are experiencing accelerated learning processes. It is therefore of utmost importance that we create spaces for reflection and sharing these experiences and insights. This book is intended to be a step in that direction.

The heightened attention for risk and crisis management and communication is also reflected by the increasing growth and institutionalization of the respective academic community in Europe. Europe has emerged as an important contributor to the global development of theory and practice in risk and crisis communication. For example, the International Association for Media and Communication Research (IAMCR) includes a working group for Crisis, Security and Conflict Communication since 2011 with 112 members in 2023 (IAMCR, 2023). However, the first international communication association to have a full permanent section of crisis communication was the European Communication Research and Education Association (ECREA). This section started as a working group in 2011 and counts 234 members by 2023. It hosts one of the two main risk and crisis communication conferences in the world that was started at Ilmenau University of Technology in Germany in 2009. The section includes members and sponsored events from Europe, Asia, Africa, and the Americas. Both the section and the conference series were an important platform to bridge the divide between crisis communication communities in the US, Europe, and – to some extent – Asia. It was also the place where the need for a journal of crisis communication was repeatedly discussed. Such a journal, the

Journal of International Crisis and Risk Communication Research (*JICRCR*), was launched in 2018 at the University of Central Florida with Timothy Sellnow as its first editor in-chief. One of the previous volume editors is co-editor of this book, and a significant number of the editorial board members are from Europe (e.g., Sweden, UK, Belgium, Germany, or Denmark) and/or members of ECREA's Crisis Communication section. While this development is hopeful, we still see a lack of integration between risk and crisis, not only in terms of theory, but also regarding the institutional academic reality. Risk communication as a field has started to become relevant in Europe in the 1980s, especially with the rise of nuclear power and large-scale accidents like Chernobyl in 1986 (Schwarz, 2016). Its development has been largely separated from crisis communication research since then. An example is the formation of the Society of Risk Analysis and its journal in the 1980s (Thompson et al., 2005), including a European chapter (founded in 1987) as well as a specialty group for risk communication in 1990 which "focuses on the communication of risk information between technical and lay audiences". The overlap between these scientific communities as well as risk and crisis communication as fields of empirical inquiry or theory development is still surprisingly thin.

However, the formation of these associations, journals, and conferences shows the significant impact of European scholars in the development of risk and crisis communication research, although the US keeps being the main source of publications and object of study. The field of risk and crisis communication emerged as a cohesive and distinctive area of study and practice, in the late 1990s and over the early 2000s has established itself as a growing field (Diers-Lawson, 2020). A literature review of crisis communication research in peer-reviewed journals – 690 articles from 1953 to 2015 – showed that after the US, Europe was the main source of research published in English language, mostly from the UK, Sweden, Netherlands, and Germany (Diers-Lawson, 2017). Another review of research on flood risks identified Europe as the most represented among the regions that were studied with countries like the Netherlands, Germany, the UK, Spain, and Switzerland (Kellens et al., 2013). Similarly, reviews of studies on social media use in emergency response to disasters (Muniz-Rodriguez et al., 2020), risk and crisis news coverage of COVID-19 (Schwarz et al., 2023), training in emergency risk communication (Miller et al., 2017), or social media use in risk and crisis communication (Rasmussen & Ihlen, 2017) revealed Europe as the second largest academic cluster in the field. However, it also shows that even within Europe, the Western bias still prevails since most research comes from or analyzes countries in Western or Northern Europe. Especially Eastern European research (published in English) is still scarce. Not only on global scale, but also within Europe there "is a lack of research focus on diverse populations (e.g., international, cultural, religious, and underserved)" (Miller et al., 2017, p. 16). In the context of global migration, climate change, and wars, Europe has become more diverse in terms of culture, languages, income, and economic development. This applies to populations within and across countries. While the lack of research attention to the Global South remains the major gap in risk and crisis communication, the lack of consideration of inner-European diversity in the context of public health crises, disasters, terrorism threats, climate change risks, or armed conflicts needs to be addressed by both European scholars and practitioners. This book contributes in two respects: First, the chapters report on research from multiple regions in Southern (e.g., Greece), Western (e.g., UK), Central (e.g., Germany), Northern (e.g., Norway), and Eastern Europe (e.g., Romania). Second, some of that research, conceptually and/or empirically intends to shed light on the role of multicultural or immigrant communities within European countries. The chapter by Björck and Farner, for example, addresses cultural and linguistic diversity Switzerland and its relevance for governmental responses to COVID-19. The chapter by Johansson et al. on migrant communities in Sweden during COVID-19 analyzes panel data from migrant-dense Swedish suburbs to identify information seeking patterns during COVID-19.

The turbulent and ever-changing landscape has pushed European-based scholars to deeply rethink and rejuvenate the scope and approaches of risk and crisis communication, also to positively impact practice and society at large. One of the critical goals of this book is in fact to make innovative research insights relevant and accessible to practitioners and non-academic audiences. Such a need for convergence and cross-fertilization of research and practice is widely felt in the scholarly community. For example, Nicolai et al. (2011) elaborate on the "rigor-relevance gap" (p. 53) in management science and highlight the lack of practical relevance in research due to the different worldviews of academics and practitioners. Other scholars advocate for more "engaged scholarship" (e.g., Van De Ven & Johnson, 2006) to break down the insular behaviors of academics. This preoccupation concerns the risk and crisis communication research community too, where one of the main challenges remains bridging the gap between academia and industry (Manias-Muñoz et al., 2019). Claeys and Opgenhaffen (2016) explicitly address the "scholar-practitioner divide" (p. 233) in crisis communication research. Their review reveals that a limited number of studies so far have examined the scholar-practitioner divide in crisis communication, and that the best practice recommendations and guidelines emerging from research evidence are scarcely applied in actual practice. They identify the roots of this gap as twofold: the "lost-in-translation gap", consisting in the inadequate conversion of academic research into publications, frameworks, methods, and tools that practitioners can employ in their daily work; and the "lost-before translation gap", related to the ineffective selection of research problems and topics where practically academic studies appear short of managerial relevance. Even in the context of COVID-19, analyses of news media content about the pandemic around the world included only few relevant implications for risk, crisis, and health communication practices of governments, health agencies, or recommendations to citizens (Schwarz et al., 2023). Recent scholarly books (Coombs

& Holladay, 2022; Jin & Austin, 2022; Schwarz et al., in preparation), however, have tried to address these gaps by stressing among their explicit goals the intent to provide useful and meaningful insights for risk and crisis communication practice and by including more practitioners as contributors.

This book addresses this emerging wake-up call for closing the research-practice gap, keeping in mind that "scholars cannot produce relevant knowledge prior to application; practice should make scientific knowledge relevant" (Claeys & Opgenhaffen, 2016, p. 233). It does so by incorporating concrete experiences and case illustrations addressing the wide range of European-based issues that have gained recent relevance in risk and crisis communication practice, and by offering practical take-aways and managerial tools intended to inspire risk and crisis communication practice. Among the practical themes emerging in risk and crisis communication research in Europe, the readers of this book will become knowledgeable about numerous crisis arenas (e.g., public health, environment, business/corporate crises, disasters, terrorist attacks, immigration, social collective action) and practice areas (e.g., risk preparedness, CSR and stakeholder communication, employee communication, political/government communication, digital mobilization, academic training).

Preview of the Chapters in This Volume

Risk and Crisis Communication in Europe: Towards Integrating Theory and Practice in Unstable and Turbulent Times draws on both the emerging state of research and theory building in risk and crisis communication as well as the lessons learned as we move beyond the COVID-19 pandemic to consider how our field has evolved and needs to continue to evolve. We, therefore, suggest this book provides a critical bridge connecting practical experience or application and the importance of theory building and evidence-informed decision-making. In this way, the volume is aligned with both the EU and WHO-European approaches to research-informed decision-making (see, e.g., Jacob, et al., 2023; WHO, 2022).

Part 1: An Evolving Field – Risk and Crisis Communication in Europe

One of the core strengths in the field's evolution to combine risk and crisis communication is that research is better aligned with practice. Risk communication is a well-established area of research with roots in risk assessment in the physical and biological sciences and risk management (see e.g., Freundberg, 1988) with authors like Sellnow and Seeger (2001) arguing two decades ago that the boundaries of crisis communication needed to be expanded to explicitly include risk as a part of crisis. However, as we note, the merger of risk and crisis communication has taken time to develop.

Part 1 of this book, however, reflects how European scholars have embraced this merger and emphasizes preparedness, resilience, and the multi-disciplinary nature of applied risk and crisis communication. For example, Eriksson's chapter provides an innovative model for the practice of preparedness in pre-crisis and pre-disaster phases. Björck and Gadgil's chapter then builds on the importance of pre-crisis preparation by focusing on how business practice merge crisis preparation and strategic planning. This chapter critically reflects on practitioner's drivers of strategic planning for crises, the role of organizational culture, and the importance of top management decision-making.

Evolutions in our understanding of risk and crisis planning, however, represent the start of the theoretical and practical contributions in Part 1. Sataøen and Renå's chapter exploring information sharing and collective sensemaking during unexpected and incomprehensible sudden events, like terrorism, provides an important contribution for both crisis planning and crisis communication by highlighting the role of power and culture in information sharing. This chapter as well as Triantafillidou and Yannas' chapter also remind readers that when we are talking about crises, we must think beyond the organization and to the stakeholders affected by crises. Triantafillidou and Yannas propose a framework for compassion and care in crisis and disaster response and recovery that is most directly applicable to disasters, which are seemingly ever growing in frequency and impact, but also applicable to other types of crises that affect populations.

As Part 1 moves from developing organizational capacity to actively considering those affected by crises, Asmolov's chapter provides readers with a rich exploration of the increasingly complex nature of crisis in Europe. This 'double chapter' challenges the reader to consider the concept of resilience arguing that instead of experiencing individual crises our societies are often subject to multiple crises and that understanding crisis-to-crisis transitions, emergent digital platforms and networks is vital. Thus, Asmolov theorizes about how all of this can contribute to building future crisis capacity at social and organizational levels. Considering *how* to build crisis resilience, especially in digital contexts, is a topic that Buzoianu and Bîră tackle directly by providing a framework for crisis simulation in social media to strengthen crisis preparedness.

Finally, the first six chapters in the volume discuss different European contexts (e.g., Swiss, Norwegian, Ukrainian, and Romanian), and the next three chapters focus on both crisis prone industries and specific case studies that scholars, students, and practitioners in Europe can learn from. For example, both Köppel and Klingelhöfer's as well as Ravazzani, Mailer, and Pollach's chapters address the airline industry – one that is crisis prone and the center of debates around climate change. Köppel and Klingelhöfer offer the case of how the German aviation industry manages multi-crises when multiple organizations and stakeholders are involved. Ravazzani et al.'s chapter tackles a relatively new phenomenon, which is connected to increasing European concern about climate change – flight shame – and how affected companies respond to it. The final case study chapter also tackles a crisis-prone industry, but one that is seldom considered in risk and crisis communication literature – the fashion industry.

Johnson's chapter provides an innovative analysis of the UK's Arcadia fashion retail group by combining a stakeholder perspective with the branding concept of value co-creation to explain failures in the company's response to the many crises that ultimately led to the company's demise.

Part 2: Lessons Learned from COVID-19 for Risk and Crisis Communication in Europe

In part 1, the chapters represent strong innovative, novel, and theoretically rich research designed to bridge the scholarship and practice divide. We suggest these chapters provide good examples of the kind of research emerging within the European risk and crisis communication community. In part 2, the chapters look ahead from the COVID-19 pandemic to try to better understand the lessons that have been learned. These chapters are not just a description of COVID-19 experiences; rather, they reflect that, as a societal level-crisis, the pandemic not only has changed our realities but it has also highlighted many different risk and crisis communication shortcomings in theory and practice.

Thus, the second of our 'double-chapters' Diers-Lawson's chapter on translating research to practice provides a pan-European summary of scientific and professional reports on emergent best practices in pandemic communication that places the role of communication as central to preserving life during major disasters and health emergencies. Zhao and Falkheimer's chapter builds on the lessons learned by highlighting findings of communication inequality across different ethnic groups during the pandemic. This finding is directly tied to what has been broadly recognized as a critical failing in risk and crisis communication – reaching out to minority and vulnerable communities. By focusing on migrant-dense communities also in Sweden, Johansson and Ghersetti's research provides insights on pandemic fatigue. Their chapter demonstrates how information seeking changes over time and by information seeking type, requiring different communication strategies to be enacted because a one-size approach is simply ineffective. Each of these chapters provides critical insights for practitioners, but Duncan's chapter provides an applied research reflection on the practitioner experience during COVID-19. He argues for the importance of more systematic engagement between practitioners and scholars to improve evidence-led risk communication and community engagement.

Part 2 begins by considering what is needed in crisis response during major national and cross-border crises, like the COVID-19 pandemic. Several chapters focus on case studies to draw out emergent themes in different national and cross-national contexts. For example, Björck and Farner's case study of the complex linguistic and cultural context for risk and crisis communication in Switzerland highlights the strategic considerations needed to manage crises at regional and national levels. Lievonen, Valentini, and Badlam's chapter focuses on a Finnish context to explore the benefits and drawbacks of using strategic ambiguity providing specific guidance for communication professionals rather than more general conclusions about government communication. Jędrzejewski, Kuźmicz, and Rae use a cross-national case comparison between Poland and the UK to critically reflect on the media's coverage of remote working and distance learning to frame those topics for their populations and consider the media's impact on the experience of populations during societal level crises. Finally, Gonçalves, Piñeiro-Naval, and Toniolo's chapter on COVID-19 communication in Portugal emphasizes the convergence of the media, government, and health care professionals during major health emergencies. Though we live in a highly mediated world with online sources growing in importance, these data demonstrate that during the pandemic most Portuguese still relied on television as their primary source for pandemic information. Yet, media sources are not necessarily trusted; Gonçalves, et al. found that experts – including health care professionals – were viewed as the most reliable sources. Their findings also suggest that those people who rely on news media are also more likely to trust the government's pandemic response. Taken together these case insights complement the findings from Diers-Lawson's pan-European research, but provide rich illustrations of the best practices and theory development.

Finally, the chapters in Part 2 also highlight the interconnectedness of experience during major disasters and health emergencies. For example, while most of the research on the pandemic focuses on government and health response, Buse, Meissner, and Sievert's chapter reminds us that during any major disaster or health emergency corporate actors still have an active role to play. Their chapter highlights the importance of socially responsible behavior from companies as well as the corporate public relations opportunities and challenges during such crises. Certainly, a meaningful part of being socially responsible – particularly during major crises – is how an organization treats its employees. Therefore, Ravazzani, Mazzei, and Butera's chapter exploring internal crisis communication in Italy in 2020 and 2021 provides an important set of insights into the growing complexity of work in a post-pandemic 'next normal' environment where we can expect more hybrid work, different employee inclusion stances, and fast-paced change.

Together, the chapters in this volume not only reflect how the field of risk and crisis communication is changing but demonstrate the strength, depth, and innovative research and theory building taking place in Europe. More than that, these chapters also reflect a strong connection between scholarly research and practice in public health, policymaking, and corporate contexts.

References

Beck, U. (2009). *World at risk*. Polity Press.

Claeys, A.-S., & Opgenhaffen, M. (2016). Why practitioners do (not) apply crisis communication theory in practice. *Journal of Public Relations Research*, *28*(5–6), 232–247, https://doi.org/10.1080/1062726X.2016.1261703.

Coombs, W. T., & Holladay, S. J. (2022). *The Handbook of Crisis Communication* (2nd ed.). Wiley-Blackwell Publishing.
Croucher, S. M. & Diers-Lawson, A. (Eds.) (2023). *Pandemic Communication*. Routledge.
Diers-Lawson, A. (2020). *Crisis Communication: Managing Stakeholder Relationships*. Routledge.
Diers-Lawson, A. (2017). A state of emergency in crisis communication an intercultural crisis communication research agenda. *Journal of Intercultural Communication Research*, *46*(1), 1–54. https://doi.org/10.1080/17475759.2016.1262891
Freundberg, W. R. (1988). Perceived risk, real risk: Social science and the art of probabilistic risk assessment. *Science*, *242*, 44–49.
IAMCR. (2023). Crisis, security and conflict communication working group. https://iamcr.org/s-wg/working-group/cri
Jacob, C., Hausemer, P., Zagoni-Bogsch, A., & Diers-Lawson, A. (2023). *The effect of communication and disinformation during the Covid-19 pandemic* (Special Committee on the COVID-19 pandemic: Lessons learned and recommendations for the future, Issue. E. Parliament. http://www.europarl.europa.eu/supporting-analyses
Jin, Y., & Austin, L. (2022). *Social Media and Crisis Communication* (2nd Edition). Routledge.
Kellens, W., Terpstra, T., & De Maeyer, P. (2013). Perception and communication of flood risks: A systematic review of empirical research. *Risk Analysis*, *33*(1), 24–49. https://doi.org/10.1111/j.1539-6924.2012.01844.x
Manias-Muñoz, I., Jin, Y., & Reber, B. H. (2019). The state of crisis communication research and education through the lens of crisis scholars: An international Delphi study. *Public Relations Review*, *45*(4), 101797.
Meissner, F. (2019). The Fukushima disaster and the "Clash of Risk Cultures": Japanese and German journalists' perceptions of a nuclear crisis. *Global Media Journal*, *9*(2), 1–23. https://doi.org/10.22032/dbt.40623
Miller, A. N., Sellnow, T., Neuberger, L., Todd, A., Freihaut, R., Noyes, J., Allen, T., Alexander, N., Vanderford, M., & Gamhewage, G. (2017). A systematic review of literature on effectiveness of training in emergency risk communication. *Journal of Health Communication*, *22*(7), 612–629. https://doi.org/10.1080/10810730.2017.1338802
Muniz-Rodriguez, K., Ofori, S. K., Bayliss, L. C., Schwind, J. S., Diallo, K., Liu, M., Yin, J., Chowell, G., & Fung, I. C.-H. (2020). Social media use in emergency response to natural disasters: A systematic review with a public health perspective. *Disaster Medicine and Public Health Preparedness*, *14*(1), 139–149. https://doi.org/10.1017/dmp.2020.3
Nicolai, A. T., Schultz, A.-C., & Göbel, M. (2011). Between sweet harmony and a clash of cultures: Does a joint academic-practitioner review reconcile rigor and relevance? *The Journal of Applied Behavioral Science*, *47*(1), 53–75. https://doi.org/10.1177/0021886310390866
Rasmussen, J., & Ihlen, Ø. (2017). Risk, crisis, and social media: A systematic review of seven years' research. *Nordicom Review*, *38*(2), 1–17. https://doi.org/10.1515/nor-2017-0393
Schwarz, A. (2016). Crisis communication research in Germany. In A. Schwarz, M. Seeger, & C. Auer (Eds.), *The handbook of international crisis communication research* (pp. 357–372). Wiley Blackwell. https://doi.org/10.1002/9781118516812.ch33

Schwarz, A., Alpers, F., Wagner-Olfermann, E., & Diers-Lawson, A. (2023). The global study of COVID news: Scope, findings, and implications of quantitative content analyses of the COVID-19 news coverage in the first two years of the pandemic. *Health Communication*, 1–14. https://doi.org/10.1080/10410236.2023.2226932

Schwarz, A., Seeger, M. W., & Kim, S. (Eds.). (in preparation). *The handbook of international crisis and risk communication research* (2nd ed.). Wiley Blackwell.

Sellnow, T. L., & Seeger, M. (2001). Exploring the boundaries of crisis communication: The case of the 1997 Red River Valley flood. *Communication Studies*, *52*(2), 153–168.

Thompson, K. M., Deisler Jr, P. F., & Schwing, R. C. (2005). Interdisciplinary vision: The first 25 years of the Society for Risk Analysis (SRA), 1980–2005. *Risk Analysis*, *25*(6), 1333–1386. https://doi.org/10.1111/j.1539-6924.2005.00702.x

Van De Ven, A. H., & Johnson, P. E. (2006). Knowledge for theory and practice. *The Academy of Management Review*, *31*(4), 802–821. https://doi.org/10.2307/20159252

WHO. (2022). *Risk communication and community engagement for COVID-19 vaccination: Implementation Tool*. https://www.who.int/europe/publications/i/item/WHO-EURO-2022-2756-42514-59053

Part 1

An Evolving Field – Risk and Crisis Communication in Europe

1 A Multi-motive Risk Communication Model for "Making" Crisis Preparedness

Mats Eriksson

Several countries in Europe today, as well as the United States, are highly committed to creating a "culture of preparedness" and/or "culture of resilience," which includes making individuals and communities well prepared to cope with future risks, crises, and catastrophes (Kapucu, 2008). The high political priority of civil preparedness and resilience issues is presently visible in the European Union's substantial investments in disaster risk reduction and in its disaster education guidelines (Benadusi, 2014). In the wake of the political precedence of crisis preparedness, several risk communication initiatives are ongoing in European municipalities (Appleby-Arnold et al., 2021; Cornia et al., 2016; Petridou et al., 2019). Nevertheless, the research community does not fully agree on how practitioners working in public authorities and local municipalities can best use risk communication to contribute to citizen and community preparedness.

This chapter combines existing theories and knowledge from several and sometimes competing fields of risk communication and preparedness research (e.g., within psychology, sociology, political science, health science, communication and public relations, social marketing, and other areas) into a basic risk communication model for crisis preparedness. The primary aim of the model is to support practitioners, such as communication managers/officers, risk, and safety managers and crisis managers, who need to "understand" and "use" multidisciplinary risk communication, public relations, and preparedness and disaster research and theory in a pragmatic way to create a reflective and holistic understanding of their own ongoing or future "practice." The proposed model especially aims to support reflections on possible multi-motive path choices in risk communication work for crisis preparedness. From a pragmatic and practitioner-oriented viewpoint, multiple paths, or a combination of individual paths, can potentially lead to the same final goal (for instance, a higher level of crisis preparedness and readiness). The word "model" is used here in the scientific sense, as referring to a simplified representation of reality. All models are "false" in so far as no representation can capture reality perfectly, but without pragmatic models of this kind, it is hard to develop a reflexive understanding of possible choices in a complex risk and preparedness communication practice.

DOI: 10.4324/9781003375296-3

The "Core" of the Model: Five Path Choices and Basic Motives Underlying Risk Communication for Crisis Preparedness

Five tentative basic motives and path choices concerning risk communication for "making" crisis preparedness are briefly presented in the following. All of them have been carefully chiseled out from the extensive body of communication-related research in different disciplines concerning the "making" of preparedness through communication, under the influence of cognitive, social, or cultural theory. The paths, in turn, represent different basic motives, practices and techniques applied to risk communication for preparedness, which are also briefly presented (Figure 1.1).

The communication practices and techniques associated with the different suggested paths can be characterized as more or less monologic or dialogic, a classical distinction that is common in both international risk communication and public relations research (Fisher, 1991; Grunig, 1984). The monologic landscape, briefly put, involves one-way linear transmission of risk information to raise awareness, educate, and persuade the public concerning preparedness behavior. The dialogic two-way landscape is more about deliberation and fostering exchange, mutual understanding and citizen-driven activities that can lead to preparedness. However, the two communication forms are not mutually exclusive, and they can even complement each other (see also Rice & Robinson, 2013).

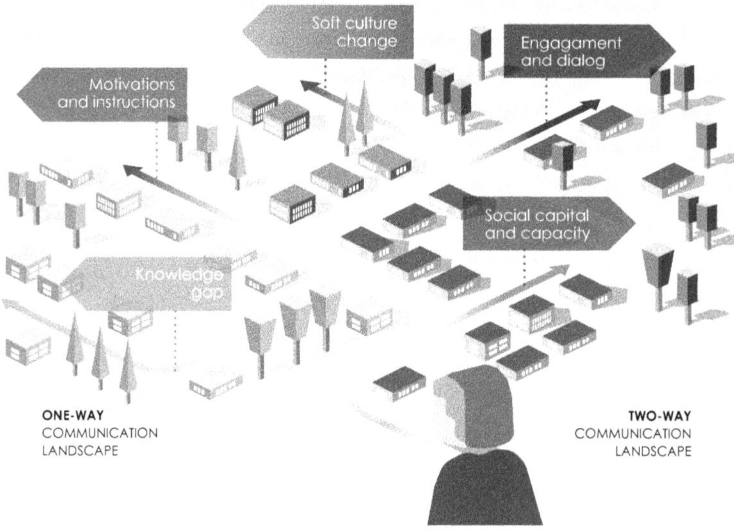

Figure 1.1 The importance of path choice.

Path 1: Knowledge Gap

The knowledge-gap path argues, in short, that lay people lack knowledge about risk, and that by giving more risk information to people ("the public") one can induce them to act more rationally in relation to risks and threats. The basis of this is the "gap" identified between how technical/scientific/health experts and laypeople/the public perceive and rank different risks. The aim of risk communication is then to design, package and transfer scientific risk assessments in a way that bridges the knowledge gap between experts' assessments and perceptions of risk (currently concerning the potential consequences of storms, floods, power outages, IT crashes, etc.) and so-called lay assessments (Renn, 2008). By closing the "gap" through successful dissemination of information, one can theoretically fulfill the universal right to access risk information in a liberal democratic society (Wardman, 2008).

Several studies, however, do not find a significant correlation between dissemination of risk information, risk knowledge, risk perception, willingness to act, and levels of risk preparedness. Instead, they identify paradox related to risk information/knowledge and risk perception (see, e.g., Wachinger et al., 2012). Studies show, for example, that well-informed individuals with high-risk knowledge often still accept risks and dangers in their neighborhoods because some perceived personal benefits (such as status, a beautiful landscape, economic gain, tradition) outweigh the negative impacts/consequences (see, e.g., Cornia et al., 2016; Lakew & Olausson, 2023). Even if individuals perceive high levels of risk, they frequently shift the responsibility for risk reduction and preparedness measures onto someone else, often municipal settings, highly trusted authorities and/or experts. Having a high level of trust in flood-protection measures seems—as a concrete example of the paradox—to reduce people's perceptions of the probability and consequences of flooding, thereby reducing high-trust individuals' willingness to prepare for floods (Terpstra et al., 2009). In practical terms, the risk-perception paradox essentially means that high levels of risk perception and knowledge rarely enhance individuals' preparedness efforts.

It is difficult, however, to begin communicating about risks and preparedness without those involved having a certain amount of basic knowledge. Therefore, purely educational risk communication activities and home preparedness campaigns are still common, and some studies still show positive effects of these (see, e.g., Maidl & Buchecker, 2015). An example is larger media attention campaigns—with clear start and stop times—conveying broad risk messages such as "watch out for disinformation" or "prepare for extreme weather" to large groups of citizens. Historically, such educational messages have been delivered through one-way channels such as advertising space in the mass media, outdoor advertising, bulletin boards and billboards, but also by personally addressed letters. Special attention is given to defining the target audience, trusted sources, and most suitable channels of communication.

Table 1.1 Summary of basic characteristics of the different path choices

Path choice	*Knowledge gap*	*Motivation and instructions*	*Soft Cultural Change*	*Community Engagement/ Empowerment*	*Social Capital and Capacity*
Basic logic	Education	Persuasion and instructions	Subtle persuasion and changes in the physical environment	Activation, involvement, and dialog	Community and trust-building support
Main type of communication	One-way	One-way	One-way	Two-way	Two-way
Main view of citizens	Passive	Passive	Passive	Active	Active
The emphasis of risk and threat messages	Central	Central	Peripheral	Peripheral	Peripheral
Time frames	Short-term	Short-term	Long-term	Long-term	Long-term
Visibility	Noticeable	Noticeable	Insidious	Fuzzy	Invisible
Evaluation	Easy	Easy	Complicated	Complicated	Complicated
Examples of risk communication activities	Educational Campaigns delivered by mass media, outdoor advertising, billboards, etc.	Campaigns with a combination of "alarming" motivational risk messages and messages highlighting what the individual can easily do to protect herself.	Short messages "sneaked into" citizens' everyday routines, but also changes in the physical environment.	Developing systems for interaction between authorities and citizens. Organizing discussion and study groups.	Developing communication efforts that activate, invite, and enable citizens, and ensure constant open risk communication.

Choosing this path of communication to "make" crisis preparedness often offers several advantages to communication, risk, and/or crisis managers. The managers can control the campaign, and it often generates public attention, thus validating the efforts. Measures of campaign impact such as "attention" or "views" are easy to assess and visualize, and it is simple to show decision makers, politicians, and colleagues media-attention effects that can legitimize the risk communication work (Wardman, 2008). However, the behavioral effect achieved by one-way mass campaigns is often limited, according to critics. One reason for this is that a wider range of psychological factors than just lack of awareness and knowledge seem to influence whether and how individuals respond to preparedness issues (Adams et al., 2017; Aitken et al., 2011).

Path 2: Motivation and Instructions

The next possible path to choose states that many individuals already have high knowledge about relevant risks, but still do not take protective actions (see, e.g., Poussin et al., 2014). Instead, the risk communication behavior problem has to do with attitude and individuals lacking motivation and confidence in their own ability to behave in an appropriate and risk-preventing manner. The influential Canadian American social cognitive theorist Albert Bandura (1982) defines the latter phenomenon in terms of the individual's level of self-efficacy, which refers to a person's level of self-confidence when it comes to carrying out things desired by the social environment, as well as achieving one's own individual desirable goals. A low level of perceived capability/self-efficacy in the preparedness context is, in turn—like in most countries—often associated with personal life experiences, financial conditions, and other socio-economic factors (Shapira et al., 2018).

The idea of a need to provide motivation and instructions stems from health behavior change models and socio-cognitive fear-appeal theory. Here, protection motivation theories (see, e.g., Rogers, 1975) argue, in short, that successful risk messages should both (1) create awareness of neglected risks and (2) motivate protective actions by generating intimidation and/or fear ("fear appeal"). In addition, successful risk messages must also (3) provide information about what the individual can easily do to protect herself and "cope" with the risk. Extended theories (Witte, 1992) based on protective motivation reasoning further claim that individuals who face dangers/risks will either try to control the dangers or try to control their own fear of the dangers. If an individual prioritizes preparing for the danger, she becomes more inclined both to take in risk messages and to protect herself, according to the theories. But if the individual is too terrified by the risk messages, she instead tries to control her own fear of the dangers and thus often rejects the essence of the messaging.

Selecting the motivation and instructions path means choosing a practice that shares social marketing's focus on the process of design, messaging strategies and implementation, as well as on the evaluation and testing of campaign messages and communication activities for the "good" of society (Okazaki et al., 2015). Therefore, like the knowledge-gap path, this path is first and foremost linked to time-limited, easily observable, classical, one-way mass-communication campaigns. These often target groups of citizens with measured low levels of perceived motivation and self-efficacy. The sole use of fear-inducing risk communication messages is said not to be a suitable messaging strategy in motivation-and-instructions preparedness campaigns. Instead, a combination of "alarming" motivational risk messages and messages highlighting what the individual can easily do to protect herself is recommended (Johansson et al., 2021). However, the appropriateness of fear appeal approaches and their behavioral effects in risk and preparedness contexts are partly disputed (Ruiter et al., 2014). The long-term effects on behavior are also uncertain (Peters et al., 2013). Several studies from different parts of the world find, for example, that it is often the "wrong" people, i.e., wealthier and already information-rich citizen groups, who above all take up and engage in educational and campaign initiatives aiming to create increased self-preparedness through fear appeal (see, e.g., Abunyewah et al., 2020).

Path 3: Soft Cultural Change

This next path highlights the need for "soft" cultural change to develop and maintain disaster preparedness behavior and culture in communities (see, e.g., Appleby-Arnold et al., 2021). The idea of soft culture partially originates from the concept of "soft power" (used in international relations studies), which refers to the use of instruments in a nation-state's arsenal that do not punish or threaten other international actors to bring about desired behavior. Soft power instead relies on soft cultural exchanges and public diplomacy activities—often taken step by step, using popular culture and mass media discourses—to help shape the desired behavior (Nye, 1990). The path of soft cultural change also bears similarities with what is popularly defined as "nudging" in, for example, economic behavior psychology and interventive health science:

> A nudge /.../ is any aspect of the choice architecture that alters people's behavior in a predictable way without forbidding any options or significantly changing their economic incentives. To count as a mere nudge, the intervention must be easy and cheap to avoid.
>
> (Thaler & Sunstein, 2009, p. 6)

In risk communication and crisis preparedness work, it can be a matter of using "sticks and carrots" instead of instruments of hard power such as education, rules, and reprimands by authorities to foster preparedness behavior (Appleby-Arnold et al., 2021). Risk communication for preparedness applying this path thus strives to align with cultural factors such as people's prevailing worldviews, values and norms, to make sustained behavioral and "soft" cultural change possible in the long term. Research within public relations and strategic communication sometimes defines all kinds of public relations and communication management activities (campaigns, media relations, publicity, citizen dialogs, meetings, etc.) as instruments of soft power, in contrast to hard power forms of governance (see, e.g., Verčič, 2008). Studies of disaster reduction recommend following more explicit communication strategies to foster "soft" cultural change in the direction of disaster preparedness over time. These include (1) using measures that build upon existing values and daily routines; (2) establishing risk communication activities that are a part of citizens' everyday-life events; and (3) emphasizing self-efficacy by showing how citizens' already existing everyday skills can be harnessed in crisis situations (Appleby-Arnold et al., 2021).

However, soft cultural change (or "nudging") as a global practice is seen as a behavioral change technology that can still contain a traditional one-way campaign design and messages, but here the campaign is explicitly designed to fit everyday habits and be "sneaked into" citizens' everyday routines, and to help them to make "easy decisions" concerning risk issues (Heath et al., 2019). This can take the form of signs, colors, and physical markings/stickers that remind people of emergency preparedness issues and changes and reminders in the environment in digital games. The biggest difference is possibly that the activities also often include making unnoticed changes in physical and digital environments to covertly create more preparedness-friendly behavior overall. So, this third path often includes both communicational activities and changes in urban planning, etc. (Thaler & Sunstein, 2009). In practice, however, the path typically includes several concrete messages using logics and techniques from the knowledge and motivation paths, but the activities/techniques are not time limited and are not always easy to observe and evaluate, because a nudge often lies "outside of conscious awareness" (Marchiori et al., 2017, p. 2).

Path 4: Community Engagement and Dialog

The fourth path does not see low levels of crisis preparedness by citizens as caused by lack of information/knowledge or of motivation/instructions. This path argues instead that the more opportunities community members have to think and talk about potential disasters and crises, the greater their sense of empowerment and intention to engage in hazard preparedness. The acronym RCCE (risk communication and community engagement), for example, has been used extensively in global Covid policy documents during the management of the pandemic (see, e.g., WHO, 2020a, 2020b). The RCCE path/perspective here includes, briefly put, an ideological turn away from a megaphone and one-way knowledge-gap approach, and toward a deliberative, participatory, and dialogic risk communication perspective where both sender and receiver are argued to be more active (see, e.g., Abunyewah et al., 2020).

Calls for community engagement (CE) in various societal processes have long been an important theme in both normative and descriptive liberal-democratic political science theory (see, e.g., Head, 2007). For several decades political scientists have also promoted the concept of active citizens in political and institutional contexts (see, e.g., Fung, 2003). However, in a crisis-preparedness context, the movement toward community engagement, empowerment and dialog also includes the sharing of responsibility, including the transfer of responsibility for preparedness issues from governments to individual citizens. This is something that is strongly requested (Abunyewah et al., 2020; Houston, 2018) but also sometimes problematized (Baker & Grant Ludwig, 2016; Hobbins, 2017).

In practice, the classic one-way preparedness campaign plays a minor role in this community engagement and empowerment path. From a public relations point of view, this path is more about having a risk communication practice that is organized and designed primarily for "the management of potential and existing communication interactive networks /.../ for the benefits of both groups" (Neff, 2005, p. 174). This preparedness-building communication path therefore blends two key themes that early became noticeable in the risk communication and public relations literature, because it features both one-way and two-way communication (see, e.g., Fisher, 1991; Grunig, 1984). The important two-way communication characteristics here are the use, in risk communication activities for preparedness, of techniques/channels/activities that support interpersonal communication, engagement, and shared actions. The procedures are considered to involve and activate the public, but also to maintain and strengthen long-term trust and confidence in the authorities and in society at large (Johnston et al., 2020). Citizens' subjective needs are central, and instead of changing citizens' behavior with the help of information, the practice is directed toward developing and changing the systems and forms of communication that facilitate the interaction between authorities and citizens. It can also be about concrete measures such as organizing discussion and study groups.

Even this choice of path is subject to criticism, a recurring example of which is that the dialog methods tend mainly to involve and activate groups of citizens who are already committed, well-educated, and engaged (Miller et al., 2012). It is also less easy to measure and demonstrate behavioral change linked to dialogical communication than in traditional one-way oriented risk communication campaigns. This path is also one that normally involves communication with relatively few individuals instead of the "masses."

Path 5: Social Capital and Capacity

Perceived self-efficacy and motivation have only limited influence on the degree to which individuals take up preparedness activities, according to this fifth path. Instead, its proponents argue for a stronger impact of knowing and trusting others (see, e.g., Bihari & Ryan, 2012; Haer et al., 2016). Supporting social capital and/or social capacity in a society is therefore seen as the core of crisis-preparedness work (Kuhlicke, et al., 2011; Meyer, 2018). Already during the 1960s, social capital was described as a network of "strong, cross-cutting personal relationships that develop over time and that create a basis for trust, cooperation and collective actions among community members" (Jacobs, cited in Ostrom, 2010, p. 19). Today, social capital is often globally associated with Putnam's (1995) ideas about the importance of human interaction and strong everyday social life in maintaining a functioning democracy.

According to several studies, aspects of social capital, such as access to social networks and group membership, have led community residents to engage in various preparedness efforts (Bihari & Ryan, 2012; Höppner et al., 2012). In the risk communication and emergency preparedness context, the closely related concept of social capacity is also connected to the abilities, skills, and competences of individuals, groups, and/or organizations when it comes to anticipating and handling crises and disasters (Kuhlicke et al., 2011). This important social capacity, in turn, depends somewhat on citizens' knowledge, attitudes, motivations, capabilities, and social and organizational capabilities regarding risks, as well as on individuals' emotional and psychological capabilities. The perspective is thus partly based on "knowledge gap" and "motivation" logics, but also on a strong and central idea about risk communication as a tool to create trusting relationships between individuals, and trust in society at large in line with the "community engagement" path/logic. In addition, the social capacity path adds the need to support positive emotions and psychological skills such as a sense of freedom of action, hope, optimism, resistance to stress, and the ability to regulate emotions through communication activities (Höppner et al., 2012).

Both theory and experience show that social capital/capacity is important for creating preparedness, but the concrete communicational processes that potentially lead to social capital are less understood and discussed. Even if in practice the social capital and capacity path partly includes classical one-way preparedness campaigns, it is more about making communication infrastructure in the municipality serve the needs of everyday risk communication efforts that run without a specific time limit. The inclusion of explicit risk messages is less central; instead, it is important to provide citizens with communication opportunities, to activate, invite, and enable them, and to ensure constant open communication. According to some preparedness literature and guidelines, a communication practice that strongly supports social capital and "community development" in the local community is the use and inclusion of social media in public administration communication. This is argued to both strengthen existing ties and create new contacts (Procopio & Procopio, 2007).

However, building social capital can also be supported by messages that highlight positive opportunities and promote an optimistic spirit in the local community by fostering neighborhood cooperation and stimulating local meeting places. Prioritizing so-called "place branding" and "citizens' innovations" as an implicit part of risk communication could then be a communication practice that potentially contributes to social capital. A dilemma for those responsible for risk communication issues is that such overall communication activities are not often associated with municipalities' preparedness levels. Public authorities that choose solely this "invisible" fifth path can then potentially be perceived as neglecting important emergency preparedness issues and responsibilities.

Summary and Final Reflections for Communication Practitioners

Even if the suggested multi-motive model for "making" crisis preparedness through risk communication contains several simplifications, it can hopefully help present and future practitioners to start reflecting about the theoretical and disciplinary roots and related philosophical and political commitments in their risk communication practice. This includes engaging in important reflections about things like basic purposes and goals, practitioners' views of citizens, the level of emphasis on risk and threats in communicated messages and time scales, as well as reflections on appropriate concrete communication practices and activities in risk communication for preparedness (see Table 1.1).

However, the basic choice of a path or combination of paths is not made in a societal or organizational vacuum or by itself. The path choices are always strongly dependent on several contextual factors, paradoxes, and/or dilemmas, which are also important for practitioners to reflect on and manage (see also Boholm, 2019b; Demeritt & Nobert, 2014; Johnston et al., 2020). Some of these are briefly highlighted and discussed in the following:

1 *The path choices concerning how to "make" preparedness through risk communication are always made in relation to governing regulations, political discourses, and commitments.* Crisis management and emergency preparedness policies in several European countries have for some time been characterized by a general shift of preparedness responsibility from the state to the regional/local municipality level, and further to households and citizens, according to several researchers. One reason for this interpretation is the increased number of government-initiated and distributed "one-way" persuasive home-preparedness campaigns that tell citizens they must prepare to manage for several days on their own in a crisis (see, e.g., Benadusi, 2014; Bergström 2018). However, the preventive risk communication work, at regional and local community level, is often highly influenced by national authorities' guidelines concerning choice of design, channels, risk messages, etc. One reason for this is that the national guidelines simplify and minimize costs at the local level. A challenge, however, is how to adapt national campaigns and other communication efforts to local risk assessments and prevailing social and cultural contextual norms (see, e.g., Sataoen & Eriksson, 2023).

2 *Multiple public administration professions are always involved in the path choices about risk communication and preparedness activities.* Communication for preparedness is not a "one man show." Studies show that the views of risks, and of citizens as active or passive recipients of risk messages, vary between the professions involved in preparedness work (Boholm, 2019a). On the one hand, this creates pluralism in internal risk communication decisions, but on the other hand it also creates potential cultural clashes between the professional groups about how to perceive local risks and if and how to persuade or involve citizens in risk decisions (Lidskog & Rabe, 2022). This means that different professional commitments always must be negotiated and adjusted as a part of the decisions about appropriate path choices concerning risk communication (Boholm, 2019b).
3 *Involved professionals' perceptions of their own roles tend to influence how risk communication for preparedness is ultimately practiced.* Professionals managing and designing strategic communication and public relations activities, like risk communication for preparedness, have historically been metaphorically described as "informers" or "propagandists," but also as "diplomats" and "agents of change". The information and propaganda roles indicate, in short, that they are devoted to one-way communication, which includes packaging and disseminating knowledge and motivating behavioral change through information and communication. The diplomat and change agent metaphors include, on the other hand, higher levels of two-way communication for dialog, symmetry, and negotiation (Dozier & Broom, 2006). Finally, radical, and postmodern ideas about the role position argue that risk communication practitioners (or "communication officers") should only represent the "audience," taking on the role of an "activist" in relation to the governing organization (Holtzhausen & Voto, 2002). The postmodern practitioner helps citizens question authorities' decisions and expert assessments regarding risk and preparedness. Obviously, the overall perception of the communication practitioner's role position, as well as the practitioners' perceptions of their own professional role in relation to citizens, is related to the possible path choices.

The main argument in the pragmatic multi-motive model is that the practitioner often needs to combine several paths, or at least elements of them, to potentially succeed in "making" preparedness through risk communication (see also Abunyewah et al., 2018; Johnston et al., 2020; Rice & Robinson, 2013). In addition, practitioners also need to make this path choice carefully in relation to their own perceived professional role positions. These ideas are supported by increasingly strong arguments in the literature stating that public agencies' risk communication efforts to create a preparedness culture should "include a wide range of techniques that work together to change behavior, including face-to-face community engagement that triggers and supports community-led preparedness activity" (Ryan et al., 2020, p. 101655). Obviously, the different paths entail different costs, comprise different time frames, and involve different types of challenges and internal and external effects that are important for the practitioner to reflect on before making decisions about the multi-motive risk communication for preparedness. Different paths and combinations of paths can also be necessary, depending on the prevailing views of democracy that characterize the national and local European communities (Lidskog, 2017).

References

Abunyewah, M., Gajendran, T., & Maund, K. (2018). Conceptual framework for motivating actions towards disaster preparedness through risk communication. *Procedia Engineering, 212*, 246–253. https://doi.org/10.1016/j.proeng.2018.01.032

Abunyewah, M., Gajendran, T., Maund, K., & Okyere, S. A. (2020). Strengthening the information deficit model for disaster preparedness: Mediating and moderating effects of community participation. *International Journal of Disaster Risk Reduction, 46*, 101492. https://doi.org/10.1016/j.ijdrr.2020.101492

Adams, R., Karlin, B., Eisenman, D., Blakley, J., & Glik, D. (2017). Who participates in the great shake out? Why audience segmentation is the future of disaster preparedness campaigns. *International Journal of Environmental Research and Public Health, 14*(11), 1407. https://doi.org/10.3390/ijerph14111407

Aitken, C., Chapman, R., & McClure, J. (2011). Climate change, powerlessness and the commons dilemma: Assessing New Zealanders' preparedness to act. *Global Environmental Change, 21*(2), 752–760. https://doi.org/10.1016/j.gloenvcha.2011.01.002

Appleby-Arnold, S., Brockdorff, N., & Callus, C. (2021). Developing a "culture of disaster preparedness": The citizens' view. *International Journal of Disaster Risk Reduction, 56*, 102–133. https://doi.org/10.1016/j.ijdrr.2021.102133

Baker, N. D., & Grant Ludwig, L. (2016). Disaster preparedness as social control. *Critical Policy Studies, 12*(1), 24–43. https://doi.org/10.1080/19460171.2016.1214075.

Bandura, A. (1982). Self-efficacy mechanism in human agency. *American Psychologist, 37*(2), 122–147. https://doi.org/10.1037/0003-066x.37.2.122

Benadusi, M. (2014). Pedagogies of the unknown: Unpacking 'culture' in disaster risk reduction education. *Journal of Contingencies and Crisis Management. 22*(3). https://doi.org/10.1111/1468-5973.12050

Bergström, J. (2018). An archaeology of societal resilience. *Safety Science, 110*, 31–38. https://doi.org/10.1016/j.ssci.2017.09.013

Bihari, M., & Ryan, R. (2012). Influence of social capital on community preparedness for wildfires. *Landscape and Urban Planning, 106*(3), 253–261. https://doi.org/10.1016/j.landurbplan.2012.03.011

Boholm, Å. (2019a). Risk communication as government agency organizational practice. *Risk Analysis, 39*(8), 1695–1707. https://doi.org/10.1111/risa.13302

Boholm, Å. (2019b). Lessons of success and failure: Practicing risk communication at government agencies. *Safety Science*, 118, 158–167. https://doi.org/10.1016/j.ssci.2019.05.025

Cornia, A., Dressel, K., & Pfeil P. (2016). Risk cultures and dominant approaches towards disasters in seven European countries, *Journal of Risk Research, 19*(3), 288–304, https://doi.org/10.1080/13669877.2014.961520

Demeritt, D., & Nobert, S. (2014). Models of best practice in flood risk communication and management. *Environmental Hazards*, *13*(4), 313–328. https://doi.org/10.1080/17477891.2014.924897

Dozier, D. M., & Broom, G. M. (2006). The centrality of practitioner roles to public relations theory. In C. H. Botan & V. Hazleton (Eds.), *Public relations theory II*. LEA.

Fisher, A. (1991). Risk communication challenges. *Risk Analysis*, *11*(2), 173–179. https://doi.org/10.1111/j.1539-6924.1991.tb00590.x

Fung, A. (2003). Associations and democracy: Between theories, hopes, and realities. *Annual Review of Sociology*, *29*(1), 515–539. https://doi.org/10.1146/annurev.soc.29.010202.100134

Grunig, J. E. (1984). *Managing public relations* (1st ed.). Cengage Learning.

Haer, T., Botzen, W. W., & Aerts, J. C. (2016). The effectiveness of flood risk communication strategies and the influence of social networks—Insights from an agent-based model. *Environmental Science & Policy*, *60*, 44–52. https://doi.org/10.1016/j.envsci.2016.03.006

Head, B. W. (2007). Community engagement: Participation on whose terms? *Australian Journal of Political Science*, *42*(3), 441–454. https://doi.org/10.1080/10361140701513570

Heath, R. L., Lee, J., & Lemon, L. L. (2019). Narratives of risk communication: Nudging community residents to shelter-in-place. *Public Relations Review*, *45*(1), 128–137. https://doi.org/10.1016/j.pubrev.2018.12.004

Hobbins, J. (2017). Between autonomy and paternalism: Crisis managers' constructions of citizens' responsibilities in the context of crises and contingencies. *Journal of Contingencies and Crisis Management*, *25*(4), 269–278. https://doi.org/10.1111/1468-5973.12151

Holtzhausen, D. & Voto, R (2002). Resistance from the margins: the postmodern Public relations practitioners as organizational activist. *Journal of Public Relations Research*, *14*(1), 57–84.

Höppner, C., Whittle, R., Bründl, M., & Buchecker, M. (2012). Linking social capacities and risk communication in Europe: A gap between theory and practice? *Natural Hazards*, *64*(2), 1753–1778. https://doi.org/10.1007/s11069-012-0356-5

Houston, J. B. (2018). Community resilience and communication: Dynamic interconnections between and among individuals, families, and organizations. *Journal of Applied Communication Research*, *46*(1), 19–22. https://doi.org/10.1080/00909882.2018.1426704

Johansson, B., Lane, D. R., Sellnow, D. D., & Sellnow, T. L. (2021). No heat, no electricity, no water, oh no!: An IDEA model experiment in instructional risk communication. *Journal of Risk Research*, *24*(12), 1576–1588. https://doi.org/10.1080/13669877.2021.1894468

Johnston, K. A., Taylor, M., & Ryan, B. (2020). Emergency management communication: The paradox of the positive in public communication for preparedness. *Public Relations Review*, *46*(2), 101903. https://doi.org/10.1016/j.pubrev.2020.101903

Kapucu, N. (2008). Culture of preparedness: Household disaster preparedness. *Disaster Prevention and Management: An International Journal*, *17*(4), 526–535. https://doi.org/10.1108/09653560810901773

Kuhlicke, C., Steinführer, A., Begg, C., Bianchizza, C., Bründl, M., Buchecker, M., de Marchi, B., di Masso Tarditti, M., Höppner, C., Komac, B., Lemkow, L., Luther, J., McCarthy, S., Pellizzoni, L., Renn, O., Scolobig, A., Supramaniam, M., Tapsell, S.,

Wachinger, G. … Faulkner, H. (2011). Perspectives on social capacity building for natural hazards: outlining an emerging field of research and practice in Europe. *Environmental Science & Policy*, *14*(7), 804–814. https://doi.org/10.1016/j.envsci.2011.05.001

Lakew, Y., & Olausson, U. (2023). When we don't want to know more: Information sufficiency and the case of Swedish flood risks. *Journal of International Crisis and Risk Communication Research*, *6*(1), 65–90. https://doi.org/10.30658/jicrcr.6.1.3

Lidskog, R. (2017). Risk governance. In *Oxford Research Encylopedia of Communication*. Oxford University Press. https://doi.org/10.1093/acrefore/9780190228613.013.246

Lidskog, R., & Rabe, L. (2022). Making climate risks governable in Swedish municipalities: Crisis preparedness, technical measures, and public involvement. *Climate*, *10*(7), 90. https://doi.org/10.3390/cli10070090

Maidl, E., & Buchecker, M. (2015). Raising risk preparedness by flood risk communication. *Natural Hazards and Earth System Sciences*, *15*(7), 1577–1595. https://doi.org/10.5194/nhess-15-1577-2015

Marchiori, D. R., Adriaanse, M. A., & de Ridder, D. T. (2017). Unresolved questions in nudging research: Putting the psychology back in nudging. *Social and Personality Psychology Compass*, *11*(1), e12297. https://doi.org/10.1111/spc3.12297

Meyer, M. A. (2018). Social capital in disaster research. In H. Rodríguez, W. Donner, & J. E. Trainor (Eds.), *Handbook of disaster research* (pp. 263–286). Springer International Publishing.

Miller, C. H., Adame, B. J., & Moore, S. D. (2012). Vested Interest theory and disaster preparedness. *Disasters*, *37*(1), 1–27. https://doi.org/10.1111/j.1467-7717.2012.01290.x

Neff, B. D. (2005). Community relations. In R. L. Heath (Ed.) *Encyclopedia of public relations* (pp. 174–177) Sage.

Nye, J. S. (1990). Soft power. Foreign Policy No. 80, Twentieth Anniversary (Autumn, 1990), pp. 153–171. https://doi.org/10.2307/1148580

Okazaki, S., Benavent-Climent, A., Navarro, A., & Henseler, J. (2015). Responses when the earth trembles: The impact of community awareness campaigns on protective behavior. *Journal of Public Policy & Marketing*, *34*(1), 4–18. https://doi.org/10.1509/jppm.13.045

Ostrom, E. (2010). What is social capital? In V. O. Bartkus & J. H. Davis (Eds.), *Social capital: Reaching out, reaching in* (pp. 17–38). Edward Elgar Publishing.

Peters, G. J. Y., Ruiter, R. A., & Kok, G. (2013). Threatening communication: A critical re-analysis and a revised meta-analytic test of fear appeal theory. *Health Psychology Review*, *7*(sup1), S8–S31. https://doi.org/10.1080/17437199.2012.703527

Petridou, E., Danielsson, E., Olofsson, A., Lundgren, M., & Große, C. (2019). If crisis or war comes: A study of risk communication of eight European Union member states. *Journal of International Crisis and Risk Communication Research*, *2*(2), 207–232. https://doi.org/10.30658/jicrcr.2.2.3

Poussin, J. K., Botzen, W. W., & Aerts, J. C. (2014). Factors of influence on flood damage mitigation behaviour by households. *Environmental Science & Policy*, *40*, 69–77. https://doi.org/10.1016/j.envsci.2014.01.013

Procopio, C. H., & Procopio, S. T. (2007). Do you know what it means to miss new orleans? Internet communication, geographic community, and social capital in crisis. *Journal of Applied Communication Research*, *35*(1), 67–87. https://doi.org/10.1080/00909880601065722

Putnam, R. D. (1995). Bowling alone: America's declining social capital. *Journal of Democracy, 6*(1), 65–78. https://doi.org/10.1353/jod.1995.0002

Renn, O. (2008). *Risk governance: Coping with uncertainty in a complex world* (Earthscan Risk in Society). Routledge.

Rice, R. E., & Robinson, J. A. (2013). Transdisciplinary approaches for twenty-first century ocean sustainability communication. In R. E. Rice & C. K. Atkin (Eds.), *Public communication campaigns*. https://doi.org/10.4135/9781544308449.N16

Rogers, R. W. (1975). A protection motivation theory of fear appeals and attitude change. *The Journal of Psychology, 91*(1), 93–114. https://doi.org/10.1080/00223980.1975.9915803

Ruiter, R. A. C., Kessels, L. T. E., Peters, G. Y., & Kok, G. (2014). Sixty years of fear appeal research: Current state of the evidence. *International Journal of Psychology, 49*(2), 63–70. https://doi.org/10.1002/ijop.12042

Ryan, B., Johnston, K. A., Taylor, M., & McAndrew, R. (2020). Community engagement for disaster preparedness: A systematic literature review. *International Journal of Disaster Risk Reduction, 49*, 101655. https://doi.org/10.1016/j.ijdrr.2020.101655

Sataoen, H. & Eriksson, M. (2023). "Striking the right balance": Tensions in municipal risk communication management for preparedness. *Journal of Communication Management, 27*(4), 601–616. https://doi.org/10.1108/JCOM-06-2022-0072

Shapira, S., Aharonson-Daniel, L., & Bar-Dayan, Y. (2018). Anticipated behavioral response patterns to an earthquake: The role of personal and household characteristics, risk perception, previous experience and preparedness. *International Journal of Disaster Risk Reduction, 31*, 1–8. https://doi.org/10.1016/j.ijdrr.2018.04.001

Terpstra, T., Lindell, M. K., & Gutteling, J. M. (2009). Does communicating (flood) risk affect (flood) risk perceptions? Results of a quasi-experimental study. *Risk Analysis, 29*(8), 1141–1155. https://doi.org/10.1111/j.1539-6924.2009.01252.x

Thaler, R. H., & Sunstein, C. R. (2009). *Nudge: Improving decisions about health, wealth, and happiness* (Revised & Expanded ed.). Penguin Books.

Verčič, D. (2008). Public relations and power: How hard is soft power? In A. Zerfass, B. van Ruler, & K. Sriramesh (Eds.), *Public relations research*. VS Verlag für Sozialwissenschaften. https://doi.org/10.1007/978-3-531-90918-9_17

Wachinger, G., Renn, O., Begg, C., & Kuhlicke, C. (2012). The risk perception paradox-implications for governance and communication of natural hazards. *Risk Analysis, 33*(6), 1049–1065. https://doi.org/10.1111/j.1539-6924.2012.01942.x

Wardman, J. K. (2008). The constitution of risk communication in advanced liberal societies. *Risk Analysis, 28*(6), 1619–1637. https://doi.org/10.1111/j.1539-6924.2008.01108.x

WHO (2020b, December 23). Covid-19 global risk communication and community engagement strategy. December 2020–May 2021. Interim Guidance. WHO/2019-nCoV/RCCE/2020.3

WHO. (2020a, March 19). Risk communication and community engagement readiness and response to coronavirus disease (COVID-19) Interim guidance.

Witte, K. (1992). Putting the fear back into fear appeals: The extended parallel process model. *Communication Monographs, 59*(4), 329–349. https://doi.org/10.1080/03637759209376276

2 Marrying Crisis Preparation and Strategic Planning

Definitions and Challenges in Business Practice

Albena Björck and Maya Gadgil

Crises are unpredictable, and complex events, that can fundamentally and sustainably change organizations (Björck, 2016). According to Deloitte Insights (2018), companies across all industries face increased uncertainty and multiple escalating risks and threats. The list of possible crises is extensive, ranging from big product recalls, data breaches, and health concerns to natural catastrophes, terrorist events, and corporate leadership failures, just to mention a few. Furthermore, the experience of an event such as COVID-19 has shown the overall vulnerability of societies (Björck et al., 2022).

A crisis is a pivotal event that puts a company's preparation, resilience, and reaction character to the test; however, most companies are surprised when a crisis hits because of a lack of systematic preparation. For boards and management teams, crisis preparation has become an important and urgent task (Deloitte, 2018). Even the best-prepared companies or organizations will face a crisis and there is rarely a perfect response. However, the ability to mitigate a crisis and avert mismanagement will be largely determined by the effectiveness of the company's crisis preventive measures and crisis response plan (Sellnow & Veil, 2016).

Strategic preparation for a crisis is highly beneficial, but still underutilized. According to Labaš (2017), better crisis preparation enables organizations to take a proactive stance and provides better crisis prediction and identification (Lanzer et al., 2020, p. 67). Being prepared for any crisis is never a waste of resources, because "the crisis you have to worry about most is the one you don't see coming" (UZH Center for Crisis Competence, 2022). Furthermore, in the modern landscape where organizations often face multiple crises at once and the environment is characterized by high uncertainty, static and tactical approaches to crisis management are insufficient (Niggemann, 2022). But why is crisis preparation still a task delegated to specialized crisis teams or communication departments?

Though multiple disciplines offer a plethora of different terms, factors, and procedures for strategic crisis preparedness, what it takes to be better equipped for crisis communication with empirical support or scholarship

DOI: 10.4324/9781003375296-4

on (strategic) crisis readiness is scarce. This chapter aims to contribute to a better understanding of the term by analyzing definitions from the literature and presenting empirical results from a study conducted in Switzerland end of 2022. Furthermore, we show the relevance of the strategic planning process to crisis management and communication to ensure strategic crisis communication readiness.

Theoretical Foundations

Preparedness in the "Pre-Crisis" Crisis Management and Communication

Crisis preparedness is treated by the academic models in the so-called pre-crisis phase (Boin & Hart, 2003; Coombs & Laufer, 2018; Fink, 1986; Mitroff et al., 1987). According to Coombs (2010), crisis management seeks to prevent or mitigate the negative consequences of a crisis, so protecting the organization, stakeholders, and/or industry and is a multi-step process that includes preventative measures, crisis management strategies, and post-crisis reviews. Crisis communication pre-crisis centers on gathering information about risks, making decisions about how to manage prospective crises, educating those who will be part in the crisis management process to ensure sufficient knowledge to address the situation (Björck, 2017). Bochenek (2019) states that there are two crises in a crisis: a "real" crisis and a communications crisis. To minimize long-term reputational problems, a dual strategy that considers both managerial and communication components is necessary to avoid reputational as well as operational concerns (Bochenek, 2019).

Crisis Communication Preparedness Models

Few academics have previously explored the topic of *crisis preparedness*. According to Sheaffer and Mano-Negrin (2003), crisis preparedness can be defined as "*the state* to foresee and effectively address internal or exogenous adversary circumstances with the potential to inflict a multidimensional crisis, by consciously recognizing and proactively preparing for its inevitable occurrence." (p. 203). According to previous research, crisis preparedness has three components: "the organization's internal functionality (rapid reaction, how informed, access to crisis management resources, effective strategic crisis preparation), the organization's capacity to handle media in a crisis, and the expected chance of a crisis striking the organization" (Rousaki & Alcott, 2006, p. 28). These three dimensions can provide a framework for crisis preparedness by first evaluating an organization's vulnerabilities and strengths within the crisis context. In many cases, low crisis response capability may be attributed to a highly bureaucratic organizational structures and cultures that slow information flow and cause information distortion (Rousaki & Alcott, 2006, p. 37).

Elsubbaugh et al. (2004) developed a *crisis preparedness level* model. The model is divided into three distinct stages and six tasks required to successfully prepare for and respond to organizational crises: In stage one we find *general preparedness* involving strategic crisis planning and a good crisis management culture; in stage two is the *identification of early warning signals* focusing on action; and in stage three there is the *specific preparedness* level – more commonly known as crisis management – which involves rapid decision-making, resource mobilization, and efficient information flow. The levels and their accompanying actions form the foundation of crisis preparedness but remain tactical in their nature. But how to attain a good crisis management culture remains unclear (Spillan & Hough, 2003).

Besides the crisis preparedness framework, the literature offers also theoretical perspectives on crisis communication preparedness. Cloudman and Hallahan (2006), developed indices grouped along three categories "crisis preparedness activities" (organizational actions), "alternative measures of preparedness" (assessments), and "predictors" (key variables for level of preparedness). According to a survey of 126 public relations practitioners in the United States, three-quarters of their companies had a documented crisis communications strategy and the organizations were reasonably prepared to respond to crises. Cloudman and Hallahan (2006) found the presence of a crisis plan and actions related to tactical development, training, contact list maintenance, and media monitoring were used to assess preparedness. Further they found preparedness was shown to be positively related to the practitioners' autonomy and delegation of power within the organization as well as organization size and a process orientation. However, crisis preparedness was not related to organization type or engagement in international versus domestic-only activities. Interestingly, practitioners from organizations with plans rated their connections with the public as less positive, but they were more confident in their capacity to respond (Cloudman & Hallahan, 2006).

The second theoretical framework that reflects indicators of crisis communication preparedness developed by Vos et al. (2011), organized in three groups "Citizens", "News media", and "Response Organization and Network". In Finland, an audit measuring of crisis communication preparation was done for 67 organizations, mostly at the national level. Under the title "Response Organization and Network" the mentioning of "communications plans and strategies" indicate a strategic approach (Figure 2.1).

Integrating the Strategic Dimension

James (2018) argues the strategic preparedness of modern enterprises is increasingly determining their competitive advantage. The alignment of an organization's human, information, and organizational capital with its strategy is referred to as both strategic change and preparedness (James, 2018). According to

RESPONSE ORGANIZATION AND NETWORK

- **Improving preparedness in the organization and in the network of the response organization**
  - Responsibilities and tasks of communication experts in relation to response management in the organization and within response network are clearly laid down
  - Agreements are made regarding coordination in the network of response organization
  - Communication plans and strategies for various crisis scenarios are developed within individual organizations as well as with other participants in the respons network

Figure 2.1 Indicators of crisis communication preparedness (own illustration, based on Vos et al., 2011, pp. 239–244).

John-Eke and Eke (2020), companies with sufficient strategic planning are better positioned to manage a crisis. Organizational strategic preparedness requires a discursive shift to manage symbolic resources like language and influence that are equally important as the allocation of financial and human resources. This implies that strategic communication units must reconsider their role in contributing to organizations' strategic readiness, which has hitherto been largely focused on preparedness for future crises and catastrophes (James, 2018). This paradigm shift from transactional and responsive work to transformational work is a process with significant consequences for strategic preparation in the context of strategic communication (James, 2018).

Despite the potential for synergetic integration, the professions of strategic planning and crisis management have evolved separately (Preble, 1997). Only recently, Haupt and Azevedo (2021) re-combined them in a strategic planning process for crisis communication preparedness. As illustrated in Figure 2.2, the non-crisis period involves seven steps, namely, identifying a planning team, crisis and risk identification, designation of roles and responsibilities, selection of organizational resources to support strategies, communication with internal and external stakeholders, and training and practice (Haupt & Azevedo, 2021, p. 174). Despite the innovation, this framework remains focused on pragmatic strategic and operational actions and less focused on creating organizational preparedness to tackle crises.

Strategic Crisis Communication Readiness in Business Practice – Perspective of Swiss Communication Experts

The purpose of this study was to identify patterns and update the current level of the understanding of *strategic crisis communication readiness.* Our study is exploratory and examines the potential elements of crisis communication readiness

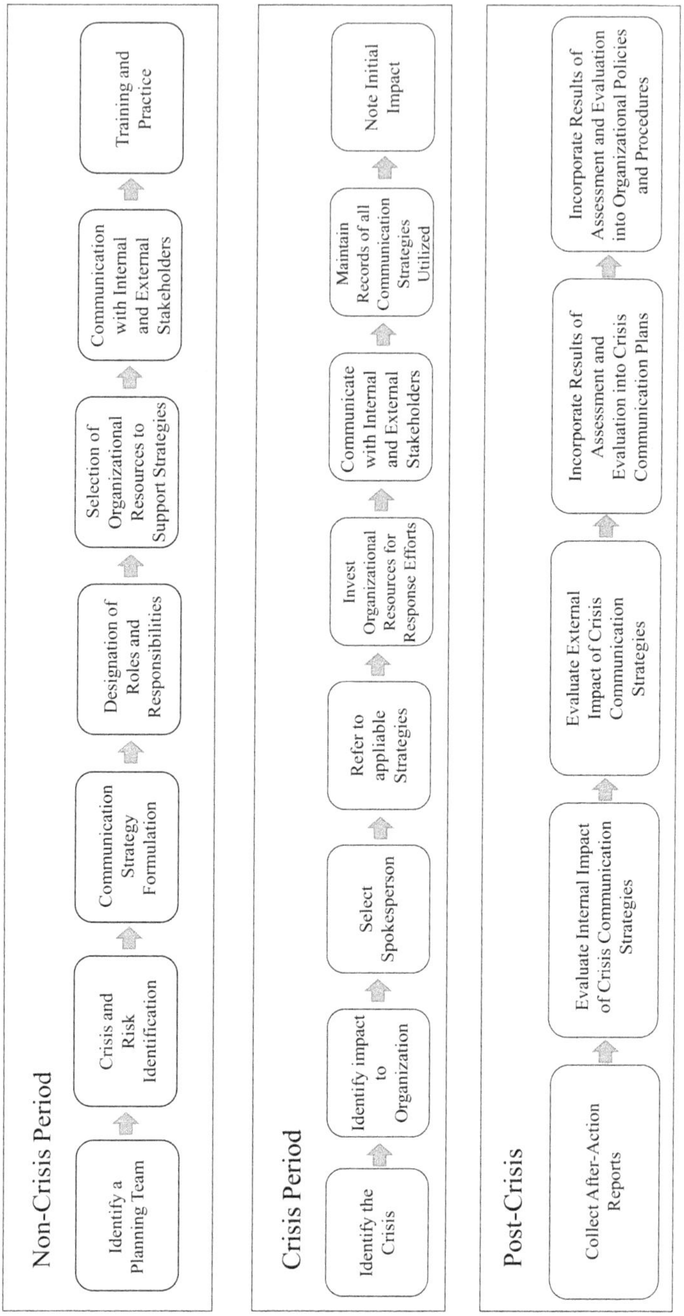

Figure 2.2 Crisis communication planning framework (adapted from Haupt & Azevedo, 2021, p. 174).

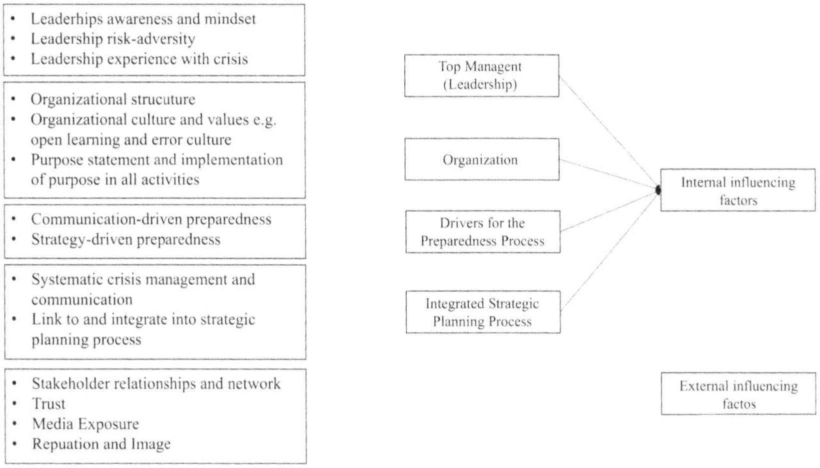

Figure 2.3 First- and second-order concepts arising from the qualitative interviews and survey.

in Swiss organizations. By applying an inductive technique, in which current organizations' activities were examined, data were evaluated, and patterns discovered to develop a better understanding of the concept (Alharahse & Pius, 2020). Data collection was triangulated including 15 in-depth, semi-structured interviews with communication consultants and a qualitative survey with more than 200 corporate communication professionals from a wide range of organizations and industries. The data from both were analyzed by using two coding cycles to generate codes and categories (see Figure 2.3).

From Preparedness to Readiness

These findings suggest that defining the difference between crisis preparedness and readiness is challenging. Crisis readiness can be described as a "state of corporate readiness to anticipate and successfully confront internal or outside adverse situations that have the potential to cause a multifaceted crisis, by consciously identifying and proactively planning for its unavoidable occurrence". The emphasis is on "consciously identifying and proactively planning" steps that can be planned before a crisis occurs. As indicated during the interviews, crisis preparedness leads to crisis readiness. Crisis preparedness is all the actions an organization undertakes to respond to a crisis, but readiness is maintaining this state.

Importance of Purpose, Values, and Culture

Most of the respondents (92.8% n = 168) confirm that defined and implemented corporate purpose is critical for an organization's ability to prepare and manage a crisis. A "need for a crisis-ready mindset at the strategic management level to ensure better crisis preparedness" was confirmed by 74.6% (n=135), while 8.9% (n=18) said No, and 13.9% (n=28) were unsure or said other. Thus, crisis preparedness can be seen as a pre-requisite that management needs to account for having a crisis-aware or crisis-ready mindset to ensure better crisis preparation. When asked if their organization's preparation for crisis management and crisis communication was systematic and linked to their organization's strategic planning process, more than half of the participants responded yes, 55.2% (n=100), while 20.4% (n=37) said no, 19.9% (n=36) were unsure, and 4.4% (n=8) replied that it was partially the case.

Strategy or Communication Driven

However, the experts disagreed on the drivers of the strategic crisis readiness inside an organization. Some believe it is predominantly strategy-driven, while others believe it is both strategy- and communication-driven. However, most agreed that strategic crisis readiness is a joint effort and an interplay between both sides is necessary.

Influencing Factors on Crisis Readiness

As identified in the theoretical framework and confirmed by empirical research, to ensure readiness for crisis communication, actions and influencing factors must be considered and integrated into strategic crisis communication planning as part of the overall crisis preparation process. First, external factors such as stakeholder management and networks, media exposure, reputation or image, and trust, influence an organization's crisis communication readiness. Second, internal influencing factors for crisis readiness are crisis awareness, crisis ready mindset, organizational culture and structure, and leadership.

Role of Top Management (Leadership)

All interviewees agreed that to reach crisis preparedness is a management task. A "crisis-aware, crisis ready" mindset, and if possible, a crisis-tested mindset", is required at the management level. Only then crisis preparation is taken seriously within the organization and seen as a necessary or even urgent topic. Prioritizing crisis management and communication cannot be delegated – knowledge and understanding must come from the very top. Furthermore, management must ensure the firm has staff that is frequently trained, well-equipped, and financially backed.

Crisis Preparedness as a Strategic Planning Process

According to the majority of experts, crisis preparation should be connected to the strategic planning process. However, several communication experts noted that while some steps within their crisis communication planning are systematized, they are frequently linked to the operational planning process rather than the strategic planning process. This is also evident from the survey, where only half of the respondents stated that in their organization the steps are systematized and linked to strategic planning. Positioning crisis preparedness to strategic planning can positively influence a higher prioritization as well as more financial and human resources.

Key Takeaways

The insights show that crisis management and communication planning need to be integrated in the strategic planning process, to increase prioritization of crisis preparation in all its facets and to finally achieve crisis readiness. Still crisis communication is often regarded as an operational task. A crucial aspect in ensuring crisis communication readiness – based on a strategic approach – is stakeholder management, internally with employees, but also with external stakeholders such as (social) media, public, politics, government, etc. Developing a trust relationship and uniting stakeholder by corporate purpose and values are key influential factors in the crisis preparation. However, this takes time, again indicating the validity of a strategic approach in preparedness planning.

A key "strategic" aspect that organizations need to consider when preparing for crisis is the mindset of management toward crisis prevention and preparation, the organizational culture, and the leadership structure. These findings suggest that crisis management and communication readiness ensure the awareness for crisis preparation not only among the communication specialists or the crisis team, but also among top management. Crisis preparation is an interdisciplinary and interrelated effort of the organization, taking inputs regarding crisis management and communication from various sources, but with top management driving the initiative.

Therefore, crisis preparedness and readiness are primarily leadership tasks. Strategy implementation is communication, and communication is strategy. Every organization needs to have a strategy associated with certain risks and activities, they also need clear communication to guide expectations from different stakeholders and ensure the organization's objectives are correctly understood. Strategy execution is communication work and should be evaluated considering the crisis probabilities; it is also a management duty to emphasize that an organization needs to be prepared.

Conclusion

A pre-crisis crisis management and communication preparedness process that is integrated in the strategic planning process has been acknowledged as a condition for achieving crisis readiness. Crisis awareness should be a part of the corporate mindset, the organizational culture, and the leadership process. It lays the grounds of strategic crisis communication readiness. The process needs to be both communication- and management-driven with a strong top management support. Finally, the discussion about a clear purpose and values of an organization is still ongoing and will undoubtedly change the perception of organizations in the years to come. However, there are already early indications derived from our empirical data that a purpose can be helpful in a crisis, especially when it is embedded in the organization's strategy and overall activities.

References

Björck, A. (2016). Crisis typologies revisited: An interdisciplinary approach. *Central European Business Review*, *5*(3), 25–37.

Björck, A. (2017, May 15). *Professionelle Krisenkommunikation*. https://www.m- q.ch/de/professionelle-krisenkommunikation/

Björck, A., Diers-Lawson A., & Dücrey F. (2022). Evolution and effectiveness of the governmental risk and crisis communication on Twitter in the Covid-19 pandemic: The Case of Switzerland. In *Proceedings of the International crisis and risk communication conference*, Vol. 5 (pp. 27–30). Nicholson School of Communication and Media. https://doi.org/10.30658/icrcc.2022.06

Bochenek, L. M. (2019). Doing good and being good or simply getting it right – corporate crisis and defensive advocacy. In *Advocacy and organizational engagement* (pp. 149–164). Emerald Publishing Limited. https://doi.org/10.1108/978-1-78973-437-920191009

Boin, A., & Hart, P. 't. (2003). Public leadership in times of crisis: Mission impossible? *Public Administration Review*, *63*(5), 544–553. https://doi.org/10.1111/1540-6210.00318

Cloudman, R., & Hallahan, K. (2006). Crisis communications preparedness among U.S. organizations: Activities and assessments by public relations practitioners. *Public Relations Review*, *32*(4), 367–376. https://doi.org/10.1016/j.pubrev.2006.09.005

Coombs, T. W. (2010). Parameters for crisis communication. In T. W. Coombs & S. J. Holladay (Eds.), *The handbook of crisis communication* (1st ed., pp. 17–53). Wiley-Blackwell.

Coombs, W. T., & Laufer, D. (2018). Global crisis management – Current research and future directions. *Journal of International Management*, *24*(3), 199–203. https://doi.org/10.1016/j.intman.2017.12.003

Deloitte Insights. (2018). *Stronger, fitter, better: Crisis management for the resilient enterprise*. Global Crisis Management Report 2018. https://www2.deloitte.com/ch/en/pages/risk/articles/crisis-management-for-the-resilient-enterprise.html.

Elsubbaugh, S., Fildes, R., & Rose, M. B. (2004). Preparation for crisis management: A proposed model and empirical evidence. *Journal of Contingencies and Crisis Management*, *12*(3), 112–127. https://doi.org/10.1111/j.0966-0879.2004.00441.x

Fink, S. (1986). *Crisis management: Planning for the inevitable*. AMACOM.

Haupt, B., & Azevedo, L. (2021). Crisis communication planning and nonprofit organizations. *Disaster Prevention and Management: An International Journal*, *30*(2), 163–178. https://doi.org/10.1108/DPM-06-2020-0197

James, M. (2018). Strategic readiness. In *The international encyclopedia of strategic communication* (pp. 1–5). Wiley. https://doi.org/10.1002/9781119010722.iesc0178

John-Eke, E. C., & Eke, J. K. (2020). Strategic planning and crisis management styles in organizations: A review of related literature. *Journal of Strategic Management, 5*(1), 36–46.

Labaš, D. (2017). The impact of organizational crisis preparedness on firm business performance. *Market-Tržište, 29*(1), 75–92. https://doi.org/10.22598/mt/2017.29.1.75

Lanzer, F., Sauberschwarz, L., & Weiß, L. (2020). *Erfolgreich durch die Krise*. Springer Fachmedien Wiesbaden. https://doi.org/10.1007/978-3-658-30543-7

Mitroff, I. I., Shrivastava, P., & Udwadia, F. E. (1987). Effective crisis management. *The Academy of Management Executive, 1*(4), 283–292.

Niggemann, L. (2022, April 28). *Von der Krisenprävention zur Crisis Readiness*. https://www.kom.de/von-der-krisenpraevention-zur-crisis-readiness/

Preble, J. F. (1997). Integrating the crisis management perspective into the strategic management process. *Journal of Management Studies, 34*(5), 769–791.

Rousaki, B., & Alcott, P. (2006). Exploring the crisis readiness perceptions of hotel managers in the UK. *Tourism and Hospitality Research, 7*(1), 27–38. https://doi.org/10.1057/palgrave.thr.6050030

Sellnow, T. L., & Veil, S. R. (2016). Preparing for international and cross-cultural crises. The role of competing voices, inclusivity, and the interplay of responsibility in global organizations. In A. Schwarz, M. W. Seeger, & C. Auer (Eds.), *The handbook of international crisis communication research*. https://doi.org/10.1002/9781118516812.ch44

Sheaffer, Z., & Mano-Negrin, R. (2003). Executives' orientations as indicators of crisis management policies and practices. *Journal of Management Studies, 40*(2), 573–606.

Spillan, J., & Hough, M. (2003). Crisis planning in small businesses. *European Management Journal, 21*(3), 398–407. https://doi.org/10.1016/S0263-2373(03)00046 X

UZH Center for Crisis Competence. (2022). *UZH Center for Crisis Competence (CCC)*. https://www.crisiscompetence.uzh.ch/en.html

Vos, M., Lund, R., Reich, Z., & Harro-Loit, H. (2011). *Developing a crisis communication scorecard: Outcomes of an international research project 2008–2011*. Jyväskylä University Printing House. https://cordis.europa.eu/docs/results/217/217889/final1-book-criscomscore-9789513942618.pdf

3 "Sharing Is Preparing"

The Role of Information-Sharing in Collective Crisis Sensemaking during the July 22 Terror Attack in Oslo

Hogne Lerøy Sataøen and Helge Renå

In the wake of fast-burning crises information-sharing and communication, within and between organizations, as well as between organizations and the public, pose perennial challenges (Boin et al., 2016; 't Hart & Boin, 2001). This is primarily because fast-burning crises are rife with uncertainty about causes, consequences, and intervention options (Ansell et al., 2010). With communication increasingly being seen as an ongoing challenge in the actual management of crises, crisis communication has emerged as a distinct and cohesive field producing a large body of research in the last ten years (Diers-Lawson, 2017). Still, the fields of crisis communication and crisis management view the role and function of communication differently. Crisis communication researchers often focus on the external aspects of crisis communication, for instance crisis-response strategies, public relations, and image-repair efforts, rather than the internal aspects: the communication within the organizations handling the crisis (Frandsen & Johansen, 2011). Consequently, limited efforts have been made to theoretically and empirically reflect upon communicational conditions, processes, and activities during an ongoing crisis (Bundy et al., 2017). Crisis management research, on the other hand, tends to play down the role of communication during ongoing crises, paying more attention to issues such as decision-making, organizational learning, and organizational cultures (Johansen et al., 2012).

This chapter addresses this paradoxical situation through in-depth analysis of the terrorist attacks in Oslo on 22 July 2011. The analysis relies on Karl Weick's sensemaking theory, which provides a valuable starting-point for understanding the role of information-sharing and communication during ongoing crises. Furthermore, the concept of *collective crisis sensemaking* (Frandsen, 2020; Stieglitz et al., 2018) has the potential to bring together insights from crisis communication and crisis management research. During an ongoing crisis, collective sensemaking processes concern how social actors create their environment by (en)acting and paying attention to some information while ignoring other information (Maitlis & Sonenshein, 2010; Young, 2018). Hence, sensemaking pertains to the process of clarifying what is going on and bracketing cues from the environment (Stieglitz et al., 2018). Sensemaking is about attributing meaning to environmental stimuli,

DOI: 10.4324/9781003375296-5

and it necessitates communication to connect cues to frames (Young, 2018). As crises typically consist of unexpected and incomprehensible events and situations, sensemaking is of the utmost importance for reducing confusion and guiding action (Waller & Uitdewilligen, 2008). Still, the actual processes whereby individuals put their different pieces of information together jointly and collectively have thus far largely been neglected (Maitlis & Christianson, 2014, p. 102).

The aim of this chapter is to contribute to filling this gap by theorizing about how collective crisis sensemaking and the actual practice of *putting together pieces of information* within and outside organizations might contribute to the crisis communication and crisis management literatures respectively. More specifically, we elucidate how power, culture and polyphonic communication have roles to play in sensemaking processes. We ask the following research questions: (How) are individuals who hold different pieces of information during an ongoing crisis able to collectively construct meaning? What challenges are involved in the processes of collective crisis sensemaking?

The empirical basis of the chapter comprises three communicative situations related to the so-called "car tip" during the two terrorist attacks in Oslo, 2011. In the aftermath of the crisis the police were strongly criticized (NOU, 2012). A quintessential example of what was widely perceived as a flawed police response was its handling of the "car tip." This tip included detailed information about an armed person in uniform who was observed leaving the government complex only minutes prior to the explosion. In the chapter, the following situations are analyzed: First, we look at how an operator assistant at the Oslo police communicated with the operations commander by a written note, causing valuable information to go missing for a significant amount of time. Second, we analyze the situation related to information about an armed man, which three separate operations operators received but did not link together. None of the operators had an overall picture, nor did they have the technology to combine the incoming information. Third, we will focus on how information shared by the Oslo police operations center was decoded differently by different police districts close to Oslo. Using unique, real-time data, we map in detail how the police handled and shared information and how they tried, but, with one exception, failed to collectively make sense of witness reports.

Theoretical Observations

Crisis Management: Sensemaking and the Ongoing Crisis

The notion of sensemaking has attracted much scholarly attention since Karl Weick's pioneering work in the 1970s and 1980s (Weick, 1976, 1979, 1988). To be sure, the sensemaking literature has offered important insights to the crisis management literature and organizational theory more generally. Weick did not define himself as a crisis theorist and only partly relied on conventional terminology from crisis management and communication research (Frandsen, 2020). Nevertheless, sensemaking has widely been utilized in crisis communication studies, in relation to discussions on situation awareness and the creation of common operating pictures.

To make sense of what is going on in a crisis, actors engage in collective sensemaking, which is understood as "a process, prompted by violated expectations, that involves attending to and bracketing cues in the environment, creating intersubjective meaning through cycles of interpretation and action, and thereby enacting a more ordered environment from which further cues can be drawn" (Maitlis & Christianson, 2014, p. 67). This definition is dense and complex, and we will explore it by discussing three principal elements: enactment, cues, and situation awareness. We conclude by summarizing important challenges related to collective crisis sensemaking in practice.

Enactment

When people act, they bring structures and events into existence and set them in motion (Renå, 2019). Enactment is the "socio-psychological phenomenon of someone 'predicting' or expecting something, and this 'prediction' or expectation comes true simply because one believes it will, and their resulting behaviors align to fulfil those beliefs" (Frandsen, 2020, p. 183). Enactment is intimately related to how Weick understands context and environment. For Weick the environment is never *given* and external. Hence, people do not react or adapt to the environment. Instead, the environment is created and shaped by enactments. This has to do with how different streams of data, information and intelligence are merged together and put into action in order to create situation awareness and common operating pictures (Wolbers & Boersma, 2013).

Cues

During an ongoing crisis, sensemaking processes concern how social actors create their environment by paying attention to some facts while ignoring others (Maitlis & Sonenshein, 2010; Young, 2018). Hence, sensemaking pertains to the process of clarifying what is going on and bracketing cues from the environment (Stieglitz et al., 2018). In a context of crisis, sensemaking entails talk and action intended to make "plausible sense of cues, in addition to the sense that is made through connecting a cue to a frame, that is, the process of meaning creation through communication behaviors in a crisis" (Young, 2018, p. 454). In a practical sense, making sense of cues involves cognitively combining different pieces of information. Paradoxically, however, an important dimension of collective sensemaking "that appears to have been relatively little pursued (...) [is] how individuals who hold different pieces of information are able to collectively construct new meaning" (Maitlis & Christianson, 2014, p. 102).

Situation Awareness and Common Operating Pictures

Situation awareness has been understood as both the ability to communicate and share information, and the pursuit of sufficient mutual understanding (Wolbers & Boersma, 2013). It is the dynamic understanding that a team or individual possess about a specific situation (Uitdewilligen & Waller, 2018, p. 732). Wolbers and Boersma (2013) see the activities involved in the creation of common operating pictures and situation awareness as pivotal parts of collective sensemaking processes. They argue that information-sharing might help the involved actors *make sense* of a crisis. Moreover, the creation of a common operating picture is a "trading zone," where actors interact, and create and share meaning. Still, the kinds of information that are shared matter. For instance, Uitdewilligen and Waller (2018) distinguish between sharing facts, interpretations, and projections. Fact-sharing is the transmission of technically accurate information about individual elements of a situation. Interpretation-sharing gives meaning to the information and creates possibilities to link elements to existing knowledge structures. Projection-sharing pertains to "the communication of projections and anticipations of future states" (ibid., p. 733).

Three Communicative Challenges in Collective Crisis Sensemaking: Power, Culture and Polyphonic Communication

In his seminal case study of the Mann Gulch fire, Weick (1993) referred to an evaluation where it was found that subordinates "mitigated" their requests and questions when communicating with superiors, which made the superiors more likely to ignore what they said. In a similar vein, research on voice delivery has demonstrated that managers and employees often regard what is being communicated differently (Burris et al., 2013). Schildt et al. (2020) show how power functions in implicit and hidden ways within sensemaking processes. Hence, in recent years there have been increasing calls to bring power into sensemaking research (Vaara & Whittle, 2022). We agree with those who situate collective sensemaking, both as a process and a result, in spoken language and written texts. But spoken language is not only about what is said, *how* we communicate is also important (Romney, 2021). Organization members enact different roles that are organized in some form of organizational structure, with a set of associated expectations involving power-relations.

Crisis responses typically involve several first responder organizations. These have their own sets of norms, procedures, and terminology, which can be barriers for effective information-sharing and meaning-construction across boundaries. One problem is that the recipients of information in crisis settings do not understand the implications of the information they receive (Wolbers & Boersma, 2013). This is because the recipients do not have exhaustive knowledge of what various parts of the information may mean for actors from other professions, because they are members of different networks of actors. For instance, information about X may make a medical responder think it is important to mobilize pediatric healthcare, while responders from the police and fire department do not draw this conclusion.

A sense of urgency is pervasive in crisis settings, and the list of pending tasks is long. This increases the risk of communicational misunderstandings because senders and recipients have not invested sufficient time to make sure that they have a shared understanding. As Wolbers and Boersma (2013) noted, "the crux is to find the appropriate balance between swift decision making and reflective meaning exchange on the information they have and possible steps further" (p. 197). Accepting communicational polyphony in such instances might be productive. For instance, researchers have documented that a behavior termed "talking to the room" (undirected talk to repeat information in the room) can facilitate effective collective sensemaking (Waller & Uitdewilligen, 2008). This communicational form has the potential to create common ground for team-members, both because everyone knows that the knowledge is shared, and because it is an input for sensemaking (Clark & Brennan, 1991). In practice, talking to the room is about stimulating polyphonic communication where actors express added information out loud, without directing it toward anyone else in particular. Polyphonic communication is seldom part of fast-response organizations' routines, as it breaks with organizational designs and hierarchical orders. Nevertheless, "dialogic coordination," for instance through cross-boundary interventions (and protocol breaking), can be time-critical actions in fast-response organizations (Faraj & Xiao, 2006).

The Case: Uncertainties and Communicational Challenges

Our empirical point of departure is the terrorist attack in Oslo on 22 July 2011 (also called 22/7). At 3:25 p.m., a large explosion was heard in central Oslo, and windows throughout the city were broken.[1] At the police headquarters, approximately two kilometers from the explosion, the blast was heard through open windows. Still, the operators did not notice the explosion, because the police operations center is situated deep in the headquarters without windows. Within seconds, however, they received alarms and incoming calls from throughout the city. Their working screens went "red," and what so far had been a "normal" day suddenly became a crisis (Renå, 2019).

Incoming calls to the police, including calls to the 112 police emergency number, are all routed to the police switchboard for a first assessment, before being re-routed to the operations center. After the explosion there was a surge of incoming calls. The operation assistants at the switchboard were unable to respond to all of them. Pending incoming calls were automatically transferred to the operations center after a fixed period. Hence, some of the incoming 112 calls were forwarded directly to the operations center, without any preassessment by the assistants. Because of the significant discrepancy between the number of incoming calls and operators, many calls were not answered at all during the first hectic hours and minutes. Between 3:00 and 4:00 p.m., 186 calls were reported, and 85 were not answered. Within an hour all ten operator desks were staffed, in addition to two extra operations commanders. However, some calls (14 out of 69) remained unanswered between 4:00 and 5:00 p.m. (Renå, 2019). This indicates a constant stream of incoming information about a novel, unexpected incident which demanded the operators' full concentration.

Data Sources

Our analysis is based on unique data sources that describe the actual and ongoing communication within and between police units. The data is best characterized as "real time data." Specifically, it consists of (a) transcripts of radio communication, (b) transcripts of phone communication, and (c) copies of PO-logs. In addition, one of the authors of this chapter conducted three days of field observations at the Oslo police operations center. These observations – where the researcher "shadowed" (Trouille & Tavory, 2019) the operations commander – provided valuable validation of the analysis. Lastly, the 480-page official evaluation report on 22/7 (NOU, 2012) also provided important context.

Phone and Radio Communication

The analysis is based on transcripts of phone and radio communication from the Oslo police, the Nordre Buskerud police, and from the fire and rescue services' 110 emergency number. The transcripts were made by internal police evaluators. As for phone communication, only calls from or to the operations centers in Oslo and Nordre Buskerud were available.

The PO-Logs

This refers to the system used by the police to register information. It is an electronic system for operating services and tasks. Transcripts from 19 (out of 27) Norwegian police districts were available for the analysis. Because the registrations in the PO-logs happen in real time, the logs provide a valuable supplement to radio and phone communication. Furthermore, in 2011 the PO-log was the most important tool used by the Norwegian police to share and transmit written information internally during ongoing events and operations.

Scrutinizing this real-time data enables us to trace how information traveled minute-by-minute through the police organization. Hence, the data provides us with a unique prism for analyzing how information-sharing and sensemaking de facto take place during an ongoing crisis.

Results

Creating Shared Ground: A Written Note on Eyewitness Observations

The first communicative situation we will examine deals with how an important incoming eyewitness observation went "missing" for 20 minutes. At 3:34 p.m., nine minutes after the bomb explosion, one of the operator assistants answered one of the many incoming emergency calls. The caller reported that (s)he

> "(...) saw something very suspicious while passing the government quarter about fifteen minutes ago (...) There was a man in a police uniform who came on foot and sat down" [...] "It's a specific tip about a car (...) a car the person drove away in (...) and I have the license plate number."
>
> (Oslo Police, phone transcript, 15:34:50–15:37:11)

As this excerpt indicates, significant information about the perpetrator is shared with the operator assistant less than ten minutes after the explosion. This incoming call contains information about a man wearing a police uniform, and it even contains the license plate number of his car. Nevertheless, the operator assistant interrupts the eyewitness: "Sorry, but I cannot take this down right now, you see, but what is your name?" The assistant ends the call by telling the eyewitness (s) he is noting the information and someone will call back.

The main task of operator assistants is to evaluate calls and forward those that seem to concern actual emergencies to the emergency operators. In this case, the assistant is certain that the call is urgent. However, (s)he is reluctant to forward the call, because (s)he does not know how long the telephone queue is, nor does (s)he know the waiting time. Unfortunately, it is not possible to give the incoming call priority in the queue, and as an assistant (s)he is not able to register the information in the PO-log. Deeming this information to be important, the assistant decides to deviate from the standard routines. Therefore, (s)he writes down a summary of the eyewitness observation and the caller's contact information in a notebook. The assistant then walks across the hall to the operations center where the operators and operations commander are located.

The operations center is a special environment with clear hierarchies and distinct norms. The operations center is always associated with *respect*. When an operator assistant enters the center, (s)he is only allowed to communicate with the one in command, namely the operations commander. When the operator assistant enters the room, the commander appears very occupied. The operator assistant puts the note on the desk and makes eye contact with the commander (NOU, 2012, p. 100). The commander nods to the assistant as a tacit "positive confirmation." No one in the operations center takes any notice of the note before 3:56 p.m.

This communicative situation is indicative of how a shared meaning is not established in the operations center, although highly important information and cues – the written note – had literally come all the way to the doorstep. From a sensemaking perspective, the cues were not sufficiently connected to a frame (cf. Young, 2018). The written note was passed on outside normal routines, and the communicative situation was saturated with power-relations. This does not create the best conditions for collective sensemaking. The assistant and the commander were assigned distinct roles, structured according to a strict hierarchy. For instance, it is a strong norm that operator assistants are only allowed to communicate with the commander, and no one else. When the assistant entered the operations center, (s)he was muted and careful in her behavior. The confirmation given by the operations commander was a tacit nod, and there was no indication that the assistant could interrupt or demand attention.

Shouting Silently: Three Operators and No Collective Sensemaking

The second communicational situation under scrutiny is the actual situation in the operations center during the first chaotic hour after the explosion. We will focus on how important eyewitness reports are not linked or related in the operations center. By 4:08 p.m., approximately 45 minutes after the detonation was heard, the operations center in Oslo had received three individual and independent eyewitness reports about an armed man in a uniform. The first, and most detailed of these three reports was the one described in the previous section, which even included information about the perpetrator's car and license plate number. However, it was not possible for the operators to make collective sense of this information and swiftly share it internally and externally.

At 3:56 p.m., after discovering the note with information about an armed man and a description of his car, one of the operators calls the eyewitness back. The eyewitness retells the story, claiming that (s)he saw a man wearing a police uniform. The perpetrator was described as having:

> (…) looked European, and I would estimate he was somewhere in his thirties. And from the little I noticed, though it was a relatively weak observation, I would estimate he was about 180 centimeters tall.
>
> (Oslo Police, phone transcript, 15:55:43–16:01:45)

Within the next six minutes, the police received five calls at the operations center where information about a man in uniform was transmitted and shared (Renå, 2022). As indicated below, no coherent situation awareness was established related to the armed man, and there were few attempts to merge information:

1 Eyewitness reports from a security guard close to the explosion are shared by the Incident Commander with the operations center. This report indicates that a man in a uniform driving a van might have had something to do with the

explosion. The operator at the operations center informs all patrols about this on the police radio. (Oslo Police, radio transcript, 16:02:43–16:03:57)

2 At 4:03 p.m. an incoming call to the operations center focuses on a "man in a police uniform." (Oslo Police, phone transcript, 16:03:28–16:07:45)

3 At 4:04 p.m. one of the operators at the operations center calls the Incident Commander on the police radio. The operator confirms that other eyewitness reports have indicated that a man in a uniform was involved. (S)he reports: "I have just talked to an eyewitness who encountered such a car and saw a man who was dressed as you described with a bullet-proof helmet and some sort of pistol, and that it drove away from the incident scene. I'm running the license plate now so you'll get more information later. Over." The Incident Commander responds: "Copy that. Delta is working further on that lead. Over." (Oslo Police, radio transcript, TG-1 16:04:26–16:05:34)

4 At 4:05 p.m. the Operations Commander (OpCom) responds to a telephone call from the desk of The National Criminal Investigation Service (KRIPOS). KRIPOS is the agency responsible for operating the internal police alert system, and it is expected to broadcast national alerts on request. In the conversation, the commander shares the information about a car and requests a national alert. The following conversation takes place: Kripos: "Is there anything – do you want any assistance from us?" OpCom: "Yes, well, you could of course, well, it could maybe be interesting to maybe alert, to put out a national alert." Kripos: "Yes, and what should it contain?" OpCom: "No, well, it is interesting that a car has been spotted here. A small, gray van. VH24605. So if you could put out a, a national alert that there has been an attack here, and that the police districts should actually keep it in mind a bit." Kripos: "The car?" OpCom: "Yes. And all other activity, because it could be interesting regarding the national borders. Maybe alert Customs, who are present at most borders at least." (Oslo Police, phone transcript, 16:04:56–16:08:03)

5 At 4:06 p.m. one of the operations center's operators calls the Delta officer in command. The operator reiterates the information about an armed and uniformed man with a helmet driving away from the explosion. The Delta commander repeats some of the information and responds: "We'll just continue assisting the rescue operation here until you have something more." (Oslo Police, phone transcript, 16:05:56–16:07:48)

Although KRIPOS was asked to broadcast a national alert, no tactical or operative measures were taken based on the information about an armed, uniformed man. Furthermore, no explicit assessments were made of the situation, or of potential operations and measures. Or at least, no such assessments were explicitly made in the operations center. Hence, no collective understanding emerged, and no collective understanding of the meaning of the information was established. Therefore, it was never possible to collectively enact a response by talking to the room (Waller &

Uitdewilligen, 2008). There was no culture, nor previous experience, of talking to the room in the operations center. Doing so would require one of the operators to step out of normal procedures. Possibly, the power structures and established routines became barriers to polyphonic communication and talking to the room.

Intra-Organizational Sensemaking: Sharing Information between Different Organizations

The third communicational situation analyzed involves the information-sharing that took place between the operations center in Oslo and the corresponding centers in three neighboring police districts (Asker-and-Bærum, Romerike, and Follo), between 4:09 and 4:17 p.m. At 4:09 the operations commander at the neighboring police district Asker-and-Bærum (ABPD) contacts the operation center in Oslo. ABPD asks if there is anything they can do to support Oslo.

Operations Operator: "We have just received a message now, I don't know if it has anything to do with the incident, but it's a bit... An eyewitness who met a man wearing some sort of uniform, a bullet-proof helmet and a pistol. Enters a van five minutes before the explosion, with the following registration number: Victor Hotel."

ABPD: "Yes"

Operations Operator: "24605"

ABPD: "24605"

Operations operator: "And drove the wrong way on a one-way street. That's the latest information I have, we don't have anything more, except several reports indicating there was a van near the explosion." (Oslo Police, phone transcript, 16:08:46–16:10:57)

The call lasts for two minutes, and ABPD concludes that Oslo does not need any particular support at the moment. However, they assume that they will be activated later on. The reports about the car (VH24605) are shared with the three patrol cars in the area.

At 4:15 p.m. an operations operator in Oslo calls the operations centers in Follo and Romerike. The call with the commander at Romerike lasts for one minute. The operator from Oslo shares the following information: "related to the explosion, there is a car that we would like to be stopped and checked if you come across it" (Oslo Police, phone transcript, 16:14:49–16:15:44). The operator gives the license plate number of the car. Still, the operator is vague when it comes to the role and status of the case. Furthermore, the man who was observed driving the car is not mentioned. The operations commander at Romerike does not follow up on the information. In the PO-log from Romerike, the license plate number of the vehicle is noted as well as a request to patrols to "check the car if seen" (Romerike politidistrikt, PO-log 22 July 2011).

At 4.16 p.m., just after the call with Romerike, the same operations operator in Oslo calls Follo police district and states that they would like to have a vehicle stopped and checked (the operator mentions the license plate number) "if a Follo patrol encounters it" (Oslo Police, phone transcript, 16:15:44–16:17:25). Contrary to the information supplied to the Romerike police district, Follo is informed that eyewitness reports indicate that the vehicle "may have something to do with it [the explosion]." This is followed by a conversation where the operator in Follo confirms what is said and asks follow-up questions. In Follo's PO-log most of the information from Oslo is described, and at 4:30 p.m. the PO-log from Follo states that all Follo units have been informed about the car. A designated patrol is even strategically placed to observe a main road (Follo politidistrikt, PO-log 22 July 2011).

As shown, the communication from the operations center in Oslo to the neighboring police districts varies. The sharing of information is always part of ongoing coding and decoding processes. For example, when communicating with Asker-and-Bærum and Romerike, no clear link was ever established between the car and the explosion. When communicating with Follo, however, the operator stated that eyewitness reports indicated the car was involved. Furthermore, both Asker-and-Bærum and Romerike were informed to "look for" the car, whereas in Follo a specific observation patrol was established. In this communicational situation, the information crosses organizational borders, where members have different norms for communication. The challenges of sensemaking are particularly evident in such instances. Reasonable solutions do exist, however, for instance setting up conversations in a better way and including contextual descriptions in addition to mere fact-sharing.

Discussion and Conclusions

Frandsen (2020) argues that collective sensemaking should be seen as a major trend in crisis sensemaking research, however it is still waiting to see its full potential. The analysis has provided us with some intriguing examples of how collective sensemaking during a crisis plays out in practice, as well as examples of barriers to collective sensemaking processes. Inspired by Uitdewilligen and Waller's (2018) distinction between "fact-sharing," "interpretation-sharing" and "projection-sharing," we structure this final discussion in line with a model that links three core concepts from Weick's perspective with evidence from the analysis. Figure 3.1 highlights how collective sensemaking is shaped both by the sharing of cues and the connecting of cues to a frame. As is evident in the analysis, receivers of information interpret it in different ways (cf. Burris et al., 2013), and they also take information into consideration for action. Hence, actors bracket cues from the environment, and put cues into broader interpretive

Cues	Connecting cues to a frame	Collective enacting of the environment
Sharing descriptive facts	Sharing interpretations where information is contextual and includes assessments of the situation	Sharing information related to implications and assessments of measures
Example: The license plate	Example: Car tip linked to the explosion	Example: Descriptions of what resources should be mobilized to stop the car

Figure 3.1 Collective Sensemaking Shaped by Cues, Frames and Enactment.

frames. They do so by merging pieces of information. Eventually, this provides a basis for enactment, where the information is used to predict outcomes and design actual measures. The possibility to do so, however, is conditioned by power relations, differences in organizational cultures, and the possibilities for, and acceptance of, polyphonic communication.

Crisis organizations are by definition hierarchical, with well-established chains of command and a clear division of tasks. Members perform distinctive roles with specific expectations and a need for effective information-sharing. However, in the analysis we observed that essential information was not shared because of how power dynamics played out internally. The dimension of power was also built into the technological structure, as the operator assistants are not authorized to register information in the PO-log. Hence, cues were not sufficiently shared. Perhaps it would have helped if the assistants received clearer signals that they are allowed to "barge into" the operations center and demand attention if they think they have vital information. This ties in with Faraj and Xiao's (2006) notion of "dialogic coordination," where cross-boundary interventions and protocol breaking are seen as time-critical actions.

Different organizations have different sets of norms, procedures, and terminologies. In short, culture plays a role in information-sharing and meaning-construction. An example from the analysis is the communication between the operations center in Oslo and the various neighboring police districts, which differed to a large degree. We also observe that communicational *forms* varied. For instance, the responses from Asker-and-Bærum and Romerike were short (mostly yes/no), whereas in Follo there were more elaborate responses. Although short responses are effective in crisis situations, they might also lead to misunderstandings. Short responses are also ineffective in explicating meaning. In Follo, the operations commander asked questions, and the operator also reiterated facts to confirm the understanding. Hence, the sender and receiver of information can mutually understand the implications of the information they share (Wolbers & Boersma, 2013).

Finally, the analysis showed how important separate eyewitness reports were not linked at the operations center. No collective understanding emerged, and no collective understanding of the meaning of the information was established. Therefore, in theoretical terms, it was never possible to engage in collective enactment by talking to the room. In our cases, as in many similar crises, the measures taken were improvised and based on individual initiatives. These individual initiatives were never merged, nor was the information meaningfully combined to enable collective sensemaking to occur. This could have been possible, however, if the value of polyphonic communication had been appreciated. "Talking to the room," as described by Waller and Uitdewilligen (2008), has the potential of creating common ground for team members.

Collective crisis sensemaking goes beyond sensemaking in teams or smaller groups, and concerns the crossing of inter-organizational, cultural, and social boundaries (Frandsen, 2020). The analysis in this chapter has shown the importance of *how* information is shared during a crisis. We have identified differences in information-sharing among different organizational units and members. The analyzed case is characterized by a high degree of uncertainty. Hence, it is difficult for the involved actors to make swift and correct decisions. It is also difficult for the actors to merge information and put together the different pieces of the puzzle. Paying deeper attention to power and culture, as well as facilitating polyphonic communication could, however, be a way forward for sensemaking during ongoing crises.

Note

1 The bombing was followed by a second terrorist attack two hours later on the island of Utøya, 40 kilometers northwest of Oslo.

References

Ansell, C., Boin, A., & Keller, A. (2010). Managing transboundary crises: Identifying the building blocks of an effective response system. *Journal of Contingencies and Crisis Management, 18*(4), 195–207. https://doi.org/10.1111/j.1468-5973.2010.00620.x

Boin, E., Stern, E., 't Hart, P. & Sundelius, B. (2016). *The politics of crisis management: Public leadership under pressure* (2nd ed.). Cambridge University Press.

Bundy, J., Pfarrer, M. D., Short, C. E., & Coombs, T. W. (2017). Crises and crisis management: Integration, interpretation, and research development. *Journal of Management, 43*(6), 1661–1692. https://doi.org/10.1177/0149206316680030

Burris, E. R., Detert, J. R., & Romney, A. C. (2013). Speaking up vs. being heard: The disagreement around and outcomes of employee voice. *Organization Science, 24*(1), 22–38. https://doi.org/10.1287/orsc.1110.0732

Clark, H. H., & Brennan, S. E. (1991). Grounding in communication. *Perspectives on Socially Shared Cognition, 13*, 127–149.

Diers-Lawson, A. (2017). *Crisis communication.* Oxford Research Encyclopedia of Intergroup Communication.

Faraj, S., & Xiao, Y. (2006). Coordination in fast-response organizations. *Management Science, 52*(8), 1155–1169. http://www.jstor.org/stable/20110591

Frandsen, F. (2020). Making sense of crisis sensemaking theory: Weick's contributions to the study of crisis communication. In F. Frandsen & W. Johansen (Eds.), *Crisis communication. Handbook in communicational science*. Mouton De Gruyter.

Frandsen, F., & Johansen, W. (2011). The study of internal crisis communication: Towards an integrative framework. *Corporate Communications: An International Journal, 16*(4), 347–361. https://doi.org/10.1108/13563281111186977

Johansen, W., Aggerholm, H., & Frandsen, F. (2012). Entering new territory: A study of internal crisis management and crisis communication in organizations. *Public Relations Review, 38*(2), 270–279. https://doi.org/10.1016/j.pubrev.2011.11.008

Maitlis, S., & Christianson, M. (2014). Sensemaking in organizations: Taking stock and moving forward. *The Academy of Management Annals, 8*, 57–125.

Maitlis, S., & Sonenshein, S. (2010). Sensemaking in crisis and change: Inspiration and insights from Weick (1988). *Journal of Management Studies, 47*(3), 551–580. https://doi.org/10.1111/j.1467-6486.2010.00908.x

NOU. (2012). *Rapport fra 22. juli-kommisjonen (NOU 2012:14)*. Oslo: Departementenes Servicesenter.

Renå, H. (2019). Police coordination in crises. Who knew what, when, where and why in managing the terrorist attacks in Oslo and Utøya in 2011? PhD-dissertation, University of Bergen.

Renå, H. (2022). *Krisehåndtering i et organisasjonsperspektiv. Politi-innsatsen 22. juli.* Oslo: Cappelen Damm Akademisk.

Romney, A. C. (2021). It's not just what you say, it's how you say it: How callings influence constructive voice delivery. *Human Relations*, 74(12), 2021–2050. https://doi.org/10.1177/0018726720945775

Schildt, H., Mantere, S., & Cornelissen, J. (2020). Power in sensemaking processes. *Organization Studies, 41*, 241–265.

Stieglitz, S. Mirbabaie, M., & Milde, M. (2018). Social positions and collective sense-making in crisis communication. *International Journal of Human–Computer Interaction.* https://doi.org/10.1080/10447318.2018.1427830

't Hart, P., & Boin, A. (2001). Between crisis and normalcy: The long shadow of post-crisis politics. In U. Rosenthal, A. Boin, & L. K. Comfort (Eds.), *Managing Crises. Threats, Dilemmas, Opportunities* (pp. 28–48). Charles C Thomas.

Trouille, D., & Tavory, I. (2019). Shadowing: Warrants for intersituational variation in ethnography. *Sociological Methods & Research, 48*(3), 534–560. https://doi.org/10.1177/0049124115626171

Uitdewilligen, S., & Waller, M. J. (2018). Information sharing and decision-making in multidisciplinary crisis management teams. *Journal of Organizational Behavior, 39*(6), 731–748. https://doi.org/10.1002/job.2301

Vaara, E., & Whittle, A. (2022), Common sense, new sense or non-sense? A critical discursive perspective on power in collective sensemaking. *Journal of Management Studies, 59*, 755–781. https://doi.org/10.1111/joms.12783

Waller, M. J. & Uitdewilligen, S. (2008). Talking to the room: Collective sensemaking during crisis situations. In R. Roe, M. J. Waller, & S. R. Clegg (Eds.), *Time in organizational research*. London: Routledge.

Weick, K. E. (1976). Educational organizations as loosely coupled systems. *Administrative Science Quarterly*, *21*(1), 1. https://doi.org/10.2307/2391875

Weick, K. E. (1979). *The social psychology of organizing* (2nd ed.). Addison-Wesley.

Weick, K. E. (1988). Enacted sensemaking in crisis situations. *Journal of Management Studies*, *25*(4), 305–317. https://doi.org/10.1111/j.1467-6486.1988.tb00039.x

Weick, K. E. (1993). The Collapse of Sensemaking in Organizations: The Mann Gulch Disaster. *Administrative Science Quarterly*, *38*(4), 628–652. https://doi.org/10.2307/2393339

Wolbers, J., & Boersma, K. (2013). The common operational picture as collective sensemaking. *Journal of Contingencies and Crisis Management*, *21*(4), 186–199. https://doi.org/10.1111/1468-5973.12027

Young, K. (2018). Enhancing employee communication behaviors for sensemaking and sensegiving in crisis situations: strategic management approach for effective internal crisis communication. *Journal of Communication Management*, *22*(4), 451–475.

4 A Caring Framework for Crises and Disasters

Amalia Triantafillidou and Prodromos Yannas

More often than ever before we witness major crises and disasters erupting and unfolding. In the European Union area from January to end of September 2022 alone there have been a multitude of disasters such as drought, fires, and floods. For example, a severe drought crisis contributed to a series of wildfires occurring throughout the summer season in Spain, Greece, Portugal, France, Italy, and Slovenia, Germany, and the Czech Republic (European Commission, EMS, Info Bulletin 163, 4 November 2022). At the same time globally, we are seeing similar disaster experiments. For example, monsoon rains caused flooding in several cities in Nigeria and Pakistan causing the loss of more than 1,200 lives and spreading devastation. This is just a small snapshot of the climate crisis that we are confronting. Droughts, wildfires, monsoon rains, tsunamis, and other extreme weather events are manifestations of a global climate crisis that has been brewing for several decades.

Central to understanding the current state of the earth is the human-nature interaction and the values that accompany it. On one side of the spectrum, humans define ourselves as rational, autonomous, invulnerable, knowledgeable, and skillful; capable of subjugating and bending non-humans for the fulfillment of our own wishes. This anthropocentric view espouses instrumental values that prioritize and calculate the benefits to humans based on an efficiency calculus and cost-benefit analysis. On the other end of the spectrum others share values that prioritize nature's inherent value, regardless of the views and design of humans. A third category of values designating how humans relate to nature and to other humans are known as relational values. Principles and social norms of what constitutes "the good life", with harmony between humans and non-humans, are derived from relationships among humans as well as of responsibilities humans have toward one another and non-humans (Chan et al., 2016). People may care for individuals and family members, the sick, the impoverished, the injured, the victims, migrants, and refugees or any other social grouping but also for natural preservation and stewardship and endowing meaning to life by taking care of non-humans.

DOI: 10.4324/9781003375296-6

In analyzing the communication of crises and disasters, we intend to provide a novel approach drawing upon elaborations of two concepts: compassion and care. These two concepts can be thought of as relational and interdisciplinary in nature, rendering them appropriate for the study of crises and disasters as an interdisciplinary endeavor. Conceptually, both can be viewed as relational and context-bound, entangling spectators and sufferers in a continuous flow of interdependent interactions that shape the identities of the subjects. Through a relational lens, instead of focusing on individuals, we focus on relationships. For example, an individual's interests are not pursued independently but taking into consideration and connecting with the interests of others. Furthermore, these conceptions acknowledge that all humans are alike in the sense that they share vulnerabilities, fears, and hopes and suggest a stewardship for other people and the world around us.

We argue that an ethic of care and compassion provides a viable approach that actors should organize disaster relief efforts. Unfortunately, the ethic of care approach into crisis/disaster management and communication has received limited attention by researchers and practitioners (Linsley & Slack, 2013). In fact, the ethic of care has been mainly studied in the context of corporate crisis management (e.g., Simola, 2003) and communication (e.g., Tao & Kim, 2017), disaster management and political leadership (Crosweller, 2022; Triantafillidou & Yannas, 2022), and social media disaster response (Boulianne et al., 2018; Hayes & Jackson, 2020). Most of these studies follow a single-agent analysis emphasizing the behaviors of corporations, leaders, or users. To our knowledge, few studies have shed light on how various disaster relief stakeholders are involved in disaster response and recovery through an ethic of care and compassion approach. Hence, this chapter intends to enrich the limited discussion at the intersection of the ethic of care approach and disaster management and communication (Linsley & Slack, 2013). We do so by proposing a taxonomy of disaster relief initiatives during the emergency response and recovery phases of natural disasters based on the notions of compassion and care. The present chapter is organized as follows: first, the concepts of compassion and care are clarified to form the basis of the proposed framework which features two types of care: caring for and caring about. Second, the proposed Crisis/Disaster Response and Recovery Framework is enriched with a taxonomy that classifies the disaster relief and recovery practices of various stakeholders during and in the aftermath of crises and disasters. For demonstrative purposes, cases originating from Greece are being used.

Compassion and Care: Crisis/Disaster Response and Recovery Framework

Compassion is an emotional reaction, a feeling of identifying with the suffering of others – humans and non-humans alike – and being compelled to do something about it. Compassion then combines feeling with purposeful action. The action part in compassion is interwoven with ethical considerations, questions of justice and concerns for a life worth living. Compassion then triggers or motivates action that is justified on ethical grounds.

Compassion elicits two major types of action responses. Under the first reaction, compassion gradually gives way to hope. Emphasis is placed on alleviating urgently the condition of the sufferers and developing forward looking policies for improving their condition. Crises and disasters are seen as opportunities for launching infrastructure and developmental projects through economic and humanitarian assistance. Unquestionably, this is the preferred reaction of political leaders, government bureaucrats, international civil servants, and business executives. These powerful decision-makers are part of national or transnational elites that assume the role of benefactors toward distant sufferers when crises and disasters erupt. This structure, unfortunately, can mask the underlying causes of crises and disasters, which can be an inherently unjust socioeconomic system. For example, the benefactors offer financial assistance and distant recipients reciprocate with expressions of gratitude accompanied by obedience to the existing social order. An emphasis on the privileged position of the benefactors may end up in the process inculcating in them a patronizing behavior. It is possible that benefactors may be acting from altruistic motivations, but it is just as likely that there is an alternative motivation. What matters is whether actions are taken to address the underlying causes of crises and disasters like injustice in social systems responsible for human calamities or structural inequalities inherent in society. Despite all the charitable acts – both with named and anonymous benefactors, it remains no coincidence that people living in impoverished areas are more vulnerable to crises and disasters.

This may prompt anger at the injustice in the system and actions to address those problems, which can also be included as compassionate acts. Compassion filtered through anger can possibly take two forms, depending on whether it is primarily directed to distant or adjacent/geographically proximate sufferers. Suffering at a distance often takes the form of public condemnation, a practice that politicians of opposition parties, academics, civil-society organizations, and activists find appropriate to engage in (Milligan & Wiles, 2010). Intimate suffering, on the other hand, is not hindered by geographic separation and tries to create bonds of solidarity and envision together with the impacted populations bottom-up community-based projects and activities (Käpylä & Kennedy, 2014). These initiatives take time to come to fruition and are usually pursued by religious organizations and charities as well as activist and volunteer groups that do not actively partake in the market economy.

Compassion in Philosophy

An issue that has occupied ancient Greek (Aristotle, Euripides) and modern (Adam Smith, Rousseau) thinkers relates to the scope of compassion as a guide to action (Nussbaum, 2003). Are we capable of extending our imaginations to include the sufferings of all humanity, animals and plants or we are constrained by our attachments to family, kin, friends, nation, ideology, etc.? Put differently, does compassion cross boundaries extending our concern for distant others or is it limited to those intimate and close to us? Examples abound to document both positions. Martha Nussbaum (1996, 2001, 2003), a philosopher known for her scholarly work on compassion, mentions two examples seen from the perspective of the nation on the axis of proximity – distance. The terrorist attack of 11 September 2001, on the twin towers in New York is a clear case of Americans feeling compassion for the victims and their families as well as the NY firefighters and first respondents. The terrorist attack brought the fear to the fore and exposed the vulnerability of people that up until the event had felt safe and secure. In this example, proximity is demonstrated with feelings toward fellow nationals. Nussbaum cites an example from the writings of Adam Smith to support the claim that catastrophic events such as earthquakes, cyclones, and disasters that occur in Asia, for example, cause significant loss of life but do not evoke feelings of compassion. This is due to the incapacity of Westerners in the example to identify emotionally with the plight of distant others, in the triple sense of (a) the geographical distance, far away from our shores, (b) the psychological distance, people not of "our" own, and (c) the short time distance, the limited period we could afford to identify with the plight of the victims and show our grief before this temporary feeling would be overtaken by paying attention to more urgent concerns in our daily lives (Nussbaum, 2003). The key point that Nussbaum makes is that a pattern of interaction between spectators and sufferers must be established for compassion to be sustained and not fade away. The emphasis on interaction shows how the relational aspect of compassion informs even an extreme case of dealing with distant others.

Although there is wide agreement that compassion is an emotion, there is disagreement whether it entails action (Herring, 2017). Compassion may provide the necessary motivational force for action but there is no certainty that action will take place. Strangers, for example, who feel the pain and understand the misfortune of the sufferers may be inclined to help but, due to circumstances, the intention is not translated into action. To capture action, compassion must be combined with the concept of care. Conceptually, compassion and care differ in some respects. One difference is that compassion stresses the motivations to address suffering whereas care focuses on the activities. Power imbalance is the second differentiating factor. Due to an uneven position that strangers and sufferers occupy across social categories of income, social status, gender, race, and ethnicity strangers as more privileged may look down or feel pity for the condition of the sufferers. Third, caring relationships foster an intimate human connection whereas compassion forges a distance between compassionate strangers and sufferers, the objects of compassion. In this sense, care can be appropriately identified as a more relational concept than compassion.

Compassion, on the contrary, is not expected to lead to intimate relationships and is better practiced at a distance. Many people, for example, out of compassion for the victims of disasters may eventually participate in fundraising activities without bothering to engage more deeply and over the long run with the sufferers. Fourth, compassion and care differ with respect to the degree of moral judgment invested in the act. Whereas compassion almost always involves a moral judgment, the moral judgment in care is only implicitly made or not made at all (Herring, 2017). For example, a firefighter who rescues individuals from the flames that are responsible for causing the spread of the fire or a doctor who treats their injuries act out of a sense of duty or in line with expectations that their professional roles prescribe. As stated, no moral judgment is involved. Equally, though, one could make the case for implicit moral judgment coloring the view of both professionals since their actions are motivated out of concern for fellow humans who happen to be less privileged than themselves.

> All theoretical treatments of care conceive it as a process and practice. The most widely known and all-encompassing definition of care is the following developed by Joan Tronto (1993,2013):a species activity that includes everything that we do to maintain, continue, and repair our 'world' so that we can live in it as well as possible. That world includes our bodies, ourselves, and our environment, all of which we seek to interweave in a complex, life-sustaining web.
>
> (p. 15)

In care, affect is attached to the practice. As Latimer and Puig de la Bellacasa (2017) succinctly state, "care indicates an affective state, but also an obligation to 'pay attention' and to actually do the care it takes to practically pay attention" (p. 160).

Authors have conceived the process of care as involving either four phases or, as geographers prefer to do (Lawson, 2007; Milligan & Wiles, 2010), collapse the four into two: care about and care for. Political theorist Tronto's (1993) fourfold breakdown associates each phase with a corresponding virtue. The first phase is "care about" and requires attentiveness of the spectators. To be attentive means to show an interest and be sensitive to the concerns of others. The second phase is "care for" and the virtues of responsibility or duty/obligation signify the care practice. "Caring for" entangles spectators in a relationship with sufferers as the latter face the particularities of their unfortunate situation. By "caring for", spectators extend themselves and reach out to the sufferers. The way the caring relationship evolves depends on the course of interaction between the two parties. (Latimer & Puig de la Bellacasa, 2017). Care giving is the third phase associated with the virtue of competence. Care giving is undertaken by benefactors that are endowed with capabilities, knowledge, and skills. Care providers originate from four sectors: households, communities, states, and markets (The Care Collective, 2020). Households are central pillars of care.

When crises or disasters strike, the love and connectedness that tie families together make their members look for one another and rush to provide help. In case of injuries or traumas that take long time to heal, family members can count on one another for the provision of continuous care. Communities include civil society actors, religious organizations, foundations and charities, volunteer associations, non-governmental organizations (NGOs), collectivities, and cooperatives. Most of these organizations foster community bonding and solidarity and engage in care provision without assessing their contributions in cost-benefit terms. Provision of goods and services to humans and non-humans are guided by cooperation, collaboration, and support. High on the priorities of organizations that make up communities are concerns of justice, of alleviating human miseries and realizing the human potential as well living in a sustainable habitat. Many of these organizations distance themselves from the utilitarian perspective of ascribing value to the transaction-based market logic of making profit. When crises or disasters occur, organizations of various trades and persuasions are among the first to appear on the scene and offer help for as long as it takes for the sufferers to overcome their unfortunate condition and return to normality. The category of states includes all administrative agencies that make up the state apparatus at the local and national levels.

Of the four phases of care mentioned, the first two "care about" and "care for" underscore the form the relationship takes between strangers and sufferers and the latter two – care giving and care receiving – highlight more the perspective of the benefactors/strangers and the sufferers respectively. Thinking of care as a practice involving two parties, the distinction between "caring for" and "caring about" seems very pertinent in analyzing responses to crises and disasters. Caring for is more personal and specific, involving the undertaking of certain tasks toward specific others, the sufferers. Caring for is assessed over the long-term and in many cases requires a life-long personal commitment. To care for means to take the required time to do things with utmost sensitivity to the needs of the sufferers for as long as it takes. Care practices employed under caring for are culturally conditioned and take the particularities of each case seriously into consideration. On the other hand, caring about entails the emotional aspects of care toward more generalized others. Caring about entails feelings of pity, empathy and compassion toward people that happen to be impacted by a crisis and/or a disaster. General categories are employed for making sense of the situation: all sufferers either are grouped together in one category or share similar characteristics depending on the type of crisis or disaster (e.g., victims of wildfires, floods, tsunamis, earthquakes, etc.). In conceptions of caring about, one is prone to deal with abstract, general categories and overlooks contextual factors that shed light to the particularities of each case. Caring about practices is more amenable to science-based theoretical formulations and technical measures or managerial best practices.

Another important dimension that is pertinent to our discussion and supplements the distinction between caring about and caring for relates to the distance factor separating strangers from sufferers. Strangers may orient their care toward either intimate/proximate or distant others-sufferers. Caring for practices is associated with an intimate human connection between strangers and sufferers whereas caring about practices are the product of geographical separation, unevenness in power and social position or evolve out of distant suffering.

A Caring Taxonomy for the Compassion and Care Disaster Response and Recovery Framework

Considering the factors that can shape the different forms of caring that arise during and after disasters and crises, a taxonomy of stakeholders based on their caring practices is developed. These stakeholders could be charity and philanthropic organizations, municipalities, the government, businesses, and groups of volunteers. The stakeholder taxonomy is portrayed on a grid based on the dimensions of (a) proximity and (b) disaster stage. Proximity can differentiate the caring practices based on whether they are directed toward geographically distant or adjacent affected communities. At the disaster stage two phases have been considered: the emergency response phase that involves the provision of assistance for the immediate needs of the affected individuals and the recovery phase that involves the long-term reconstruction and rebuilding efforts of actors for facilitating community resilience.

Four categorizations of stakeholders are produced (see Table 4.1). The first group (A) refers to stakeholders that provide long-term care to victims with whom they develop close relationships, and the second group (B) is related to stakeholders that take care of the immediate needs of the victims and affected communities at the site of the disaster. The next group of stakeholders (C) is associated with caring practices that are provided to distant victims during the recovery stage while the fourth type of stakeholders (D) are groups who help the affected communities remotely during the intense phase of the disaster.

The proposed taxonomy also takes into consideration the motivation of the stakeholders to provide care. Herein, two broad forms of motivation to care are considered: (a) compassion that is driven out of hope or anger and (b) sense of duty that originates from the professional role that key actors enact (Käpylä & Kennedy, 2014). Thus, stakeholders in the same group may be driven by different motives to help disaster victims. For example, during the response phase, groups such as the Scouts of Greece driven by their compassion are willing to provide care to victims on the site whereas the local government of the affected area helps victims due to their duty and responsibility.

Table 4.1 Taxonomy of caring initiatives during natural disasters adjusted to fit cases in Greece

		Disaster Phase	
		Recovery	*Response*
Proximity	**Intimate/ Adjacent Victims**	(A) • *Salvia.org* • *Federation for Mental Health Institutions (Argo)* • *Prolepsis Institute* • *Theseus Rehabilitation Center*	(B) • *Greek Action of Volunteer Veterinarians* • *Scouts of Greece* • *Local Governments* • *Government-Prime Minister*
	Distant Victims	(C) • Philanthropic Organizations • Government • European Commission	(D) • *Municipalities outside the affected areas* • *Greek Diaspora Organizations* • *Philanthropic Organizations* • *Environmental NGOs* • *Government – Prime Minister* • *Businesses*

Note: Stakeholders in italics represent groups that are motivated by their compassion to help others.

Table 4.1 illustrates the proposed taxonomy of stakeholders. Italics represent stakeholders that are driven out of compassion.

(A) Recovery Phase – Intimate/adjacent Sufferers

Stakeholders of this category (section A in Table 4.1) are mainly groups of volunteers who are in close and intimate relationships with the disaster victims, provide them long-term care that extends across the disaster recovery phase, and are motivated by feelings of compassion. These endeavors might represent forms of "caring for" the victims. "Care for" activities vary from addressing the physical needs, being close to family members, to aiming at the emotional well-being and resilience of affected citizens (O'Connor & Takahashi, 2014). These activities are related to a continuous face-to-face involvement with the sufferers throughout the recovery process and are driven by a sense of emotional connection (Nodding, 2002; O'Connor & Takahashi, 2014).

On the other hand, "care about" practices are directed to distant others and/or are associated with short-term or long-term, task-oriented practices during the immediate aftermath of a disaster (medical attention, provision of shelter, food and first aid material) (Nodding, 2002; Leeson, 2010). In the 2018 wildfires in Eastern Attica suburbs (Mati), almost 102 people lost their lives, 150 individuals were hospitalized and 60 of them were severely burned. Two residents of Mati, Alexandros Andronopoulos, and Marina Karyda founded the Salvia Burn Association that is dedicated to support burn survivors along the continuum of care that involves the various recovery phases (e.g., immediately after the injury, during the hospital treatment, the plastic and reconstructive surgery processes, rehabilitation treatment). These two volunteers searched for the burn victims, collaborated with plastic surgeons, the Latsis Public Benefit Foundation, other Greek and International bodies, and the Government (Leivadaros, 2021) and provided financial, social, and psychological support for 60 burn victims of the Mati disaster. They also took a special interest for the specialized medical treatment of the victims. The Salvia Organization has been committed to the provision of an integrated program that creates a trusting relationship with the burn victims and their families helping them daily in all aspects of life (Grous, 2019). In a similar vein, the Theseus Rehabilitation Center under the Latsis Foundation's financial support assumed the treatment of burn victims for many months.

Another endeavor that falls into the long-term care toward victims, is the program entitled "365+ days of care" of the Prolepsis Institute directed toward elderly people of the affected communities in the 2018 wildfires at the Eastern Attica suburbs. The program continued almost two years after the wildfires and included the provision of everyday meals to elderly based on their medical history and special dietary needs. This program had a positive impact on their physical and psychological health and reduced their insecurity. The program was financially supported initially by Syn-Enosis, the Greek Shipowners' Social Welfare Company, the Hellenic Initiative Canada, the Bodossaki Foundation, the South Bridge Europe Mezzanine, and Eurobank (H anagki, 2020).

An additional "care for" practice was performed by the bodies of the Federation of Mental Health Institutions (ARGO) after the 2021 devastating fires in Northern Evia. One year after the fire erupted, these bodies continued to support the residents of Evia in mental health issues. This support took the form of weekly visits to villages, psychotherapy sessions, counseling of children and vulnerable groups of people. These initiatives are funded by the Greek Ministry of Health.

(B) Emergency Response Phase – Intimate/adjacent Sufferers

Groups in section B of the grid (Table 4.1) represent stakeholders that provide care to victims on the site of the disaster as soon as the disaster strikes to support the immediate needs of human and non-human victims. These groups could be driven either by a sense of compassion or duty.

For example, groups of volunteers are primarily motivated by feelings of compassion to provide relief and to instill hope for the future. The Scouts of Greece at the first week of the disaster, delivered daily first aid supplies, and non- prescription drugs and provided door-to-door meal delivery to the affected citizens (Oi proskopoi, 2018). The Greek Action of Volunteer Veterinarians (EDKE) during the first days of the Evia wildfires in 2021 sent a group of veterinarians at the burned areas of North Evia to treat the wounds of almost 70 burned animals. Moreover, they established a first aid station at the Olympic Village to help the animals of farmers in Attica (Sterea Ellada, 2021).

Whereas the above relief efforts are driven mainly from feelings of compassion, several actors, such as the government or local government officials might be activated to help the affected citizens mainly due to their professional roles and sense of duty. These initiatives take the form of physical presence at the disaster site, communication with empathy and compassion toward the victims. However, one cannot deny that certain actors will also be driven by feelings of compassion as well as their sense of duty and be more empathetic and caring at their initial responses. Primary examples of these caring practices are related to the disaster rituals that are performed by public leaders in the aftermath of disasters (Helsloot & Groenendaal, 2017). One day after the 2020 flash floods in Central Evia, Prime Minister Kyriakos Mitsotakis, visited the affected areas and discussed with residents (Episkepsi, 2020). Besides being physically present and interacting with the residents, local governments of the affected communities might provide immediate relief measures to victims. In August 2021, simultaneously with the devastating fire in Northern Evia similar scenes were unfolded across the country in Attica and Peloponnese. To provide immediate relief to the affected citizens, the municipality of East Mani in Laconia (Peloponnese), offered accommodation in hotels to 200 persons after the fire burned down almost 56 houses (Evia, 2021).

(C) Emergency Response Phase – Distant Other Sufferers

Caring about distant sufferers at least at the initial stages could be triggered by feelings of compassion associated with enhancing hope or expressing anger but also by a sense of duty that is expected due to the actors' societal and professional role. These actors are represented in section C of the grid (Table 4.1) and could be several philanthropical organizations, businesses, and the government that mobilize their resources to provide immediate relief assistance. It could be argued that these initiatives are driven by the organizational mission or the social corporate responsibility endeavors of these entities that aim at serving the public welfare.

These activities are often viewed as "an expected obligation" to support victims of disasters. For example, the Coca-Cola company donated €100,000 to cover the immediate needs of the affected citizens in northern Evia in cooperation with the Bodossaki Foundation (Coca Cola, 2021). The public also expects the Government and the Prime Minister to engage in meaning making by providing immediate support to the affected communities and inspiring hope and resilience after the disaster strikes (Boin et al., 2013). This support could take the form of communication and compensation announcements. Few days after the 2021 wildfires in Attica and Evia, the Prime Minister, Kyriakos Mitsotakis, made a public announcement, apologizing and identifying with distant citizens that had been affected by the disaster and lost their properties and homes.

Moreover, he announced immediate compensations to disaster victims through a simple online process (Diamantis, 2021). These activities could be seen as part of the wider crisis management responsibilities of the government in times of disaster that are not necessarily pursued out of compassion and feelings of empathy toward the affected communities.

However, several "caring about" initiatives are driven out of feelings of compassion toward distant others who have been affected by a catastrophe. According to Zaki (2020) in the aftermath of disasters certain prosocial behaviors (e.g., donations) are initiated out of "catastrophe compassion" that enhance solidarity and feelings of resilience. In the 2021 wildfires in Evia, many municipalities geographically distant from the affected areas collected essential goods such as food, clothes, and other supplies and distributed them to the citizens at the disaster sites (Pyrkagies, 2021). Diaspora Greeks and the American Hellenic Educational Progressive Association (AHEPA) responded immediately to the 2021 Evia wildfires by organizing a fundraising campaign for the provision of emergency financial relief and humanitarian aid to the sufferers (Bissarionos, 2021).

NGOs are also expected to be caring agents to distant sufferers by recognizing the issues associated with the disaster (Orgad, 2017). NGOs' caring initiatives during the emergency phase of the disaster directed toward distant others could take the form of public condemnation and accusations of the government that are emboldened by compassion produced by justice-oriented anger (Käpylä & Kennedy, 2014). One week after the Mati wildfires eleven environmental organizations issued a common statement regarding the devastating fires adopting the frame of "loss and damage" (Allan & Hadden, 2017) and assigning responsibility to the current as well as previous governments. Moreover, they communicated the need to eliminate the causes of the disaster by proposing critical changes and proactive strategies to the government (Epistoli, 2018).

(D) Recovery Phase – Distant Other Sufferers

Stakeholders in section D of the grid engage with the affected communities during the recovery phase of disasters and are represented by organizations that continue to support victims and citizens mainly through financial aids and rebuilding programs. These initiatives are long-term projects aiming at the reconstruction of the disaster sites, crisis preparedness, and enhancement of community resilience. The Greek government proposed a strategic regeneration plan for the burned areas in Northern Evia that included reforestation and flood protection initiatives, reconstruction of road networks, and programs for enhancing the local economy (Tratsa, 2022). The financial support the European Commission offered to Greece under the European Solidarity mechanism one year after the Mediterranean cyclone "Ianos" that affected Ionian Islands, Western Greece, Thessaly and Central Greece in September 2020 also falls under the category of "caring about" practices toward distant sufferers (Greece, 2018). It should be noted that these initiatives are undertaken by state and European agencies whose responsibility is to expedite the recovery process after disasters.

However, several philanthropic organizations try to establish more long-lasting relationships with the affected communities governed by compassion. For instance, the Stavros Niarxos Foundation nominated grants to non-profit organizations supporting the local economy (programs directed to beekeepers, resin producers, forestry workers, farmers) for an extended period (Fire relief, 2022).

Conclusion

In this chapter, we proposed an alternative relational framework for understanding the disaster relief and recovery efforts of different types of stakeholders that emerge after natural disasters based on the notions of compassion and care. Based on the taxonomy, "care for" initiatives that span from the emergency to the recovery phase, are primarily induced by feelings of compassion and altruism and require a long-term commitment toward adjacent sufferers. "Care for", is mainly practiced through attentiveness and responsiveness to the needs of the victims through trusted relationships. On the other hand, "caring about" takes the form of immediate relief efforts toward adjacent and distant others through financial support, provision of essential goods for the affected citizens, fundraising campaigns and framing strategies and communication rituals. Moreover, "caring about" could also be related to strategically oriented recovery and reconstruction efforts of philanthropic, state, and international agents. The proposed stakeholder typology provides an alternative approach to stakeholder identification and analysis that is based on the relational notion of care. Disaster managers could use this typology to identify crisis stakeholders with similar caring practices and motivations and encourage them to collaborate. In addition, the typology could enable disaster managers to decipher and incorporate in their decisions the care motives of crisis stakeholders during the different phases of the disaster. This segmentation could be tested and validated empirically in the aftermath of disaster and could be also applied to other types of crises as well, such as corporate crises, migration crisis, technological disasters, etc. Moreover, the Compassion and Care Disaster Response and Recovery framework could be extended to encompass other disaster phases such as the mitigation and preparedness stages.

References

Allan, J. I., & Hadden, J. (2017). Exploring the framing power of NGOs in global climate politics. *Environmental Politics*, *26*(4), 600–620. https://doi.org/10.1080/09644016.2017.1319017

Bissarionos, N. (2021, August 8). *Australia: H Ahepa Viktorias sto plevro ton pyroplikton [Australia: Ahepa Victoria stands by the fire victims]*. Ertnews. https://www.ertnews.gr/omogeneia/ipa-h-axepa-sto-pleyro-ton- pyroplikton/

Boin, A., Kuipers, S., & Overdijk, W. (2013). Leadership in times of crisis: A framework for assessment. *International Review of Public Administration, 18*(1), 79–91. https://doi.org/10.1080/12294659.2013.10805241

Boulianne, S., Minaker, J., & Haney, T. J. (2018). Does compassion go viral? Social media, caring, and the Fort McMurray wildfire. Information, *Communication & Society, 21*(5), 697–711. https://doi.org/10.1080/1369118X.2018.1428651

Chan, K., Balvanera, P., Karina Benessaiah, K., Chapman, M., Díaz, S., Baggethun, E. G., Gould, R., Hannahs, N., Jax, K., Klain, S., Luck, G., Martín-López, B., Muraca, B., Norton, B., Ott, K., Pascual, U., Satterfield, T., Tadaki, M., Taggart, J., and Turner, N. (2016). Why protect nature? Rethinking values and the environment. *PNAS, 113*(6), Opinion. https://doi.org/10.1073/pnas.1525002113

Coca Cola: Dorea 100.000€ se pyropliktous kai pyrosvestiki [Coca Cola: Donation of 100.000€ to fire victims and fire service] (2021, August 23). *Businessnews*. https://www.businessnews.gr/epixeiriseis/item/217071-coca-cola- dorea-100-000-se-pyropliktous-kai-pyrosvestiki

Crosweller, M. (2022). Disaster management and the need for a relational leadership framework founded upon compassion, care, and justice. *Climate Risk Management, 35*. https://doi.org/10.1016/j.crm.2022.100404

Diamantis, A. (2021, August 9). *Mitsotakis gia tis foties: Signomi gia tis opoies adynamies – Tha apodothoun euthunes [Mitsotakis on fires: Sorry for any shortcomings - Responsibilities will be attributed]*. Ethnos. https://www.ethnos.gr/Politics/article/169709/mhtsotakhsgiafotiessygnomhgiatisopoiesadyna miesthaapodothoyneythynes

Episkepsi tou prothipourgou Kyriakou Mitsotaki stis pleigises periohes tis Evias [Prime Minister Kyriakos Mitsotakis visits the affected areas of Evia] (2020, August 10). *Prime Mininster.gr*. https://primeminister.gr/2020/08/10/24575

Epistoli pente perivallontikon organoseon: Matia zois gia to mellon [Letter from five environmental organizations: A lifetime vision for the future] (2018, July 30). To Vima. https://www.tovima.gr/2018/07/30/society/epistoli-pente-periballontikwn-organwsewn-matia-zwis-gia-to-mellon/

European Commission. (2022). Exceptional mobilisation of Copernicus emergency management service during the 2022 wildfire crisis. *Emergency Management Service Information Bulletin, 163*. https://emergency.copernicus.eu

Evia: Me ta cheria tous svinoun tis flogs oi polites sto Pfki, I fotia sinexizei na proxoraei [Evia: Citizens extinguish the flames in Pefki with their hands, the fire continues to progress] (2021, August 9), *H Efimerida ton Sintakton*. https://www.efsyn.gr/ellada/koinonia/305591_eyboia-me-ta-heria-toys- sbinoyn-tis-floges-oi-polites-sto-peyki-i-fotia

Fire relief initiative for Northern Evia (2022). Stavros Niarchos Foundation. https://www.snf.org/en/grants/fire-relief-initiative-for-north-evia/

Greece to receive €35.9 million in EU disaster relief funds (2021, August 24). EKathimerini. https://www.ekathimerini.com/news/1168521/greece-to-receive-e35-9-million-in-eu-disaster-relief-funds/

Grous, D. (2019, July 22). *Mati, enas hronos meta: Aftoi pou thymountai tous egkavmaties [Mati, one year later: Those who remember the burn victims]*. Athens Voice. https://www.athensvoice.gr/epikairotita/ellada/565050/oi-egkaymatiesapo-mati-1-hrono-meta/

H anagki gia stiriksi ton ilikiomenon pligenton sto Mati paramenei megali gia dyo hronia meta tis katastrofikes pyrkagies [The need for support of the elderly victims in Mati remains high two years after the devastating fires] (2020). *Prolepsis Institute.* https://www.prolepsis.gr/en/news/i-anagki-gia-stirixi-ton-ilikiomenon-pligenton-sto-mati-paramenei-megali-duo-xronia-meta-tis-katastr/

Hayes, P., & Jackson, D. (2020). Care ethics and the responsible management of power and privacy in digitally enhanced disaster response. *Journal of Information, Communication and Ethics in Society, 18*(1), 157–174. https://doi.org/10.1108/JICES-02-2019-0020

Helsloot, I., & Groenendaal, J. (2017). It's meaning making, stupid! Success of public leadership during flash crises. *Journal of Contingencies and Crisis Management, 25*(4), 350–353. https://doi.org/10.1111/1468-5973.12166

Herring, J. (2017). Compassion, ethics of care and legal rights. *International Journal of Law in Context, 13*(2), 158–171. https://doi.org/10.1017/S174455231700009X

Käpylä, J., & Kennedy, D. (2014). Cruel to care? Investigating the governance of compassion in the humanitarian imaginary. *International Theory, 6*(2), 255–292. https://doi.org/10.1017/S1752971914000025

Latimer, J. & Puig de la Bellacasa, M. (2017). Re-thinking the ethical: Everyday shifts of care in biogerontology. In N. Priaulx & A. Wrigley (Eds.), *Ethics, Law and Society* (Vol. *V*, pp. 153–174). London: Routledge.

Lawson, V. (2007). Geographies of care and responsibility. *Annals of the Association of American Geographers, 97*(1), 1–11. https://doi.org/10.1111/j.1467-8306.2007.00520.x

Leeson, C. (2010). The emotional labour of caring about looked-after children. *Child & Family Social Work, 15*(4), 483–491.

Leivadaros, M. (2021, November 17). *Alexandros kai Marina: Oi dyo katoikoi apo to Mati pou ezisan ton efialti tis fotias kai afierothikan sti stiriksi ton egkavmation [Alexandros and Marina: The two residents from Mati who lived the nightmare of the fire and dedicated themselves to supporting burn victims].* Iefimerida. https://www.iefimerida.gr/stories/andronopoylos-karyda-organosi-salvia-egkaymaties

Linsley, P. M., & Slack, R. E. (2013). Crisis management and an ethic of care: The case of Northern Rock Bank. *Journal of Business Ethics, 113*(2), 285–295. https://doi.org/10.1007/s10551-012-1304-8

Milligan, C., & Wiles, J. (2010). Landscapes of care. *Progress in Human Geography, 34*(6), 736–754. https://doi.org/10.1177/0309132510364556

Nodding, N. (2002). *Starting at home: Caring and social policy.* Berkeley: University of California Press.

Nussbaum, M. (1996). Compassion: The basic social emotion. *Social Philosophy and Policy, 13*(1), 27–58. https://doi.org/10.1017/S0265052500001515

Nussbaum, M. (2001). *Upheavals of Thought: The Intelligence of Emotions.* Cambridge: Cambridge University Press.

Nussbaum M. (2003). Compassion & terror. *Daedalus, 132*(1), 10–26.

O'Connor, P., & Takahashi, N. (2014). From caring about to caring for: Case studies of New Zealand and Japanese schools post disaster. *Pastoral Care in Education, 32*(1), 42–53.

Oi Proskopoi dipla stous pyropliktous – Kathimerina dekades ethelontes prosferoun ergo koinonikis seinisforas stis pyropliktes perioxes [The Scouts next to the fire victims - Every day dozens of volunteers offer social contribution to the fire-stricken areas] (2018, July 30). *Soma Hellinon Proskopon.* https://www.sep.org.gr/en/normal/21308/ViewAnnouncement

Orgad, S. (2017). Caring enterprise in crisis? Challenges and opportunities of humanitarian NGO communications. In I. B. Seu & S. Orgad (Eds.), *Caring in Crisis? Humanitarianism, the Public and NGOs* (pp. 83–109), Springer. https://doi.org/10.1007/978-3-319-50259-5_6

Pyrkagies: "Karavani" voitheias kai allileggiis apo dimous tis Attikis stous pyropliktous [Wildfires: "Caravan" of aid and solidarity from Attica Municipalities to fire victims] (2021, August 11). *Proto Thema*. https://www.protothema.gr/greece/article/1151293/purkagies-karavani-voitheias-kai-allilegguis-apo-dimous-tis-attikis-stous-puropliktous/

Simola, S. (2003). Ethics of justice and care in corporate crisis management. *Journal of Business Ethics*, *46*(4), 351–361. https://doi.org/10.1023/A:1025607928196

Sterea Ellada: H apostoli mas stis fylakes koridallou [Central Greece: Our mission to Korydallos Prison] (2021). *Edke*. https://www.edke.gr/geolocation/%CF%83%CF%84%CE%B5%CF%81%CE%B5%CE%AC-%CE%B5%CE%BB%CE%BB%CE%AC%CE%B4%CE%B1/

Tao, W., & Kim, S. (2017). Application of two under-researched typologies in crisis communication: Ethics of justice vs. care and public relations vs. legal strategies. *Public Relations Review*, *43*(4), 690–699. https://doi.org/10.1016/j.pubrev.2017.06.003

The Care Collective. (2020). *The Care Manifesto. The politics of interdependence*. London & New York: Verso.

Tratsa, M. (2022, November 13). Voreia Evia: 381 ekat. evro gia 71 erga anasigkrotisis [North Evia: €381 million € for 71 reconstruction projects]. Oikonomikos Taxidromos. https://www.ot.gr/2022/11/13/green/voreia-eyvoia-381-ekat-eyro-gia-71-erga-anasygkrotisis/

Triantafillidou, A., & Yannas, P. (2022). Coping with natural disasters: Political leadership framing of the 2018 wildfires in Greece. *Journal of Contingencies and Crisis Management*. https://doi.org/10.1111/1468-5973.12431

Tronto, J. (1993). *Moral boundaries. A political argument for an ethic of care*. London: Routledge.

Tronto, J. (2013). *Caring democracy: Markets, equality and justice*. New York: New York University Press.

Zaki, J. (2020). Catastrophe compassion: Understanding and extending prosociality under crisis. *Trends in Cognitive Sciences*, *24*(8), 587–589. https://doi.org/10.1016/j.tics.2020.05.006

5 The Agents of Resilience

Generativity and Durability of Digital Platforms in Crisis-to-Crisis Transition

Gregory Asmolov

Over a decade after I started studying crisis-related mobilization there is one topic that puzzles me a lot. This is what happens with successful crisis-related digital projects that emerge in response to a specific crisis. For instance, an Internet domain of the *Floodaid* project (http://floodaid.com.au) created by a group of activists to facilitate mutual aid in response to floods in Brisbane, Australia, in January 2011 is now owned by a legal company offering emergency-related insurance services. In the case of another Australian platform, *Bushfireconnect*, an Ushahidi-based deployment that was actively used to crowdsource information about bushfires starting from 2010, the project's domain now belongs to a gambling website. In Russia, a domain that was used by volunteers to facilitate mobilization in response to severe floods in the Amur region in the Russian Far East (http://amur13.ru) is also now dedicated to gambling. A similar dynamic can be seen around the domains of platforms that were used to facilitate political protests. The *White Circle* platform (feb26.ru), used to create a live 13-km chain of people around the Moscow Kremlin in protest against electoral fraud in 2012, is now a fashion blog. The pages of some of these projects on social media platforms like Twitter or Facebook seem to be more resilient and to have a longer life, continuing to link to websites that no longer exist. At the same time, we can see that spontaneous, crisis-related online communities decline over time. For instance, some of the hyperlocal UK-based COVID-related WhatsApp mutual aid groups have been hijacked by distributors of spam once the crisis was over, either forcing admins to close the groups or members to leave these groups.

There are some evident reasons why these spontaneous, crisis-related platforms become victims of cybersquatters. On the one hand, such websites generate a high volume of traffic in a short period of time. On the other hand, the websites are likely to lose the support of their owners once the crisis is over and they stop paying domain extension and hosting fees. However, interest in past crisis-related projects may go beyond the digital archeology and history of crisis response. The ephemeral nature of crisis-related deployments evokes a feeling of missed opportunity and concern. Some of these projects could be used in future crises and contribute to overall crisis preparedness.

DOI: 10.4324/9781003375296-7

This chapter has been made available under a CC-BY 4.0 license.

That said, while in some cases we see a failure to sustain crisis-related networks in post-crisis situations, in other cases digitally mediated crisis-related networks do not necessary disperse.

Some scholars suggest that the value of specific crisis-related platforms should be seen beyond a specific type of crisis situation, while a link between mobilizations around different types of event may exist, even if the events are very different in social and political nature. For instance, Patrick Meier (2012), one of the founders of the crisis-mapping movement, underlines the interrelation between mobilization in response to natural disasters and participation in political protests:

> Whether they are political activists on one day and volunteer humanitarians on another, the individuals behind the efforts described above use the same tools to mobilize and coordinate. And they build social capital in the process—strong and weak ties—regardless of whether they are responding to repressive policies or 'natural' disasters (online).

The need for this type of analysis is particularly visible in crisis-prone regions facing different types of crisis situation including natural disasters, armed conflicts and political protests in a relatively short period of time. In Europe this type of situation can be seen in Russia and Ukraine. Both countries continuously face different types of natural disaster. They have also experienced major political protests, as in the case of the protests against electoral fraud in Russia in 2011–2012 and of the Euromaidan protests in 2013–2014 in Ukraine. Finally, Ukraine has faced a continuous security threat from Russia starting with the occupation of Crimea in 2014 and continuing with the full-scale Russian invasion of Ukraine in 2022. Relying on an analysis of the role of social media in mobilization in Ukraine, Metzger and Tucker (2017) note that

> Deeper work on the way that networks have transitioned from working on issues of protests towards working on issues about the crisis and ongoing violence can help give us insight into the way that social media can make networks more flexible.
>
> (p. 189)

A focus on Ukraine and Russia offers an empirical opportunity to explore the role of digital platforms and digital networks in crisis-to-crisis transitions beyond a specific type of crisis.

The link between different types of crises is particularly important in empirical cases related to authoritarian regimes, as in the case of Russia, or in empirical cases of countries under a political and military threat from authoritarian neighbors, as in the case of Ukraine. This is because civil society in such cases often needs to address a double threat from nature and from political institutions

(Asmolov, 2022a). However, a crisis-to-crisis transition can also be seen in contexts that are not related to authoritarian regimes. For instance, some scholars recognize a close link between the role of digital platforms in supporting various forms of social and political activism and the role of platforms in crisis response, as in the case of mutual aid networks in response to COVID-19 in the UK (Kavada, 2020). In this light, it is important to explore what factors may contribute to persistence and continuity when it comes to the role of innovative digital platforms, digital practices, and digital communities in crisis response.

The question of whether networks that self-organize in response to a crisis fall apart when the crisis is over or can be reactivated in the case of a new crisis is important given the increasing attention dedicated to the role of digital platforms in the development of social resilience in the context of emergencies and global risks. The idea that each crisis can potentially be considered as an opportunity to build a capacity to address future risks relies on understanding resilience as the adaptive potential of all living systems to survive perturbation. Holling (2000) highlights the nature of resilience in terms of "never-ending adaptive cycles of growth, accumulation, restructuring, and renewal" (p. 7). The concept of resilience considers a crisis as an external shock creating an opportunity for a socio-political transformation that increases the capacity to address future risks by relying on the resources of the public (Cannon & Müller-Mahn, 2010; Tierney, 2014).

The cycle-based nature of resilience offers an analytical opportunity to explore the role of digital platforms in linking different cases of response to crisis. This may suggest that, to understand the role of digital innovation in mobilization in response to a specific threat, we need to look at the dynamics of previous cycles of mobilization. A focus on these cycles can help us to consider how these forms of mobilization are transferred to and applied within different contexts. In this sense, a focus on cycles allows both an exploration of the expanding scope of mobilization and a diversification of the forms of mobilization. However, the post-crisis destiny of crisis-related platforms and of networks of Internet users that have taken part in crisis response has often remained beyond the scope of investigation. Most research has been focused on the role of social media in the context of specific crisis situations (Reuter et al., 2018; Liu et al., 2018; Vera-Burgos & Griffin Padgett, 2020). Some scholars have conducted a comparative analysis of disaster response in different emergencies such as hurricanes and COVID-19 (Mirbabaie et al., 2020; Momin et al., 2023). While the literature offers analytical insights relying on a comparison of different types of crises, less attention has been dedicated to the links and transitions between different cases of crisis response.

Exploring how such a transition may operate is challenging. This is because the literature is inclined to distinguish between investigation of the social mobilization around different types of crises like natural disasters, political crises, health-related crises or armed conflicts. This type of distinction imposes conceptual limitations on the investigation of crisis-to-crisis transition. To open a window of opportunity for this type of analysis, one should first identify a definition of a crisis that allows us to bypass these limitations and to recognize the commonalities of different crisis situations.

Some concepts recognize that different types of crisis situation can be interrelated. This relationship is highlighted by the notions of a "complex emergency" and of "cascading events" (Sellnow & Seeger, 2013). The relationship between different crisis situations is also addressed in the literature as a link between triggering crises and secondary crises (Diers-Lawson, 2020). That said, most of these frameworks focus on the chain-effect relationship between crisis situations. A more flexible and holistic framework can be supported by definitions that consider crises in terms of people's perception. For instance, "a crisis may be defined as a specific, unexpected, non-routine event or series of events that creates high levels of uncertainty and a significant or perceived threat to high priority goals" (Seeger et al., 2003, p. 7). Weick (1993) addresses a crisis as a cosmological episode, where "people suddenly and deeply feel that the universe is no longer a rational, orderly system" (p. 633). Some scholars highlight ways in which the role of social media in the representation of a disaster, in sensemaking and in collective meaning-creation (sense-giving) are associated with potential forms of action by audiences in response to a disaster (Hannigan, 2012; Jasanoff, 2015; Mirbabaie et al., 2020; Weick, 1993).

In this light, the perception of a crisis as a threat to high-priority goals can be considered as a property linking very different types of crises and transforming any crisis into an attractor of mobilization driven by efforts either to restore order, or to lead to a new point of equilibrium accepted by the members of a social group whose perception of order has been disrupted. A holistic definition going beyond a focus on a specific crisis allows us to switch attention from the role of information and communication technologies (ICTs) in a specific crisis to the role of ICTs in crisis-to-crisis transition, and to explore the factors that shape the role of ICTs in supporting such transitions.

This research is concerned with mapping different pathways of transition of digital platforms from one crisis to another, and identifying the factors that may either increase or diminish the durability of networks and platforms through crisis-to-crisis transition. The chapter considers several empirical cases of shifts in the purpose of online communities and adjustment of digital innovation from one crisis to another, relying on data on the role of digital platforms in crises collected in Russia and Ukraine and including the following types of transition:

- from natural disasters to political protests
- from protests to armed conflicts
- from natural disasters to conflicts.

To analyze the role of digital platforms in the context of this transition, it relies on the notion of activity systems (Engeström, 1987), which allows us to follow whether the same digital platforms continue to play a role when the object of activity changes. This framework should help us to underline the association between digitally mediated mobilization around different crises, and to explore whether previous crisis situations contribute to a capacity to address different types of crisis situation, on both a social and a technological level. This discussion should contribute to the literature on the role of digital platforms in developing social resilience in the face of global catastrophic risks (Avin et al., 2018; Kreienkamp & Pegram, 2021).

Theoretical Framework: Crisis as a "Runaway Object"

There are several conceptual challenges that need to be resolved to investigate the factors that shape the role of digital platforms in crisis-to-crisis transitions. First, we should offer a flexible framework that allows us to explore the link between various types of crises even if there is no specific link connecting these emergencies. Second, we should address the nature of digital platforms as both shaping the perception of the crisis and offering an opportunity to address the crisis through the mobilization of digital users. Third, we need to offer a space both for digital platforms and for digital communities in the context of a changing crisis-to-crisis transition. Finally, this framework should offer a space for considering the fluid nature of digital platforms as constantly changing artifacts that may experience some form of transition alongside the transition from crisis to crisis.

The purpose of this framework is to address the role of digital users and digital platforms, and to allow us to offer an association between these two actors in the context of a crisis response to follow the transition in their role from one crisis to another. There is a rich diversity of concepts that address both the potential socio-political role of online communities (boyd, 2011; Dutton, 2009) and the role of digital platforms in various forms of socio-political mobilization (Bennett & Segerberg, 2011; Chon & Park, 2020; Diers-Lawson, 2023; Sandoval-Almazan & Gil-Garcia, 2014). Some of these concepts highlight how digital media offer new forms of mobilization without relying on organizational frameworks, while others focus on the ease of connectivity as an affordance that simplifies rapid mobilization. A connective mobilization that offers an opportunity for crisis-related activity without the sharing of a common organizational affiliation can be seen in the context of crowdsourcing platforms. These platforms enable the mobilization of a variety of user resources in relation to a crisis (Asmolov, 2015).

That said, while most of these concepts are useful for considering the role of digital platforms in the context of a specific crisis, the challenge of how to explore the role of digital platforms from crisis to crisis remains. The notion of generativity may help us to address the unpredictable nature of potential transformations going beyond the initial purpose of a specific platform. According to Zittrain (2008), generativity is considered "a capacity to produce unanticipated change through unfiltered contributions from broad and varied audiences" (p. 70). Digital platforms offer great flexibility since they allow the separation of "function from form," and of "contents from medium" (Yoo et al., 2010). The intentional incompleteness of digital platforms makes them unpredictable and fluid (Nambisan, 2017). In this light, the changing, dynamic, and fluid nature of crises can be linked to the flexibility of digital objects used to address these situations.

Scholars who rely on Cultural Historical Activity Theory (CHAT) suggest a link between generativity and the role of digital platforms in the mediation of new forms of relationships between users and their environment. In this context, generativity can be addressed as the capacity of information technologies to "produce new activities and outputs and to structure behaviour beyond original creators' intentions" (Karanasios et al., 2021, p. 245). Relying on the conceptual apparatus of activity theory, and specifically on the notion of "activity systems" (Engeström, 1987) may help us to explore how the generativity of a digital platform operates in the transition to a new crisis.

The conceptual framework of CHAT offers a focus on tool-mediated and object-oriented activity as a major level of analysis. In this way, digital platforms that mediate activity in relation to a crisis can be considered as digital tools and mediating artefacts (Kaptelinin, 2014). An analytical framework for the analysis of activity systems as systems of collaborative human practice, relying on mediating artifacts, allows us to make a link between users, tools, and crises (as shown in Figure 5.1).

The *subject* in this case is the individual. The *object* is something located in the external environment of the subject that is also a goal and an expected outcome of an activity. The artifact is something that mediates activity as a form of subject-object relationship. The notion of *community* suggests the conceptualization of a group of subjects that share a common object. The notion of *division of labor* suggests that different subjects can accomplish different tasks as part of their object-oriented activity. An activity system is also based on a set of *rules* shared by members of its community.

Relying on Engestrom's model, we can address the role of digital platforms during crises as that of tools that mediate different forms of user activity in relation to a crisis. In this case, we consider the crisis as the object of activity. We can consider the users involved in crisis-related activity through common digital platforms as a community. Therefore, analysis of the transition of crisis-related digital networks from crisis to crisis should focus on situations where the object of activity has changed and should explore whether any elements of previous activity systems, communities, and/or mediating tools remain following the transition of the object.

The model of activity systems helps us to connect individual users, communities, digital platforms, and crisis situations. Accordingly, it builds a foundation for exploring the role of digital platforms and digital communities in

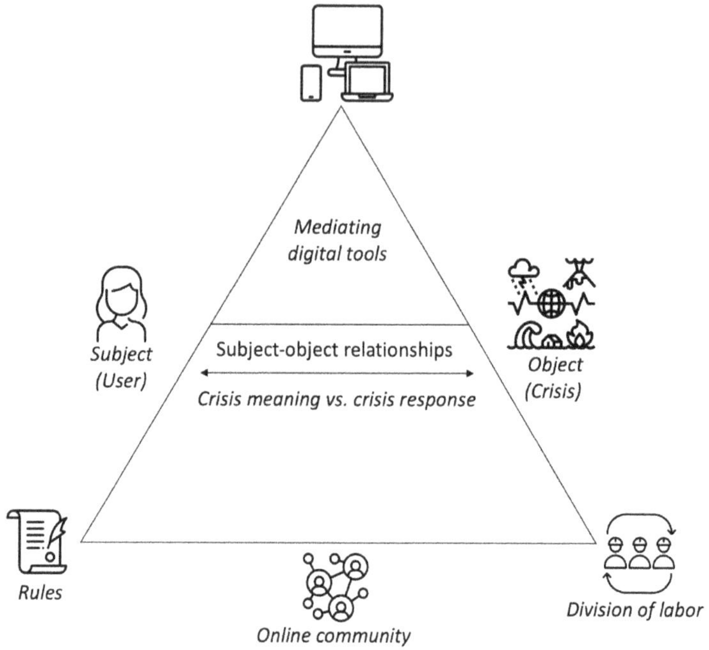

Figure 5.1 The structure of a crisis-related activity system (adapted from Engeström, 1987, p. 78).

crisis-to-crisis transition. Either the same mediating tools are used to respond to a new type of crisis, or a different type of tool is used to mediate the activity of the same community members in response to a new crisis. The scenario, however, that would be consistent with the maximal degree of durability and flexibility of crisis-related digital networks is one where the activity of the same community members addresses a new object by relying on similar digital tools.

CHAT also offers us an opportunity to question whether we should consider a new crisis as a new object or whether it may potentially be seen as a dynamic change of objects within the same system. Engeström (2007) has addressed the situation where the object of an activity system continuously changes, while the activity system remains relatively stable, as one of "runaway objects." He developed the notion of a "runaway object" in terms of a large-scale, complex object that is "pervasive and its boundaries are hard to draw" (Engeström, 2007, p. 5). This notion offers an opportunity to go beyond focus on a specific crisis, and to expand the boundaries within which the object of analysis may link different types of crises including natural disasters, political protests and armed conflicts. For instance, we could consider the transition from the Euromaidan protests in Ukraine against the government to the defence of the country against the Russian invasion in 2014 as one of a "runaway object."

Finally, the framework also addresses the challenge, which concerns the link between perception and activity. The flexibility and boundlessness of runaway objects highlight the dual position of objects in the context of activity systems. The object is not only a fixed and bounded external threat that we need to address, but also an outcome of perception and of a constant process of construction. We can see subject-object relationships in the context of a dynamic change in the narrative concerning potential threats and risks (Asmolov, 2022b). In other words, members of a community both construct and address such runaway objects within an activity system. This highlights how members of an activity system may consider very different types of crises as a continuation of one "runaway object" threatening their high-priority goals. In such a case, the perceived continuation of a crisis as a runaway object, even if the crisis changes, sustains the activity system and keeps it, or at least some of its elements, relatively stable. This approach is also supported by the literature highlighting the importance of the collective creation of meaning and sensemaking in crisis response.

The theoretical framework here suggests that we consider a hypothesis whereby, if the members of a specific community that mobilized around a specific crisis also share a perception highlighting the connection between different type of crises, they may sustain the crisis as an object of continuous activity. In this case we may see that the same communities of users use the same or similar digital tools to address different types of crisis situation, including natural disasters and conflicts (See Figure 5.2). This framework allows us to identify for the purpose of empirical analysis several theoretical cases, whereby:

1 The digital platform that mediates the relationship between the crisis and the community of users remains the same.
2 The community is the same, but the platforms for mediating relationships are different.
3 The platform is the same, but the community is different.
4 Neither platform nor community is the same following crisis-to-crisis transition.

The methodological section below suggests how this framework informed data collection and data analysis to explore the role of digital platforms in transition from crisis to crisis.

Methodology: Mapping the Role of Online Communities and Digital Tools in Crisis-to-Crisis Transitions

The purpose of this analysis is to consider empirical cases of a shift in the purpose of online communities and digital tools from one crisis to another. The analysis explores a potential association between participation in different types of crisis situation relying on digital mediation. It focuses on how the digital tools

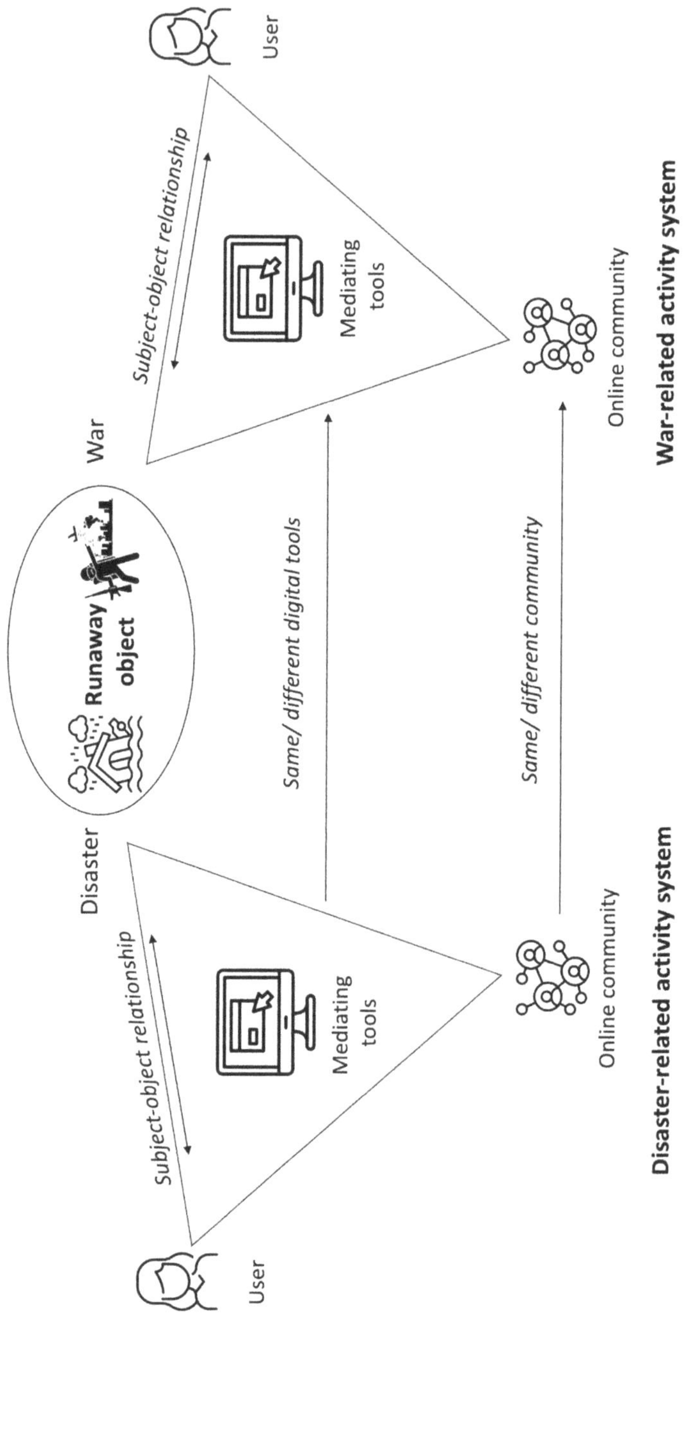

Figure 5.2 Runaway object and transformation of a crisis-related activity system.

used to mediate user-crisis relationships in a specific crisis can be linked to tools developed in the context of previous crisis situations.

The conceptual apparatus of CHAT offers a methodological direction for exploring the factors that shape the role of digital platforms in transition from crisis to crisis. The notion of "knotworking" suggests how activity systems operate in the context of a dynamic runaway object. "Knotworking" may be seen as a "collaborative performance between otherwise loosely connected actors and activity systems" that are "characterized by a movement of tying, untying, and retying together seemingly disparate threads of activity" (Engeström, 2008, p. 228). Spinuzzi highlights how *knotworking* is "oriented toward a runaway object, one that is shared by multiple activities with variable actors occupying different locations and collaborating irregularly" (2014, p. 462). By following the links between different threads of digitally mediated crisis-related activity, our analysis should explore the factors that shape a crisis-to-crisis transition.

Relying on this theoretical framework, our analysis of the transition considers whether there are changes in the community and in the digitally mediated tools. The empirical analysis operates on two levels. First, it follows the changes in specific platforms. Second, it examines the role of specific existent platforms in driving the innovation and development of new platforms for crisis response. In addition, specific attention has been dedicated to analysis of the relationship between crowdsourcing platforms and the social networking pages/communities linked to these platforms. For instance, if we explore war-related mobilization in the case of the Ukrainian response to Russian aggression, we need to consider the history of previous crisis-related mobilizations and to establish whether the same digital tools or/and the same online communities took part in the response to other crisis situations. If we can establish links through platforms or through communities to previous instances of crisis response, then we can explore the factors that help to explain a particular type of transition.

This approach suggests that we may identify a type of genealogical structure that links different types of crisis response. The purpose of genealogical mapping is to identify the nature of connections between different instances of response and to explore what has contributed to the development of these links. For this purpose, we need to address two empirical goals. First, to examine the links between two specific crisis situations and see which of the four theoretical cases presented in Figure 5.2 can be seen in the context of transition from crisis to crisis. If the platforms and communities that were used to address different crisis situations are not the same, we may want to see to what extent the later instance can be linked to previous instances by evidence of reliance on similar practices, tools and community members. For this purpose, we apply a retrospective analysis, while taking the later crisis and exploring the extent to which the response to this crisis can be linked to previous instances of crisis response. Second, once we establish a particular mode of transition, we need to explore the factors that can explain why we see this type of transition.

Mapping the threads of crisis-related activity and the relationship between different communities and mediating artifacts in the context of runaway objects relies on several datasets from

1 the collection of an archive database of crowdsourcing platforms and communities that emerged in response to crisis.
2 interviews with founders, developers, and admins of crowdsourcing projects.
3 secondary sources including research conducted into the role of digital platforms in different crises and into media sources related to specific crisis-related mobilizations.

We need to clarify that not only dedicated crowdsourcing platforms, but also social networking pages can be considered as tools that mediate activity around a particular crisis. Our analysis of the role of communities in the transition from crisis to crisis followed whether the same admins, moderators and significantly active users remained active around various types of crises. It also considered data from interviews, social media and other media sources that allowed us to explore whether the same users have participated in activity around different types of crises.

To consider crisis-to-crisis transitions, the research for this chapter had to identify an initial empirical case for a retrospective analysis following the relationships between disparate threads of digitally mediated crisis-related activity. This needed to be a case allowing us to address the links between responses to different types of crisis situation including natural disasters, political protests and armed conflicts. The ideal case would allow us to see the same platform in the context of at least two transitions and to address three different types of crisis situation: natural disasters, political protests and armed conflicts. This type of case can be considered as a starting point for the exploration of a runaway activity system that can be linked to a variety of crisis situations.

The search for this case relied on empirical data concerning crisis-related crowdsourcing platforms in Russia and Ukraine. Both countries offer an opportunity for empirical analysis of digital platforms in the context of a diversity of crisis situations including natural disasters, internal political crises, and armed conflict. The analysis identified the Ukrainian crowdsourcing platform Galas as one that offered an opportunity to analyze two transitions, and this was therefore identified as a starting point for empirical investigation. Galas was used, in response to extreme snowfall in Kyiv, to support activists taking part in the Euromaidan protests and to facilitate mobilization in face of the Russian invasion.

The data was analyzed by relying on a thematic analysis informed by activity systems elements (see Figure 5.1). The coding and analysis was based on NVivo software, which enabled the consideration of different sets of data within the same coding framework. Each platform was coded according to the type of technology (e.g. Ushahidi), type of practice (e.g. crowdsourcing), type of community (identities of admins and whether the same community pages were used previously in other contexts) as well as the innovative roots of the platforms (whether the founder argued that the platform was inspired by any other cases, and if yes, how). This analysis allowed us to construct a genealogical map of all instances, and then to identify which model could be seen in each transition. This type of mapping allowed us to address the question: "What factors may explain a particular type of transition?"

Empirical Discussion

The Transformation of Crisis Mapping and Crowdsourcing in Ukraine: The Case of Galas

The significance of the transition from crisis to crisis in the case of Ukraine has been noted by scholars exploring the role of social media in the Euromaidan protests (2014). Metzger and Tucker (2017) consider three possibilities of what could happen with networks of people that have taken part in protests:

> One possibility, for example, is that these looser networks will be better at monitoring the state and making people aware of political situations in the country than those who organized the Orange Revolution were, perhaps because they are less directly connected to the state. Another possibility is that these networks will fall apart as soon as the crisis is over. Yet a third is that they will exist as loose networks which can be reactivated in crisis, but which will play little role in day-to-day politics.
>
> (p. 190)

Dickinson (2014) argues that "social networks have proved to be remarkably durable and flexible" (p. 82) in the transition from participation in political protests in Kiev in 2014 to working on issues related to the conflict in eastern Ukraine. She points out that there has been a seamless transition on social media networks from "gathering support for protests" to "monitoring the actions of the interim government" and to "sharing geolocation analyses for videos uploaded to Vkontakte by Russian soldiers suspected of firing into Ukrainian territory and crowdsourcing clothing and supplies for the Ukrainian army" (pp. 82–83).

The nature of such a transition can be illustrated through an empirical focus on the crowdsourcing platform Galas (galas.org.ua), which has addressed three different types of crises. Galas (Ukrainian for "clamor") was introduced in March 2013 as an "interactive map of mutual aid for emergency situations." According to the Facebook page of Galas, the development of the project was technically supported by the Russian platform Virtual Rynda, an "atlas of mutual aid" created by the founders of the Help Map for Russian wildfires. According to Vladimir Valdman, the founder of Galas, the idea of developing the platform emerged in March 2013 during extreme snowfalls in Kyiv (Alekseev, 2013). The map was developed by relying on the Ushahidi platform. The project relied on the idea that a crowdsourced map can facilitate mutual aid by connecting those who need help and those who can offer their resources. It addressed a variety of emergencies including floods and local urban issues.

A year later, in November 2014 during the first phase of EuroMaidan protests, IT manager Dmytro Leader and designer Ihor Sklyarevskyi decided to create a site for coordination of mutual aid to support people taking part in the protests. According to the founders of the updated version of Galas, they decided to launch the map after seeing efforts to provide participants in the protest with warm sweaters and food, while also witnessing a shortage of disposable dishes and gloves. According to Lokot (2016, online), the founders saw that "the management and distribution of resources was chaotic and inefficient." They looked for a crowdsourcing solution to this problem. Then, they "recalled that a real-time alert platform had already been tested during the heavy snowfalls in Kyiv the previous winter" (Lokot, 2016). Valdman, who created the first version of Galas, offered the domain galas.org.ua and technical assistance to support the new map. The map was used to coordinate assistance based on 30 volunteers. The most frequent needs and offers included food, fuel, firewood for heating, transport, housing, and warm clothes (Klimovich, 2014).

According to Lokot (2016),

> the flexibility of the resource management and volunteer operations structure also meant that Galas, as a project, was able to adapt quickly to the changing needs of Euromaidan, going from collecting camping gear, tea, and phone chargers at the start to crowdsourcing medical equipment and bulletproof vests when the protests turned violent.

Lokot highlights how "Galas has continued operating beyond Euromaidan, although on a smaller scale, managing resources during the conflict in Eastern Ukraine, including refugee assistance and collecting donations for the Ukrainian army and volunteer brigades." That said, most of the activity moved to the Galas Facebook group. Starting from spring 2014, the group shared requests for diverse forms of support including equipment and transport for tactical medic units, food supplies for military units, and night-vision devices for artillery. The Galas Facebook group continued to show limited activity in 2022, although control of the Galas domain (galas.org.ua) seemed to have been lost by the founders of the map (the domain galas.org.ua is now occupied by a blog mainly dedicated to car advertisements).

It should be noted that Galas was a relatively small project in comparison with other digital initiatives that emerged during Euromaidan events and the following war. Therefore, it is important to consider Galas in the context of the ecosystem of platforms and online communities that emerged in response to each crisis.

For instance, different forms of protest-related mobilization took place through a broad range of platforms during the EuroMaidan events. These included the Facebook pages EuroMaydan and EvromaidanSOS. Some activities were also supported by the affordances of hashtags on Twitter. Mutual aid also relied on dedicated websites, as in the case of, as well as on offline coordination centers including the IT Tent on Maidan, a physical tent which "evolved into a space where technology specialists met and collaborated with professional activists on a number of ICT-enabled social projects" (Bohdanova, 2014, p. 138).

However, the purpose of this empirical mapping is not to establish the significance of specific platforms but to identify potential cases of links between platforms and communities responding to different type of crisis and to explore the factors that may explain these transitions. The case of Galas remains important since it allows us to follow how one digital artifact can be seen in the context of three different types of crisis-related activity systems, including natural disasters, political protest and military conflict. This transition has also been supported by the Facebook page of the project, which shifted its focus.

The Transformation of Crisis Mapping and Crowdsourcing in Russia[1]

As mentioned above, the initial version of Galas was supported by the Russian platform Virtual Rynda, an "Atlas of Mutual Aid." In this case, the link was not limited to offering a source of inspiration with one crisis mapping deployment informed by another. There was a direct contact between the key people in both projects, involving technical assistance in creating the map. Accordingly, we can see a link between digital tools used in crisis response in Ukraine and in Russia, although the platforms relied on different communities. The Virtual Rynda platform was created by the same team that developed the Help Map, the first Russian crowdsourcing and crisis mapping deployment in response to wildfires in summer 2010. Although the Russian and Ukrainian threads of crisis-related activity seem to be disparate, the existence of a relationship between "Galas" and "Virtual Rynda" suggested that we consider the genealogical development linked to the Help Map and explore the transformation of crisis mapping and crowdsourcing in Russia. The following discussion explores the links between digital platforms used in response to natural disasters and as part of political protests in Russia.

In summer 2010, wildfires broke out in different locations in western Russia and Moscow was covered by smog. More than 60 people died, while the unofficial number of casualties was higher. The Russian wildfires of 2010 may be considered as a first case of an emergency response relying significantly on different forms of digital innovation supporting a broad participation of the Russian public. This included various forms of crisis mapping relying on platforms such us Open Street Map. In addition, we saw social networking platforms including

Facebook and Vkontakte, as well as the blogging platform LiveJournal, being used by the online community of Russian Internet users to participate in mapping the crisis and for engagement in responding to various aspects of the crisis.

While some tools were mainly supporting the mapping of the crisis, and others supported the development of networks of people willing to participate in crisis response, an application of the Ushahidi platform (used several months earlier for response to an earthquake in Haiti) was used to link efforts to map the crisis and engagement of the community in response to the issues mapped. The crowdsourcing platform Help Map (Russian-fires.ru) offered to connect those who needed help and those who could help, relying on a permanent aggregation of the data on fires, needs, and resources. Unlike in the case of Haiti, where the mapping connected local affected communities and external responders, both those requiring help and those responding to the emergency were members of the Russian public (Meier, 2015). Later, Ushahidi was used in Russia to address the cold winter of 2010–2011 (Holoda.info), the floods in the Kuban region (south Russia), and the mapping of radiation in the Russian far-east following the nuclear disaster at the Fukushima power station in Japan. The founders of the Help Map also developed a new mapping tool, An Atlas of Help (Rynda.org), that was able to host multiple maps to facilitate people's participation in a variety of crisis situations. This project failed, however, and the Rynda.org domain was used to create a free WordPress mapping plugin, shMapper, which allows the creation of crowdsourcing maps based on OpenStreetMap.

So far, we have followed the transitions related to the role of similar crowdsourcing platforms in response to natural disasters. In this case, one may argue, the digital tool is not only a specific crowdsourcing deployment, but an Ushahidi platform that allows an advanced degree of generativity to use crowdsourcing for shaping the perception of the crisis and mobilizing people's resources in response to this crisis by relying on common perceptions. However, the question is to what extent the same or similar tools, practices and communities could be seen in other areas including different forms of social and political activism, and what are the links between crisis-related and political mobilization. Exploring links can help us to understand whether we may be facing the transformation of the same activity system around a runaway object or the rise of a new system potentially "inspired" to some extent by the existing ones.

In 2010, the prominent Russian political activist Alexey Navalny[2] wrote on his blog that the Help Map could be considered as a model for a platform to address the condition of Russian roads. In a blog post titled "Ushahidi on the potholes," he offered the concept of a website that could be used to gather photos of potholes and submit official complaints to the authorities. Navalny pointed out that "the most well-known website relying on Ushahidi –the Help Map, was created in order to provide help for the victims of fires and proved to be efficient."[3] In October 2010, the platform was released. In May 2011, Navalny announced that the project had moved to a new platform, and with a new name, RosYama (Russian Pothole). In 2015, Navalny launched a new version of the website for the mapping of crowdsourced data on potholes and argued that in four years the project had been able to eliminate at least 20,000 potholes.

One may argue that this example suggests how innovation comes to be diffused, moving from crisis-related activism to other spheres of digitally mediated citizen participation, specifically urban activism. That said, RosYama was not the only crowdsourcing platform developed by Navalny and the Anti-Corruption Foundation launched by him. These included ROsZhkh, an online platform for monitoring Russian Communal Services, as well as RosPil, a platform crowdsourcing the fight against corruption by relying on the analysis of open data on the Russian procurement system. At the beginning of 2012, the same ideas were used to support the monitoring of the Russian presidential elections to be held in March 2012. The RosVybory (RusElections) platform was used for the mobilization of observers and monitoring of polling stations with the highest likelihood of fraud.

Navalny and his team were not the only activists using innovative solutions for election monitoring to be inspired by the experience of crowdsourcing in the context of natural disasters. In Autumn 2011, prior to the parliamentary elections of December 2011, an online mapping and crowdsourcing platform, Karta Narusheniy (Map of Violations), was developed by the election-monitoring NGO Golos and the online liberal media portal Gazeta.ru. The chief editor of Gazeta.ru, Mikhail Kotov, learned about Ushahidi and the Help Map during his visit to MIT in 2010. He returned to Russia with an idea of creating a map that would allow the gathering of information from readers. Kotov's first experiment was the creation of a map to monitor the increase in gasoline prices. That map, however, faced challenges due to a limited number of contributions and to problems with verification.

The next idea was to create a crowdsourcing map for the monitoring of electoral fraud. Kotov invited the developers of the Help Map to study the experience of the project and to use it as part of the development of an election monitoring map. To increase outreach and address the challenge of verification, Gazeta.ru partnered with the election-monitoring NGO Golos. As well as RosYama, Karta Narusheniy relied on a new dedicated platform developed specifically for the purpose of election monitoring. As a part of this collaboration, the map was managed by Golos, while Gazeta.ru used the project to identify the most significant cases of fraud requiring additional verification before being covered by the media. Eventually, the Russian authorities started to be concerned about the increasing impact of the new crowdsourcing platform and Gazeta.ru was forced to revoke the partnership with Golos.

Consideration of the link between the Help Map, RosYama and the Map of Violations demonstrates that potential reliance on crowdsourcing and online mapping are not limited to the Ushahidi platform. Crisis mapping can be considered as a methodology for the mobilization of the resources of digital users that can be used to address a set of social and political challenges relying on similar practices. The diffusion of innovation does not necessarily have to be linear in nature when the same platform is used in different contexts. The data suggests that disaster response, urban activism and political activism have relied on the same imaginaries of crowdsourcing as practices that can support the identification of problems, hold the authorities accountable, and facilitate collective action to address these problems.

In this case, the concept of "runaway objects" is not sufficient to identify the links in a transition from crisis to crisis, since such a transition does not rely on the same tools or the same communities. The concept of Internet imaginaries (Flichy, 2007; Mansell, 2012) and sociotechnical imaginaries as "collectively held and performed visions of desirable futures" relying on digital innovation (Jasanoff, 2015, p. 25) may help us to conceptualize the common denominator linking different projects. The proliferation of these imaginaries seems able to rely on links and interactions between the developers of different crisis-related platforms. These links have supported the diffusion of technological ideas from the field of disaster response to that of political activism.

The cases of crowdsourcing maps in Russia focus attention on platforms created to address a particular crisis. However, at the same time, each crisis can also be linked to a variety of online community pages based on social networks. In the case of the Russian wildfires, dedicated community pages were created on several platforms including LiveJournal, Vkontakte, and Odnoklassniki. In many cases, the communities that emerged in the context of a crisis remained passive and gradually declined. However, since, unlike websites, these do not require any investment in maintenance (e.g., paying for hosting and domain), they may remain in a dormant form following a crisis. The transition of social networking pages that have no association with a particular website differs from the transition of platforms. The case of the Facebook community "Help to victims of Kuban floods" offered an opportunity to follow a transformation in the purpose of a dormant community.

The group was created in 2012 following unprecedented floods in the Kuban area (south Russia). Following the end of that response, the group remained inactive until the Russian occupation of Crimea in 2014 and the beginning of the war in eastern Ukraine, after some areas were occupied by pro-Russian separatists. In 2014, two years after the floods, one of the admins of the group published an announcement that the group was going to refocus from assistance to victims of floods to assistance to refugees coming from eastern Ukraine to Russia. The announcement indirectly recognized the political sensitivity of this transformation. The admin mentioned that "if you don't like this change, you may leave the group." However, the group stopped operating soon after the change in its purpose.

At the same time, the Pozar_ru Facebook group, created in 2014 as an extension of the LiveJournal community from 2010, continued to be active as recently as 2022, focusing mainly on issues related to wildfires. It seems that the long-term development of crisis-related communities depends on the rules or operation of the community that are introduced and enforced by admins of the group. In other words, the rules that define both the topics allowed to be raised and the forms of behavior prohibited seem to play a key role in defining the role of online communities in the mediation of the relationship between users and crisis, as well as in the degree of generativity and the potential scale of flexibility to address new types of crises beyond the initial intent. Crisis-related online social media groups may survive longer since these do not, like websites, require maintenance including domain and hosting support. This means that the direction of the pages and the forms of the transition mainly depend on the decisions of the users that have been assigned as admins.

Discussion

The empirical discussion above allows us first to identify forms of transition from crisis to crisis and to address the descriptive question of the dominant forms of transition (see Figure 5.3).

Here I offer an illustration of three types of transition. First is a transition within the same platform, as in the case of Galas, which has been used as a crowdsourcing tool to collect data and engage users as part of a response to a natural disaster, of internal political protests or of a response to external military aggression. Second is a transition related to the diffusion of innovation through a common network of founders and activists sharing similar socio-technological imaginaries. This can be seen in the case of the links between the role of crowdsourcing platforms in response to disasters, in supporting urban activism, and in supporting political activism in Russia. Third is a transition in the purpose of crisis-related groups on existent social networking platforms. Such a transition may take one of two forms. If the group is related to a particular website, then the transition may follow the transition of the website, as in the case of Galas (where these transitions are interrelated). If there is no specific website related to a social networking page, then the transition is mainly driven and authorized by the admins of the page (as in the case of the page dedicated initially to emergency response to floods in southern Russia).

Following consideration of mapping, the next question to ask is what factors may support the generativity of platforms and the durability of a network in a transition from crisis to crisis, and particularly why in some cases digitally mediated activity systems remain despite a change in the nature of the object, while in other cases once the object is no longer there (that is, once a specific crisis ends), the digital object loses its function and the system dissolves. One may consider three potential explanations that can help to address this question. First, the capacity of the system to avoid dissolution may depend on the nature of the mediating digital tools and their affordances. Second, the transition may depend

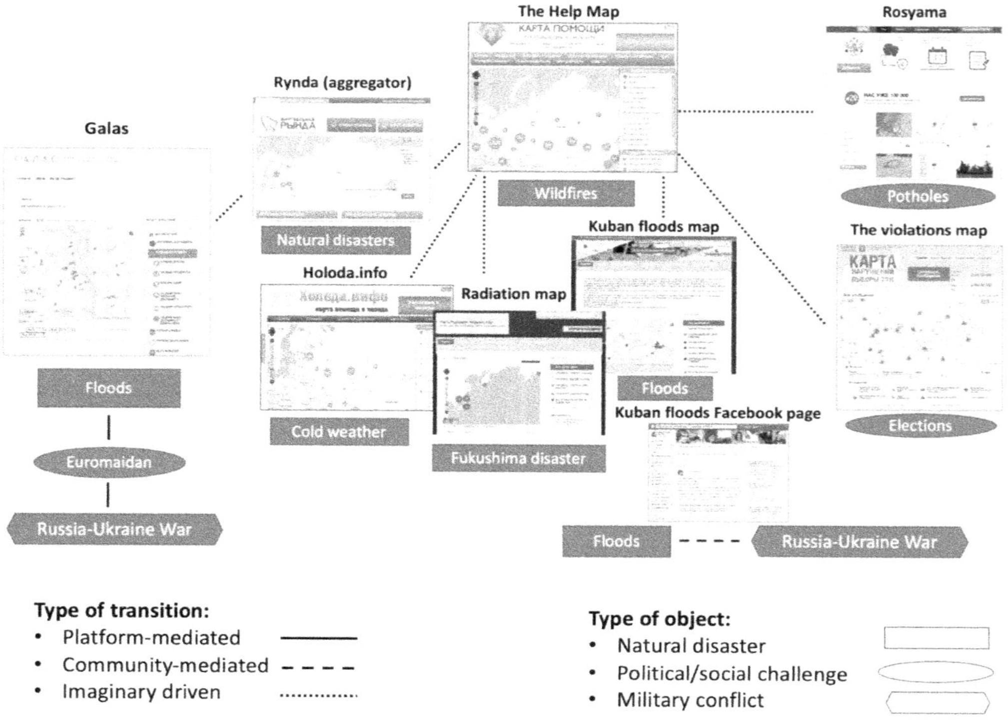

Figure 5.3 Mapping of the role of digital tools in crisis-to-crisis transitions.

on the nature of the online communities and on the perception of crisis-to-crisis transition among the members of these communities. Third, the transition may also depend on the nature of the digital ecosystem either creating favorable conditions for generativity or restricting transitions enabling the existence of digitally mediated activity systems that follow "runaway objects."

The empirical cases mentioned allow us to identify two types of digital tools, distinguishing between situations where the crisis response relies on the same platforms or on the same networks of users. The first are *object-oriented tools* created mainly to address a specific crisis. The central element of the platform in such a case concerns the representation of a crisis (e.g., a map), while the mediating function of the platform mainly concerns the classification, mobilization, and allocation of resources in relation to the crisis (crisis-related sourcing). This can be seen in the case of crisis-related crowdsourcing platforms. Platforms of this type often do not have an opportunity to register the personal profiles of users, while the networking affordances are supported through affiliated groups on social networks. The identity of users has a secondary role, and often they are not required to register to participate in various forms of activity. For instance, the Help Map was created to address wildfires, while also having some affiliated communities on Facebook and Vkontakte.

The second type are *subject-oriented* digital tools that support the development of a specific community of users. Subject-centered platforms are developed to offer the user an opportunity to register her/his own page in order to carry out various forms of activity, including communication, data generation and data consumption. These are mainly social networking platforms relying on the personal profiles of users as the central element of operations. This can be seen in the case of Facebook community groups, where the role of digital platforms is to provide an affordance for the existence of a particular network. The distinction between object-oriented and subject-oriented tools may also help us to address the question of which platforms are more likely to perish during the period between different crisis situations, and which ones may demonstrate more durability.

One may argue that the above distinction allows us to differentiate between platform-driven and community-driven crisis responses. However, the empirical cases described highlight how most platforms offer a combination and integration of both object-oriented and subject-oriented tools. That said, one may also argue that the transition from crisis to crisis of object-oriented and of subject-oriented tools may follow different paths. This is because the structure of subject-oriented tools is mainly shaped by rules enforced by moderators/admins, while the structure of object-oriented tools seems to rely more on the code, design, and specific affordances of the platform. One may therefore argue that subject-oriented tools are more generative and durable since, on the one hand, their structure may potentially be less focused on a specific crisis, and, at the same time, the maintenance of these tools does not require investment. Object-oriented tools seem to be more vulnerable, since their maintenance requires support (e.g., paying for domain and hosting, as well as updating code), while their structure offers less space for generativity. Therefore, subject-oriented tools may remain dormant between crises, but can be brought back to life more easily by comparison with crowdsourcing platforms.

An additional factor that should be considered is the temporal proximity of one crisis to another. For instance, in the case of the transition from protests to armed conflict in Ukraine, the events took place without a break, and therefore a transition relying on object-oriented tools was more likely. In addition, networking platforms offer more flexibility to support some forms of communication to maintain the community between crisis situations, while object-oriented crowdsourcing platforms do not offer an option for conducting activity between crisis situations (unless they are repurposed for long-term recovery efforts or start to be used to address everyday-life issues, e.g., hyperlocal problems). Therefore, the act of repurposing requires more effort and resources in the case of object-oriented platforms.

That said, object-oriented tools may potentially contribute to the diffusion of crisis-related innovation, while also inspiring the creation of new tools through the introduction of new socio-technical imaginaries. The Russian case allows us to establish some links between crowdsourcing platforms created for disaster response and crowdsourcing platforms used to address various political and urban challenges. Moreover, empirical discussion demonstrates a link between Russian and Ukrainian platforms, since the development of the first prototype of Galas was associated with a socio-technological imaginary introduced earlier by the Help Map platform. The core element of that imaginary suggests that we consider digital platforms as a tool of mutual aid that can offer a bridge for connecting those who need help and those who want to help in the context of crisis mapping.

In order to address the main research question we should consider these findings in the context of the notion of a runaway object. On the one hand, the notion of a runaway object challenges the idea of differentiation between different types of crises. On the other hand, it proposes that we consider which crisis-to-crisis transitions can be considered as cases where the activity system remains resulting from technological mediation, and in which cases we can see a rise of new crisis-related activity systems. The empirical data suggests that subject-oriented tools have a better capacity to contribute to the continuity and durability of crisis-related activity systems. We can see that social networking groups have a longer life and can more easily be reactivated in the context of a new crisis.

That said, object-oriented tools can also contribute to the durability of activity systems in the context of crisis-to-crisis transitions. First, the case of Galas demonstrates that when there is a temporal proximity between various crisis situations this enables the repurposing of a crowdsourcing project in the context of a changing object. The durability of an object-oriented platform is also reinforced by the existence of subject-oriented platforms (social networking groups) that are more durable in the long term. The second pathway for this identifies how the role of object-oriented tools in crisis-to-crisis transition can be considered in the context of diffusion innovation. In such a case, we may see new platforms giving rise to new crisis-related activity systems, but these activity systems rely on similar socio-technological imaginaries.

The existence of a crisis as a "runaway object" that maximizes the generativity of digital platforms in response to a crisis and supports the continuous long-term existence of a crisis-related activity system depends, however, on an additional factor concerning the ambivalent role of digital artifacts in constructing the object of activity and mediating activity in relation to the constructed object. This highlights the essential role of sensemaking and collective meaning-creation (sense-giving) in the existence of runaway objects. The need for a common meaning to support the operation of a network highlights how distinguishing between the transformation of a runaway object within the context of an existing activity system and the rise of a new activity system around a new crisis depends on a community's shared perception of the object. If, despite the changes in the nature of the crisis, the community around specific digital tools agrees to accept an object, this object can be considered as a runaway. In other words, the basic condition for the continuation of activity systems is a shared perception of a crisis by the members of a community, even when the situation changes.

For instance, in the case of the transformation from political protests to armed conflict in Ukraine, a significant part of the community continued to share a common perception of the crisis, and therefore the crisis could be considered as a runaway object. However, in the case of the transformation from response to floods in south Russia to a refugee crisis linked to the war in Ukraine, sustaining a shared perception of the crisis was rejected because of disagreement among community members. Therefore, we could see the discontinuation of the crisis both as a runaway object and as the decline of a community. In this light, this chapter suggests that a shared perception of a crisis is a fundamental condition for the existence of crisis-related runaway activity systems. This is where we can see that, while the object of activity changes, the system remains and continues to operate, relying on the same or similar digital tools including both subject-oriented and object-oriented platforms.

The last aspect that should help us to address factors related to the role of digital platforms in crisis-to-crisis transition is the structure of a digital ecosystem, and specifically the role of state-sponsored regulation. This factor is particularly evident when comparing the Russian and Ukrainian cases. In the Russian case, we can see that once the runaway objects started moving from natural disasters toward political activism, this raised a particular concern from the perspective of the state. Starting from 2011, Russian authorities made significant efforts to introduce different forms of Internet regulation in order to restrict and eliminate any forms of digitally mediated independent mobilization. This included not only new forms of filtering and censorship that restricted crisis mapping and the bottom-up construction of a shared threat, but also the development of state-sponsored volunteering platforms as a form of vertical crowdsourcing (Asmolov, 2015), which was seen particularly in the context of the COVID-19 pandemic (Asmolov, 2022c). In this sense, autocratic regulation seeks to eliminate and discontinue potential transitions that support runaway objects. In other words, the existence of activity systems around runaway objects becomes a political threat that is addressed through regulative and disconnective powers of the state.

At the same time, we have not seen a disruption of runaway objects because of political regulation in the Ukrainian case. The Ukrainian ecosystem gives a space for the flourishing of horizontal networks and enables a maximization of the generative potential of digital tools. This could be seen particularly in the rise of a broad range of digitally mediated forms of participation in response to Russian aggression (Asmolov, 2022b). In this sense, those factors that enable the continuation of runaway objects in Ukraine have played a key role in the development of Ukrainian resilience since the full-scale Russian invasion in 2022. While our initial empirical analysis shows some links between the socio-technical imaginaries that shaped the role of digital platforms in crisis response in Russia and Ukraine, the further implementation of these imaginaries in these two countries has moved in different directions. This is due to the difference between the political systems and, specifically, to the role of regulation in shaping the role of digital tools in crisis-to-crisis transition.

Conclusion

This chapter explores the factors that shape the role of digital platforms in transitions from crisis to crisis. It addresses what types of platform may be considered more generative and flexible to allow the switching of user mobilization from one crisis to another, while relying on previous experience and existent technological infrastructure. This question is particularly important in the context of discussions about how digital platforms may support social resilience as an outcome of continuous cycles of crisis-related mobilization. The analysis of empirical cases suggests that we focus on three potential pathways of transition that can be associated with the mediating role of digital tools. It proposes that a continuation of crisis-related engagement may be driven either by the same community, by the same digital platforms, or by the same imaginaries as were related to a previous case of digitally mediated crisis response.

The highest degree of adaptability to a new type of crisis seems to be seen in the cases of communities that rely on social networks (this can also apply to messengers, e.g., WhatsApp or Telegram). This can also be seen in the case of hyperlocal COVID-related mutual aid groups, which remain beyond the focus of the analysis in this chapter (Kavada, 2020). While these tools do not offer specific affordances for the representation and classification of an object, they enable community-building based on the affordances of personal profiles and interaction around specific topics. In this way, these networks allow the development of "crowd capital" (Prpić & Shukla, 2013), which can be mobilized in the context of different crisis situations. That said, since networking platforms do not have specific affordances for the mapping of subjects as a common denominator of activity, to operate in a crisis situation these networks require a shared understanding of the challenge. This is where we can see a space for synergy between subject-oriented and object-oriented tools. The first can sustain a community between crises. The second can offer meaning for the mobilization of networks in the context of a specific crisis and identify opportunities for specific forms of response.

More work is required to address how social media can make networks more generative, and how each cycle of crisis-related mobilization relying on a digital platform can contribute to the development of social resilience in the context of emerging global catastrophic risks. For instance, the role of specific leaders and innovators in sustaining online communities and in the development of new tools of crisis-related mobilization requires more analytical attention. Further analysis of the role of specific forms of innovation, including generative AI and blockchain, may also help us to identify how to sustain community through an ongoing change of objects and how to support the diffusion of innovation enabling each community to foster a shared perception of a crisis and to develop new object-oriented tools in relation to that crisis.

Notes

1 Crisis mapping and crowdsourcing are usually mentioned in the context of the same platforms, and it may seem that the terms are used interchangeably. However, these two concepts may represent two separate functions of the same platform. Crisis mapping refers to the development of a fully dynamic picture of the crisis relying on the aggregation of information from a diversity of sources, and to the visualization of this information through a map. The crowdsourcing element concerns the mobilization of crowd resources in relation to the crisis that has been mapped. In this sense, the sourcing cannot operate without mapping, and both elements can be considered as object-oriented activities. The first layer concerns the construction of the object, while the second addresses the challenges related to the object-related allocation of crowd resources.

2 Alexey Navalny has been prosecuted by the Russian authorities, which consider him as an "extremist" due to his political activism and struggle against corruption. In 2021, 2022 and 2023 Navalny was sentenced to 19 years in Russian prison. "Navalny," a film about the poisoning and imprisonment of Alexei Navalny, won the Academy Award for best documentary feature in 2023. Alexei Navalny died in an Arctic penal colony on February 16, 2024. According to his political allies, Russian authorities killed him to sabotage a prisoner swap.

3 http://navalny.livejournal.com/500765.html.

References

Alekseev, K. (2013). "Galas" – Ukrainian map of mutual aid. Teplitza Socialnyh Technologiy, April 22. https://te-st.ru/entries/galas/

Asmolov, G. (2015). Vertical crowdsourcing in Russia: Balancing governance of crowds and state–citizen partnership in emergency situations. *Policy & Internet*, *7*(3), 292–318.

Asmolov, G. (2022a). Crisis communication in authoritarian systems and digital innovation. How do autocracies resolve the dictator's dilemma in crisis situations? In W. T. Coombs & S. J. Holladay (Eds.), *The handbook of crisis communication* (2nd ed., pp. 209–227). John Wiley & Sons.

Asmolov, G. (2022b). The transformation of participatory warfare: The role of narratives in connective mobilization in the Russia–Ukraine war. *Digital War Journal*, *3*(1), 25–37. https://doi.org/10.1057/s42984-022-00054-5

Asmolov, G. (2022c). Internet regulation and crisis-related resilience: From Covid-19 to existential risks. *The Communication Review*, *25*(3–4), 235–257. https://doi.org/10.1080/10714421.2022.2129124

Avin, S., Wintle, B. C., Weitzdörfer, J., Ó hÉigeartaigh, S. S., Sutherland, W. J., & Rees, M. J. (2018). Classifying global catastrophic risks. *Futures*, *102*, 20–26.

Bennett, W. L., & Segerberg, A. (2011). The logic of connective action. *Information, Communication & Society*, *15*(5), 739–768.

Bohdanova, T. (2014). Unexpected revolution: The role of social media in Ukraine's Euromaidan uprising. *European View*, *13*(1), 133–142.

boyd, D. (2011). Social network sites as networked publics: Affordances, dynamics, and implications. In Z. Papacharissi (Ed.), *A networked self: Identity, community, and culture on social network sites* (pp. 39–58). Routledge.

Cannon, T., & Müller-Mahn, D. (2010). Vulnerability, resilience and development discourses in the context of climate change. *Natural Hazards*, *55*, 621–635.

Chon, M.-G., & Park, H. (2020). Social media activism in the digital age: Testing an integrative model of activism on contentious issues. *Journalism & Mass Communication Quarterly*, *97*(1), 72–97. https://doi.org/10.1177/1077699019835896

Dickinson, J. (2014). Prosymo Maksymal'nyi Perepost! Tactical and discursive uses of social media in Ukraine's EuroMaidan. *Ab Imperio*, *3*, 75–93.

Diers-Lawson, A. (2020). *Crisis communication: Managing stakeholder relationships*. Routledge.

Diers-Lawson, A. (2023). iScotland: Building a unified model of activism in multi-platform communication environments from traditional PR theory. *Corporate Communications: An International Journal* (ahead of print). https://doi.org/10.1108/CCIJ-12-2022-0153

Dutton, W. H. (2009). The fifth estate emerging through the network of networks. *Prometheus* *27*(1), 1–15.

Engeström, Y. (1987). *Learning by expanding: An activity-theoretical approach to developmental research*. Orienta-Konsultit Oy.

Engeström, Y. (2007). From communities of practice to mycorrhizae. In J. Hughes, N. Jewson, & L. Unwin (Eds.), *Communities of practice: Critical perspectives* (pp. 41–54). Routledge.

Engeström, Y. (2008). *From teams to knots: Studies of collaboration and learning at work*. Cambridge University Press.

Flichy, P. (2007). *The internet imaginaire*. MIT press.
Jasanoff, S. (2015). Future imperfect: Science, technology, and the imaginations of modernity. In S. Jasanoff & S-H Kim (Eds.), *Dreamscapes of modernity: Sociotechnical imaginaries and the fabrication of power* (pp. 1–33). University of Chicago Press.
Hannigan, J. (2012). *Disasters without borders. The international politics of natural disasters*. Polity.
Holling, C. S. (2000). Theories for sustainable futures. *Conservation Ecology*, *4(*2), 7.
Kaptelinin, V. (2014). The mediational perspective on digital technology: Understanding the interplay between technology, mind and action. In S. Price, C. Jewitt, & B. Brown (Eds.), *Sage handbook of digital technology research* (pp. 203–217). Sage.
Karanasios, S., Nardi, B., Spinuzzi, C., & Malaurent, J. (2021). Moving forward with activity theory in a digital world. *Mind, Culture, and Activity*, *28*(3), 234–253.
Kavada, A. (2020). Creating a hyperlocal infrastructure of care: COVID-19 mutual aid groups. *OpenDemocracy*, https://www.opendemocracy.net/en/openmovements/creating-hyperlocal-infrastructure-care-covid-19-mutual-aid-groups
Klimovich, S. (2014) З чого складається Майдан. Дослідження груп, котрі забезпечують життя Майдану (What does the Maidan consist of? Study of the groups that provide life to the Maidan), Texty. https://texty.org.ua/articles/50821/
Kreienkamp, J., & Pegram, T. (2021). Governing complexity: Design principles for the governance of complex global catastrophic risks. *International Studies Review*, *23*(3), 779–806.
Liu, W., Lai, C-H., & Xu, W. (2018). Tweeting about emergency: A semantic network analysis of government organizations' social media messaging during Hurricane Harvey. *Public Relations Review*, *44*(5), 807–819.
Lokot, T. (2016). *Galas: Mobilizing and managing volunteer humanitarian efforts online during Euromaidan protests in Ukraine.* https://medium.com/civic-media-project/galas-mobilizing-and-managing-volunteer-humanitarian-efforts-online-during-euromaidan-protests-in-35c284b37e3f
Mansell, R. (2012). *Imagining the Internet: Communication, innovation, and governance*. Oxford University Press.
Meier, P. (2012). *How civil disobedience improves crowdsourced disaster response (and vice versa)*. https://irevolutions.org/2012/08/22/civil-resistance-improve-disaster-response/
Meier, P. (2015). *Digital humanitarians: How big data is changing the face of humanitarian response*. CRC Press.
Metzger, M. M., & Tucker, J. A. (2017). Social media and EuroMaidan: A review essay. *Slavic Review*, *76*(1), 169–191. https://doi.org/10.1017/slr.2017.16
Mirbabaie, M., Bunker, D., Stieglitz, S., Marx, J., & Ehnis, C. (2020). Social media in times of crisis: Learning from Hurricane Harvey for the coronavirus disease 2019 pandemic response. *Journal of Information Technology*, *35*(3), 195–213.
Momin, K. A., Kays, H. M. I., & Sadri, A. M. (2023). Identifying crisis response communities in online social networks for compound disasters: The case of Hurricane Laura and COVID-19. *Transportation Research Record*, *0*(0), 1–19.
Nambisan, S. (2017). Digital entrepreneurship: Toward a digital technology perspective of entrepreneurship. *Entrepreneurship Theory and Practice*, *41*(6), 1029–1055.
Prpić, J., & Shukla, P. (2013). *The theory of crowd capital.* Proceedings of the Hawaii international conference on systems sciences #46, Maui, Hawaii, January 7–10. IEEE Computer Society Press. http://papers.ssrn.com/sol3/papers.cfm?abstract_id=2193115

Reuter, C., Hughes A. L., & Kaufhold, M-A. (2018). Social media in crisis management: An evaluation and analysis of crisis informatics research. *International Journal of Human–Computer Interaction, 34*(4), 280–294. https://doi.org/10.1080/10447318.2018.1427832

Sandoval-Almazan, R., & Gil-Garcia, J. R. (2014). Towards cyberactivism 2.0? Understanding the use of social media and other information technologies for political activism and social movements. *Government Information Quarterly, 31*(3), 365–378. https://doi.org/10.1016/j.giq.2013.10.016

Sellnow, T. L., & Seeger, M. W. (2013). *Theorizing crisis communication.* Wiley-Blackwell.

Seeger, M. W., Sellnow, T. L., & Ulmer, R. R. (2003). *Communication and organizational crisis*. Greenwood Publishing Group.

Spinuzzi, C. (2014). How nonemployer firms stage-manage ad-hoc collaboration: An activity theory analysis. *Technical Communication Quarterly, 23*(2), 88–114.

Tierney, K. (2014). *The social roots of risk: Producing disasters, promoting resilience.* Stanford University Press.

Vera-Burgos, C. M., & Griffin Padgett, D. R. (2020). Using Twitter for crisis communications in a natural disaster: Hurricane Harvey. *Heliyon, 6*(9), 1–10.

Weick, K. E. (1993). The collapse of sensemaking in organizations: The Mann Gulch disaster. *Administrative Science Quarterly, 38*(4), 628–652.

Yoo, Y., Henfridsson, O., & Lyytinen, K. (2010). The new organizing logic of digital innovation: An agenda for information systems research. *Information Systems Research, 21(*4), 724–735.

Zittrain, J. (2008). *The future of the Internet – And how to stop It.* Yale University Press.

6 Bridging Theory and Practice Through Crisis Simulation

A Framework Designed to Address the Current Development of Risk Assessment and Crisis Communication in Romania

Corina Buzoianu and Monica Bîră

As in the case of other post-communist countries, in Romania communication and public relations, risk, and crisis communication do not have a substantial tradition (see Schwarz et al., 2016). They have been developed by borrowings from Western theories and practices (Craig, 1999; 2013; Taylor & Lindlof, 2013), as well as based on knowledge transfer from well-established academic programs available in Romanian universities (in the fields of philology and philosophy). In many instances, communities of practice in the field of communication and PR in Romania were aggregated alongside the development of the business environment and the market penetration of North American and Western-European corporations. They were subsequently followed by the set-up of dedicated academic training and programs, with a mixed teaching staff of practitioners and academic pioneers. The field's professionalization started during the late 1990s and the beginning of the 2000s with local public relations agencies, professional associations, and first-generation BA and MA in communication and public relations. More than a decade later, although public relations and communication are established disciplines, risk, and crisis communication in Romania appear to still search their own path in terms of theories and practices. This is reflected both in academia and in the business field. Compared with other areas, risk and crisis communication and management have a small share in academic programs and organizational structures of agencies and PR service providers.

To situate crisis communication simulation in a broader and relevant context for higher education in Romania, we need to address two layers that, during the last three decades, built up this branch of crisis communication and management. The first layer regards communication teaching and learning in relation to the development of communication as a field and, subsequently, as an academic discipline in universities and markets across Eastern European societies. It covers both formal academic teaching and training (BA and MA degrees) and practice training (professional training on the job). The second layer includes the

DOI: 10.4324/9781003375296-8

ongoing process of integrating new technologies into higher education, which is closely related to the emerging way of producing and sharing knowledge in universities (Adi & Scotte, 2016).

The development of communication as a field in Eastern European countries has followed the path of an "imported" discipline, first brought in during the 1990s by public relations and advertising practices. At that time, the required practical and technical knowledge in communication was supplied by what we may call "proxies" for formal academic training in communication. During that period, journalism, modern languages and literature (including English), sociology, and philosophy served as substitutes and worked as proxies for communication studies. Partially, this pathway of developing communication studies in Eastern European countries has been researched with a focus on journalism and related fields (Casmir, 2012; Ivan et al., 2014; Jirak & Kopplova, 2008; Klyukanov, 2011; Peruško & Vozab, 2015). There is still much to cover in relation to the process of institutionalizing communication as an academic field, especially in tracing the career paths of public relations practitioners and in mapping out how formal academic training is shaping the domain and, in its turn, how companies' practices influence the development of the field, expectations and the jobs they offer (Buzoianu et al., 2019).

Extant literature shows that there is evidence for a need to revise the traditional approaches to education in communication (Diers-Lawson, 2021), as they are lacking in meeting the learners' expectations and the labor market's needs (Ewing et al., 2018; Neill & Schauster, 2015). Consequently, academic programs are expected to rethink their content, methods, and tools to benefit from the digital environment's development. In addition, we must consider how today's students refer to the learning experience (Diers-Lawson, 2021) and the need for new communication and public relations competencies in social media (Macnamara et al., 2015; Manias-Muñoz et al., 2019) and the digital environment. The changes envisaged by the spread of social media, digital communication, affiliate marketing, and performance media are challenging the anatomy, means, and practices of communication and public relations (Morgan & Wilk, 2021; Utz et al., 2013). To all these, it is worth adding that both academics (Macnamara et al., 2015; Macnamara & Zerfass, 2017) and practitioners tackle the pressure that public relations practitioners feel to upskill to stay relevant in the digital ecosystem (AMEC, 2023; Sprout Social Index – UK and Ireland, 2021; State of Nordic PR, 2022; Zerfass et al., 2021, 2022).

If, for experienced PR specialists, the ongoing adjustment to the digital environment is a challenge, forming the next generation of PR professionals poses yet another set of specific difficulties. The growing gap between technology transformation and the pace at which universities manage to deliver appropriate training and expertise for young graduates in working with social media (Kim & Freberg, 2017; King, 2015) as well as different expectations that senior and mid-level PR professionals might have from newly graduates (Krishna et al., 2020) are concerns addressed both by academia and the industry.

It is relevant that, according to recent studies, the core skills required to work in PR are still revolving around competencies that don't directly depend on digital technology, such as writing, listening, and creativity (Krishna et al., 2020), with an added layer of intercultural competencies (Miño & Gibson, 2020) for people generally aiming to assume roles as global communicators in strategic communication and journalism. However, once these prerequisites are checked, being able to answer properly to a hostile online environment (deal with an online reputation crisis, communicate effectively in today's environment of disinformation, and build a crisis response plan) brings once more into focus the fact that understanding the online environment and social media (see Manias-Muñoz et al., 2019) as well as having the appropriate training becomes critical. As the social media landscape is rapidly changing and an entire new universe is being created (e.g., metaverse), there is a need to enhance collaboration with the industry's own solutions and certification programs (e.g., Hootsuite Academy, Google Academy) and with tools and platforms developers for risk and crisis communication (see Cowley et al., 2021; Kinsky, et al., 2016; Laverie at al., 2020; Staton, 2016).

Crisis Simulation: Theory-Based Communication Practice

Initially designed for media training and disaster management, crisis simulations in communication have been developed to help communication professionals and managers be prepared to respond to crises based on scenarios and different difficulty levels (Chung, 2016;'t Hart, 1997). Because crisis simulations have proven to be very efficient in training (Borodzicz & Van Haperen, 2002; Klabbers, 2018), they have been gradually used in academic programs in communication (Delaney & Meister, 2021; Veil, 2010) to develop active learning experiences (Aertsen et al., 2013; Diers-Lawson, 2021) and help students apply theories and models to solve problems and respond to issues and crises (e.g., Harvard Business Publishing simulations for different disciplines). Generally, crisis simulations are experience-based learning (Borodzicz & Van Haperen, 2002), where students or practitioners apply theories, models, and concepts to solve realistic crisis situations (Veil, 2010). In most cases, simulations are designed to build core communication skills that any communication practitioner is expected to have (Anderson et al., 2014; Diers-Lawson, 2021): the ability to analyze the situation (Coombs, 2001), to make sense of contextual data, oral and written communication skills, navigate tensions and public outrage, deal with media buzz and work in teams (Wang, 2017). Consequently, crisis simulation in social media can also be referred to as a solution for bridging theory and practice in communication and increasing trust in the practical applicability of theory and its relevance for practitioners.

Crisis simulations have been considered essential for crisis management and communication (Boin & Lagadec, 2000;'t Hart, 1997) due to their substantial contribution to preparing for threats, issues, and crises. It has been underlined that crisis simulations' efficiency relies on the key factor of "being there" in the sense of being present in a situation and taking part in the decision-making process (Wang, 2017). The subjective feeling of being present (see Barfield et al., 1995) triggers students' engagement and commitment to the assignment and enables collaborative learning. As scholars point out (Boin et al., 2004; Wang, 2017), crisis simulations are attractive to both students and practitioners due to their entertaining dimension (Diers-Lawson, 2021). Crisis simulations are considered more fun and inspiring experiences than traditional learning and knowledge transfer. In addition, they manage to produce high levels of cognitive learning (Delaney & Meister, 2021) and increase student satisfaction in class (Anderson et al., 2014). As interactive learning environments (see Klabbers, 2018), crisis simulations enhance learning through practice (Coombs, 2001), communication, and joint work. Moreover, simulations generate critical thinking using worse-case scenarios and probabilities and increase decision-making (Boin et al., 2004).

Since Weber Shandwick launched FireBell, the in-house developed social crisis simulator in 2010 (2010, November 18), to offer clients a real-time experience of being under attack on social media channels, the design and implementation of crisis simulations in academic training have been put under scrutiny (see Anderson et al., 2014). Although very useful for communication practitioners, simulations designed for media training and looking to develop disaster management skills are perceived as insufficient to manage the dynamics of crisis communication today and to deal with different categories of stakeholders and their expectations. The cross-channel crises and the key role that social media platforms play in creating and spreading an event must be considered in any crisis simulation to help students develop relevant skills for crisis communication. For this, some instructional design and pedagogy changes must be considered, along with both software and hardware infrastructure in classes. As scholars note (Anderson et al., 2014), there is evidence of the efforts made to develop innovative learning techniques in crisis communication programs (see Aertsen et al., 2013; Pyle, 2017; Veil, 2010), but in most cases, the simulations do not include events unfolding in social media, due to lack of resources (Moizer et al., 2009), means, and practices. Although it is known that free and easy-to-use software is used to run simulations, progress is still needed. Besides existing software and hardware-related challenges, existing literature on crisis simulation design in social media is scarce. Furthermore, options for scenario building and practice through problem-based learning in online environments are insufficiently covered and lack diversity. While in recent years, public relations agencies, multinational companies, and training providers have developed several crisis simulation platforms, they are still very little used in academic programs for crisis communication students.

Crisis Communication Simulation in the Romanian Context

Drawing on extant literature on teaching crisis communication (Borodzicz & Van Haperen, 2002; Coombs, 2001; Pyle, 2017), instructional design (Riforgiate et al., 2019; Sellnow & Sellnow, 2010), learning preferences (Evans et al., 2010; Frisby et al., 2013), and problem-solving (Allen & Rooney, 1998; Jonassen, 2010), we developed an educational project on crisis simulation in social media to enhance learning and support students in acquiring crisis communication skills, like identifying threats, analyzing problems and responding to a crisis that is very likely to occur (see Coombs, 2001). The design and means are envisaged to create a learning environment where students use theories, models, and techniques throughout crisis simulations. Thus, throughout our project, we seek to support students' practice and increase their knowledge and expertise in teams working around scenarios and collaborating to solve specific situations.

The educational project was initiated in 2017 and was dedicated to MA students in social media at the College of Communication and Public Relations, SNSPA, Romania. The project aligns with academic programs' efforts to gain recognition from communication and public relations practitioners and increase relevance for the labor market. Initially based on a partnership with public relations agencies and multinational companies, the educational project was set up as a response to the hesitancy of communication practitioners toward academic programs and courses in crisis communication. From the early beginning, the crisis simulation project looked to bridge scholars' outputs with PR and communication practitioners and to promote new means and practices in for academic training. We designed this educational project to meet MA students' expectations of a crisis communication course, as they were looking for interactive learning experiences around social media and online communication environments. The crisis simulation project was initially set up in cooperation with a multinational company headquartered in the USA and a nonaffiliated local public relations agency. Other communication, public relations, and digital agencies joined our project in the following years as we extended the project to BA programs. Currently, all crisis communication classes at the College of Communication and Public Relations, SNSPA, include a crisis simulation tailored to the class's objectives, level of knowledge, comprehension, competencies, and students' expectations and professional interests.

In this educational project, crisis simulations have been designed to take account of events unfolding in social media and include boycotts, buzz, and several types of stakeholders stepping in through different channels and platforms. Since 2017, approximately 2,000 students from BA and MA programs in communication have attended the crisis simulation project in on-site and online formats. The high number of students involved, the different study levels and formats, and the diverse range of scenarios, industries, and anatomies of events and crises have been instrumental in improving the crisis simulation project, from design to implementation, debriefing, and grading. As other studies reveal (e.g., Anderson et al., 2014), this type of activity is highly appreciated by students; the yearly internal quality evaluation process conducted by the faculty indicates that students consider the activity as being one of the most engaging learning experiences in their program and very useful in shaping their professional skills and practice.

Over the years, the crisis simulation educational project we developed at the College of Communication and Public Relations has been subject to many changes and adjustments in terms of instructional design, scenarios, means, tools, and formats. In the initial stages of implementing this educational project, it is important to frame the activities as derived from the experience of communication and public relations practitioners. In doing so, we emphasize their relevance to the professional path of our students. We depart from the idea that the learning experience should be both entertaining (Moyer-Gusé, 2008) and rigorous (Diers-Lawson, 2021) and thus seek to create an environment appropriate to obtain an increased interest in theory (Denker et al., 2022; Mazer, 2013) and facilitate learning. To ensure conditions for successful collaborative work (Fransen et al., 2011; Loh & Ang, 2020) and increase cohesion, students must work in teams, take up a name, and submit a team presentation where each team member's communication and creative thinking competencies are highlighted. It is important to create a trustful and safe learning environment where students can share knowledge, give and receive constructive feedback (Ashby-King et al., 2021), and get acquainted with self-evaluation. Teams get to present their work and receive feedback, and in some class meetings, teams are asked to self-evaluate their work according to guidelines, best messages, and outcomes for crisis response. During the project, students get to exercise and increase their adaptability, negotiation, and communication skills since, at least in Romania, in most cases, practitioners involved in crisis communication and management do not have exact roles and responsibilities; instead, they switch between different tasks and positions. Therefore, unlike other crisis simulation projects and team assignments (see Aertsen et al., 2013; Pyle, 2017), students do not have specific roles assigned to each of them within the team.

In our educational project, the crisis simulation content creation departs from real-life situations as (1) it goes along with the current dynamics of social media platforms' algorithms (Ewing et al., 2018; Neill & Schauster, 2015) and (2) considers different categories of stakeholders that may be involved during a crisis (see Diers-Lawson, 2019, 2020). The crisis simulation exercise is developed and tailored for each class according to learning objectives, students' previous knowledge, competencies, and the academic program objectives they are enrolled in.

A Framework for Developing Crisis Simulations for Social Media Crises

In this section, we focus on the development of crisis simulations in communication, addressing the process, methods, steps, and guidelines for the design and implementation. In designing a crisis simulation, one has the mission to align expectations and perceptions that are not necessarily divergent but still difficult to negotiate. First, crisis simulations should be an entertaining and interactive learning experience (Diers-Lawson, 2021) and therefore need solid preparation and a multi-stages organization (Anderson et al., 2014). Second, crisis simulations should merge the class's learning objectives with students' expectations and professional interests, especially for MA students. Third, the activity should prove valuable for the learner's professional development (Delaney & Meister, 2021; Diers-Lawson, 2021). Crisis simulations are mostly efficient when designed and planned as a part of an educational project, wherein several weeks of work with students are scheduled. Thus, a series of learning activities are preceding the crisis simulation, in most of the time a minimum of 10 weeks of class work is needed.

Unlike in the past decade, when all crisis simulations were built in PowerPoint, nowadays, several options are available to host crisis simulations in communication, ranging from easy-to-use open access to sophisticated, highly secured subscription platforms that are principally adapted to this end. The landscape of tools and means has changed to such a degree that if the exercise uses ongoing crises, some of these platforms may be employed to foresee threats, as they can send real-time alerts based on keywords and probabilities. Also, the learners may post cross-channel content when submitting the response and see it in real-time. As a result, from the point of view of software and technical solutions, crisis simulations and exercises have diverse options to create engaging, appealing, and realistic crisis examples. The only real limitation in working with these tools is linked with having access to them, both for teaching staff and students. However, like all other available technologies for content creation, instructional design, and learning experiences, they also incur the downside of soliciting more time for users to adapt and efficiently handle them.

Learning Journey

Efficiency and added value to student training in the case of crisis simulation are derived by its being not a single-event activity but rather the final event of a learning chain that starts at the beginning of the semester. In this logic, crisis simulation exercises become memorable activities (Diers-Lawson, 2021; Klabbers, 2018) along a learning journey wherein the teacher enables the acquisition of knowledge and creates occasions for the development of crisis communication skills. It is, therefore, important to bear in mind that a sequence of class meetings where progressively higher levels of effort and difficulties are required to meet learning objectives, as opposed to a one-time event.

When examining crisis simulation as a learning journey, several factors come into play, alongside outcomes and experiences (Gibson, 2017; Northcote et al., 2015). In this process, students advance through moments of decision-making, feedback loops, and thoughtful analysis of crisis response (see Sadowska & Laffy, 2017). Therefore, the acquisition of skills (Coombs, 2001; Neill & Schauster, 2015; Sellnow & Sellnow, 2010) in addition to the learning environment (Borodzicz & Van Haperen, 2002; Diers-Lawson, 2021; Moyer-Gusé, 2008) are to be considered together with the way in which students' expectations are acknowledged and met. In support of this approach, drawing on the extant literature, we put together a list of questions that may be helpful for designing crisis simulations in social media (see Figure 6.1).

Instructional Design and Crisis Content Creation

Unlike crisis simulations based on events unfolding in traditional media, crisis simulations in social media need a different instructional strategy since they must replicate the social media crisis' volatility and multiple dimensions. If, in the case of traditional media, crisis response is based on a series of theories and guidelines, in social media, due to a wider range of stakeholders envisaged and multiple platforms involved, the situation requires a different approach. Consequently, designing a crisis simulation in social media should start with the diverse threats organizations face in online environments and social media platforms. Based on the problems that are likely to happen, a scenario is built, and dedicated content and crisis simulation-related materials are produced. For the scenario to be credible and resemble a real crisis in social media, it should present events unfolding similarly on Facebook, Twitter, TikTok, or any other platform. It should mention all data that any organization may have from the early beginning of the crisis (e.g., posts, shares, comments, tweets, reactions, audiences, attitudes, and sentiments) and gradually introduce emerging events and new audiences stepping in. To reach the expected student engagement, all materials should use the same visual elements and content as on the social media platform. The scenario also has to consider that social media platforms' algorithms favor negative posts and reactions and will likely boost the buzz and outrage; therefore, regardless of the good approach in crisis communication, negative conversations will continue to grow and tackle the organization. Depending on the events unfolding and the crisis-related topics, the crisis simulation may consider expanding the situation from one channel to another and moving the conversations and attacks to new layers.

MULTIPLE-STAGE APPROACH

As mentioned, developing a crisis simulation is a process that needs preparation and several dedicated activities. Achieving the learning objectives and creating

QUESTIONS TO CONSIDER FOR DESIGN EVALUATION

CATEGORY	QUESTIONS	REFERENCES
The learning environment	• Do we use adequate pedagogical and training methods to make students feel comfortable when expressing/defending their viewpoints? • Are students encouraged often enough to engage in debates? • Do students have enough occasions to cooperate during classes? • Are students forming effective teams? • Are storytelling techniques properly used in terms of frequency and content? • Is class communication both entertaining and rigorous?	• Borodzicz & Van Haperen, 2002 • Diers-Lawson, 2021 • Moyer-Gusé, 2008 • Loh & Ang, 2020 • Ashby-King et al., 2021 • Frasen, 2011 • Evans et al., 2010
Knowledge acquisition	• Are there enough instances for students to internalize theories, principles and methods? • Are we discussing best practices and inadequate approaches in crisis response? • Are theories and models used to discuss and explain crises in different contexts? • Do we enable the anticipation of worse-case scenarios? • Is there a time set apart for feedback and case debriefing?	• Coombs, 2001 • Veil, 2010 • Ashby-King et. al., 2021 • Mazer, 2013 • Denker et al., 2022; • Sellnow & Sellnow, 2010 • Borodzicz & Van Haperen, 2002 • Frisby et al., 2013
Developing skills	• Do students demonstrate various abilities to identify threats, diagnose crisis and manage different situations? • Do students demonstrate the ability to construct an appropriate crisis response? • Do students manage to navigate through different stakeholders' expectations? • Do students experience diverse roles in crisis management and communication? Are they able to make sense of contextual data?	• Anderson et al., 2013 • Diers-Lawson, 2021 • Fransen, 2011 • Loh & Ang, 2020 • Coombs, 2011 • Pyle, 2017 • Neill & Schauster, 2015

Figure 6.1 List of questions to consider for design evaluaticn.

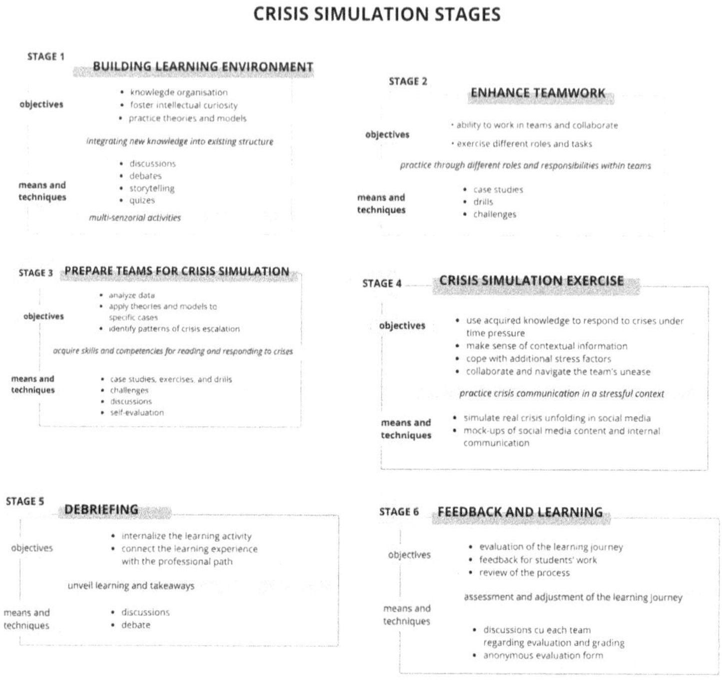

Figure 6.2 Crisis simulation stages.

memorable and valuable learning experiences need time, resources, and consistency. The instructional strategy referred to in this current paper consists of six stages for designing, planning, implementing, and evaluating the crisis simulation, which are summarized in Figure 6.2.

STAGE 1 – BUILD A LEARNING ENVIRONMENT ON THEORY-BASED COMMUNICATION PRACTICE

From the beginning, all activities must be designed to build a learning environment on theory-based communication practice. Different means and techniques must be used to facilitate knowledge acquisition and a solid understanding of concepts, models, theories, and practices in crisis communication. Class activities should enable critical thinking, stimulate intellectual curiosity, and constantly highlight relevance.

STAGE 2 – ENHANCE TEAMWORK TO PUT THEORY INTO PRACTICE

In this stage, teamwork and cooperation must be facilitated. Students enroll in a team to gain new skills and practice different roles and tasks. Teams analyze and discuss crises, best crisis responses, and organizational mistakes. Working in teams enables students to listen, negotiate ideas, and navigate tensions and disagreements. Exercising different roles, in turn, helps students gain perspective and adjust their expectations to a real-life work environment, attuned to practices common to most public relations departments and/or agencies.

STAGE 3 – PREPARE TEAMS FOR CRISIS SIMULATION BY USING REAL-LIFE SITUATIONS AND DRILLS

In direct connection with stage 2, in stage 3 teams are trained for the crisis simulation exercise by practicing real-life crises and drills. By looking into real crises and examining the anatomy of the events and the crisis communication techniques and strategies, students will be able to understand situations and consequences better and use contextual data. On the other hand, drills give students learning opportunities to imagine scenarios and probabilities, not affected by their attachment to organizations and brands. In this stage, at least one trial activity of the crisis simulation is to be organized. Mock-up social media accounts, websites, social media metrics charts, and other materials are created.

STAGE 4 – CRISIS SIMULATION EXERCISE

In this stage, the crisis simulation is organized. Students are graded based on their capacity to analyze, make use of data and contextual information, examine crisis-related conversations and sentiments, foresee crisis escalation, and determine the most appropriate crisis response. The exercise is basically the result of previous building-up activities, with additional stress factors, such as time limits for each of the two parts it contains.

STAGE 5 – DEBRIEFING

At the end of the crisis simulation, a debriefing must be conducted. This stage is important for both the learning outcomes and value for the student's future career in communication. Debriefing is key for internalizing the activity and its connection to professional development and integrating the decision-making process in crises.

STAGE 6 – FEEDBACK, FOLLOW UP & LEARNING

Feedback includes teachers' feedback for students on the quality of their work, team dynamic, and role assuming. It also has students' feedback on the activity, and the entire learning journey, with specific questions asked to gain insights related to student expectations and perceptions.

Conclusions

The educational project we designed for crisis simulation in social media aligns with our academic programs' efforts to become relevant for the labor market and to prove their effectiveness. From the early beginning, we sought to create crisis communication academic training in response to the labor market expectations. Grounded in the idea that academic programs should enhance learning and bridge theory and practice (Coombs, 2001), we designed a crisis simulation project based on an interactive learning environment where students acquire knowledge and develop skills (Diers-Lawson, 2021) key to identifying threats and issues, analyze, manage, and respond to crises in social media.

Since it was set up in 2017, the educational project has been subject to changes and upgrades to meet the need for critical interpretation of social media analytics in relation to the shifting landscape of social media platforms and their impact on risk and crisis communication. Designed as a multiple-stage approach, our project envisages a learning journey that enables students to develop relevant skills for crisis communication in social media. It does so by constructing an adequate learning environment grounded on theory-based communication practice, enhancing teamwork, exercising through real-life simulations and drills, facilitating decision-making, making sense of contextual data in social media, identifying threats and managing crisis response in stressful situations. In its final stages, the educational project for crisis simulation in social media uses students' reflections on the learning journey and self-evaluation of their performance. Throughout debriefing, feedback and follow-up, teachers acquire insights related to design, means and tools, content development and scenario building as well as class instruction and communication.

While we are aware that crisis communication and events unfolding in social media may vary by country-specific contexts and are influenced by a series of factors, there are still transferable lessons that could be applied more broadly. Among these lessons, three may prove useful. First, crisis simulation should be part of a multiple-stage educational project, with a series of gradual difficulty class meetings and exercises to acquire knowledge and develop skills for events and crises unfolding in social media. Second, teamwork and peer learning have proved to be very helpful in bridging theory with practice and in coping with stressful events. Third, meeting learning objectives and developing an effective crisis simulation rely on resources for instructional design and content creation as well as tools and platforms for simulations. In many instances, having access to these resources may prove challenging for academia, as cost and logistics are significant barriers.

However, we anticipate an increase in collaboration between universities, agencies, and different tools and platform developers for designing and developing interactive learning formats and materials in realistic settings (Manias-Muñoz et al., 2019) for crises in social media.

References

Adi, A., & Scotte, C. G. (2016). Barriers to emerging technology and social media integration in higher education: Three case studies. In *Professional development and workplace learning: Concepts, methodologies, tools, and applications* (pp. 1161–1182). IGI Global. https://doi.org/10.4018/978-1-4666-2970-7.ch017

Aertsen, T., Jaspaert, K., & Van Gorp, B. (2013). From theory to practice: A crisis simulation exercise. *Business Communication Quarterly, 76*, 322–338. https://doi.org/10.1177/1080569913482575

Allen, R., & Rooney, P. (1998). Designing a problem-based learning environment for ESL students in business communication. *Business Communication Quarterly, 61*(2), 48–56. https://doi.org/10.1177/108056999806100020

AMEC. (2023). *Measurement Month*, https://amecorg.com/measurement-month/

Anderson, B., Swenson, R., & Kinsella, J. (2014). Responding in real time: Creating a social media crisis simulator for the classroom. *Communication Teacher, 28*(2), 85–95. https://doi.org/10.1080/17404622.2013.865766

Ashby-King, D. T., Mazzone, R., & Anderson, L. B. (2021). Defining feedback: Understanding students' perceptions of feedback in the introductory communication course. *Journal of Communication Pedagogy, 4*, 70–84.

Barfield, W., Zeltzer, D., & Slater, M. (1995). Presence and performance within virtual environments. In W. Barfield & T. A. Furness (Eds.), *Virtual environments and advanced interface design* (pp. 473–541). Oxford University Press.

Boin, A., Kofman-Bos, C., & Overdijk, W. (2004). Crisis simulations: Exploring tomorrow's vulnerabilities and threats. *Simulation & Gaming, 35*(3), 378–393. https://doi.org/10.1177/1046878104266220

Boin, A., & Lagadec, P. (2000). Preparing for the future: Critical challenges in crisis management. *Journal of Contingencies and Crisis Management, 8*(4), 185–191. https://doi.org/10.1111/1468–5973.00138

Borodzicz, E., & Van Haperen, K. (2002). Individual and group learning in crisis simulations. *Journal of Contingencies and Crisis Management, 10*(3), 139–147. https://doi.org/10.1111/1468–5973.00190

Buzoianu, C., Bira, M., & Duduciuc, A. (2019). Building a discipline. The setup of communication as an academic discipline in Romania. *Studies and Scientific Researches. Economics Edition*, (30). https://doi.org/10.29358/sceco.v0i30.445

Casmir, F. L. (2012), *Building communication theories: A socio/cultural approach.* Routledge.

Chung, S. (2016). Simulations for crisis communication: The use of social media. In *Proceedings of the International Conferences on Internet Technologies & Society (ITS), Education Technologies (ICEduTECH), and Sustainability, Technology and Education (STE)* 2016, Melbourne, Australia, December 6–8. 272–276. Research Collection Lee Kong Chian School of Business. https://ink.library.smu.edu.sg/lkcsb_research/6946

Coombs, W. T. (2001). Teaching the crisis management/communication course. *Public Relations Review, 27*(1), 89–101.

Cowley, S., Humphrey, Jr., W., & Muñoz, C. (2021). Industry certifications in digital marketing and media education: An examination of perceptions and use among educators. *Journal of Marketing Education, 43*(2), 189–203. https://doi.org/10.1177/0273475320948570

Craig, R. T. (1999). Communication theory as a field. *Public Relations Review*, *9*, 119–161.

Craig, R. T. (2013). Constructing theories in communication research. In P. Cobley & P. J. Schulz (Eds.), *Theories and models of communication* (39–57). De Gruyter.

Delaney, A. L., & Meister, S. (2021). Crisis simulation scenarios: Applying crisis communication lessons to an app mishap, a public health misstep, and a college athletics calamity. *Communication Teacher*, *35*(4), 313–319. https://doi.org/10.1080/17404622.2020.1869280

Denker, K. J., Knight, K., Carroll, R. K., Bradley, K. R., Bonine, P. J., Lauck, S. M., ... & Storr, M. L. (2022). Assessing student mindset, interest, participation, and rapport in the post-pandemic public speaking classroom: Effects of modality change and communication growth mindset. *Journal of Communication Pedagogy*, *6*(1), 14.

Diers-Lawson, A. (2019). *Crisis communication: Managing stakeholder relationships*. Routledge.

Diers-Lawson, A. (2020). Applying the stakeholder relationship model as an issue management and risk communication tool. In B. S. Peksevgen (Ed.), *Themes in issues, risk and crisis communication: A multi-dimensional perspective*. Peter Lang Publishers. https://doi.org/10.3726/b17931

Diers-Lawson, A. (2021). Eureka: Identifying what it means to practice student-centered teaching in a hypermodern age. *Journal of Communication Pedagogy*, *4*, 110–120. https://doi.org/10.31446/JCP.2018.02

Evans, C., Cools, E., & Charlesworth, Z. M. (2010). Learning in higher education–How cognitive and learning styles matter. *Teaching in Higher Education*, *15*(4), 467–478.

Ewing, M. E., Kim, C. M., Kinsky, E. S., Moore, S., & Freberg, K. (2018). Teaching digital and social media analytics: Exploring best practices and future implications for public relations pedagogy. *Journal of Public Relations Education*, *4*(2), 51–86.

Fransen, J., Kirschner, P. A., & Erkens, G. (2011). Mediating team effectiveness in the context of collaborative learning: The importance of team and task awareness. *Computers in Human Behavior*, *27*(3), 1103–1113.

Frisby, B. N., Sellnow, D. D., Lane, D. R., Veil, S. R., & Sellnow, T. L. (2013). Instruction in crisis situations: Targeting learning preferences and self-efficacy. *Risk Management*, *15*, 250–271. https://doi.org/10.1057/rm.2013.7

Gibson, D. (2017). Big data in higher education: Research methods and analytics supporting the learning journey. *Technology, Knowledge and Learning*, *22*, 237–241.

Ivan, L., Daba-Buzoianu, C., & Gray, B. (Eds.) (2014). *Mapping Heterogeneity: Qualitative research in communication*. Tritonic.

Jirak, J., & Kopplova, B. (2008). Communication as an academic field: Eastern Europe and Russia. *The International Encyclopedia of Communication*. Wiley Online Library https://doi.org/10.1002/9781405186407.wbiecc060

Jonassen, D. H. (2010). *Learning to Solve Problems: A Handbook for Designing Problem-Solving Learning Environments*. Routledge. https://doi.org/10.4324/9780203847527

Kim, C., & Freberg, K. (2017). The state of social media curriculum: exploring professional expectations of pedagogy and practices to equip the next generation of professionals. *Journal of Public Relations Education*, *2*(2). 62–82.

King, M. D. (2015). Why higher ed and business need to work together. *Harvard Business Review*. https://hbr.org/2015/07/why-higher-ed-and-business-need-to-work-together

Kinsky, E. S., Freberg, K., Kim, C., Kushin, M., & Ward, W. (2016). Hootsuite university: Equipping academics and future PR professionals for social media success. *Journal of Public Relations Education, 2*(1), 1–18.
Klabbers, J. H. (2018). On the architecture of game science. *Simulation & Gaming, 49*(3), 207–245. https://doi.org/10.1177/1046878118762534
Klyukanov, I. (2011). Russian journal of communication: A new journal on the block. *Review of Communication, 11*(3), 229–237. https://doi.org/10.1080/15358593.2011.578256
Krishna, A., Wright, D. K., & Kotcher, R. L. (2020). Curriculum rebuilding in public relations: Understanding what early career, mid-career, and senior PR/communications professionals expect from PR graduates. *Journal of Public Relations Education, 6*(1), 33–57.
Laverie, D., Humphrey, W., Manis, K. T., & Freberg, K. (2020). The digital era has changed marketing: A guide to using industry certifications and exploration of student perceptions of effectiveness. *Marketing Education Review, 30*(1), 57–80. https://doi.org/10.1080/10528008.2020.1716806
Loh, R. C. Y., & Ang, C. S. (2020). Unravelling cooperative learning in higher education: A review of research. *Research in Social Sciences and Technology, 5*(2), 22–39.
Macnamara, J., Lwin, M., Adi, A., & Zerfass, A. (2015). *Asia-Pacific Communication Monitor 2015/16. The state of strategic communication and public relations in a region of rapid growth. Survey results from 23 countries*. APACD: Hong Kong. http://www.communicationmonitor.asia/media/APCM-2015-16-Report.pdf
Macnamara, J., & Zerfass, A. (2017). Evaluation stasis continues in PR and corporate communication: Asia-Pacific insights into causes. *Communication Research and Practice, 3*(4), 319–334. https://doi.org/10.1080/22041451.2017.1275258
Manias-Muñoz, I., Jin, Y., & Reber, B. H. (2019). The state of crisis communication research and education through the lens of crisis scholars: An international Delphi study. *Public Relations Review, 45*(4), 101797.
Mazer, J. P. (2013). Student emotional and cognitive interest as mediators of teacher communication behaviors and student engagement: An examination of direct and interaction effect. *Communication Education, 62*(1), 253–277. https://doi.org/10.1080/03634523.2013.777752
Miño, P., & Gibson, R. (2020). Intercultural competencies needed for evolving media professions: Educating the next generation of globally minded communicators. *Journalism & Mass Communication Educator, 75*(3), 259–274. https://doi.org/10.1177/107769581989386
Moizer, J., Lean, J., Towler, M., & Abbey, C. (2009). Simulations and games: Overcoming the barriers to their use in higher education. *Active Learning in Higher Education, 10*, 207–224. https://doi.org/10.1177/1469787409343188
Morgan, A., & Wilk, V. (2021). Social media users' crisis response: A lexical exploration of social media content in an international sport crisis. *Public Relations Review, 47*(4), 102057. https://doi.org/10.1016/j.pubrev.2021.102057
Moyer-Gusé, E. (2008). Toward a theory of entertainment persuasion: Explaining the persuasive effects of entertainment-education messages. *Communication Theory, 18*(3), 407–425.
Neill, M. S., & Schauster, E. (2015). Gaps in advertising and public relations education: Perspectives of agency leaders. *Journal of Advertising Education, 19*(2), 5–17.

Northcote, M., Gosselin, K. P., Reynaud, D., Kilgour, P., & Anderson, M. (2015). Navigating learning journeys of online teachers: Threshold concepts and self-efficacy. *Issues in Educational Research*, *25*(3), 319–344.

Peruško, Z., & Vozab, D. (2015). The field of communication in croatia. In P. Simonson & D. W. Park (Eds.), *The international history of communication study* (pp. 213–235). Routledge.

Pyle, A. S. (2017). Teaching PEACE: A plan for effective crisis communication instruction. *Communication Teacher*, *32*(4), 209–214.

Riforgiate, S. E., Gattoni, A., & Kirby, E. L. (2019). Organizing the organizational communication course: Content and pedagogical recommendations. *Journal of Communication Pedagogy*, *2*, 7–11.

Sadowska, N., & Laffy, D. (2017). The design brief: inquiry into the starting point in a learning journey. *The Design Journal*, *20*(sup1), S1380–S1389.

Sellnow, T. L., & Sellnow, D. D. (2010). The instructional dynamic of risk and crisis communication: Distinguishing instructional messages from dialogue. *Review of Communication*, *10*(2): 112.

Schwarz, A., Seeger, M. W., & Auer, C. (Eds.). (2016). *The handbook of international crisis communication research*. John Wiley & Sons.

Sprout Social Index – UK and Ireland. (2021). *Sprout social*. https://sproutsocial.com/insights/data/uk-ireland-index-2021/

State of Nordic PR & Communication. (2022). *MyNewsDesk*. https://library.mynewsdesk.com/state-of-pr

Staton, M. G. (2016). Improving student job placement and assessment through the use of digital marketing certification programs. *Marketing Education Review*, *26*(1), 20–24. https://doi.org/10.1080/10528008.2015.1091665

Taylor, B. C., & Lindlof, T. R. (2013). Traveling methods: Tracing the globalization of qualitative communication research. *Romanian Journal of Communication and Public Relations*, *15*(3), 11–30. https://doi.org/10.21018/rjcpr.2013.3.192

't Hart, P. (1997). Preparing policy makers for crisis management: The role of simulations. *Journal of Contingencies and Crisis Management*, *5*(4), 207–215. https://doi.org/10.1111/1468–5973.00058

Utz, S., Schultz, F., & Glocka, S. (2013). Crisis communication online: How medium, crisis type and emotions affected public reactions in the Fukushima Daiichi nuclear disaster. *Public Relations Review*, *39*(1), 40–46. https://doi.org/10.1016/j.pubrev.2012.09.010

Veil, S. R. (2010). Using crisis simulations in public relations education. *Communication Teacher*, *24*(2), 58–62. https://doi.org/10.1080/17404621003680906

Wang, M. (2017). Using crisis simulation to enhance crisis management competencies: The role of presence. *Journal of Public Relations Education*, *3*(2), 96–109.

Weber Shandwick. (2010). Weber Shandwick launches social media crisis simulator, FireBell. *PRNewswire*. http://www.prnewswire.com/news-releases/webershandwick-launches-social-crisis-simulator-firebell-108940364.html

Zerfass, A., Buhmann, A., Tench, R., Verčič, D., & Moreno, A. (2021). *European Communication Monitor 2021. CommTech and digital infrastructure, video-conferencing, and future roles for communication professionals. Results of a survey in 46 countries.*

Brussels: EUPRERA/EACD. https://www.communicationmonitor.eu/2021/05/21/ecm-european-communication-monitor-2021/

Zerfass, A., Moreno, A., Tench, R., Verčič, D., & Buhmann, A. (2022). *European Communication Monitor 2022. Exploring diversity and empathic leadership, CommTech and consulting in communications. Results of a survey in 43 countries.* Brussels: EUPRERA/EACD. https://www.communicationmonitor.eu/2022/07/07/ecm-european-communication-monitor-2022/

7 Coordination in Multi-crises

The German Aviation Industry

Carolin Köppel and Janina Klingelhöfer

The COVID-19 pandemic, as one example, has raised awareness of crises that affect several organizations simultaneously. Especially industries with a high degree of interconnectedness between organizations such as the aviation industry experience so-called multi-crises (Biesiadecka, 2009). Crashes in particular cause crises that have the "tendency to resonate throughout the industry, affecting not only victims and the airline in crisis, but other stakeholders as well" (Ray, 1999, p. 9).

A multi-crisis evokes challenges that can only be overcome by joint action from all impacted parties (Ansell et al., 2010; Frandsen & Johansen, 2017, 2018). Due to their complexity, the scope of their consequences and their frequency in an increasingly networked economy, multi-crises attract "a growing interest in studying the interorganizational dimension of crises, focusing on negative spillovers from the corporate level to the industry level" (Frandsen & Johansen, 2018, p. 92). Organizations, however, "are porous letting internal communication leak out, and external communication leak in" (Frandsen & Johansen, 2011, p. 356). This means both the intra- and inter-organizational levels are equally constitutive for organizational survival (Frandsen & Johansen, 2011, 2017, 2018; Jaffee, 2001). Nonetheless, the importance of the internal or intra-organizational level in crisis communication is rather slowly integrated in crisis communication research (Frandsen & Johansen, 2011, 2017, 2018; Heide and Simonsson, 2015; Johansen et al., 2012; Ravazzani, 2016).

The main objective of this study is to explore who coordinates with whom in times of crisis in the civil aviation industry. We thereby focus on crises that affect not only one airport or airline but multiple simultaneously.

Dimensions of Organizational Crises

An organizational crisis is "an event perceived by managers and stakeholders as highly salient, unexpected, and potentially disruptive" and "can threaten an organization's goals" (Bundy et al., 2017, p. 1662). The effects of a multi-crisis go beyond one organization, hitting on at least two organizations and their

DOI: 10.4324/9781003375296-9

stakeholders (Frandsen & Johansen, 2017). Frandsen and Johansen (2017) differentiate between two types. Horizontal multi-crises affect organizations located at the same level of operation (e.g: spillover crises). Vertical multi-crises have an impact on organizations located at different levels (e.g., supply chain crises).

Airports and airlines do not operate on the same level, but their operations are highly interdependent. A crisis that disturbs one airport or airline is very likely to cause trouble for others as well. Such crises can be considered multi-crises simultaneously occurring horizontally and vertically. They can be the result from a variety of causes such as labor strikes, security issues, airplane crashes or natural disasters. The volcanic eruption in 2010 with devastating consequences for civil air traffic can be used as an example for the latter (Alexander, 2013).

From Single-Crisis to Multi-Crisis

To thoroughly manage stakeholder relations in crises, organizations must fully understand the interests and expectations of their internal and external stakeholders (Jin et al., 2012). Ahrne and Brunsson (2005) even state that the "very existence of organizations is dependent on the tolerance and support of their particular environment, and much of what organizations do can be explained by aspects of this environment" (p. 431). While this is true under normal circumstances, it becomes particularly important in times of crisis.

Most studies in crisis communication take a single organization-centered perspective, although there is a complex social space opening in a crisis with "many senders and receivers [...] communicating about, to, with, past or against each other" (Frandsen & Johansen, 2018, p. 94). Instead of taking a single perspective, the Rhetorical Arena Theory (RAT) assumes that many voices "struggle with each other on how to interpret not only the crisis itself but also how to handle it" (Frandsen & Johansen, 2018, p. 94). RAT therefore enables a deeper analysis of different perspectives making it a suitable approach for research on multi-crises. By assigning the most relevant stakeholder voices to the intra-organizational respectively inter-organizational level, this study deepens the theoretical assumptions of RAT and allows an integrative analysis of multi-crises.

Crisis Management Team

A crisis management team (CMT) is responsible for important decisions "such as when to activate the crisis preparedness and how to coordinate the response activities" (Frandsen & Johansen, 2017, p. 77). Often, "the CMT is a cross-functional group consisting mainly of middle managers representing the key functions of the organization: corporate communication, security, finance, production, marketing, and human resource management" (Frandsen & Johansen, 2017, p. 77). With their deep knowledge of the organization and expertise in relevant fields, the members of CMTs create and enact the crisis management plan, and handle any difficulties related to crisis prevention and management (Coombs, 2019).

Multi-crises evoke the necessity of CMTs of different organizations to coordinate their attempts (Ansell et al., 2010). Seeger et al. (2003) emphasize that CMTs which match both the characteristics of the respective organizations and the specifics of a particular crisis can perform best. CMTs are "designed to function under stress and uncertainty" (Seeger et al., 2003, p. 186). Multi-crises further require special treatment in terms of aligning strategies and resources between the CMTs of multiple organizations. As there are different coping strategies and measures, the crisis management teams of the different organizations facing the same crisis must coordinate in order not to act counterproductively (Benoit, 1997, 2015; Coombs, 1995, 2006, 2007; Coombs & Holladay, 2002). To avoid contrary actions, some sort of coordination is necessary to fulfill the different roles and responsibilities when facing a multi-crisis (Boin & Bynander, 2015; Christensen et al., 2016; Ödlund, 2010).

Coordination can be viewed from two perspectives: while the top-down perspective describes coordination as achieved by hierarchical means and command, the bottom-up perspective understands coordination to be achieved by network arrangements without central guidance (Boin & Bynander, 2015; Christensen et al., 2016; Ödlund, 2010). Although it is a deep-rooted, widespread presumption that coordination lacking some form of guidance cannot be the most efficient way to solve interdependent tasks, coordination in crises that affect more than one organization often does not follow hierarchical processes or routine plans (Ansell et al., 2010). The relations on the inter-organizational level "can range from dyadic, involving just two organizations, to multiplicitous, involving huge networks of many organizations" (Cropper et al., 2010, p. 4).

Employee Empowerment in Crisis Communication

Ahrne and Brunsson (2005) emphasize that "members are necessary if organizations are to exist and to act at all, and members determine to some extent what organizations do" (p. 431) and thereby highlight the importance of the intra-organizational level. According to Lee (2019), "it can be assumed that employees' communicative actions will either enhance or damage an organization's reputation through diverse channels during a crisis" (p. 3). Words of employees "may have significant influences on how these external publics' view and evaluate an organizational crisis" (p. 2). Based on these assumptions, this study agrees with Coombs and Holladay (2014) stating that all "that communicate during crises should be considered crisis communicators as well" (p. 51).

Even though employees' behaviors are especially important during crises, "little research has provided a comprehensive approach to understand what organizational efforts affect employees' communicative behaviors in a crisis situation" (Mazzei et al., 2019, p. 196).

Mazzei et al. (2019) found out that employees "who evaluate their company as authentic in their actions and who feel empowered in the workplace are more likely to forward and share positive information with other people [...] when a company is undergoing a crisis" (p. 205). Kim and Rhee (2011) argue that employees can be regarded "as one of the most important strategic constituencies because they interact with external publics on a daily basis" (p. 243). They further state that "it is desirable and feasible for individual organization members to enact their environmental scanning roles and become agents for intraorganizational information circulation" (p. 247). With the term *microboundary spanning*, Kim and Rhee (2011) refer "to nonnominated (nondesignated) employees' voluntary communication behaviors to (a) disperse positive information for one's organization, (b) search and obtain valuable organization-related information from internal and external constituencies, and (c) disseminate acquired information internally with relevant internal personnel and groups" (p. 249). Similarly, Frandsen and Johansen (2017) differentiate between designated "formal ambassadors" and "informal ambassadors." While the former are strategically employed and coordinated with a top-down approach by the corporate communications team of an organization, the latter support the organization in building and maintaining strong relationships with other relevant stakeholders on their own initiative.

On the intra-organizational level, CMTs can make use of internal resources and competencies of employees from different departments (Maurer, 2017). On the inter-organizational level, aviation requires to coordinate with public authorities due to the industry's high degree of regulation (BDF, 2018). As public authorities can be viewed as the executive, the legislative being politics and their representatives also require consideration. The liberalization of civil air traffic in the European Union in 1992 has attracted many players to found airports and airlines (European Commission, 2017). With strong competition there is also a tendency to join forces through strategic alliances (Iatrou and Oretti, 2016; Oum et al., 2000). That is why both competitors and partners can also be counted in on the inter-organizational level.

As air traffic requires a multitude of services such as baggage handling or offering leisure opportunities until boarding, it makes sense to include all types of service providers as they are critical to the successful operation (Appold & Kasarda, 2013; Stevens, 2006). Furthermore, the media, likely to reporting on events of public interest and therefore interested in all matters related to civil air traffic, can also be assigned to the inter-organizational level (Bachmann, 2017).

With this theoretical knowledge in mind, this study examines with whom and how airports and airlines coordinate their communication in multi-crises on both the (1) intra- and (2) inter-organizational level. Based on the key findings, the study argues for an integrative approach in multi-crises as communication permeates through both levels.

Study Design

The study took a qualitative approach to acknowledge the sensitivity of information in crises. In-depth interviews with communication experts working in the civil aviation industry were found suitable as exclusive knowledge needed to be retrieved, and qualitative interviews are better able to capture individual attitudes, experiences, and opinions than quantitative surveys (Brosius et al., 2022; Meyen et al., 2019). Eight of the fifteen interviewees work for Germany's largest and most important airports and seven for the respective airlines. In daily business, all interviewees have direct reporting lines to the CEO of their organization. During crises they may additionally report to the leader of their organization's crisis management team. Except for one personal interview, the interviews were conducted by telephone from April to September 2018. Once a certain degree of insight had been gathered through the interviews and the study reached the criteria of theoretical saturation, there were no further interviews conducted (Glaser & Strauss, 1970).

The interview questions were divided into three main sections: Asking the interviewees about their (1) *personal background* helped to develop a better understanding of the interviewees' convictions and professional experiences. With the answers to the icebreaking questions the replies to the subsequent questions about crisis communication could be contextualized (Hoffmann, 2017; Kaiser, 2014). To better understand who coordinates with whom in multi-crises within air traffic, the study then addressed the (2) *specific structures and processes of organizational communication within airports and airlines.* The interviewees had to outline the number of personnel working for their communication department, the reporting lines and different functional roles and responsibilities. The answers of this section were used to identify potential changes when the industry faces a multi-crisis. Focusing on (3) *organizational communication within air traffic in multi-crises*, the interviewees were asked to explain which incidents they consider to be crises and what characterizes crises within air traffic. Depending on the crisis scenarios that the interviewees mentioned, they had to elaborate on which internal and external stakeholders they would ask for support, in which way they could support their CMT and what specifics they had to consider when coordinating their crisis communication with these stakeholders. The interviewees had to describe how they believe such crises can be communicatively handled best and what challenges they are facing in crisis communication.

Results

The key insights from the expert interviews are now presented along both the intra- and inter-organizational levels. Later, the key findings are summarized with a focus on their interconnectedness, suggesting integrating them for further consideration.

Coordinating Crisis Communication in Air Traffic on the Intra-organizational Level

Airlines and airports are organized into aviation services and non-aviation services (Biesiadecka, 2009). In times of crisis, representatives of both are permanent members of their organizations' CMTs. This includes, for example, air traffic control, terminal management and passenger control on the aviation services' side; corporate communication, legal and IT on the non-aviation services' side.

According to the interviewees, the CMT is the central point from which all operative and communicative efforts of the respective organization are coordinated. As previous research highlighted, the individual scenario decides who needs to coordinate with whom within and beyond their own CMT (e.g., Seeger et al., 2003). That is why the CMTs need to have a modifiable structure to be able to manage various multi-crises: "In principle, the team includes a representative of all relevant departments involved with flight operations – but it depends on the matter at hand who needs to coordinate with whom to best handle the situation."

In contrast to Seeger et al. (2003), the interviewees do not consider the Chief Executive Officers (CEOs) of the affected organizations to be leading the CMTs. While CEOs lead in daily business, the usual procedures of top-down coordination are replaced by leading functions of the CMT. However, the interviewees stress the CEOs' function to communicate with shareholders or politics or be the main spokespersons aside from their Chief Communication Officers (CCOs). These findings go in line with previous research (Coombs, 2019). In this context, one airline representative differentiates between a *gold team* dealing with strategic questions with high coordination effort, and a *silver team* coordinating the crisis locally. As the local plus superior handling of a crisis cost valuable time, for almost all interviewees the management of a crisis by a CMT on site is ranked first. One participant noted: "This is a question of efficiency, of speed, and to avoid major coordination rounds."

Furthermore, the interviewees acknowledge a rising potential from employee empowerment in crisis communication. They thereby include non-communication experts acting as formal and informal ambassadors, as Frandsen and Johansen (2017) differentiate, to ensure that all stakeholders' information and communication needs are met sufficiently: "In general, even though it is often overlooked, employees can often be the strongest weapon in controversial topics." This finding fits well with previous research suggesting that internal communication and employee empowerment are gaining importance in crises (Frandsen & Johansen, 2017; Mazzei et al., 2019).

As formal ambassadors in multi-crises, special assistant teams (SATs) complement immediate crisis responders and are coordinated with a top-down approach:

> I am thinking especially of the Special Assistance Team. They take care of passengers or, in the worst case, the surviving relative. Not in a psychological way, but to be there for them and provide them the most basic needs.

This participant's example illustrates how much responsibility some employees must take on in times of crisis when quick reaction is needed.

The influence of informal ambassadors seems particularly strong in crisis communication on social media. When heated discussions occur online, CCOs of airports and airlines often lack the personnel to handle the enormous flood of information, which is why they seek support from other departments. With the help of corporate ambassadors who argue for the organization and try to mediate and moderate the discussion, the organization can prevent further damage. The interviewees emphasize that employees with no professional communication background may appear more genuine and trustworthy as they use alternative verbiage when supporting the key messages.

Previous studies also indicate the positive effects on organizational reputation of non-professional employee communication (Lee, 2019; van Zoonen & van der Meer, 2015). Lee (2019) argues that the public not only relies on official corporate communication. It is also interested in what employees say as a cue for evaluating organizations facing a multi-crisis.

In contrast to formal ambassadors, informal ambassadors are coordinated with a bottom-up approach, which underlines the argument that in crises hierarchical structures must be broken up (Ansell et al., 2010). While acknowledging the importance and potential of employee empowerment, all interviewees admit that it is practically still underperformed in the aviation industry.

To summarize: Coordination on the intra-organizational level can build a solid basis for effective crisis communication beyond organizational boundaries. Airports and airlines highly depend on agile CMTs supported by highly qualified SATs as well as by formal and informal ambassadors. For employee empowerment, bottom-up coordination becomes more and more important when facing multi-crises. When working with agile CMTs without the CEO as their lead, airports and airlines break through rigid organizational structures and processes with the hierarchies of daily business.

Coordinating Crisis Communication in Air Traffic on the (2) Inter-organizational Level

Participants noted that coordinating crisis communication on the inter-organizational level between airports and airlines as well as affiliated organizations is heavily challenged by the common practice of outsourcing certain services in the aviation industry. For example,

> in a strongly regulated industry such as ours, even in the simplest things, many process partners are involved. The federal police are responsible for the security checks, for example, however, they outsource these services to service providers. Now, you already have three process partners: airport, federal police and Securitas, the service provider.

In general, all coordination efforts in crisis communication strongly depend on the specific crisis case on the one hand, and the preparedness of all affected organizations on the other hand. The interviewees mention that most of their affiliated organizations have their own CMTs or at least previously defined emergency contacts. However, some have none of the above, even though it is essential in multi-crises to know who to contact and how to reach these contacts: "We initially give new employees the task of calling all emergency contacts and updating them." Considering crises usually go through a pre-crisis phase, crisis phase and post-crisis phase, organizations could gain an overview of who to coordinate with under normal circumstances.

A further aspect highlighted by the interviewees is coordination demanding mutual benefit and a deep understanding for the associated partners' information and communication needs. Creating a coordination culture is therefore of utmost importance. This is particularly important considering diverse corporate and leadership cultures, communication habits, language barriers as well as conflicting interests. According to our participants, these difficulties can only be overcome by joint training and meetings as well as ongoing communication. The interviewed airports even create centralized operation centers where the CMTs of different organizations can meet physically or virtually to discuss the best way to handle crisis situations. Such operation centers, however, are still to be established at most airports.

According to Pinsdorf (1991), the aviation industry is characterized by its international environment and 24/7 operations. To master these industry specific challenges impacting multi-crises, the interviewees act according to the principle *think global, act local*: "This is where I get the right to talk to any operational unit because I am the one to explain the situation to the public, and therefore must be the best-informed person." The crisis-related empowerment of the CCO once again shows that traditional top-down approaches are demolished during crises.

Even though multi-crises affect more than one organization, the interviewed airport and airline representatives are often held responsible by the public even for problems they did not cause or for which they lack competencies or authority for handling the situation:

> If there is a problem with security checks at the terminal, there is no valid option to direct the responsibility to the federal police and their service providers – even though it is within their field of competence – as the public will ultimately blame the airport itself and would interpret the factually correct information as an excuse to not take action.

Consequently, they are often expected to take the lead in crisis communication even though they do not have the authority to do so. Incidents in air traffic are often being revealed from all sides. However, when related to human harm or loss, public authorities (e.g., Ministry of Transportation, German Federal Aviation

Authority, Federal Police) immediately take the lead: "to announce the number of and details about injured or dead is primarily the job of the public authorities, mostly the police and their associates."

In such cases, airports and airlines must connect to the public authorities' communication (e.g., by re-tweeting their content). It therefore depends on whether the affected organizations have some sort of hierarchy in claiming authority when it comes to which of the organizations is taking the lead and coordinating crisis communication (Kalkman et al., 2018). Kalkman et al. (2018) use the example of a terrorist attack to illustrate that in such cases the state authorities often claim sole leadership, while the stakeholders of the other affected organizations expect them to assume responsibility as well. In such cases, the coordination of all CMTs involved is often complicated by the fact that it is unclear who has which competencies and powers.

When it comes to different stakeholders that must be addressed in crisis communication, the interviewed communication experts specifically name their customers / passengers and the media. Stakeholders such as workers on site that are usually employed by tenants and service providers are often overlooked and thus, not included in internal communication (e.g., no access to the intranet of the focal airline or airport). But these individuals are often in direct contact with other stakeholders such as customers / passengers or journalists reporting from the scene of events. That is why this study argues that due to their local and emotional proximity, non-contractual employees must be addressed equally to contractual employees. At this point, it becomes obvious that the borders between the intra-organizational and inter-organizational level are porous, allowing incoming and outgoing flows of communication (Frandsen & Johansen, 2011).

When involved in internal (crisis) communication efforts, non-contractual employees can become formal or informal ambassadors. However, despite their efforts on the ground or in the air, the interviewed communicators from airports and airlines emphasize existing problems of being in appropriate information and communication relations with stakeholders such as tenants or suppliers. They may be denied access to certain communication channels such as the intranet or might be using different tools or platforms through which they are informed by their superiors due to difficulties in aligning different structures and processes.

Despite these difficulties, economic pressure and high competition in air traffic, the aviation industry stands out with mutual respect and support in times of crisis: "In a crisis – and this is really distinguishing – all of a sudden the aviation-world is one big family." The interdependence between airports and airlines, beyond previously established strategic partnerships and alliances, is comparable to the connection of members of trade organizations which "coordinate the exchange of important information among member organizations, but more importantly, they all serve as crisis counsellors for the members in crisis" (Frandsen & Johansen, 2018, p. 103).

To summarize: Airports and airlines are increasingly striving for cross-organizational communication channels and platforms that enhance coordination in daily business as well as in multi-crises. They need to further strengthen their attempts to stay in regular contact with as many affiliated organizations, their CMTs and non-contractual employees as possible to enhance coordination culture.

Connecting Crisis Communication Coordination from Both Levels

Instead of distinguishing between internal and external stakeholders, multi-crises demand integrated communication toward all stakeholders:

> These days you cannot differentiate between target groups: The relatives of customers are also the recipients of social media messages. [...] The journalists who do research and the inquiring authorities who want answers from us are also on Twitter and Facebook.

The blurring lines between senders and receivers of crisis related information and communication become particularly apparent due to new communication technologies: "That is why we always have to keep in mind both the internal as well as the external environment." The interviewed airports and airlines therefore differentiate between issues and communication channels rather than between internal and external communication. Most of them have already established or are aiming to establish cross-media newsrooms managing communication with all relevant stakeholders. However, as one noted "in theory, we acknowledge the importance of internal crisis communication, but in real cases we often miss to consider internal stakeholders on an equally important level as external stakeholders."

To coordinate communication in multi-crises, the participants also propose to establish either a vital intranet and extranet or create a common virtual space integrating all stakeholders on a single platform to ensure most efficient information and communication flows between the intra- and inter-organizational levels. One of the airports interviewed is about to establish not only a commentary function within its intranet but also to create a socialized intranet with real time chat rooms opening new possibilities to engage with both those who are directly employed as well as personnel employed by on-site service providers. By granting these stakeholders direct access to traditionally internal communication channels such as the intranet, airports and airlines can make use of synergy effects in information distribution: "With the expanded intranet we can reach out to local transportation services, for example, letting them know not to approach the airport in an actual crisis situation." Ultimately, such platforms can be used to enhance coordination for not only handling acute crises but also to prevent potential crises.

The implementation of such projects is time- and cost-intensive as cultural as well as structural differences between the joining organizations must be overcome. This is why despite increasing efforts to get as many different stakeholders on board as possible, the interviewed airports and airlines still struggle with integrated communication.

As a result, they rather use direct messenger services such as SMS, e-mail, or mobile applications. Especially reaching out to personnel on site is facilitated by such communication technologies.

To summarize: Instead of artificially distinguishing between internal and external stakeholders, multi-crises demand an equal consideration of stakeholders with different information and communication needs and habits. Therefore, the aviation industry is establishing and strengthening structures and processes enabling integrated crisis communication such as common virtual spaces.

Conclusion

Crisis communication research is yet to mature and expand its interest to both the intra-organizational and inter-organizational level of organizations when analyzing multi-crises. Air traffic organizations with their high exposure to such crises serve as a good example to investigate crisis communication in and within both levels. This study confirms that both the intra- and inter-organizational levels as well as their interconnection are crucial for efficiently coordinating crisis communication.

Concerning the intra-organizational level, employee empowerment that is independent of departmental affiliation supports and strengthens agility, flexibility, and adaptability of resources in multi-crises. On the inter-organizational level, affiliated partners working on site have high influential potential, including employees of tenants and service providers. Airports and airlines, however, tend to ignore workers on site despite their particular information needs derived from experiencing most crises up close. By granting them access to all communication channels, airports and airlines can integrate them into their overall crisis communications.

Instead of differentiating between internal and external stakeholders, the study advocates an integrated organizational communication policy that includes all possible senders and recipients of crisis communication at both the intra- and inter-organizational levels. The theoretical conceptualization with the two levels helps to map all relevant stakeholders while its boundaries are still porous. At the same time the conceptualization needs to be agile in case the focus changes from one organization to another. Multi-crises force airports and airlines to coordinate their crisis communication efforts beyond organizational boundaries which is time- and cost-intensive. Corporate cultural differences, language barriers, diverging leadership styles as well as organizational structures and processes regarding not only (crisis) communication but other operations as well make it difficult for multiple affected organizations to align their resources and competencies.

For theory building and development, we would suggest removing all artificial distinctions between internal and external stakeholders and directing communication activities toward specific needs. By distinguishing between needs rather than internal and external audiences, communication activities can be more solution oriented. This perspective would fit very well with the Rhetorical Arena Theory, considering that the many voices in the arena raise awareness to their different communication needs. Therefore, different needs need to be identified such as *obtaining pure factual information* or *receiving moral support*.

For future research, the study suggests looking at other industries such as critical infrastructure, other means of transportation or chemical corporations that are likely to experience multi-crises to add further knowledge about the coordination in crisis communication. Including crisis communication documents (e.g., emergency manual, coaching guidelines) and research observations would also support a better understanding of how organizations coordinate to reduce the impact of multi-crises. Conducting in-depth interviews with different (potential) designated and non-designated crisis communicators would further add to the knowledge on preventing and handling multi-crises.

Regarding the practice of crisis communication, it can be assumed that the trend toward establishing newsrooms in organizations, as it is described by the interviewees, will further lead to less distinction between stakeholders as such and rather channel-specific adaptations of content.

References

Ahrne, G., & Brunsson, N. (2005). Organizations and meta-organizations. *Scandinavian Journal of Management*, *21*(4), 429–449. https://doi.org/10.1016/j.scaman.2005.09.005

Alexander, D. (2013). Volcanic ash in the atmosphere and risks for civil aviation: A study in European crisis management. *International Journal of Disaster Risk Science*, *4*(1), 9–19. https://doi.org/10.1007/s13753-013-0003-0

Ansell, C., Boin, A., & Keller, A. (2010). Managing transboundary crises: Identifying the building blocks of an effective response system. *Journal of Contingencies and Crisis Management*, *18*(4), 195–207. https://doi.org/10.1111/j.1468-5973.2010.00620.x

Appold, S. J., & Kasarda, J. D. (2013). The airport city phenomenon: Evidence from large US airports. *Urban Studies*, *50*(6), 1239–1259.

Bachmann, P. (2017). *Medienunternehmen und der strategische Umgang mit Media Responsibility und Corporate Social Responsibility*. Springer VS.

BDF. (2018). *Bedeutung des Luftverkehrs*. http://www.bdf.aero/themen/wirtschaftliche-bedeutung/

Benoit, W. L. (1997). Image restoration discourse and crisis communication. *Public Relations Review*, *23*(2), 177–186.

Benoit, W. L. (2015). Image restoration theory. In W. Donsbach (Ed.), *The concise encyclopedia of communication* (1st ed.). John Wiley & Sons, Ltd. https://doi.org/10.1002/9781405186407.wbieci009.pub2

Biesiadecka, G. M. (2009). *Krisenpräventives Kommunikationsmanagement am Flughafen: Ein Modell der Public Relations für den erfolgreichen Umgang mit Krisen* (1st ed.). VS Verlag für Sozialwissenschaften.

Boin, A., & Bynander, F. (2015). Explaining success and failure in crisis coordination. *Geografiska Annaler: Series A, Physical Geography, 97*(1), 123–135. https://doi.org/10.1111/geoa.12072

Brosius, H.-B., Haas, A., & Unkel, J. (2022). *Methoden der empirischen Kommunikationsforschung: Eine Einführung*. Springer Fachmedien.

Bundy, J., Pfarrer, M. D., Short, C. E., & Coombs, W. T. (2017). Crises and crisis management: Integration, interpretation, and research development. *Journal of Management, 43*(6), 1661–1692. https://doi.org/10.1177/0149206316680030

Christensen, T., Danielsen, O. A., Laegreid, P., & Rykkja, L. H. (2016). Comparing coordination structures for crisis management in six countries: Comparing coordination structures for crisis management. *Public Administration, 94*(2), 316–332. https://doi.org/10.1111/padm.12186

Coombs, W. T. (1995). Choosing the right words: The development of guidelines for the selection of the "appropriate" crisis-response strategies. *Management Communication Quarterly, 8*(4), 447–476.

Coombs, W. T. (2006). The protective powers of crisis response strategies: Managing reputational assets during a crisis. *Journal of Promotion Management, 12*(3/4), 241–260. http://dx.doi.org/10.1300/J057v12n03_13

Coombs, W. T. (2007). Protecting organization reputations during a crisis: The development and application of situational crisis communication theory. *Corporate Reputation Review, 10*(3), 163–176.

Coombs, W. T. (2019). *Ongoing crisis communication: Planning, managing, and responding* (5th ed.). SAGE Publications.

Coombs, W. T., & Holladay, S. J. (2002). Helping crisis managers protect reputational assets: Initial tests of the situational crisis communication theory. *Management Communication Quarterly, 16*(2), 165–186. https://doi.org/10.1177/089331802237233

Coombs, W. T., & Holladay, S. J. (2014). How publics react to crisis communication efforts: Comparing crisis response reactions across sub-arenas. *Journal of Communication Management, 18*(1), 40–57. https://doi.org/10.1108/JCOM-03-2013-0015

Cropper, S., Huxham, C., Ebers, M., & Ring, P. S. (Eds.). (2010). *The Oxford handbook of inter-organizational relations* (2nd ed.). Oxford University Press.

Frandsen, F., & Johansen, W. (2011). The study of internal crisis communication: Towards an integrative framework. *Corporate Communications: An International Journal, 16*(4), 347–361. https://doi.org/10.1108/13563281111186977

Frandsen, F., & Johansen, W. (2017). *Organizational crisis communication*. SAGE Publications.

Frandsen, F., & Johansen, W. (2018). Voices in conflict? The crisis communication of meta-organizations. *Management Communication Quarterly, 32*(1), 90–120. https://doi.org/10.1177/0893318917705734

Glaser, B. G., & Strauss, A. L. (1970). Theoretical sampling. In N. K. Denzin (Ed.), *Sociological methods. A sourcebook* (pp. 105–114). Aldine. http://doi.org/10.4324/9781315129945-10

Heide, M., & Simonsson, C. (2015). Struggling with internal crisis communication: A balancing act between paradoxical tensions. *Public Relations Inquiry*, *4*(2), 223–255. https://doi.org/10.1177/2046147X15570108

Hoffmann, D. (2017). Experteninterviews. In L. Mikos & C. Wegener (Eds.), *Qualitative Medienforschung. Ein Handbuch* (2nd ed.). UVK.

Iatrou, K., & Oretti, M. (2016). *Airline choices for the future: From alliances to mergers*. Routledge.

Jaffee, D. (2001). *Organization theory: Tension and change*. McGraw Hill.

Jin, Y., Pang, A., & Cameron, G. T. (2012). Toward a publics-driven, emotion-based approach in crisis communication: Testing the Integrated Crisis Mapping (ICM) model. *Journal of Public Relations Research*, *24*(3), 266–298. https://doi.org/10.1080/1062726X.2012.676747

Johansen, W., Aggerholm, H. K., & Frandsen, F. (2012). Entering new territory: A study of internal crisis management and crisis communication in organizations. *Public Relations Review*, *38*(2), 270–279.

Kaiser, R. (2014). *Qualitative Experteninterviews: Konzeptionelle Grundlagen und praktische Durchführung*. Springer VS.

Kalkman, J. P., Kerstholt, J. H., & Roelofs, M. (2018). Crisis response team decision-making as a bureau-political process. *Journal of Contingencies and Crisis Management*, *26*(4), 480–490. https://doi.org/10.1111/1468-5973.12243

Kim, J. N., & Rhee, Y. (2011). Strategic thinking about employee communication behavior (ECB) in public relations: Testing the models of megaphoning and scouting effects in Korea. *Journal of Public Relations Research*, *23*(3), 243–268. https://doi.org/10.1080/1062726X.2011.582204

Lee, Y. (2019). An examination of the effects of employee words in organizational crisis: Public forgiveness and behavioral intentions. *International Journal of Business Communication*, *Online First*, 1–23. https://doi.org/10.1177/2329488419877236

Maurer, A. (Ed.). (2017). *Handbuch der Wirtschaftssoziologie* (2nd ed.). Springer VS.

Mazzei, A., Kim, J.-N., Togna, G., Lee, Y., & Lovari, A. (2019). Employees as advocates or adversaries during a corporate crisis: The role of perceived authenticity and employee empowerment. *Sinergie Italian Journal of Management*, *37*(2), 195–212. https://doi.org/10.7433/s109.2019.10

Meyen, M., Löblich, M., Pfaff-Rüdiger, S., & Riesmeyer, C. (2019). *Qualitative Forschung in der Kommunikationswissenschaft: Eine praxisorientierte Einführung* (2., aktualisierte und erweiterte Auflage 2019). Springer Fachmedien Wiesbaden GmbH.

Mobility and Transport, European Commission. (2017). *European civil aviation handbook*. European Commission – Directorate General for Mobility and Transport.

Ödlund, A. (2010). Pulling the same way? A multi-perspectivist study of crisis cooperation in government. *Journal of Contingencies and Crisis Management*, *18*(2), 96–107. https://doi.org/10.1111/j.1468-5973.2010.00605.x

Oum, T. H., Park, J.-H., & Zhang, A. (2000). *Globalization and strategic alliances: The case of the airline industry* (1st ed.). Pergamon.

Pinsdorf, M. K. (1991). Flying different skies: How cultures respond to airline disasters. *Public Relations Review*, *17*(1), 37–56. https://doi.org/10.1016/0363-8111(91)90005-6

Ravazzani, S. (2016). Exploring internal crisis communication in multicultural environments: A study among Danish managers. *Corporate Communications: An International Journal*, *21*(1), 73–88. https://doi.org/10.1108/CCIJ-02-2015-0011

Ray, S. J. (1999). *Strategic communication in crisis management: Lessons from the airline industry*. Quorum Books.

Seeger, M. W., Sellnow, T. L., & Ulmer, R. R. (2003). Crisis teams and decision making. In M. W. Seeger, T. L. Sellnow, & R. R. Ulmer (Eds.), *Communication and organizational crisis* (pp. 185–199). Praeger.

Stevens, N. J. (2006). City airports to airport cities. *Queensland Planner*, *46*(1), 37.

van Zoonen, W., & van der Meer, T. (2015). The importance of source and credibility perception in times of crisis: Crisis communication in a socially mediated era. *Journal of Public Relations Research*, *27*(5), 371–388. https://doi.org/10.1080/1062726X.2015.1062382

8 The Arcadia Crisis Postmortem

Lessons Learned for the Fashion Industry in Stakeholder Relationship Management and Value Co-creation

Sophie Louise Johnson

In November 2020, the UK fashion industry suffered a huge loss of one of the biggest fashion retail groups in the country. Home to high street king and queen Topshop and Topman, as well as Burton, Dorothy Perkins and BHS, the group had previously been perceived as the heart of the British High Street. Though successful, the group was well accustomed to crisis, both internally and externally. CEO Phillip Green often made UK and international headlines for the 2016 BHS pensions scandal and his alleged decades-long tax evasion. Finally, in 2018 the group was close to filing for bankruptcy but was saved before succumbing to further financial pressures during the COVID-19 pandemic in 2020. The Arcadia Group was quick to blame the pandemic as a principle factor for their closure, however it seems the retailer group had been on a steady decline due to financial problems, lack of consumer engagement and communities and a lack of competitive strategy. Over the last decade, the fashion industry has seen many changes including evolving digital landscapes, sustainability scrutiny and supply chain pressures, as well as a boom in fast fashion retailers and a changing high street (Vänskä & Gurova, 2022). This chapter will explore the lack of value co-creation in their communication strategy and the importance of stakeholder engagement in crisis-prone organizations.

The global fashion industry is worth $1.7 trillion (Statista, 2022). In just 2022, its growth projections ranged from 3% to 8% (McKinsey, 2022). As one of the biggest global industries, it is also inherently crisis prone (Gistri et al., 2018). However, with the industry's changing landscape, increased media attention, and social media crises more visible today than ever before – focusing on stakeholder interests becoming increasingly critical in strategic communication. This heightened skepticism includes criticism of sustainability initiatives, working conditions, and challenges in the supply chain. Some crises emerge as internal problems and unsustainable supply chain decisions. For example, in 2021 BooHoo.com was exposed for poor factory conditions and modern-day slavery (Stevenson, 2021). Everlane was also exposed as lacking diversity and unfair treatment behind closed doors. Everlane is particularly interesting because an anonymous on Instagram account named 'The Ex-Wives Club' outed the

DOI: 10.4324/9781003375296-10

organization and encouraged consumer boycott (Nytimes.com, 2022). Unsafe working conditions were highlighted in 2013 with the collapse of the Rana Plaza in Bangladesh, injuring and killing a total of 1,134 workers (Clean Clothes Campaign, 2021). The collapse happened after concerns had already been expressed from workers who produced clothing for Mango, Primark, H&M, WalMart (Asda in the UK), and Matalan (Auke & Simaens, 2019) as well as luxury retailers Dior and St Laurent (Pelikánová et al., 2021). Additionally, external factors such as natural disasters, war, and recessions have had a widespread effect on many parts of the industry. Since 2020, no single industry has been able to ignore the impact of the COVID-19 but for the fashion industry the pandemic created financial, health, and supply chain complications (Zhao & Kim, 2021).

Due to both disruptions and advancements in recent decades – globalization, communication, technology, and the recent economic crisis – organizations are investing more time and research in crisis management. This is certainly true of the fashion industry as it is noted to be fragmented, and a victim of extreme globalization (Chan et al., 2017). Fashion brands are increasingly vulnerable, not only to crisis, but also to the amplification of this crisis in the media. Media coverage of the industry can often be described as 'cutthroat' having damaging reputational repercussions (Jung & La, 2020).

Thus, the fashion industry is a 'crisis-prone industry' which has seen some notable crises (Gistri et al., 2018) and has faced many different types of risks and challenges in the last decade alone. Fashion is most certainly an industry that is determined by change, whether that be adapting to short-term fads or long-term trends, which then has a direct effect on production, creativity, and marketing (Easey, 2009). Crisis communication should be a priority for fashion organizations moving forward to help prevent and manage a crisis. Yet Gistri et al. (2018) found that the fashion industry is a significantly understudied area of crisis management and communication. They suggest that the relevance of the industry is far reaching and that more should be done to examine customer interactions, brand reactions, and the deeper impact of crisis in this arena. Gistri et al. (2018) also discuss the cultural impact of the industry illustrating how fashion consumers play a unique role in pressuring brands so retailers should pay more attention to their input. To summarize, with the fast-moving pace of the industry, and is clear vulnerability to crisis, more should be done to examine how crisis can be prevented and managed.

Literature Review

The Fashion Industry and Crisis

Despite the fashion industry's crisis-prone status, the industry is seldom meaningfully addressed in risk and crisis communication literature; it suffers from a lack of research and theory development. Moreover, while case-based research on crises in the fashion industry has emerged in industry literature, they typically suffer from a lack of expertise in risk and crisis communication.

Vulnerability to crisis for fashion retailers is higher than ever before, with increased consumer pressure and the watchful eye of social media. Von Busch (2019) states that power can be defined by the simplest question of 'who rules' and tackles this conversation by examining three categories of power in the fashion industry. She suggests that those brands are losing power agency because the digital shift of fashion highlights that the brands no longer rule the world of fashion, due to more complex relationships with their consumers. The growth of online communities and vulnerability to scandal has, in turn, created a megaphone effect where communities of consumers fuel word-of-mouth as collective voices (Vänskä & Gurova, 2022). However, brands are not truly powerless – the volume of their voices depends on their initial response or reaction when they face crises. Brennan et al., (2013) define two key brand responses in the context of the fashion industry crisis. Brands may either respond in a positive state of acceptance or combine apologies and promises in order to positively face the crisis. In contrast, other brands are seen to ignore or dispute misconduct and responsibility, choosing instead to take a defensive approach. Yet this is not a particularly sophisticated understanding of crisis response in the fashion industry because it does not take into account different factors influencing crisis response.

Diers-Lawson (2019) identifies four types of crisis including: transgressions, disasters, reputational and events. Viewed in a progression of blame attribution where the organization cannot reasonably be blamed for the emergence of the crisis (i.e., disasters) to situations where the organization is materially at fault for the crisis (i.e., transgressions), the heuristic argues that how organizations respond to a crisis should depend on the degree to which stakeholders would hold the them accountable *and* the severity of the crisis (Diers-Lawson, 2019). In the context of the fashion industry, disasters are probably the least relevant; however, they commonly face reputational crises (e.g., online complaints, negative attributions, and negative coverage), events (e.g., economic downturns, supply chain problems), and transgressions (e.g., safety risks, environmental damage, or worker's rights violations). However, even in instances like COVID-19, where the industry cannot be directly blamed for the crisis, organizations in the fashion industry must still be careful to manage their relationships with their stakeholders, actively using crisis management strategies (Peiyu, 2020).

Stakeholder Relationship Management

The stakeholder relationship model (SRM) explores the intersections of the relationships between organizations, their stakeholders, and the issues that affect both (Diers-Lawson, 2019). SRM emphasizes the stakeholder perspective, as this enables organizations to put their stakeholder interests and values at the heart of their communication practices. Diers-Lawson (2019) states that the more engaged and connected stakeholders feel to issues surrounding the organization, the more likely stakeholders are to act in times of crisis. Applications of SRM have also found that crises meaningfully influence stakeholder evaluations of reputation, trust, perceived consumer knowledge, attitudes, evaluations, and behaviors (Diers-Lawson & Croucher, 2017). Relationships with stakeholders can become threatened when an organization suffers a crisis (Gistri, 2018). The outcome can be that people lose confidence in the organization as 'crisis-prone', which can lead to other negative implications when critical stakeholders lose confidence in the organization. The vulnerability of organizations in the fashion industry is heightened because the stakeholders surrounding the industry and their roles are constantly fluctuating because of the frequent and radical changes in the fashion landscape (Scheffer, 2019). The consequences of this instability create changes in relationships between stakeholders such as retailers, consumers, and supply chain.

Due to the perceived shift of brand power in the fashion industry (Von Busch, 2019), stakeholder relationships are growing in importance (Black, 2020) and can be separated into both direct and indirect groups. Direct stakeholders are retailers, suppliers, designers, and sometimes consumers. Indirect stakeholders being government, surrounding businesses, councils, and activists, and sometimes consumers. Consumers *can* fall into both groups because, as Gistri et al. (2018) argue, consumers are the 'final stakeholder' in the chain of a fashion product and understanding their reactions to fashion crisis is vital. Their study analyzed the emotional impact and behaviors of consumers when a fashion brand is facing a crisis, finding that brand identification and personal crisis relevance were crucial factors influencing consumer behavior. This is an interesting application to the fashion industry as many fashion crises do not have a direct effect on the consumer, making them indirect stakeholders at times. For example, the Rana Plaza collapse in 2013 saw loss of lives and affected the direct community surrounding the factory; however, consumers thousands of miles away were considered indirect, but were emotionally affected and acted on social media and through boycotting actions. Gistri et al. (2018) examined how negative consumer reactions to a fashion retailer in crisis can have a profound effect on the organization. Though not directly affected, these types of crises do seem to affect consumers financially, mentally, and physically. It can be suggested that when developing crisis management strategies that considering the relationships with their consumers both directly and indirectly is imperative to the crisis impact. Though SRM can be effectively applied to explain these phenomena, what is missing is the triggering factor that shifts the consumer from a 'passive recipient' not directly affected by an issue to an 'active co-designer of value' for the organization (Kaczorowska-Spychalska, 2018).

Brand Communities and Value Co-creation

The concepts of brand communities and value co-creation complements the SRM perspective and provides the missing link explaining how some stakeholders can shift between being direct and indirect in their influence over a company. Value co-creation can be defined as a contemporary management paradigm, evaluating the relationship between an organization and its stakeholders as one where the value of both stakeholders are elevated because of their relationship (Galvagno & Dalli, 2014). Until recently, value co-creation has been dominated by the service industry, but it is now considered to be more important in product-related industries. The concept has emerged from the works of Vargo and Lusch (2004) who explore the movement from 'Goods Dominant Logic' to 'Service Dominant Logic'. They define this alongside value co-creation as *an ongoing voluntary process that works as an exchange between social and economic actors, i.e., individuals or organizations*. In the context of the fashion industry, the adaption of value co-creation could help further support these relationships between stakeholders and issues in order to both prevent and manage crisis. From this perspective, value co-creation argues that stakeholders are no longer fully separate from the retailers they use because their interactions ultimately create new business and consumption opportunities (Galvagno & Dalli, 2014). Yet, value co-creation has not been fully developed in the context of industries that focus on goods or product consumption and its relevance needs to be better developed (Peñaloza & Venkatesh, 2006). Surely, there can be no better context to explore and apply value co-creation than in one of the biggest consumption industries in the world – fashion. Moreover, because value co-creation explores the exchanges between social and economic actors, it may serve as a central glue connecting stakeholders, issues, and organizations in the context of SRM.

Certainly, this would be why there has been some exploration of value co-creation in the fashion industry in recent years. For example, Jain et al. (2022) explores the relationship between a fashion rental organization and its customers, stating that involving customers in its processes is very important as they can leverage technology to encourage value co-creation. Prete (2022) also explored value co-creation relationship factors between stakeholders and fast fashion retailers to identify recommendations for retailers interested in sustainable fashion. Considering value co-creation beyond consumers, Millspaugh and Kent (2016) place further emphasis on the impact of these activities and relationships within the fashion industry network. Concentrating on SME fashion design enterprises, the study finds that co-creation between surrounding stakeholders such as competitors, collaborators, and supply chain, has an impact on brand identity and growth as retailers in a global marketplace. Emphasis here is placed on identity and interpretation and considers how value co-creation in the form of stakeholder feedback, requests, opinions, and impressions is just as important as producer-consumer interaction and calls for a multi stakeholder perspective in the fashion industry.

To underscore this point, a critical component of value co-creation are brand communities, which are characterized by a new kind of brand involvement or engagement. Brand communities are virtual communities connected by their mutual admiration of a brand (Muniz & O'Guinn, 2001). Molina-Prados et al. (2021) emphasizes the importance of fashion retailers enabling and supporting the evolution of brand communities for their consumers because, as Laroche et al. (2012) note, they build brand trust and loyalty. Though building brand communities also enables emergent online activism whether these engagement activities create or destroy a brand's value may largely depend on the organization's response to the activist engagement (Sandoval-Almazan & Gil-Garcia, 2014). However, no matter whether we think about brand communities as a virtual community of admiration or advocacy, it highlights the importance of embedding value co-creation into stakeholder relationship management processes.

However, in the context of crises, Mortiz and Youn (2020) suggest that established online communities can be used to a brand's advantage. Brand communities that are treated as value co-creators can significantly benefit retailers in these contexts for a number of reasons (Nyadzayo et al., 2020). First, as members of brand communities, stakeholders prolong engagement with and about brands (Yang et al., 2016), facilitate interactions around shared values and content (Richter & Koch, 2007), and support or enable brands to cope with crises (Yuan et al., 2020). Certainly, social media enables reputational crises and negative word of mouth but can also be a useful brand tool to mediate the impact of a crisis through stakeholders (Mishra & Sharma, 2018). However, Santos et al. (2022) points out that if retailers have not created a value co-creation set of relationships with consumers before a crisis, value co-destruction could take place. We can think of *value co-destruction as a brand losing its relationships with stakeholders, including negative engagement and the formation of brand hate communities*.

A Value Co-creation Approach to Stakeholder Relationship Management

The SRM ValCo model (Stakeholder Relationship Management – Value Co-Creation) adds an additional layer to the existing model (see Figure 8.1). This model allows the notion of value co-creation to be considered as a factor that can influence the relationship between the fashion organization, the consumer, and the perceived issue i.e., the crisis itself. The notion of value co-creation and the importance of stakeholder relationships in the fashion industry presents the opportunity to further develop the model, considering value co-creation as key part of examining relationships pre-crisis. This could have practical implications for businesses to not only understand the stakeholder relationships and the issues facing both, but also to explore value co-creation as a mitigating factor to prevent crisis. Therefore, building a

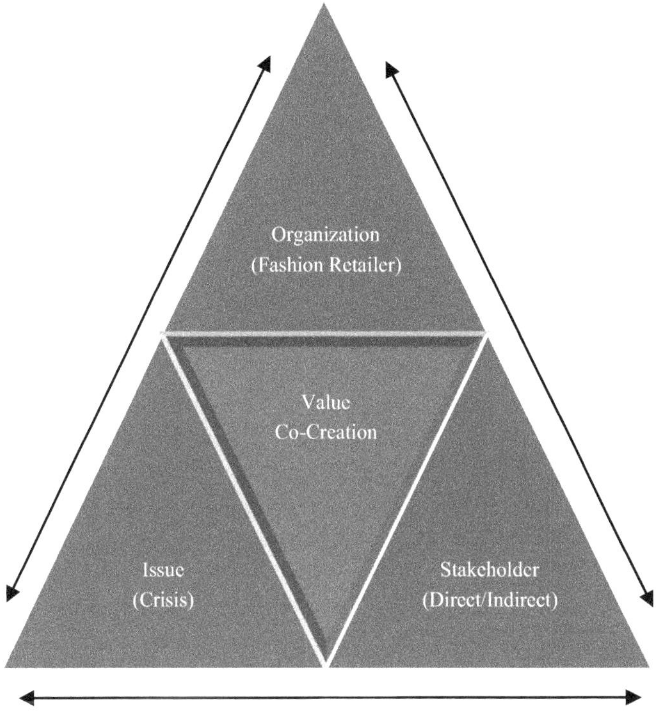

Figure 8.1 SRM val-co model.

model with multiple stakeholder perspectives and converging it with value co-creation, could be an effective way to approach crisis response in the fashion industry. Yet, this also problematizes the connection to media coverage of the fashion industry.

Value co-creation has been seen in other contexts to mitigate crisis and create solidarity (Johnson & Buhalis, 2023) maintains and protects customer and stakeholder relationships (Zen et al., 2022) and behavior shifts pre, during, and post crisis (Edvardsson & Tronvoll, 2021). While value co-creation may be essential to emerging and existing online brand communities, connecting this to media coverage of crisis in the fashion industry also represents a black hole in our understanding of crisis in the fashion industry. Therefore, given the lack of direct connection between stakeholder relationship management, value co-creation, and the fashion industry this chapter asks the simple question: in the context of media coverage of a major brand crisis, like the fall of the Arcadia group, what evidence of value co-creation and stakeholder relationship management is reported on in the national news and trade publications?

Methodology

This chapter focuses on a case study because it can be used to apply the concepts of SRM and value co-creation with a retrospective view on what lessons can be learned from a fashion retailer crisis. Multiple case studies using the same organization, therefore, allow us to identify trends over time in how the organization may have managed its relationships and value co-creation with its direct and indirect stakeholders.

The Organization

Phillip Green and the Arcadia Group are no stranger to crisis. Knighted on the recommendation of Tony Blair, the award-winning retail group was named 'retailer of the year' numerous times and called upon by former Prime Minister David Cameron to support Charity Initiatives and UK government efficacy (Nelken & Levi, 2018). It can be argued that the arrogant attitude Green instilled within his retail group, coupled with his personal reputation as an individual, are jointly responsible for the downfall of the group An interview with Sam Preston, previously a buyer for Topshop discussed the arrogance of the organization prior to its demise, and described its attitude as 'untouchable'. This insider perspective during the time of its reign shows the key issues that existed within the head office mentality. This was also evidenced in Phillip Green himself through various times of crisis that affected the organization toward the end of the group's reign. Overall, the Arcadia Group has been incredibly crisis prone across its high street reign and built a poor reputation due to its poor relationship management and handing from Philip Green, CEO and a lack of value co-creating activities. This case study approach will address four crises that took place in the last decade, directly effecting Topshop and BHS (see Table 8.1 for a summary of the crises).

Data Collection

To analyze the media coverage of stakeholder responses during the times of the four chosen crisis, trade publication *Retail Gazette* was chosen to collate articles within the crisis time frames. As a trade publication, *Retail Gazette* offers industry insight specific to stakeholder needs and covering factors that directly affect retail stakeholders. Utilizing a stakeholder led publication allows the relationships to be analyzed better and the impact of crisis on stakeholder attitudes and behaviors. Church et al. (2020) noted the relevance of using trade publications in a weather crisis context. Journalists of trade related publications such as Retail Gazette can attenuate risk due to its targeted nature, as opposed to public news outlets who have an agenda to appease national interests. However, Church et al. (2020) also note that using both together can be a useful combination. In addition to the article search using *Retail Gazette*, a sampling of national news

Table 8.1 Multiple crisis case studies for Arcadia group

Crisis	*Crisis Type*	*Crisis Summary*	*Brands Affected*	*Stakeholders Affected*
BHS Pension Scandal	Transgression Reputational	In 2015, 16 years after selling BHS to his wife's offshore company for just £1, Phillip Green caused intentional debt to the organization which ultimately effected the pensions of thousands of employees of BHS. Philip Green committed 'lawful looting' and at points refused to work with the UK government to ensure the £363 million owed to its employees (Clark, 2019). The crisis was the result of illegal corporate behavior, however, can be deemed reputational as other parts of the organizational group continued to flourish for a while longer.	BHS	Government Employees Consumers Media
#MeToo	Transgression	Following the 2016 #MeToo scandal, in 2018 Phillip Green was announced publicly in parliament as the 'British Me Too case'. Green denied all allegations, but further rumors followed, This crisis saw the end of relationships with female celebrities such as Kate Moss and Beyonce Ivy Park.	Topshop, Topman, Miss Selfridge, Burton Evans, Dorothy Perkins, Wallis, Outfit, BHS, Ivy Park	Government Employees Consumers Media
Administration	Disaster (Covid-19), Reputational	The Arcadia group has openly struggled financially over the years previous to covid, being no stranger to financial transgressions and near administration in 2019. The impact of Covid-19 in 2020 finally saw the retail group close its doors permanently in November (Davey, 2020).	Topshop, Topman, Miss Selfridge, Burton Evans, Dorothy Perkins, Wallis, Outfit, BHS	Government Employees Consumers Media
Tax Evasion	Transgression	Named as 'The Face of British Capitalism' Philip Green has been no stranger to financial transgressions since acquiring the Arcadia Group. Ohen describes Green's activities as a toxic cocktail of 'bankruptcy, loss, offshore status and wealth with the love of limelight, celebrities, yachts and parties' (Nelken & Levi, 2018). Allegations surfaced that Green paid out a large dividend from Arcadia, not to himself but to his wife Tina Green At the time of this transaction his wife lived outside of the UK, which meant this transaction was not taxed and Green did not have to pay £300 million to the HMRC (Nelken & Levi, 2018).	Topshop, Topman, Miss Selfridge, Burton Evans, Dorothy Perkins, Wallis, Outfit, BHS	Government Employees Consumers Media

articles was taken to complement the industry-led content. The sample collected here allows for consideration of the top trending news stories while each of the crises were relevant.

Analysis of Media Coverage

A total of 740 articles appears in the *Retail Gazette* in relation to Arcadia Group Crisis. For each of the four crises the following search terms were used 'BHS Pension', 'Philip Green Me Too', 'Arcadia Administration' and 'Arcadia Tax Evasion/Philip Green Tax Evasion'. All articles were screened for repetitive themes and the ones included in this study were deemed relevant with links to stakeholder relationships and value co-creation. 270 articles appeared in the *Retail Gazette* search for BHS Pension Scandal but only 117 were deemed relevant. For the #MeToo scandal, 160 articles appeared in the search but only 7 were chosen. A total of 210 articles appeared in the search for Arcadia Administration, but only 46 were selected in the screening process. It is also key to note that pre-2020, the organization suffered initial creditor problems and were on the brink of administration, for this period nine articles were collected. Arcadia filed for administration in November 2020 and 37 articles were collected from this time. In total, 740 articles were scaled down to 216 based on direct relevance. A collation of 210 articles from *Retail Gazette* were combined with 20 mainstream news articles from national press outlets in the UK. This allows triangulation of regular British press and trade journalism to balance the coverage and context.

Results and Discussion

Overall, the analysis shows little evidence of value co-creation activities or even broader stakeholder relationship management. While the mainstream media coverage could be criticized as focusing on the sensational, the consistent findings in the trade industry publication suggests that from a public stakeholder perspective the Arcadia group showed a distinct lack of co-creation and very little stakeholder relationship management over time, which was certainly reflected in the negative tone of the mainstream media coverage.

Trade publications not only cover organizations over time, but also provide direct and indirect stakeholder reflections on them. Throughout the articles *Retail Gazette* often interview retailer stakeholders for commentary on each of the crises. Philip Green's credibility is described throughout articles as 'sour' and commentary is made on Arcadias link with a 'toxic association with Sir Philip Green' and state he represents the unacceptable face of capitalism'. Commentary is also made on the retailers' lack of relevance in a contemporary fashion market as Arcadia is described as struggling 'to remain relevant in a younger, socially aware digital' marketplace. Michael Rolph, Chief Executive of YoYo, was quoted in describing Arcadia Group as complacent and lacking integration of digital technologies. This connects back to the value co-creation literature that connects the digitization of business and use of technology as a value co-creating activity (Jain et al., 2022). A sheer lack of digitization with the business shows a disconnect with the demands of fashion consumption and brand community engagement.

Other retail stakeholders commented that the Arcadia Group, in particular Topshop, were key trendsetters on the high-street but notes due to consumer shifts complacent brands are never immune. It is also noted that Greens distraction due to crisis may have impacted the strategic side of the business. Again, this illustrates the sheer disconnect with its consumers and therefore a lack of opportunity to co-create. As defined previously by (Galvagno & Dalli, 2014), value co-creation activities are dependent up on a two-way relationship between a stakeholder and the organization. In the fashion market, and in regard to this particular case study, consumers themselves serve as large participants in the collaborative nature of value co-creation (Peñaloza & Venkatesh, 2006). It seems as though, in practice, the Arcadia group saw its relationship with its consumers as a one-way street; the group just did not realize where the street was going.

Crisis (Issue) and Value Co-creation

In the case of the four key crises analyzed, there is a substantial lack of value co-creation seen before the crises, evidenced by the lack of a digital strategy, no brand community development, and seemingly no value co-creation with any of its direct and indirect stakeholders. This lack of SRM and value co-creation was particularly problematic because most of the crises the company faced were transgressions – where the company was at fault. As such, when the company was losing reputational value, doing nothing to improve its value co-creation, as it faced a reputational crisis, it had no brand community to defend it because its relationships with its stakeholders was already damaged.

It became clear in the media coverage that the financial scandals that have followed Philip Green from the BHS pension crisis, many stakeholder relationships were destroyed – particularly with its indirect stakeholders like the government and media. According to the press commentary, initially Green and his wife showed no regret or apologies and this lack of remorse seemed to generate more negative press coverage. Their morals and values were often questioned and while they were one of the richest couples in the UK, they continued to purchase property while other properties and assets were being seized. These actions do not align with value co-creating activities during the crisis and gave stakeholders more reason to question their relationships or even end them. Press commentary questioned his approach to many of the crises stating 'Sir Philip Green needed to honor his promises', offer other opportunities to the 'blameless, dedicated and loyal staff' and commented on the delay in his proposals to appease the situations.

Stakeholders and Value Co-creation

Although many stakeholders can be affected by a crisis in the fashion industry, the majority of crises only adversely affect the direct stakeholders. For example, in a fashion supply chain crisis, only the workers, manufacturers may be directly affected; however, indirect consumers feel they also have a stake and may respond accordingly. However, as these data suggest, relationships with indirect stakeholders still matter because when organizations fail to build and maintain value and relationships, not only are opportunities to buffer the organization in crisis lost, but it can seemingly lead directly to value destruction because stakeholders' *want* to see the organization fail. In the context of the Arcadia group, over time the word-of-mouth, trade industry coverage, media coverage, and government relationships all became increasingly negative.

When we track the group's stakeholder problems over time, we consider several stakeholder groups whose negative relationships clearly emerge. For example, BHS employees were one the first substantial groups to be directly affected by the actions of Green. In the industry and popular media coverage, the scorned responses from employees held no sympathy for the company. Across the cases, it was also evident that a negative crisis history also created additional problems for the Arcadia group because there was no room for forgiveness from those directly or indirectly affected. For example, in response to the #MeToo crisis, key celebrity stakeholders that were once the bread and butter for Arcadia's reputation in the industry publicly ended their relationships with the retail group. Most notably, as allegations of bullying and sexual harassment further surfaced, both Beyonce and Kate Moss were publicly ended ties with Topshop (Baker & Milligan, 2019).

Although not directly affected by the BHS pension scandal, Arcadia consumers were quick to respond negatively press outlets. With a lack of a brand community, no evidence of stakeholder relationship management, and an apparent lack of value co-creation, the Arcadia group's crisis history meant it was losing its core consumer group. As further financial indiscretions involving Arcadia, the indirectly affected consumers voted with their feet. After a considerable range of crisis as outlined above, the group's financial struggles hit the headlines as more and more consumers either lost interest in the brand or made conscious decisions not to shop at any of the Arcadia Group's stores. Meanwhile surrounding businesses recorded record profits such as the BooHoo group in 2019 with a 48% increase in profit in February 2019. Other competitors were taking advantage of the UK retail hole, that was seemingly shrinking around the Arcadia brands.

Concluding Thoughts

This chapter discusses the key events surrounding the Arcadia group reign and demise. The literature highlights the importance of connecting crisis communication, the fashion industry, and the co-creation of value by using the de-evolution of the Arcadia Group through crisis after crisis. These cases demonstrate not only the importance of accounting for both direct and indirect stakeholders during crises but also the applicability and revision of the SRM in the fashion industry. When we can better understand the relationships between organizations, issues, and stakeholders we can better plan or evaluate an organization's response to crises. However, this chapter does more than just re-affirm the value of the SRM framework, it provides an important addition by demonstrating that the concept of value co-creation can improve the framework's explanation of how stakeholder relationship management works to also explain what holds it together. Certainly future research should explore this through different data sources, methods, and corporate contexts; however, these data demonstrate an effective starting point for systematically improving the field's understanding of crises in the fashion industry – or any other retail-based industry.

References

Auke, E., & Simaens, A. (2019). Corporate responsibility in the fast fashion industry: How media pressure affected corporate disclosure following the collapse of Rana Plaza. *International Journal of Entrepreneurship and Innovation Management*, *23*(4), 356. https://doi.org/10.1504/ijeim.2019.10021652

Baker, S., & Milligan, E. (2019). *Topshop's Philip Green met his match with #metoo*. Bloomberg.com. Retrieved October 21, 2022, from https://www.bloomberg.com/news/articles/2019-07-11/topshop-s-philip-green-met-his-match-with-metoo

Black, S. (2020). Fashion in a time of crisis. *Fashion Practice*, *12*(3), 327–330. https://doi.org/10.1080/17569370.2020.1823624

Brennan, N. M., Merkl-Davies, D. M. and Beelitz, A. (2013). 'Dialogism in Corporate Social Responsibility Communications: Conceptualising verbal interaction between organisations and their audiences', Journal of Business Ethics, *115*(4), pp. 665–679. doi:10.1007/s10551-013-1825-9.

Buckley, C. (2011). Fashion & Luxury: Between Heritage & Innovation. In *Fashion & Luxury: Between Heritage & Innovation: Conference Proceedings* (pp. 61–68). Paris: Institut Français de la Mode (IFM).

Chan, A., Ngai, E., & Moon, K. (2017). The effects of strategic and manufacturing flexibilities and supply chain agility on firm performance in the fashion industry. *European Journal of Operational Research*, *259*(2), 486–499. https://doi.org/10.1016/j.ejor.2016.11.006

Church, S. P., Bentlage, B., Weiner, R., Babin, N., Bulla, B. R., Fagan, K., Haigh, T., Carlton, J. S., & Prokopy, L. S. (2020). National print media vs. agricultural trade publications: Communicating the 2012 midwestern us drought. *Climatic Change*, *161*(1), 43–63. https://doi.org/10.1007/s10584-019-02630-3

Clark, I. (2019). The British home stores pension scheme: Privatised looting? *Industrial Relations Journal*, *50*(4), 331–347. https://doi.org/10.1111/irj.12261

Clean Clothes Campaign. (2021). *Rana Plaza, clean clothes campaign*. https://cleanclothes.org/campaigns/past/rana-plaza (Accessed: December 29, 2022).

Davey, J. (2020). Philip Green's Arcadia UK fashion group falls into administration. *Reuters*. Retrieved October 21, 2022, from https://www.reuters.com/article/us-britain-retail-green-idUSKBN28A2TQ

Diers-Lawson, A. (2019). *Crisis communication*. Routledge.

Diers-Lawson, A., & Croucher, S. M. (2017). Sports, culture, and financial crisis: A cross-cultural comparison of the social media responses of struggling sports associations in the United States and the United Kingdom. In L. L. Austin & Y. Jin (Eds.), *Social media and crisis communication* (pp. 353–373). Routledge.

Easey, M. (2009). *Fashion marketing*. Wiley-Blackwell.

Edvardsson, B., & Tronvoll, B. (2021). Crisis behaviors as drivers of value co-creation transformation. *International Journal of Quality and Service Sciences, 14*(5), 1–15. https://doi.org/10.1108/ijqss-01-2021-0001

Galvagno, M., & Dalli, D. (2014). Theory of value co-creation: A systematic literature review. *Managing Service Quality, 24*(6), 643–683. https://doi.org/10.1108/msq-09-2013-0187

Gistri, G., Corciolani, M., & Pace, S. (2018). The interaction effect between brand identification and personal crisis relevance on consumers' emotional reactions to a fashion brand crisis. *Journal of Global Fashion Marketing, 9*(3), 252–269. https://doi.org/10.1080/20932685.2018.1461021

Jain, R., Jain, K., Behl, A., Pereira, V., Del Giudice, M., & Vrontis, D. (2022). Mainstreaming fashion rental consumption: A systematic and thematic review of literature. *Journal of Business Research, 139*, 1525–1539. https://doi.org/10.1016/j.jbusres.2021.10.071

Johnson, A.-G., & Buhalis, D. (2023). Legitimacy in co-creating tourism value through customer-to-customer (C2C) online travel communities. *Tourism Recreation Research*, 1–17. https://doi.org/10.1080/02508281.2023.2196488

Jung, E., & La, S. (2020). Wear your heart on your sleeve: Exploring moral identity as a moderator across CSR authenticity, consumer admiration, and engagement in the fashion industry. *Asia Marketing Journal, 22*(2), 19–57. https://doi.org/10.15830/amj.2020.22.2.19

Kaczorowska-Spychalska, D. (2018). Shaping Consumer Behaviour in the Fashion Industry by Interactive Communication Forms. *Fibres & Textiles in Eastern Europe, 26*(4), 13–19.

Laroche, M., Habibi, M. R., Richard, M.-O., & Sankaranarayanan, R. (2012). The effects of social media based brand communities on brand community markers, value creation practices, brand trust and brand loyalty. *Computers in Human Behavior, 28*(5), 1755–1767. https://doi.org/10.1016/j.chb.2012.04.016

McKinsey. (2022). *The state of fashion 2022*. Retrieved from https://www.mckinsey.com/~/media/mckinsey/industries/retail/our%20insights/state%20of%20fashion/2022/the-state-of-fashion-2022.pdf

Millspaugh, J., & Kent, A. (2016). Co-creation and the development of SME designer fashion enterprises. *Journal of Fashion Marketing and Management, 20*(3), 322–338. https://doi.org/10.1108/jfmm-10-2015-0085

Mishra, M. S., & Sharma, R. W. (2018). Brand crisis-sentiment analysis of user-generated comments about @Maggi on facebook. *Corporate Reputation Review, 22*(2), 48–60. https://doi.org/10.1057/s41299-018-0057-4

Mortiz, A., & Youn, S.-yi. (2020). You could do it better! Consumer negative responses toward moral crisis in the fashion industry. *Pivoting for the Pandemic*. https://doi.org/10.31274/itaa.12156

Molina-Prados, A., Muñoz-Leiva, F., & Prados-Peña, M. B. (2021). The role of customer brand engagement in the use of Instagram as a "shop window" for fashion-industry social commerce. *Journal of Fashion Marketing and Management: An International Journal*, *26*(3), 495–515. https://doi.org/10.1108/jfmm-12-2020-0275

Muniz, A. M., & O'Guinn, T. C. (2001). Brand community. *Journal of Consumer Research*, *27*(4), 412–432. https://doi.org/10.1086/319618

Nelken, D., & Levi, M. (2018). Sir Philip Green and the unacceptable face of capitalism. *King's Law Journal*, *29*(1), 36–57. https://doi.org/10.1080/09615768.2018.1480886

Nyadzayo, M. W., Johnson, L. W., & Rossi, M. (2020). Drivers and outcomes of brand engagement in self-concept for luxury fashion brands. *Journal of Fashion Marketing and Management: An International Journal*, *24*(4), 589–609. https://doi.org/10.1108/jfmm-05-2018-0070

Nytimes.com. (2022). Everlane's promise of 'Radical Transparency' unravels (Published 2020). *Nytimes.com*. Retrieved 26 August 2022, from https://www.nytimes.com/2020/07/26/fashion/everlane-employees-ethical-clothing.html

Peiyu, W. (2020). Analysis on the Different Response of Fast Fashion Brands and Luxury Brands to the Epidemic. *Advances in Economics, Business and Management Research*, *55*.

Pelikánová, R. M. G., Němečková, T., & MacGregor, R. K. (2021). CSR statements in international and Czech luxury fashion industry at the onset and during the COVID-19 pandemic—slowing down the fast fashion business? *Sustainability*, *13*(7), 3715. https://doi.org/10.3390/su13073715

Peñaloza, L., & Venkatesh, A. (2006). Further evolving the new dominant logic of marketing: From services to the social construction of Markets. *Marketing Theory*, *6*(3), 299–316. https://doi.org/10.1177/1470593106066789

Prete, M. D. (2022). Mindful sustainable consumption and sustainability chatbots in fast fashion retailing during and after the COVID-19 pandemic. *Journal of Management and Sustainability*, *12*(1), 19. https://doi.org/10.5539/jms.v12n1p19

Richter, A., & Koch, M. (2007). *Social Software –Status quo und Zukunft*. Fak. für Informatik, Univ. der Bundeswehr München.

Sandoval-Almazan, R., & Ramon Gil-Garcia, J. (2014). Towards cyberactivism 2.0? Understanding the use of social media and other information technologies for political activism and social movements. *Government Information Quarterly*, *31*(3), 365–378. https://doi.org/10.1016/j.giq.2013.10.016

Santos, Z. e. R., Cheung, C. M. K., Coelho, C., & Rita, P. (2022). Consumer engagement in social media brand communities: A literature review. *International Journal of Information Management 63*.

Scheffer, M. (2019). *Crisis and long terms challenges: Responsibility in the clothing industry*. Kies voor de toekomst. Retrieved January 5, 2023, from http://michielscheffer.nl/?p=420

Statistia. (2022). *Topic: Apparel market worldwide*. Statista. Retrieved 26 August 2022, from https://www.statista.com/topics/5091/apparel-market-worldwide/#topicHeader__wrapper.

Stevenson, M. (2021). Hidden in plain sight: The bystander effect and the mobilisation of modern slavery whistleblowing. *Supply Chain Management: An International Journal*, *27*(1), 128–139. https://doi.org/10.1108/scm-08-2020-0373

Vänskä, A., & Gurova, O. (2022). The fashion scandal: Social media, identity and the globalization of fashion in the twenty-first century. *International Journal of Fashion Studies*, *9*(1), 5–27. https://doi.org/10.1386/infs_00045_1

Vargo, S. L., and Lusch, R. F. (2004). Evolving to a new dominant logic for marketing. *Journal of Marketing*, *68*(1), 1–17.

von Busch, O. (2019). A crisis of power in fashion: Is there agency for change? *Fashion Practice*, *11*(3), 302–308. https://doi.org/10.1080/17569370.2019.1662234

Yang, S., Lin, S., Carlson, J. R., & Ross, W. T. (2016). Brand engagement on social media: Will firms' social media efforts influence search engine advertising effectiveness? *Journal of Marketing Management*, *32*(5–6), 526–557. https://doi.org/10.1080/0267257x.2016.1143863

Yuan, D. Lin, Z., Filieri, R., Liu, R., &, Zheng, M. (2020). Managing the product-harm crisis in the digital era: The role of consumer online brand community engagement. *Journal of Business Research*, *115*, 38–47. https://doi.org/10.1016/j.jbusres.2020.04.044

Zen, A. C., Bittencourt, B. A., & Spohr, R. (2022). Co-creation strategies in times of crisis: The case of warren. *The International Journal of Entrepreneurship and Innovation*, *23*(2), 144–150. https://doi.org/10.1177/14657503221092969

Zhao, L., & Kim, K. (2021). Responding to the COVID-19 pandemic: Practices and strategies of the global clothing and textile value chain. *Clothing and Textiles Research Journal*, *39*(2), 157–172. https://doi.org/10.1177/0887302x21994207

9 Managing a Legitimacy Crisis

Airline Sensemaking in the Context of Flight Shame

Silvia Ravazzani, Carmen Daniela Maier and Irene Pollach

This chapter considers a wicked problem central for contemporary crisis communication: climate change, which is "the defining crisis of our time" (United Nations, n.d.). Due to its nature as a wicked problem, climate change can be characterized as complex, embedded in landscapes that change rapidly and unexpectedly, intertwined with social, political, and cultural differences across countries yet urgently requiring global and integrated responses (Sun & Yang, 2016). The airline industry has long been attributed at least partial responsibility for climate change due to emissions from airplanes as well as radiative forcing (Coles et al., 2014; Peeters et al., 2019). Since there are no alternatives to fuel-driven planes in the foreseeable future, the de-carbonization of the industry is next to impossible (Dunn, 2019). Consequently, the airline industry is increasingly stigmatized as a key contributor to global warming (Chiambaretto et al., 2021; Gössling et al., 2020). Given that COVID-19 has led to disastrous economic losses for the aviation industry, airline companies find themselves in the paradoxical crisis that they urgently need to encourage people to fly again to bring back their business, while having to deal with the blame for climate change.

Consumers' concerns over air travel culminated in the coinage of the term "flight shame", which emerged in Sweden around 2018 and has become recognized as "an individual's uneasiness over engaging in consumption that is energy-intense and climatically problematic" (Gössling et al., 2020, p. 1), which translates into perceiving air travel as environmentally harmful and socially undesirable (Extrakt, 2018). Airlines have responded to this legitimacy crisis by arguing that flying is a necessary and valuable service function as well as the safest way of travel (Walker, 2019). Low-fare airlines have always been under attack, being accused of encouraging unnecessary travel (Mann, 2004), which these airlines tend to counter by arguing that they offer "more socially equitable travel" (Coles et al., 2014, p. 71). As a more passive response, green advertising by airlines has become common, suggesting to travellers that the airlines' environmental performance is satisfactory (Neureiter & Matthes, 2023).

DOI: 10.4324/9781003375296-11

Against this backdrop, this chapter studies airline communication from a crisis communication perspective. Specifically, it *explores the discursive strategies adopted by airline companies when engaging in processes of crisis sensemaking and in the context of "flight shame" on social media.* It presents a framework suitable for the investigation of how generative sensemaking (Höllerer et al., 2018; Weber & Glynn, 2006) and interpretive sense-giving (Höllerer et al., 2018; Smerek, 2011) processes get materialized in corporate crisis communications. Such a framework is concretely showcased through the systematic and in-depth discourse analysis of social media content posted by the airline company Ryanair in the period 2020–2022. This allows, from a corporate perspective, to extrapolate the discursive strategies adopted by the company when engaging in processes of crisis sensemaking and sense-giving around "flight shame" on social media. The sensemaking perspective was chosen over other possible theoretical underpinnings, such as discursive legitimation (Vaara et al., 2006), impression management (Elsbach et al., 1998) or guilt management (Pollach et al., 2022), because of its focus on meaning-making processes and subsequent discursive constructions as well as its considerable impact on crisis research (Maitlis & Sonenshein, 2010). The main novelty of this work derives from adopting a methodological approach like discourse analysis which is an alternative to more common quantitative and qualitative content analyses in crisis communication research (Dunn & Eble, 2015). The chapter also includes implications for both scholarship and practice as well as future research prospects.

Literature Review

This section will first present relevant previous research on the topic of flight shame before it reviews the literature on discursive sensemaking and sense-giving as the theoretical foundation for the empirical study.

Previous Research on Flight Shame

Previous research has investigated how consumers deal with, react to, and promote flight shame. First, experiments have been used to study how and when people experience flight shame. Specifically, Doran et al. (2022) found that perceived moral obligations are a driver of feelings of flight shame. Neureiter and Matthes (2023) studied whether green advertising can reduce feelings of flight shame, but were not able to prove such an effect. Further, surveys have been used to gauge people's feelings towards and behavioural responses to the environmental impact of aviation. This stream of research includes Chiambaretto et al.'s (2021) study on "carbon literacy", which found that people overestimate the carbon emissions attributable to air travel. They view this lack of knowledge as a causal effect for the flight shame movement. Further, based on self-reported survey data, Gössling et al. (2020) report that people have not changed their travel behaviour significantly, but would be willing to accept market-based policy measures that increased the cost of flying. A third stream within consumer studies has drawn on social media data to study the implications of the flight shame movement. Mkono and Hughes (2022) used Reddit data to study how consumers resolve the tensions between their desire to travel and their awareness of the environmental impact of travelling. Becken et al. (2021) investigated the dissemination of the concept of "flight shame" and its Swedish equivalent "flygskam" on Twitter over time and geographies, starting in 2016.

Another strand of research has focused on airlines' communication efforts against the backdrop of climate change, yet without an explicit focus on flight shame. A content analysis of CSR reports of airlines found that airlines overemphasize their economic responsibilities relative to their environmental responsibilities (Yang et al., 2020). Further, a discourse analysis of airline websites has revealed that airlines present themselves as green by pointing to the possibility of carbon offset purchases and the potential for innovation in green fuels in the future (Burns & Cowlishaw, 2014). Coles et al. (2014) coupled their content analysis of CSR reports of low-fare airlines with interviews with managers in an integrated study of how airlines address sustainability demands, finding that their CSR communication is very fragmented and distributed over multiple channels. Against this backdrop, this chapter delves into the "flight shame" phenomenon and airline responses from a crisis communication perspective since this is an under-researched area. Specifically, this chapter adopts discursive crisis sensemaking and sense-giving as its theoretical foundation to shed light on flight shame from a corporate perspective and supplement previous research on consumer responses to flight shame as well as research on the CSR communication of airlines.

Crisis Sensemaking

Since the publication of Weick's (1995) seminal work "Sensemaking in Organizations", sensemaking and sense-giving have been articulated in many ways while being researched across multiple disciplines (e.g., organization studies, management, communication) and contexts (e.g., newcomer leaders, organizational change, news media discourse). Scholars highlight how research on these two concepts has grown varied and fragmented over time (Maitlis & Christianson, 2014) as well as how sensemaking and sense-giving are indeed difficult to split up. Höllerer et al. (2018) regard them as "intertwined processes" (p. 618) and Rouleau (2005) as "two sides of the same coin – one implies the other and cannot exist without it" (p. 1415).

Sensemaking and sense-giving, while being closely related, focus on different aspects of the meaning-making process. Sensemaking is considered both a retrospective process (Smerek, 2011) where people attribute meaning through "labeling and categorizing to stabilize the streaming of experience" (Weick et al.,

2005, p. 411) and a prospective process (Maitlis & Christianson, 2014) where people form expectations about how the future will unfold. While reducing uncertainty, sensemaking is also seen as a generative process that creates new objects of knowledge (Höllerer et al., 2018; Weber & Glynn, 2006). Sense-giving instead is conceived as an interpretative process through which people "attempt to intentionally alter how people attribute meaning, with no assurance that the intended meaning is adopted" (Smerek, 2011, p. 81). Therefore, sense-giving is about the intentional attempts made to establish an alternate or desired interpretation and persuade target audiences (Höllerer et al., 2018; Maitlis & Christianson, 2014; Maitlis & Sonenshein, 2010).

Sensemaking and sense-giving are key processes in crisis communication. Again, Weick's (1988, 1995) sensemaking work has powerfully inspired the crisis research field in thinking very differently about crises (for a comprehensive review, see Maitlis & Sonenshein, 2010). A crisis inherently yields disorientation and ambiguity, which requires sensemaking to clarify what is going on and sense-giving to communicate about the crisis, guide interpretations and gain support (Coombs, 2015; Kim, 2018; Maitlis & Christianson, 2014).

Recent research shows the richness of foci and perspectives in uncovering the role and mechanisms of sensemaking and sense-giving in crisis situations. For example, Stieglitz et al. (2018) stressed the critical role of social media to facilitate collective crisis sensemaking and fill in the possible information vacuum left by official channels or mainstream media. Kim (2018) considered sensemaking and sense-giving in connection to the employee communication behaviours of actively seeking out organization-related information (sensemaking) and disseminating it (sense-giving) to influence the meaning construction of internal and external constituencies. Höllerer et al. (2018) scrutinized the global financial crisis communication by business news media highlighting their double role as crisis sensemakers and sense-givers in constructing a public arena that gives visibility to multiple actors and their own crisis meaning-making strategies. More recently, Cuevas Shaw (2021) examined the scholarly communications community's public-facing communications in response to the pandemic based on both sensemaking (e.g., in relation to the crisis and the actors' role in it) as well as sense-giving (e.g., in relation to how this crisis work should be carried out) discursive strategies. While Yeomans and Bowman (2021), again in the context of the COVID-19 health crisis, focused on university leaders' employee-focused sense-giving narratives.

In this chapter, we adhere to the understanding of sensemaking as the generative process (Höllerer et al., 2018; Weber & Glynn, 2006) by which meaning is socially constructed through communication. As for sense-giving, we follow its conceptualization as an interpretive process (Höllerer et al., 2018; Smerek, 2011) by which others' sensemaking or meaning construction is influenced towards a preferred understanding of reality. As both processes are closely related to narratives and discursive constructions (Höllerer et al., 2018;

Maitlis & Christianson, 2014) and crises as such are the embodiment of rhetorical problems (Heath & Millar, 2004), we look at crisis sensemaking and sensegiving from a discursive perspective, which enables us to scrutinize in detail how they get materialized in crisis communication. Additionally, we also acknowledge the critical role played by the two processes in the early stages of the objectification of novel ideas and practices (Höllerer et al., 2018) and therefore decided to focus on the recently raised issue of flight shame and the related legitimacy crisis for the airline industry.

Methodological Framework

We conducted our analysis in the form of a case study of Ryanair, whose business model as a low-cost carrier is particularly challenged by climate change concerns. On its corporate website (Ryanair, 2023a), the company showcases its sustainability efforts by detailing its programme for decarbonization and net-zero emissions by 2050 that aligns to the Paris Agreement, the UN Sustainable Development Goals and the aviation industry's Destination 2050. To sustain its claim of representing "the greenest and cleanest airline in Europe" (Ryanair, 2023a), it also reports current data about its ESG ratings, the amount of investment in greener aircraft, as well as carbon emissions data on a monthly basis since January 2021 (Ryanair, 2023b). Public recognition of such efforts has been documented in 2021 and 2022 by CDP, one of the largest and independent environmental reporting and ranking no profit organizations, with a "B" rating assigned to the company on climate protection (CDP, 2023).

The basis of our qualitative research design are the data units selected for this analytical work: Ryanair's 37 Facebook posts and 33 Twitter posts appearing during 2019, 2020 and 2021. The selection of the posts has been made by employing a series of key terms: *flight shame, crisis, sustainable/sustainability, responsibility, climate/climate change, environment/environmental, CO2/carbon/ emissions*, and *green*. The overarching theme is the promotion of a company involved in a wide range of sustainability-related activities and keen on improving not only their relations with their customers and the flight industry, but also the whole global environmental situation.

Gee's work on discourse and discourse analysis (e.g., 2008, 2011, 2017) has been chosen for informing the present analytical work. Gee provides a series of discourse definitions from "stretches of language which 'hang together' to make sense to some community of people" (Gee, 2008, p. 115) to "the design of language-in-use" (Gee, 2008, p. 119), and considers that discourse analysis is primarily "the study of language-in-use" (Gee, 2011, p. 8). His understanding of discourse and discursive work is based on the idea that through language we can create or build things in particular ways in seven interrelated areas of "reality": *significance, activities* (*practices*), *identities, relationships, connections, politics*, and *sign systems and knowledge* (Gee, 2011). From Gee's perspective, the task of discourse analysts is to uncover the strategic representation of these seven areas of "reality" by asking specific questions about each of them. Even though Gee (2011) notes that such an analysis does typically not focus on the whole picture, we started analysing all seven building tasks of language to open the enquiry. However, at the end of the first stage of the analysis, it became clear that only the first five tasks had a central relevance for the proposed research focus. According to Gee, when *significance* is explored, the analysis is focused on how specific things – from institutions to problems – are rendered significant or not to signal their relevance in a certain context. The investigation of *activities* (*practices*) implies uncovering what activities (practices) are institutionally or culturally supported and socially recognized as going on in a certain context. Analysing *identities* contributes to explaining what and how specific types of identities are attributed to people involved in specific situations. *relationships* are analysed to clarify what social relationships with other people and/or other institutions are signalled as being consequential. Finally, the relevance of one thing to another (be it an institution or a past, present, and future issue) is explained by focusing on *connections*.

In the first part of the analysis, we focused on mapping the discursive building tasks that are accomplished for promoting the image of sustainable company in each of the selected data units. During the 2nd stage of the analysis, at the level of each discursive building task, we discerned the sensemaking and sense-giving processes through which the respective task was accomplished. For discerning the sensemaking and sense-giving processes, we adopted the understanding of these terms provided by Weber and Glynn (2006) and Smerek (2011). More specifically, Weber and Glynn (2006) take into consideration the generative aspect of sensemaking, arguing that "institutions are part of sensemaking because they shape signification (meaning making) via interpretation and communication" (p. 1643), and that the institutional context is an essential part of sensemaking. This understanding of institutional sensemaking is relevant for the present study because the crisis context in which Ryanair is forced to communicate determines the sensemaking processes that are selected when accomplishing the discursive building tasks. Sensemaking also complements Gee's perspective, who considers that "to understand sense-making in language it is necessary to understand the ways in which language is embedded in society and social institutions" (2008, p. 115). As far as sense-giving is concerned, we adopted Smerek's interpretative understanding of this term, as he highlights the fact that "if sensemaking is about how people come to construct meaning, then sense-giving is *intentionally* trying to influence how other people attribute meaning" (2011, p. 81). Sense-giving therefore also complements Gee's perspective when looking at language as an instrument to build and present things in particular ways. As Cuevas Shaw (2021), by coupling Gee's discursive building tasks with these understandings of sensemaking and sense-giving processes, we have been able to perform the proposed discourse analysis and to elaborate on the existing terms of sensemaking and sense-giving.

Analysis

In what follows, we structure our findings related to the five discursive building tasks into three topics, viz. the discursive building of a green identity, of sustainable activities and their significance, and of relationships and connections. We further illustrate how sensemaking and sense-giving processes are materialized in Ryanair's social media communication. In relation to each building task identified, we explain how sensemaking and sense-giving are employed by the company to implicitly negotiate the contemporary flight shame crisis that has marked the whole aviation industry due to global climate change. Although the findings related to the discursive building tasks are separated in the following explanations, many posts accomplish several tasks simultaneously despite their brevity. Accordingly, all the building tasks constitute an interrelated network "within which each of the components or aspects simultaneously gives meaning to all the others and get meaning from them" (Gee, 2008, p. 102).

Building a Green Identity

During the first stage of the analysis, our focus has been on the identification of the sensemaking, and sense-giving processes involved in building a green corporate identity that is based on exceptional sustainability expertise and, consequently, on environmental leadership.

A series of sensemaking and sense-giving processes are used to select specific aspects of the company's identity which is built on such sustainability expertise that also confers them a leadership status as far as the environmental protection is concerned. This green identity is enacted not only at the company level, but also at the level of its management and products. In many social media posts, the sensemaking processes intertwine these levels through strategic discursive selections. For example:

> *We are delighted to launch the Ryanair Sustainable Aviation Research Centre in partnership with Trinity College Dublin. Thomas Fowler, Director of Sustainability discusses how this exciting new initiative will help support research around Sustainable Aviation Fuels, Zero Carbon Aircraft Propulsion System and Noise Mapping.*
>
> (Ryanair, 29 April 2021)

When this expertise-based identity meant to elevate the status of the company's sustainability efforts is built through sensemaking processes at the product level, the same intertwining strategy is employed. However, in this case, the environmental leadership status is also highlighted as being part of the green corporate identity: *The brand-new Boeing 737–8200 "Gamechanger" will further enhance Malta Air and the Ryanair Group's environmental leadership* (Ryanair, 28 July 2021). In these examples, sensemaking is accompanied by sense-giving as the future is also envisaged. Consequently, these processes contribute to reassuring the customers that this green corporate identity will be preserved and, presumably, also strengthened beyond the present crisis.

The focus on reassuring the customers about the validity of this green corporate identity is also evident though a plethora of sense-giving processes that are employed in rhetorical questions and answers such as:

> *Did you know Ryanair is the greenest way to fly? As Europe's largest airline, we are aware that we have an important responsibility, and we are fully committed to leading the way to a green, decarbonized future. Here is how.*
>
> (Ryanair, 12 May 2021)

Sense-giving can also be detected when the customers are addressed through imperatives meant both to convince them about this green corporate identity and to bring them closer to the company: *As Europe's most environmentally efficient major airline, we're committed to making travel more sustainable. Try our new Carbon Calculator and Fly Greener today!* (Ryanair, 30 July 2021). All the sense-giving processes that are involved in building this green corporate identity are usually based on superlative adjectives such as above. Involving the present and prospective customers in their sustainability-related activities while building their green corporate identity is also supposed to have a beneficial effect on the customers' identity as sustainable individuals. Conclusively, the company projects itself discursively as *Europe's greenest major airline* (Ryanair, 5 September 2019) that has nothing to be ashamed of and neither do their customers. Consequently, the company implicitly invalidates flight shame and its consequences by discursively implying that there are only reasons to be proud of both for the company and its customers.

Building Sustainable Activities and their Significance

As the findings suggest, sensemaking and sense-giving processes employed during the crisis are meant to discursively build a corporate green identity at three levels – at the company, the management, and the product level. Simultaneously, multiple sensemaking and sense-giving processes are also meant to build the network of the company's sustainable activities that are related to sustainable aviation practices, sustainable aviation research and initiatives for global environmental protection.

In this regard, the significance of their sustainable activities is established by using sensemaking and sense-giving processes that build and nuance a wider range of activities meant to enhance the sustainable image of the company. For example, sensemaking is employed to highlight the company's involvement in repairing activities related to environmental sustainability even if they have not been the direct culprits. For example:

> *Back in 2018, the Monique area of the Algarve was destroyed by wildfires. Today, we presented a check for €250,000 to plant thousands of new trees in the area – as part of our Carbon Offset Initiative funded by customers.*
>
> (Ryanair, 22 October 2019)

Once again, by drawing customers in as "helpers", the company succeeds to empower them, transforming them from passive fliers to active sustainability enablers. Thus, they eliminate also in this way the possibility of experiencing flight shame. Furthermore, the significance of the corporate involvement in supporting activities related to sustainability even if these are not related to aviation practices is also built through intertwined sensemaking and sense-giving:

> *Meet our partner First Climate. We've worked together since 2019 supporting Uganda Cookstove Project, which distributes efficient cookstoves to households in the Kampala region.*
>
> (Ryanair, 19 May 2021)

More sense-giving processes are also discernible here as a sense of temporality and numbers are provided to emphasize the extent and impact of this corporate endeavour. When temporality and exceptional efforts are emphasized, they can be seen as an attempt to influence the customers' perceptions through sense-giving processes that pinpoint the ongoing character of the company's efforts. Thus, the significance of their sustainable activities is built through such sense-giving processes amplifying this ongoing aspect. Furthermore, in the first example, by mentioning the customers' role in bringing to life this initiative, the distance between company and customers is once again minimized.

Finally, the significance of their activities is also generated through sensemaking and sense-giving processes meant to highlight their usage of both scientific methods for proving the sustainability of their practices, and of transparency methods for recurrently defending it. Both sensemaking and sense-giving build the significance of their sustainable flight practices based on constant scientific methods:

> *Our carbon offset calculator allows passengers to fully offset their flight emissions in one simple click. These carbon contributions help to fund carbon offset projects in Europe and Africa.*
>
> (Ryanair, 14 August 2021)

The significance of their transparent methods employed for defending the sustainability of their aviation practices is built through sensemaking and sense-giving processes meant to evaluatively underline their recurrency:

> *CO2 per passenger/km is the most transparent way to accurately measure every airline operating in Europe. We'll publish our monthly CO2 emissions to show our environmental commitment and call on all other EU airlines to do the same.*
>
> (Ryanair, 5 June 2019)

By building an extended range of recurrent sustainability-related activities and their significance through strategic sensemaking and sense-giving, the company seeks to demonstrate discursively the extent and relevance of everything they do, not only for themselves but also for their customers, the airline industry and ultimately the whole world.

Building Relationships and Connections

The building of the green corporate identity and of sustainability-related activities is discursively assisted by sensemaking and sense-giving performed by the company to clarify the relationships and connections that contribute to this corporate greening. Apart from the relationships established with prestigious universities meant to elevate the company's sustainable status (see above Ryanair, 29 April 2021), the company has relationships with other European aviation companies and environmental partners. Based on these relationships, several connections are also discursively established through sensemaking and sense-giving: between the company's sustainable goals and research funding, between the company's initiatives and various geodemographic contexts, between the company's sustainable projects and their donating customers, and between the company's sustainability commitment and the carbon neutral future. The discursive building of such relationships and connections is meant to improve the company's sustainable image and to clarify their pro-collaboration attitude when it comes to sustainable initiatives.

The sense-giving processes accompanying the sensemaking processes involved in the discursive building of sustainability-related relationships and connections are characterized by repeated displays of positive emotions such as:

> *We are delighted to join the "Fuelling Flight Initiative" in our pledge to support Sustainable Aviation Fuels for a carbon neutral future* (Ryanair, 3 March 2021), or *For Biodiversity Day, we joined The Native Woodland Trust (...) and we're proud to support them on their mission.*
>
> (Ryanair, 22 May 2019)

The choice of continuous form for the verbs is also a characteristic of sense-giving because by highlighting the ongoing character of the relationship with environmental organizations, the company forces the reader to reconsider the flight shame issue:

> *Happy #EarthDay2021. The 2018 wildfire left the region of Serra de Monchique in Portugal devastated. Over the last two years, we've been working with our environmental partner GEOTA* (link) *to restore the area and support the local community by planting over 135,000 trees.*
>
> (Ryanair, 22 April 2021)

In this example, a sensemaking process also establishes a connection between a natural disaster and the company to highlight the relevance of their activity in a specific geodemographic context.

Through sensemaking and sense-giving, the connection between the company's sustainable projects and their donating customers is also discursively built once again:

> *Next time you're flying with us offset the carbon cost of your flight through our voluntary offset scheme at the end of the booking process. By donating just €2 you can support causes like our environmental partner First Climate's cookstove project in Uganda.*
>
> (Ryanair, 26 August 2020)

Implicitly, the company accomplishes this building task through a sensemaking process that implies not only an obvious connection but also an indispensable connection that has an impact on the customers' sense of responsibility and flight shame too. As in the case of the other building tasks accomplished discursively in the selected data (i.e., the discursive building of the green identity and of sustainability-related activities), the recurrent presence of the customers in the sustainable relationships and connections is strategically capitalized on. By discursively using the customers when accomplishing these building tasks, the company succeeds to construe recurrent situations that cannot relate to the flight shame crisis either by the present or prospective customers.

In conclusion, the sensemaking and sense-giving processes that are materialized through the accomplishment of the discursive building tasks are used to produce and reproduce the image of a sustainable company with a green corporate identity, involved in a wide range of sustainability-related activities, and supported by a sustainable network of relationships and connections that is supposed to elevate Ryanair above the current flight shame crisis.

Table 9.1 provides an overview of the sensemaking and sense-giving processes materialized through the accomplishment of the discursive building tasks.

Conclusions

According to our findings, although Ryanair never mentions flight shame in their social media posts, they implicitly try to deter the amplification of this crisis by using a series of sensemaking and sense-giving processes for the

Table 9.1 Sensemaking and sense-giving processes materialized through the accomplishment of discursive building tasks

Discursive building tasks	*Cognitive processes materialized through the accomplishment of the discursive building tasks*	
	Sensemaking processes	*Sense-giving processes*
Identities	Green expertise-based identity of company, management, and products	Emphasis on the future Rhetorical questions and imperatives
Activities	Sustainable business practice Sustainability-related research Initiatives for global environmental protection	Emphasis on the impact of the company's sustainable activities by providing numbers and evaluations
Significance	Involvement in repairing activities related to environmental sustainability when they haven't been the culprits Involvement in supporting activities related to environmental sustainability even if unrelated to their own practices	Emphasis on the ongoing character of the company's repairing and supporting sustainable activities
	Usage of scientific methods for proving the sustainability of their practices	Evaluations suggesting the excellence of their scientific methods
	Usage of transparency methods for recurrently defending the sustainability of their practices	Evaluations suggesting the leading role of the company in transparently communicating about their environmental impact
Relationships	Relationships with environmental partners	Emphasis on the ongoing character of partnership activities
	Relationships with sustainable European industry peers	Expression of positive emotions and evaluations of the relationship
	Relationships with universities	Evaluations suggesting the impact of the relationship
Connections	Connection between the company's initiatives and various geodemographic contexts	Expression of positive emotions and evaluations of the relationship
	Connection between the company's sustainable goals and research funding	Emphasis on the connection's relevance for sustainable practice through numbers
	Connection between the company's sustainability commitment and the carbon neutral future	Emphasis on the connection's relevance for sustainable projects through numbers
	Connection between the company's sustainable projects and their donating customers	Emphasis on the connection's relevance for sustainable practice through numbers and evaluations

discursive building of a green corporate identity, of sustainable activities and their significance, and of respectable relationships and connections. By discursively highlighting exceptional sustainability expertise and environmental leadership as fundamental characteristics of the company's green identity, a potential flight shame stance is cancelled out. Similarly, when sustainable aviation practices, sustainable aviation research, and initiatives for global environmental protection are in focus, the rationality of flight shame is undermined. Finally, the company's continuous involvement in a sustainable network of multiple relationships and connections is discursively built to both strengthen their legitimacy and share responsibility. Taken all together, these discursive selections in Ryanair's social media communication contribute to downplay the threat of the flight shame crisis while minimizing their distance from (environmentally concerned) customers and instead presenting the company as active protagonist of the climate change fight.

Taking into consideration the fact that the flight shame crisis is an ongoing legitimacy crisis, these findings can offer implications both for scholars and practitioners. As scholars need to accelerate their research input and take into consideration new methodological frameworks to keep track of any crisis' rapid developments, such a study can be a relevant example of readdressing qualitative approaches to discourse analysis through the lens of crisis sensemaking and sense-giving processes. Practitioners can also employ the perspective of this study as a useful resource when they are involved in crisis communication. They can adjust their communicative strategies by taking into consideration how sensemaking and sense-giving can discursively shift the attention of audiences and create new centres of interest. Whether and how organizations should employ the described discursive strategies meant to deter flight shame (and in general sustainability issues) on social media remains an ethical decision to be made with organization- and context-specific sensitivity.

This chapter provides a rigorous discourse analysis of the communication strategies adopted by an airline company when engaging in processes of crisis sensemaking and sense-giving for deterring flight shame on social media. The novelty of this research approach resides in the application of Gee's framework to the discourse analysis of crisis sensemaking and sense-giving processes in corporate social media communication. Complementing Gee's perspective with crisis sensemaking and sense-giving proved highly valuable for a systematic analysis of language used as a strategic instrument in corporate crisis communication to shape reality and influence interpretations in particular ways.

Based on this work, other potential research avenues can be opened by extending the number of companies or/and data choices. New data can include other semiotic modes than text such as still and moving images. This model of addressing the discursive strategies meant to deter flight shame can be adopted when approaching other types of ongoing crises too.

References

Becken, S., Friedl, H., Stantic, B., Connolly, R. M., & Chen, J. (2021). Climate crisis and flying: Social media analysis traces the rise of "flightshame". *Journal of Sustainable Tourism*, *29*(9), 1450–1469. https://doi.org/10.1080/09669582.2020.1851699

Burns, P. M., & Cowlishaw, C. (2014). Climate change discourses: How UK airlines communicate their case to the public. *Journal of Sustainable Tourism*, *22*(5), 750–767. https://doi.org/10.1080/09669582.2014.884101

CDP (2023). *Data and insights*. https://www.cdp.net/en/responses?queries%5Bname%5D=ryanair

Chiambaretto, P., Mayenc; E., Chappert, H., Engsig, J., Fernandez, A. -S., & Le Roy, F. (2021). Where does flygskam come from? The role of citizens' lack of knowledge of the environmental impact of air transport in explaining the development of flight shame. *Journal of Air Transport Management*, *93*, 102049. https://doi.org/10.1016/j.jairtraman.2021.102049

Coles, T., Fenclova, E., & Dinan, C. (2014). Corporate social responsibility reporting among European low-fares airlines: Challenges for the examination and development of sustainable mobilities. *Journal of Sustainable Tourism*, *22*(1), 69–88. https://doi.org/10.1080/09669582.2013.790391

Coombs, W.T. (2015). *Ongoing crisis communication: Planning, managing, and responding* (4th ed.). Sage Publications.

Cuevas Shaw, L. (2021). From sensemaking to sensegiving: A discourse analysis of the scholarly communications community's public response to the global pandemic. *Learned Publishing*, *34*, 6–16. https://doi.org/10.1002/leap.1350

Doran, R., Pallesen, S., Böhm, G., & Ogunbode, C. A. (2022). When and why do people experience flight shame? *Annals of Tourism Research*, *92*, 103254. https://doi.org/10.1016/j.annals.2021.103254

Dunn, C., & Eble, M. (2015). Giving voice to the silenced: Using critical discourse analysis to inform crisis communication theory. *Journal of Business Ethics*, *132*(4), 717–735. https://doi.org/10.1007/s10551-014-2315-4.

Dunn, K. (2019, November 18). *Flight shame is 'Our biggest challenge,' air france CEO Says*. Fortune. https://fortune.com/2019/11/18/flight-shame-air-france-anne-regail/

Elsbach, K. D., Sutton, R. I., & Principe, K. E. (1998). Averting expected challenges through anticipatory impression management: A study of hospital billing. *Organization Science*, *9*, 68–86.

Extrakt (2018, June 1). *Flygskam minskar inte resandet*. https://www.extrakt.se/flygskam-minskar-inte-resandet/

Gee, J. P. (2008). *Social linguistics and literacies. Ideology in discourses*. Routledge.

Gee, J. P. (2011). *An introduction to discourse analysis. Theory and method*. Routledge.

Gee, J. P. (2017). *Introducing discourse analysis. From grammar to society*. Routledge.

Gössling, S., Humpe, A., & Bausch, T. (2020). Does 'flight shame' affect social norms? Changing perspectives on the desirability of air travel in Germany. *Journal of Cleaner Production*, *266*, 122015. https://doi.org/10.1016/j.jclepro.2020.122015

Heath, R. L., & Millar, D. P. (2004). A rhetorical approach to crisis communications: Management, communication processes, and strategic responses. In R. L. Heath & D. P. Millar (Eds.), *Responding to crisis: A rhetorical approach to crisis communication* (pp. 1–17). Routledge.

Höllerer, M. A., Jancsary, D., & Grafström, M. (2018). 'A picture is worth a thousand words': Multimodal sensemaking of the global financial crisis. *Organization Studies, 39*(5–6), 617–644. https://doi.org/10.1177/0170840618765019

Kim, Y. (2018). Enhancing employee communication behaviors for sensemaking and sensegiving in crisis situations: Strategic management approach for effective internal crisis communication. *Journal of Communication Management, 22*(4), 451–475. https://doi.org/10.1108/JCOM-03-2018-0025

Maitlis, S., & Christianson, M. (2014). Sensemaking in organizations: Taking stock and moving forward. *The Academy of Management Annals, 8*, 57–125, https://doi.org/10.5465/19416520.2014.873177

Maitlis, S., & Sonenshein, S. (2010). Sensemaking in crisis and change: Inspiration and insights from Weick (1988). *Journal of Management Studies, 47*, 551–580. https://doi.org/10.1111/j.1467-6486.2010.00908.x

Mann, D. (2004). *Calls to control low-cost flights*. BBC. http://news.bbc.co.uk/2/hi/science/nature/3625931.stm

Mkono, M., & Hughes, K. (2022). Sustainability paralysis in travel consumption: A Reddit study. *Tourism and Hospitality Research*. https://doi.org/10.1177/14673584221110370

Neureiter, A., & Matthes, J. (2023). Comparing the effects of greenwashing claims in environmental airline advertising: Perceived greenwashing, brand evaluation, and flight shame. *International Journal of Advertising, 42*(3), 461–487. https://doi.org/10.1080/02650487.2022.2076510

Peeters, P., Bouwer, J., Bongaerts, R., & Eijgelaar, E. (2019). Airlines and corporate responsibility: Issues and challenges. In D. Lund-Durlacher, V. Dinica, D. Reiser, & M. S. Fifka (Eds.), *Corporate sustainability and responsibility in tourism* (pp. 163–180). Springer.

Pollach, I., Ravazzani, S., & Maier, C. D. (2022). Organizational guilt management. *Group & Organization Management, 47*(3), 487–529.

Rouleau, L. (2005). Micro-practices of strategic sensemaking and sensegiving: How middle managers interpret and sell change every day. *Journal of Management Studies*, 42, 1413–1441. https://doi.org/10.1111/j.1467–6486.2005.00549.x

Ryanair (2019). *For biodiversity day, we joined the native woodland trust* [Embedded video]. Facebook.

Ryanair (2019). *CO2 per passenger/km is the most transparent way to accurately measure every airline operating in Europe* [Attached image]. Twitter.

Ryanair (2019). *We're Europe's greenest major airline* [Attached image and link to corporate website]. Facebook.

Ryanair (2019). *Back in 2018, the Monique area of the Algarve was destroyed by wildfires.* [Attached image and link to corporate website]. Facebook.

Ryanair (2020). *Next time you're flying with us offset the carbon cost of your flight* [Attached image and link to project website]. Facebook.

Ryanair (2021). *We are delighted to join the 'Fuelling Flight Initiative' in our pledge to support Sustainable Aviation Fuels* [Attached image and link to corporate website]. Facebook.

Ryanair (2021). *Happy #EarthDay2021* [Embedded video]. Facebook.

Ryanair (2021). *We are delighted to launch the Ryanair Sustainable Research Centre* [Embedded video]. Facebook & Twitter.

Ryanair (2021). *Did you know Ryanair is the greenest way to fly?* [Attached image and link to corporate website]. Facebook & Twitter.

Ryanair (2021). *Meet our partner First Climate* [Embedded video]. Facebook.

Ryanair (2021, July 28). *The brand-new Boeing 737–8200 "Gamechanger" will further enhance Malta Air and the Ryanair Group's environmental leadership* [Attached image and link to corporate website]. Facebook & Twitter.

Ryanair (2021). *As Europe's most environmentally efficient major airline, we're committed to making travel more sustainable* [Attached image and link to corporate website]. Facebook.

Ryanair (2021). *Our carbon offset calculator allows passengers to fully offset their flight omissions* [Embedded video]. Facebook.

Ryanair (2023a). *Sustainability*. https://corporate.ryanair.com/sustainability/

Ryanair (2023b). *Our Emissions*. https://corporate.ryanair.com/facts-figures/our-emissions/

Smerek, R. (2011). Sensemaking and sensegiving: An exploratory study of the simultaneous "being and learning" of new college and university presidents. *Journal of Leadership & Organizational Studies*, *18*(1), 80–94. https://doi.org/10.1177/1548051810384268

Stieglitz, S., Mirbabaie, M., & Milde, M. (2018). Social positions and collective sense-making in crisis communication. *International Journal of Human–Computer Interaction*, *34*(4), 328–355. https://doi.org/10.1080/10447318.2018.1427830

Sun, J., & Yang, K. (2016). The wicked problem of climate change: A new approach based on social mess and fragmentation. *Sustainability*, *8*, 1312. https://doi.org/10.3390/su8121312

United Nations (n.d.). *The climate crisis – A race we can win*. Retrieved June 15, 2020, from https://www.un.org/en/un75/climate-crisis-race-we-can-win

Vaara, E., Tienari, J., & Laurila, J. (2006). Pulp and paper fiction: On the discursive legitimation of global industrial restructuring. *Organization Studies*, *27*(6), 789–810.

Walker, K. (2019, July/August). There's no shame in buying a flight ticket. *Transportation World*. https://aviationweek.com/air-transport/safety-ops-regulation/editorial-theres-no-shame-buying-flight-ticket

Weber, K., & Glynn, M. A. (2006). Making sense with institutions: Context, thought and action in Karl Weick's theory. *Organization Studies*, *27*(11), 1639–1660. https://doi.org/10.1177/0170840606068343

Weick, K. E. (1988). Enacted sensemaking in crisis situations. *Journal of Management Studies*, *25*, 305–17. https://doi.org/10.1111/j.1467-6486.1988.tb00039.x

Weick, K. E. (1995). *Sensemaking in organizations*. Sage Publications.

Weick, K. E., Sutcliffe, K. M., & Obstfeld, D. (2005). Organizing and the process of sensemaking. *Organization Science*, *16*(4), 409–421. https://doi.org/10.1287/orsc.1050.0133

Yang, L., Ngai, C. S. B., & Lu, W. (2020). Changing trends of corporate social responsibility reporting in the world-leading airlines. *PLoS One*, *15*(6), e0234258. https://doi.org/10.1371/journal.pone.0234258

Yeomans, L., & Bowman, S. (2021). Internal crisis communication and the social construction of emotion: University leaders' sensegiving discourse during the COVID-19 pandemic. *Journal of Communication Management*, *25*(3), 196–213. https://doi.org/10.1108/JCOM-11-2020-0130

Part 2

Lessons Learned from COVID-19 for Risk and Crisis Communication in Europe

10 Translating Research to Practice

Identifying Best Practice in Pandemic Communication

Audra Diers-Lawson

The COVID-19 pandemic has been very different from previous pandemics (e.g., Zika, Ebola, H_1N_1, or MERS) because of the magnitude of its effects on all aspects of government, business, and everyday lives. Though it has only been about three years since the beginning of the pandemic, there has already been a global effort to understand the pandemic with well over 125,000 of scientific articles and reports published (Fraser et al., 2021) with national and cross-national comparisons of COVID-19 experiences and policies from Asia (Azadeh et al., 2020; Dai et al., 2020; Nguyen et al., 2020), to Europe (Betsch et al., 2020; Breakwell & Jaspal, 2020; Meier et al., 2020), or the Americas (Bruine de Bruin & Bennett, 2020, Glenn et al., 2020). More specifically, in the context of pandemic communication, there has been a disproportionate amount of research focusing on the United States (US) (Diers-Lawson et al., 2021); however, the largely US-biased research does provide a benchmark for understanding national contexts where initial COVID-19 responses were relatively unsuccessful. Additionally, US-based research also reveals three important themes for consideration across national contexts

1 The documented emergence of the infodemic with rampant problems associated with misinformation, disinformation, and so-called 'fake news' limiting the adoption of self-protective behaviors (Balarabe & Kumar, 2020; Cheng & Luo, 2020).
2 The challenges in developing an effective government response and communication when the pandemic and its actors are politicized (Bruine de Bruin et al., 2020; Salvi et al., 2021).
3 The need to develop communication strategies that improve the public's willingness to adopt self-protective behaviors (Papageorge et al., 2021; Sun et al., 2020).

Aside from being US-centric, there is also little cohesive analysis comparing findings across cultures, research contexts, theories, and findings to provide guidance for theory building and practice. Before the pandemic was declared

DOI: 10.4324/9781003375296-13

as no longer a public health emergency, globally, public health organizations, researchers and governments were already beginning to reflect on the lessons learned during the acute stages of the pandemic in the first two or three waves to improve pandemic response, recognizing the increased importance of placing risk and crisis communication alongside medical interventions as mission-critical endeavors to respond to health crises (WHO, 2022). Therefore, the central objective of this piece is to translate emergent academic and public health research across Europe to: (1) provide a summary and cross-national comparison of scientific publications and institutional reports related to the COVID-19 pandemic between 2020 and 2022; (2) identify theoretically grounded best practices for research and practice; and (3) critically reflect on the importance of a stakeholder-contingency approach to risk and crisis communication. Europe provides an important cross-national set of comparisons because with approaching 800 million people in 44 countries it represents a diverse population, different types of governments, and different pandemic responses.

Research-Based Approaches to Document Analysis

In an analysis of the scholarly research on crisis communication from 1953 to 2015, Diers-Lawson (2020) found more than 100 different frameworks and theories had been applied to risk and crisis communication contexts. Though the common narrative about crisis communication often focuses on a very narrow and organization-centric set of theories, the reality is that risk and crisis communication frameworks span across disciplines like communication, management, public health, sociology, and social psychology. They also typically focus on one of three perspectives – the institution, the message, or the stakeholder. Frameworks focusing on the institution are predominantly interested in protecting or developing the institution's interest(s) and reputation. Those exploring risk and crisis messages highlight the construction of messages and message channels (e.g., social media, interpersonal interventions, mass media, etc.) that different types of groups find compelling enough to change behaviors. Finally, stakeholder-focused frameworks explore the convergence of situation, institution, and message. As such, the literature analyzing pandemic communication supports the need for an effective stakeholder relationship management framework (Diers-Lawson, et al., 2021). The stakeholder relationship management (SRM) framework (see Figure 10.1) focuses on the interactions between the institutions managing pandemics, citizen interests, and pandemic related issues that lead to self-protective behaviors being enacted. However, it also recognizes that these interactions occur within a complex multi-platform information environment (*e.g.,* social media, legacy media, and face-to-face communication) where there are often contradictory messages and different actors competing for citizen attention (Diers-Lawson, 2020). SRM, therefore, addresses both the complicated personal factors (e.g., political ideology or existing attitudes) in considering the citizen-related attitudes but also the broader organizational context, as well as how the relationships between institutions, citizens, and issues like COVID-19 are influenced by challenges like disinformation or the politicization of health issues (Diers-Lawson, 2020).

The SRM framework also complements traditional risk and crisis communication in practice, which considers three factors as a part of the communication strategy: the channel or platform for communication, the source of the message, and the message strategy (WHO, 2022). Message strategy categories analyzed across the European context were based on a theoretical review of primary crisis response strategies (Diers & Donohue, 2013). The instructive communication category is based on the IDEA model (Sellnow et al., 2017), which emerged after Diers and Donohue's (2013) analysis of crisis response categories and represents a meaningfully different message-response strategy. This analysis was then applied to each of the countries to summarize and evaluate available knowledge about best practices.

Additionally, within both public relations as well as risk and crisis communication, contingency approaches are increasingly favored for applying research to experience to improve the effectiveness of communication and engagement strategies (Cameron et al., 2001; Kulkarni, 2017; Pang et al., 2020). A contingency approach argues that rather than using a rigid theory that may not adequately apply across situations, using previous research to create a comprehensive list of factors influencing citizen behaviors and attitudes better allows researchers and practitioners to be more agile in designing and evaluating communication in complex situations, like COVID-19 (Diers-Lawson, et al., 2021). Diers-Lawson, et al., (2021) analysis of pandemic crisis response in Vietnam and the Republic of Korea provides a template for a contingency approach to analyzing risk and crisis communication strategy.

Pandemic Communication across Europe

Overall, in a review of the enacted risk and communication strategies across Europe, evidenced in the scientific and institutional reports, a cohesive set of themes and best practices emerge. This section highlights the overview of the findings, common themes for each of the countries analyzed, and factors influencing risk and crisis communication across the region. The analysis was taken in two stages. First, articles and reports addressing pandemic communication specifically were analyzed to identify different platforms, 'expert' sources used, and communication strategies applied to respond to COVID. Second, articles and reports analyzing any factors influencing citizen message acceptance and self-protective behaviors were analyzed using a contingency approach to evaluating the research (see Diers-Lawson et al., 2021).

Cross-National Comparisons of Platform, Source, and Strategy

This analysis provides a summary and cross-national comparison of scientific publications and institutional reports related to the COVID-19 pandemic between 2020 and 2022 in Europe. There were 236 publications and reports directly related to risk and crisis communication from Europe reviewed for this analysis. However, to provide a deeper country comparison, this analysis focuses on nine countries that represent the diverse population, governments, and pandemic responses across Europe including: Bulgaria, France, Germany, Hungary, Italy, Lithuania, the Netherlands, Portugal and Sweden using the search term 'COVID and communication <country>' in an exhaustive Google Scholar search as well as identifying English-language reports from the countries, WHO-Europe, and the EU. These countries were selected as part of the EU's COVID-19 review as exemplars of the diverse economies, geographies, and governments in the EU. Therefore, for each of the 100 different scientific articles and reports related to the nine countries compared for this document, the platform, source, and message strategy were analyzed (see Table 10.1 and Appendix A).

Bulgaria

There were no cross-national comparisons between Bulgaria and any other country identified in the 236 articles reviewed. Three common themes emerged in the analysis of Bulgaria's COVID-19 communication strategy:

- As a source of information, the Bulgarian government has a credibility gap attributable to citizen perceptions of governmental corruption (Popova & Valkov, 2022).
- Culturally relevant messaging – especially for minority communities like the Roma community – is essential for improving health outcomes in those communities (Kamburova & Georgieva, 2021).
- Digital communication integration is a critical innovation for community engagement (Todorova & Padareva-Ilieva, 2021).

France

National and cross-national analyses of the French government's response to the COVID-19 pandemic placed very little emphasis on the platforms used for communication; there was a much stronger focus on the institutional response and message features in the French communication environment with two common themes emerging:

- Evaluations of the French response demonstrated that while early recommendations were not adopted (Gagneux-Brunon et al., 2022) the strict measures that followed were clearly communicated to citizens and were more successful (OECD, 2021).

Table 10.1 Crisis communication strategies during the COVID-19 pandemic

Strategy Category	*Strategy*	*Description*	*Bulgaria*	*France*	*Germany*	*Hungary*	*Italy*	*Country Lithuania*	*Netherlands*	*Portugal*	*Sweden*
Platform	Face-to-Face	Interpersonal communication – direct interventions (e.g., health care settings)	✓ [1]						✓ [70, 72]		
	Legacy Media	Messages designed for traditional mass media channels via print or television media organizations	✓ [4]	✓ [7, 21]	✓ [26, 27, 28, 33, 34, 36]	✓ [44]	✓ [33, 34, 51]	✓ [61, 62, 66]	✓ [33, 34, 36, 68, 70, 71, 74]	✓ [77, 80, 82, 84]	✓ [28, 36]
	Digital Media	Messages designed & communicated on new media platforms (e.g., Facebook, Twitter, meeting platforms)	✓ [1, 3]		✓ [22, 23, 25, 26, 27, 28, 31, 33, 34, 35, 36, 37, 38, 39, 40, 41]	✓ [45, 46]	✓ [33, 34, 48, 54, 55, 59]	✓ [38, 65]	✓ [33, 34, 35, 36, 48, 68, 69, 70, 74]	✓ [37, 76, 78, 80, 82, 83, 84, 86, 91]	✓ [28, 35, 36, 59]
Source	Government	Inclusive of political government sources (e.g., local, regional, national elected leaders)	✓ [1, 2]	✓ [5, 6, 7, 13, 16, 19, 20, 21]	✓ [5, 16, 19, 20, 21, 26, 28, 29, 36, 37, 38]	✓ [21, 42, 43, 44, 46, 47]	✓ [5, 13, 16, 29, 49, 50, 51, 52, 53, 54, 55, 58]	✓ [13, 38, 63, 65]	✓ [5, 13, 36, 67, 68, 72, 74, 75]	✓ [36, 37, 53, 76, 78, 79, 83, 86, 89, 91]	✓ [13, 19, 20, 21, 28, 93, 94, 95, 96, 97, 98, 99]

(*Continued*)

Table 10.1 (Continued)

Strategy Category	*Strategy*	*Description*	*Bulgaria*	*France*	*Germany*	*Hungary*	*Italy*	*Country Lithuania*	*Netherlands*	*Portugal*	*Sweden*
	Public Health/ Science	Inclusive of all public health and science-related sources (e.g., health institutions, doctors, virologists, etc.)	✓[1, 2, 3]	✓[5, 13, 14, 15, 17, 20]	✓[17, 20, 26, 27, 28, 30, 39, 40]	✓[45, 46]	✓[5, 13, 17, 49, 52, 55, 56, 59]	✓[13, 64, 66]	✓[5, 13, 17, 68, 74]	✓[17, 80]	✓[13, 20, 28, 59, 92, 97, 100]
Message Strategy	Self-Enhancement	Brand-based communication, image promotion, image advertising related to the crisis	✓[4]	✓[5, 8, 9, 11, 16, 20]	✓[5, 11, 16, 20, 35]	✓[11, 47]	✓[5, 9, 11, 16, 58]	✓[9]	✓[5, 68]	✓[78, 83]	✓[11, 20]
	Routine Communication	Non-crisis specific contexts like daily information releases, parliamentary debates that address the crisis		✓[5, 11]	✓[5, 11, 37, 38, 40]	✓[11]	✓[5, 11, 49, 53, 58]	✓[38, 64, 65]	✓[5, 67, 71, 72]	✓[37, 53, 77, 89]	✓[11, 20, 96, 98]

Instructive Communication	Providing people with clear guidance (either voluntary or non-voluntary) to support self-protective behavior during crises.	✓ 1, 3	✓ 5, 6, 7, 9, 10, 11, 12, 13, 14, 15, 16, 17, 18, 19, 20, 21	✓ 5, 10, 11, 12, 16, 17, 18, 19, 20, 21, 22, 23, 24, 26, 27, 29, 30, 31, 32, 33, 34, 36, 39	✓ 10, 11, 21, 45	✓ 5, 9, 10, 11, 13, 16, 17, 29, 33, 34, 50, 52, 54, 55, 56, 57, 60	✓ 9, 13, 63, 66	✓ 5, 13, 17, 33, 34, 36, 68, 69, 70, 72, 73, 74, 75	✓ 17, 36, 77, 78, 79, 80, 81, 82, 83, 84, 85, 86, 87, 88, 90, 91	✓ 10, 11, 12, 13, 18, 19, 20, 21, 36, 92, 94, 95, 97, 99, 100
Framing the Crisis	Providing an account of the crisis to improve sensemaking, situational clarity, status updates		✓ 7, 8, 9, 11, 12, 14, 17, 18, 19, 20, 21	✓ 11, 12, 17, 18, 19, 20, 21, 22, 23, 24, 26, 27, 28, 29, 31, 33, 34, 36, 37, 39	✓ 11, 21, 42, 45	✓ 9, 11, 17, 29, 33, 34, 36, 50, 51, 52, 53, 59, 60	✓ 9, 61, 62, 65, 66	✓ 17, 33, 34, 36, 67, 68, 69, 70, 71, 74	✓ 17, 36, 37, 53, 78, 79, 80, 81, 84, 85, 86, 87, 88, 90	✓ 11, 12, 18, 19, 20, 21, 28, 36, 59, 91, 99, 100
Framing the Organization	Providing information about the organization's role and performance in the crisis	✓ 4	✓ 5, 11, 13, 16, 18, 19	✓ 5, 11, 16, 18, 19, 29, 35, 36, 37	✓ 11, 42, 44, 47	✓ 5, 11, 13, 16, 29, 58	✓ 13	✓ 5, 13, 35, 36, 67, 70	✓ 37, 76, 78, 84, 90	✓ 11, 13, 18, 19, 35, 97
Defensive	Messages that try to mitigate or shift blame about crisis away from the organization or diminish the risk of the situation.		✓ 7		✓ 42, 44, 47	✓ 5				

(Continiued)

Table 10.1 (Continued)

Strategy Category	*Strategy*	*Description*	*Bulgaria*	*France*	*Germany*	*Hungary*	*Italy*	*Country* *Lithuania*	*Netherlands*	*Portugal*	*Sweden*
	Accommodative	Messages that focus on the organization's actions to protect & build stakeholder efficacy in actions	✓ 1, 2	✓ 10, 11, 14, 15, 18, 19, 20	✓ 10, 11, 18, 19, 20, 22, 24, 26, 30, 32, 33, 34, 35, 40	✓ 10, 11, 45	✓ 10, 11, 33, 34, 36, 56, 57, 59, 60	✓ 66	✓ 5, 33, 34, 35, 68, 69, 73	✓ 36, 79, 81, 83, 84, 85, 87, 88, 89, 90	✓ 10, 11, 18, 19, 20, 35, 59, 99
	Excellence/ Renewal	Messages that demonstrate the effectiveness of the organization during the crisis – forward looking (beyond the crisis), highlights citizen engagement		✓ 5, 9, 11, 13, 16, 18, 19, 20	✓ 5, 11, 16, 18, 19, 20, 23, 26, 27, 28, 29, 30, 35, 36	✓ 11, 43, 45	✓ 5, 9, 11, 13, 16, 29, 36, 50, 54, 56, 59	✓ 9, 13	✓ 5, 13, 35, 36, 67, 68, 69, 70, 75	✓ 36, 78, 83, 86	✓ 11, 13, 18, 19, 20, 28, 35, 36, 59, 97
	Emphasizing Interorganizational Relationships	Messages that emphasize positive or negative relationships with other organizations as a way of contextualizing the organization's response to the crisis	✓ 2	✓ 5, 8, 9, 13, 16, 18, 20	✓ 5, 16, 18, 27, 28, 36	✓ 44, 47	✓ 5, 9, 13, 16, 49, 50, 59	✓ 9, 13, 64	✓ 5, 13, 67, 68, 72, 74		✓ 13, 18, 28, 36, 59, 96, 97, 100

Notes: See Appendix A for the full source list for the table.

- The message strategies France used converged on a cohesive approach emphasizing instructive communication, framing the crisis and excellence strategies (Table 10.1) that highlighted efforts to build the case for the restrictions imposed and community engagement.

Germany

There is already a significant amount of research published on the German response to the COVID-19 pandemic, including both national and cross-national analyses. Across the literature, two clear themes emerge (see Table 10.1):

- The German response to the pandemic emphasized the digitization of information available (Dadaczynski et al., 2021). This included both the government's effort in using different digital channels (e.g., social media, blogs, and applications) and citizens' consumption of digital content.
- The German government's message strategies used converged on a cohesive and centralized approach to government pandemic response emphasizing instructive communication, framing the crisis, accommodation, and excellence strategies that highlighted explanation for the government's actions (Lindholt et al., 2021).

Hungary

While there were few cross-national comparisons including Hungary, this analysis identified three themes in the Hungarian government communication strategy that highlights some critical limitations in its potential for success in risk mitigation:

- The most effective source for health messages were health officials (Gabay et al., 2021; Mihelj et al., 2022), not the government because of a highly politicized and adversarial political environment (Bene & Boda, 2021).
- Because recommendations about self-protective behaviors were viewed by citizens as an issue of freedom, emphasizing the voluntary nature of the behaviors was key to citizen adoption (Bíró-Nagy & Szászi, 2022).
- Government responses focused on message strategies that were defensive, shifted the blame for failures, and attacked its opponents (Szabó & Szabó, 2022).

Italy

There is a substantial amount of crisis communication research analyzing the Italian government's COVID-19 response both because Italy was the place in Europe where COVID-19 was first identified and because of the severity of the crisis in the country. Across this research three key themes emerged (see Table 10.1):

- Because of the prolonged lockdowns, there is a substantial amount of research connecting the usefulness of digitization and digital community engagement in addressing issues of loneliness and social isolation (Mori et al., 2021).
- Communication about government coordination at the local/regional and national levels, including the clarity of applicable rules emerged as a central theme (Bosa et al., 2021).
- The Italian government's message strategies converged on a combination of instructional communication,[1] framing the crisis, accommodation, and excellence, to highlight citizen engagement and develop citizen efficacy in the risk mitigation behaviors.

Lithuania

Much of the COVID-19 pandemic communication research on Lithuania was focused on business practices and not governmental communication making research in this national context different compared to the other countries. However, identification and evaluation of government response highlighted some limitations in the communication strategy across three themes (see Table 10.1):

- The Lithuanian government enacted risk mitigation policies, but with limited information and explanation from either government or public health sources (Stankutė et al., 2021).
- Among citizens there was a heightened sense of information dissatisfaction and desire for more governmental engagement across platforms – especially, more personal communication (Buneviciene et al., 2021). In part, this was complicated by the multiple language and migration issues facing Lithuania during the pandemic.
- The legacy media[2] was central in communicating and encouraging self-protective behaviors (Černikovaitė, 2022).

Netherlands

Analyses of government communication in the Netherlands identified four recommendations for pandemic communication and a cohesive message strategy (see Table 10.1):

- Governmental communication strategy should:
  - demonstrate cross-platform and media integration (de Vries et al., 2022)

    - use branding techniques as an important part of crisis response (te Poel et al., 2021)
    - tailor messaging to diverse populations (Buijzen et al., 2021)
    - coordinate cross-government and across sectors (Ashraf, 2021)

- The Dutch government's message strategies converged around instructional communication, framing the crisis, and active demonstration of community engagement (Minderhout et al., 2021).

Portugal

Analyses of the Portuguese government's communication strategy focused more on the institutions as communicators rather than the citizens as stakeholders compared to other countries. The two critical themes emerging were (see Table 10.1):

- The Portuguese strategy highlights a clear cross-platform communication approach with branding and visual communication strategies as central to the approach (Jiménez-Sánchez et al., 2020)
- The government's message strategy converged around a pandemic response emphasizing instructive communication, framing the crisis, and citizen efficacy in risk mitigation (Padeiro et al., 2021).

Sweden

Analyses of the Swedish government's communication strategy also focused more on how the government institutions were communicating and coordinating the public health response rather than emphasizing stakeholder needs. This is largely attributable to the Swedish government choosing a different crisis management strategy than lockdowns and restrictions. However, two central communication themes emerged (see Table 10.1):

- The Swedish government's strategy was grounded by a distinctively Nordic high institutional trust environment that improved citizen crisis resilience throughout the pandemic (Johansson et al., 2021).
- The government's message strategy converged around instructional communication, excellence, and accommodation (Ihlen et al., 2022).

Best Practices for Pandemic Communication for Platform, Source, & Strategy

A key question emerging from this analysis is: what is the transferrable knowledge that can be drawn from a pan-European analysis for risk and crisis communication? Most of the countries included in this analysis demonstrate several effective pandemic communication strategies. For example, the French, German,

Italian, Dutch, Portuguese, and Swedish *communication strategies all centred on explaining to their citizens what self-protective behaviors should be taken and why*, within each country's national contexts. Beyond that, the findings suggest that, in a pandemic, the most successful government communication strategies adopt a positive tone supporting citizen confidence in acting, communicating engagement and responsiveness whereas the least successful government strategies focus on defensive messages, shifting the blame for problems in the government's response, or fear-based messaging. This suggests *an overall citizen preference for transparency* as well as a need for more constructively managing the fear and anxiety emerging in a global health pandemic (see Table 10.1).

Additionally, in countries like France, the Netherlands, and Portugal, *two-way communication or community engagement* was a central feature in their relative communication success. It was also recognized across countries – regardless of relative success – that *tailoring the messages to meet different demographics' information needs and attitudes* about government was essential. For example, analyses from Bulgaria and the Netherlands both directly recognized the importance of adapting messages and reaching out to minority communities within their countries. Finally, regardless of relative success in managing the pandemic, a central – if not *the central feature of communication success – is trust in the institutions communicating.* In countries with low levels of institutional trust, this represents a chasm to the success of any health intervention whereas in countries with high levels of institutional trust, it meaningfully increases citizen willingness to enact recommendations from governments and/or public health institutions.

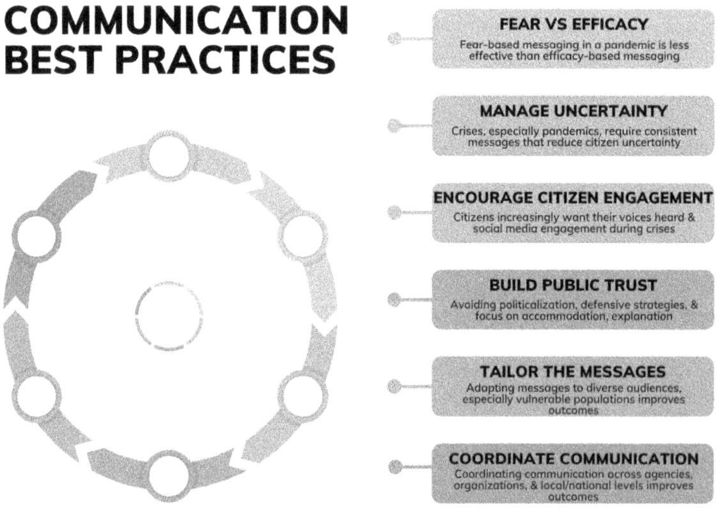

Figure 10.1 European best practices in pandemic communication.

Figure 10.1 summarizes the best practices emerging from the literature by focusing on the six communication practices that are recognized within the countries by practitioners and identified in the scientific research. These best practices align with, for example, the World Health Organization's framework for risk communication and community engagement and demonstrate transferrable lessons for future health crises and disasters.

Factors Influencing Citizen Message Acceptance and Self-Protective Behaviors

Broadly speaking, while no nation's response was perfect, France, Germany, Italy, the Netherlands, Portugal, and Sweden all demonstrated good communication practices. Likewise, based on the analysis there were limitations or challenges to effective communication practice identified in Bulgaria, Hungary, and Lithuania. Certainly, political, economic, and social factors all contribute to the relative success of any country's pandemic communication and community intervention efforts; however, at a most basic level in the case of COVID-19, the number of deaths suggests there is a relationship between effective government communication, citizens enacting self-protective behaviors, and proportionately fewer deaths (see Figure 10.2). Therefore, the 'success' of a communication effort could be thought of in terms of both evidence of lower deaths and improved citizen adoption of self-protective behaviors.

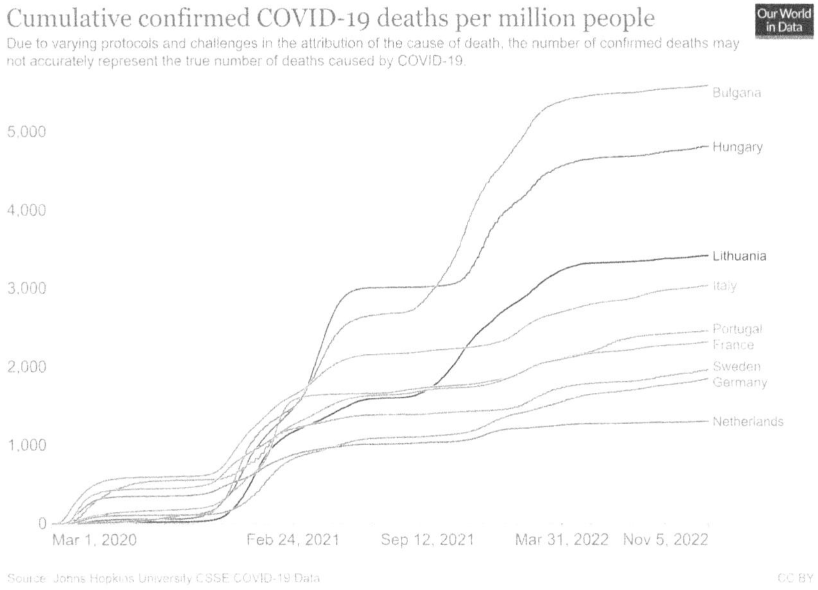

Figure 10.2 Comparative deaths per million people in sampled countries.

Figure 10.3 SRM and contingency factors influencing self-protective behavior adoption.

While communication strategy seems to improve crisis outcomes, the story is not so simple. To understand the nuanced differences in the relative success of crisis communication strategies and therefore improve those strategies in the future, it is important to understand other factors that either enable or inhibit citizens willingness and ability to act based on their governments' recommendations or mandates. Therefore, this section summarizes factors that governments should also consider when designing crisis communication strategies that will be accepted by their citizens and places that within the SRM framework to develop a more cohesive understanding of pandemic communication.

By combining the SRM with a contingency approach, we can begin to better understand complex pandemic communication environments (see Figure 10.3). As a starting point, the framework identifies four factors that critically influence message acceptance: issue-related, institutional, citizen, and information factors. Additionally, because the COVID-19 crisis context is unique and many communication theories have overlapping concepts (e.g., efficacy, perceived threat, or subjective knowledge), Diers-Lawson, et al (2021) argued that instead of employing traditional theoretical approaches to identify and evaluate effective communication practice, a contingency approach exploring the factors known to influence self-protective behaviors would better enable scholars and practitioners to design, execute, and evaluate pandemic communication strategy.

This part of the analysis focuses on the 33 scientific articles and reports that directly analyzed factors influencing citizens' self-protective behaviors during the COVID-19 pandemic in the nine countries of focus. Additionally, the United Kingdom (UK) and US were included because many of the 236 articles reviewed used one or both countries as points of comparisons (see Table 10.2 and Appendix B).

Table 10.2 Factors influencing citizen selfprotective behavior during COVID-19

Factor	*Description*	*Bulgaria*	*France*	*Germany*	*Hungary*	*Italy*	*Country Lithuania*	*Netherlands*	*Portugal*	*Sweden*	*UK*	*US*
Cognitive Elaboration / Uncertainty Discrepancy	Extent to which people think about a message depends on association with prior knowledge about health crises and emotional arousal – it can be a way to manage threat.	✓ [30, 33]		✓ [18]		✓ [6, 22, 24, 27]		✓ [3, 28]	✓ [26]		✓ [27]	✓ [2, 20]
Demographics	Who the person is can affect information processing. For example, gender, language, age, culture	✓ [30, 31]	✓ [29]	✓ [1, 17, 29]	✓ [10]	✓ [29]	✓ [4]	✓ [3, 8, 28, 29]	✓ [7, 29]	✓ [15]	✓ [29]	✓ [23]
Efficacy	Belief both in the ability to perform a behavior and/or by performing the action, protecting self from the hazard/risk (i.e., self and response efficacy).		✓ [16]	✓ [16, 18, 19]	✓ [16]	✓ [16, 24]			✓ [5]	✓ [16]	✓ [9, 16]	✓ [16, 23]

(Continiued)

Table 10.2 (Continued)

Factor	*Description*	*Bulgaria*	*France*	*Germany*	*Hungary*	*Italy*	*Country* *Lithuania*	*Netherlands*	*Portugal*	*Sweden*	*UK*	*US*
Epistemic Mistrust	Combination of trust violation, threat/uncertainty/trauma, xenophobia, and suspiciousness (conspiracy theory)	✓ [30, 32]	✓ [14]	✓ [1]		✓ [14]	✓ [12, 14]					
Information Insufficiency	Degree to which person lacks information about a risk issue	✓ [32]		✓ [1, 17]	✓ [10]	✓ [17, 22, 24]			✓ [13, 26]		✓ [9]	
Information Equivocality	Degree to which multiple conclusions can be reasonably drawn from information presented				✓ [10]				✓ [13]			
Information Fatigue	Degree to which an excess of information causes people to stop paying attention to messaging			✓ [17]		✓ [17]	✓ [4]					

Institutional Trust	Trust in agencies responsible for managing harms related to technology, environment, and public health; making decisions to protect public	✓ [30, 31, 32]	✓ [21, 29]	✓ [17, 18, 21, 29]		✓ [6, 17, 29]	✓ [12]	✓ [8, 29]	✓ [7, 29]	✓ [15, 21]	✓ [21, 29]	✓ [20, 21]
Misinformation Processing	Combination for certainty, uniqueness, biases (confirmation, attribution, and perceptual), with lack of analytic thinking, science illiteracy	✓ [30, 32]	✓ [14]	✓ [1, 11]		✓ [14]	✓ [14]		✓ [13]			
Negative Affect	Emotions including anxiety, fear, uncertainty, or anger towards risk issue	✓ [30, 33]			✓ [10]				✓ [5]			✓ [2]
Perceived Risk (Threat Appraisal)	A combination of problem recognition, susceptibility, and severity in judging risky behavior or issues	✓ [30]	✓ [16]	✓ [16, 19]	✓ [10, 16]	✓ [6, 16, 22, 24, 27]	✓ [4, 12]	✓ [3, 8, 28]	✓ [7, 26]	✓ [16, 25]	✓ [9, 16, 27]	✓ [2, 16, 20]

(*Continued*)

Table 10.2 (Continued)

Factor	*Description*	*Bulgaria*	*France*	*Germany*	*Hungary*	*Italy*	*Country Lithuania*	*Netherlands*	*Portugal*	*Sweden*	*UK*	*US*
Self-Other Gap (Third Person Effect)	Assumption that media messages, issues have greater effect on others, not themselves					✓[6]		✓[3]				
Social Support	Resources exchanged through social ties. It is comprised of tangible, emotional, esteem, and appraisal support. It also includes social distance.	✓[33]		✓[1]				✓[3, 28]	✓[7]			
Source Accessibility	Ease of access of the information by information seekers	✓[32]		✓[1, 11]	✓[10]			✓[8]	✓[13, 26]		✓[9]	
Source Credibility	Belief the source of information itself is credible – particularly scientific knowledge		✓[29]	✓[11, 18, 29]	✓[10]	✓[6, 29]	✓[12]	✓[8, 29]	✓[29]		✓[29]	✓[20]
Subjective Knowledge	What people think/ believe they know		✓[14, 29]	✓[1, 18, 29]		✓[14, 27, 29]	✓[4, 14]	✓[28, 29]	✓[26, 29]		✓[27, 29]	

Notes: See Appendix B for the full source list for the table. Categorization of factors is based on a theoretical review of 13 communication theories related to information seeking in health crises (including COVID-19). See Diers-Lawson, et al. (2021).

Issue-Related (COVID-19) Factors

Across the EU, UK, and US literature, citizens' evaluations of COVID-19's (perceived) risk to themselves and their subjective knowledge were most often identified as significant predictors of their likelihood to enact self-protective behaviors. Cognitive elaboration, which combines the uncertainty of the crisis context with emotional arousal based on prior experience with health crises was also found to influence citizen behaviors, especially in Italy.

Issue-related factors influence strategy in a number of ways. For example, within the context of the COVID-19 pandemic, people were already afraid – among most populations there were already high levels of perceived risk. Therefore, it makes more sense within this context to focus on building efficacy rather than using fear-based messages because public health needs to concentrate on making people feel like they can positively affect their own safety by adopting simple self-protective behavioral recommendations. Whereas countries that used fear-based messaging or emphasized punishment for non-compliance had lower levels of citizen compliance with instructional messages. This means that government and public health need to know what their citizens understand (i.e., subjective knowledge) about the situation to determine how to approach the communication of scientific information needed to explain *why* people need to enact different types of self-protective behaviors (see Table 10.2).

Institution-Related Factors

Institutional trust is the single biggest factor across countries to explain why citizens may or may not adopt self-protective behaviors (see Table 10.2) based on government and/or public health recommendations. Whether research was analyzing the high-trust environments in Sweden or explaining why political polarization damaged institutional trust and adoption of self-protective behaviors in countries like the US, UK, Bulgaria, and Hungary, institutional trust emerged as central to citizen behavior.

There are two factors that align with institutional trust. The first, is understanding citizen views of the government's and/or public health's credibility in discussing the pandemic. This is particularly important within a context like COVID-19 where the knowledge of the disease was evolving as were the recommendations. Second, where populations have suspicion about the government's or public health's *real* intentions in acting (i.e., epistemic mistrust), it creates additional challenges for persuading people to adopt the recommended behaviors. Epistemic mistrust can describe, for example, minority populations mistrust of government, perceptions of government corruption, or even belief in conspiracy theories. All of these influence whether citizens will pay attention to government recommendations or laws. Credibility and epistemic mistrust are a long-term challenge for governments but highlights the importance of governments taking action that builds trust and transparency in both crisis and non-crisis periods with different citizen populations – it explains why reputation and trust matter as essential tools for governments and public health to manage future pandemics (Mihelj et al., 2022; Varghese et al., 2021).

Citizen-Related Factors

Citizen-related factors highlight the demographic and attitudinal predispositions for people to enact (or not) self-protective behaviors. Research on COVID-19 clearly demonstrates that demographics, like gender, culture, age, religious identification, or minority status influence citizens' propensity to enact self-protective behaviors. The challenge is that these demographic factors are not stable nor consistent enough across countries to lead to broadly generalizable conclusions; they must be constantly evaluated on a country-by-country basis (see Table 10.2).

A more consistent citizen-related factor is efficacy – both self and response efficacy. The evidence from across the countries clearly concludes that as governments and public health authorities explain what people should be doing and why, they also need to give clear instructions on how to correctly perform the behavior (self-efficacy) *and* they need to show citizens that there is a benefit for them in performing the behaviors (response-efficacy).

Information-Related Factors

It is widely recognized in popular media and has been consistently found in scientific research that the COVID-19 'infodemic' poses a serious challenge in risk mitigation through persuading citizens to take self-protective behaviors (Ghebreyesus, 2020) because once false beliefs take hold in a population, they are difficult to undo (Lewandowsky et al., 2013). Director General of the WHO, Tedros Ghebreyesus, used the term *infodemic* at the height of the COVID-19 pandemic to describe an overabundance of information – some accurate, some not – that spreads alongside a disease outbreak (Ghebreyesus, 2020). Infodemics amplify public risk during pandemics (Bursztyn et al., 2020) by creating mental noise (Covello et al., 2001) and affecting how audiences receive and interpret information (Baron et al., 2000). Although the term is yet to be established in social science research, it complements Nielsen et al.'s (Nielsen et al., 2020) observation of how news and information around COVID-19 is harder to clearly and cleanly separate into information and misinformation, true and false, reliable, and unreliable. Yet credible information and instructive guidance from governments and health officials is essential for saving lives by reducing risk, reinforcing desirable health attitudes, and building institutional trust (Marks et al., 2000). One of the biggest threats is when citizens feel that they do not have enough quality information from their governments and public health authorities because this might lead them to fill perceived information gaps from other sources (see Table 10.2).

Additionally, in such a prolonged crisis, several pieces of research also identified a new challenge related to information fatigue. Information fatigue emerged as a prominent factor in Germany, Italy and Lithuania but in the research on COVID-19 is not adequately measured despite the long-established literature on information overload that even connects it to sharing misinformation (Laato et al., 2020). Finally, the importance of information literacy is also well-established in previous research (Fitzpatrick & Muelemans, 2011) and was likewise found to influence self-protective behaviors in the research related to COVID-19. In this case, when there is lower information literacy, citizens are more resistant to adopting self-protective behaviors recommended (or required) by governments and public health institutions.

Conclusions

In the final evaluation, while it is obvious to say that 'good pandemic communication practice' is necessary to manage the public health, economic, and general well-being threats posed by a pandemic like COVID-19, good pandemic communication practice requires planning, adaptability, and a strong understanding of citizen attitudes. Specifically, in reviewing practice, reflection from the countries, and research in across different countries in the EU, I have identified six distinctive pandemic communication best practices and I have also identified issue-specific, institutional, citizen, and information-related factors that modify those best practices. These findings suggest that combining a risk and crisis communication approach with direct community engagement both during crises and as a part of building better relationships between governments and its citizens all improves societal security during health crises.

Acknowledgments

VVA International and the European Parliament for asking me to be a part of the post COVID-19 evaluation process. These data have also been reported as a part of a larger document but represent the author's contribution to the larger document (see Jacob et al., 2023).

Notes

1 ***Instructional communication*** in the context of COVID-19 focuses on governments providing specific and concrete recommendations and explanations regarding the purpose or value of specific for self-protective behaviors such as wearing facemasks, handwashing, social distancing, or staying at home.

2 ***Legacy media*** is a term used to refer to traditional news sources (e.g., newspapers, media outlets) no matter the platform or channel that the information is shared on.

References

Ashraf, A. (2021). Lessons learned from COVID-19 response for disaster risk management. *Natural Hazards*, *107*(2), 2027–2032. https://doi.org/10.1007/s11069-021-04658-0

Azadeh, M., Ramezani, T., & Taheri-Kharameh, Z. (2020). Factors affecting workplace protective behaviors against Covid-19 disease in employees of crowded public offices: Application of protection motivation theory. *Iran Occupational Health*, *17*, 1–11.

Balarabe, U. B., & Kumar, R. (2020). Perspectives and impacts of social media, fake news and misinformation narratives about coronavirus. *Journal of Humanities and Social Science*, *25*(7), 62–66. https://doi.org/10.9790/0837-2507086266

Baron, J., Hershey, J. C., & Kunreuther, H. (2000). Determinants of priority for risk reduction: The role of worry. *Risk Analysis*, *20*(4), 413–428. https://doi.org/10.1111/0272-4332.204041

Bene, M., & Boda, Z. (2021). Hungary: Crisis as usual—Populist governance and the pandemic. In *Populism and the Politicization of the COVID-19 Crisis in Europe* (pp. 87–100). Springer. https://doi.org/10.1007/978-3-030-66011-6_7

Betsch, C., Korn, L., Sprengholz, P., Felgendreff, L., Eitze, S., Schmid, P., & Bohm, R. (2020). Social and behavioral consequences of mask policies during the COVID-19 pandemic. *Proceedings of the National Academy of Sciences*, *117*(36), 21851–21853. https://doi.org/10.1073/pnas.2011674117

Bíró-Nagy, A., & Szászi, Á. J. (2022). The roots of COVID-19 vaccine hesitancy: Evidence from Hungary. *Journal of Behavioral Medicine*, 1–16. https://doi.org/10.1007/s10865-022-00314-5

Bosa, I., Castelli, A., Castelli, M., Ciani, O., Compagni, A., Galizzi, M. M., Garofano, M., Ghislandi, S., Giannoni, M., & Marini, G. (2021). Corona-regionalism? Differences in regional responses to COVID-19 in Italy. *Health Policy*, *125*(9), 1179–1187. https://doi.org/10.1016/j.healthpol.2021.07.012

Breakwell, G. M., & Jaspal, R. (2020). Identity change, uncertainty and mistrust in relation to fear and risk of COVID-19. *Journal of Risk Research*, *24*(3/4), 1–17. https://doi.org/10.1080/13669877.2020.1864011

Bruine de Bruin, W., & Bennett, D. (2020). Relationships between initial COVID-19 risk perceptions and protective health behaviors: A national survey. *American Journal of Preventative Medicine*, *59*(2), 157–167. https://doi.org/10.1016/j.amepre.2020.05.001

Bruine de Bruin, W., Saw, H. W., & Goldman, D. P. (2020). Political polarization in US residents' COVID-19 risk perceptions, policy preferences, and protective behaviors. *Journal of Risk and Uncertainty*, *61*, 177–194. https://doi.org/10.1007/s11166-020-09336-3

Buijzen, M., Anschütz, D., de Leeuw, R. N., Bleize, D. N., Sadza, A. J., de Droog, S. M., & Rozendaal, E. (2021). Behind the policy frontline in the Netherlands during the Corona crisis. *Journal of Children and Media*, *15*(1), 49–54. https://doi.org/10.1080/17482798.2020.1858899

Buneviciene, I., Bunevicius, R., Bagdonas, S., & Bunevicius, A. (2021). COVID-19 media fatigue: predictors of decreasing interest and avoidance of COVID-19–related news. *Public Hhealth*, *196*, 124–128. https://doi.org/10.1016/j.puhe.2021.05.024

Bursztyn, L., Rao, A., Roth, C. P., & Yanagizawa-Drott, D. H. (2020). *Misinformation during a pandemic* (D1,I31,Z13). (NBER Working Paper 27417, 114 pages).

Cameron, G. T., Cropp, F., & Reber, B. H. (2001). Getting past platitudes: Factors limiting accommodation in public relations. *Journal of Communication Management*, *5*(3), 242–261. https://doi.org/10.1108/13632540110806802

Černikovaitė, M. E. (2022). Manifestation of panic in mass media: Covid 19 case in Lithuania. 6th World Conference on Media and Mass Communication MEDCOM 2020+ 1, 17–19 June 2021, Cagliari, Italy, Online Conference: Book of Abstract,

Cheng, Y., & Luo, Y. (2020). The presumed influence of digital misinformation: Examining US public's support for governmental restrictions versus corrective action in the COVID-19 pandemic. *Online Information Review*. https://doi.org/10.1108/OIR-08-2020-0386

Covello, V. T., Peters, R. G., Wojtecki, J. G., & Hyde, R. C. (2001). Risk communication, the West Nile virus epidemic, and bioterrorism: Responding to the commnication challenges posed by the intentional or unintentional release of a pathogen in an urban setting. *Journal of Urban Health*, *78*(2), 382–391.

Dadaczynski, K., Okan, O., Messer, M., Leung, A. Y., Rosário, R., Darlington, E., & Rathmann, K. (2021). Digital health literacy and web-based information-seeking behaviors of university students in Germany during the COVID-19 pandemic: cross-sectional survey study. *Journal of Medical Internet Research*, *23*(1), e24097. https://doi.org/10.2196/24097

Dai, B., Fu, D., Meng, G., Liu, B., Li, Q., & Liu, X. (2020). The effects of governmental and individual predictors on COVID-19 protective behaviors in China: A path analysis model. *Public Administrative Review*. https://doi.org/10.1111/puar.13236

de Vries, H., Verputten, W., Preissner, C., & Kok, G. (2022). COVID-19 vaccine hesitancy: The role of information sources and beliefs in Dutch adults. *International Journal of Environmental Research and Public Health*, *19*(6), 3205. https://doi.org/10.3390/ijerph19063205

Diers-Lawson, A. (2020). *Crisis communication: Managing stakeholder relationships*. Routledge.

Diers-Lawson, A., Johnson, S., Clayton, T., Kimoto, R., Tran, B. X., Nguyen, L. H., & Park, K. (2021). Pandemic communication: Information seeking, evaluation, and self-protective behaviors in Vietnam and the republic of Korea. *Frontiers in Communication*, *6*(731979), 160. https://doi.org/10.3389/fcomm.2021.731979

Diers, A. R. (2012). Reconstructing stakeholder relationships using 'corporate social responsibility' as a response strategy to cases of corporate irresponsibility: The case of the 2010 BP spill in the Gulf of Mexico. In R. Tench, W. Sun, & B. Jones (Eds.), *Corporate social irresponsibility: A challenging concept* (Vol. 4, pp. 177–206). Emerald. https://doi.org/10.1108/S2043-9059(2012)0000004017

Diers, A. R., & Donohue, J. (2013). Synchronizing crisis responses after a transgression: An analysis of BP's enacted crisis response to the Deepwater Horizon crisis in 2010. *Journal of Communication Management*, *17*(3), 252–269.

Fitzpatrick, M. J., & Muelemans, Y. N. (2011). Assessing an information literacy assignment and workshop using a quasi-experimental design. *College Teaching*, *59*, 142–149. https://doi.org/10.1080/87567555.2011.591452

Fraser, N., Brierley, L., Dey, G., Polka, J. K., Pálfy, M., Nanni, F., & Coates, J. A. (2021). The evolving role of preprints in the dissemination of COVID-19 research and their impact on the science communication landscape. *PLoS Biology*, *19*(4), e3000959. https://doi.org/10.1371/journal.pbio.3000959

Gabay, G., Gere, A., Fehér, O., Bellissimo, N., & Moskowitz, H. (2021). Rapid discovery of optimal messages for behavioral intervention: the case of Hungary and Covid-19. *Heliyon*, *7*(12), e08535. https://doi.org/10.1016/j.heliyon.2021.e08535

Gagneux-Brunon, A., Botelho-Nevers, E., Bonneton, M., Peretti-Watel, P., Verger, P., Launay, O., & Ward, J. K. (2022). Public opinion on a mandatory COVID-19 vaccination policy in France: a cross-sectional survey. *Clinical Microbiology and Infection*, *28*(3), 433–439. https://doi.org/10.1016/j.cmi.2021.10.016

Ghebreyesus, D. T. (2020). *Director general speeches detail Munich security conference*. World Health Organization. Retrieved July 30, 2021 from https://www.who.int/director-general/speeches/detail/munich-security-conference

Glenn, J., Chaumont, C., & Dintrans, P. V. (2020). Public health leadership in the times of COVID-19: Acomparative case study of three countries. *International Journal of Public Leadership*, *17*(1), 81–94. https://doi.org/10.1108/IJPL-08-2020-0082

Ihlen, Ø., Johansson, B., & Blach-Ørsten, M. (2022). Experiencing COVID-19 in Denmark, Norway and Sweden: The role of the Nordic Model. In R. Tench, J. Meng, & A. Moreno (Eds.), *Strategic Communication in a Global Crisis* (pp. 184–198). Routledge. https://doi.org/10.4324/9781003184669

Jacob, C., Hausemer, P., Zagoni-Bogsch, A., & Diers-Lawson, A. (2023). *The effect of communication and disinformation during the Covid-19 pandemic* (Special Committee on the COVID-19 pandemic: Lessons learned and recommendations for the future, Issue. E. Parliament. http://www.europarl.europa.eu/supporting-analyses

Jiménez-Sánchez, Á., Margalina, V.-M., & Vayas-Ruiz, E. (2020). Governmental communication and brand advertising during the COVID-19 pandemic. *Tripodos*, *2*(47), 29–46. https://doi.org/10.51698/tripodos.2020.47p29-46

Johansson, B., Sohlberg, J., Esaiasson, P., & Ghersetti, M. (2021). Why Swedes don't wear face masks during the pandemic-a consequence of blindly trusting the government. *Journal of International Crisis and Risk Communication Research*, *4*(2), 335–358. https://doi.org/10.30658/jicrcr.4.2.6

Kamburova, M., & Georgieva, S. (2021). The impact of the COVID-19 epidemic and anti-epidemic measures in the Roma neighborhood in Bulgaria. *European Journal of Public Health*, *31*(Supplement_3), ckab164. 244.

Kulkarni, V. (2017). Contingency theory. *The International Encyclopedia of Organizational Communication*, 1–6. https://doi.org/10.1002/9781118955567.wbieoc041

Laato, S., Islam, A. K. M. N., Islam, M. N., & Whelan, E. (2020). Why do people share misinformation during the COVID-19 pandemic? *European Journal of Information Systems*. https://doi.org/10.1080/0960085X.2020.1770632

Lewandowsky, S., Gignac, G. E., & Oberauer, K. (2013). The role of conspiracist ideation and worldviews in predicting rejection of science. *PloS One*, *8*(10), e75637. https://doi.org/10.1371/journal.pone.0075637

Lindholt, M. F., Jørgensen, F., Bor, A., & Petersen, M. B. (2021). Public acceptance of COVID-19 vaccines: Cross-national evidence on levels and individual-level predictors using observational data. *BMJ Open*, *11*(6), e048172. http://dx.doi.org/10.1136/bmjopen-2020-048172

Marks, D., Murray, M., Evans, B., & Willig, C. (2000). *Health psychology: Theory, practice and research*. Sage publications.

Meier, K., Glatz, T., Guijt, M. C., Piccininni, M., van der Meulen, M., Atmar, K., Jolink, A. C., Kurth, T., Rohmann, J. L., & Zamanipoor Najafabadi, A. H. (2020). Public perspectives on protective measures during the COVID-19 pandemic in the Netherlands, Germany and Italy: A survey study. *PloS One*, *15*(8), e0236917. https://doi.org/10.1371/journal.pone.0236917

Mihelj, S., Kondor, K., & Štětka, V. (2022). Establishing trust in experts during a crisis: Expert trustworthiness and media use during the COVID-19 pandemic. *Science Communication*, *44*(3), 292–319. https://doi.org/10.1177/10755470221100558

Minderhout, R. N., Baksteen, M. C., Numans, M. E., Bruijnzeels, M. A., & Vos, H. M. (2021). Effect of COVID-19 on health system integration in the Netherlands: A mixed-methods study. *Journal of the American College of Emergency Physicians Open*, *2*(3), e12433. https://doi.org/10.1002/emp2.12433

Mori, E., Barabaschi, B., Cantoni, F., & Virtuani, R. (2021). Local governments' communication through Facebook. Evidences from COVID-19 pandemic in Italy. *Journal of Public Affairs*, *21*(4), e2551. https://doi.org/10.1002/pa.2551

Nguyen, N. P. T., Hoang, T. D., Tran, V. T., Vu, C. T., Siewe Fodjo, J. N., Colebunders, R., Dunne, M. P., & Vo, T. V. (2020). Preventive behavior of Vietnamese people in response to the COVID-19 pandemic. *PloS One*, *15*(9), e0238830. https://doi.org/10.1371/journal.pone.0238830

Nielsen, R. K., Fletcher, R., Newman, N., Brennen, J. S., & Howard, P. N. (2020). *Navigating the 'infodemic': How people in six countries access and rate news and information about coronavirus*. Reuters Institute.

OECD. (2021). *First lessons from government evaluations of COVID-19 responses: A synthesis* (Tackling Coronavirus (COVID-19): Contributing to a Global Effort, Issue. https://www.oecd.org/coronavirus/policy-responses/first-lessons-from-government-evaluations-of-covid-19-responses-a-synthesis-483507d6/

Padeiro, M., Bueno-Larraz, B., & Freitas, Â. (2021). Local governments' use of social media during the COVID-19 pandemic: The case of Portugal. *Government Information Quarterly*, *38*(4), 1–20. https://doi.org/10.1016/j.giq.2021.101620

Pang, A., Jin, Y., Kim, S., & Cameron, G. T. (2020). Contingency theory: Evolution from a public relations theory to a theory of strategic conflict management. In F. Frandsen & W. Johansen (Eds.), *Crisis communication* (pp. 141–164). Walter de Gruyter GmbH & Co KG.

Papageorge, N. W., Zahn, M. V., Belot, M., van den Broek-Altenburg, E., Choi, S., Jamison, J. C., & Tripodi, E. (2021). Socio-demographic factors associated with self-protecting behavior during the Covid-19 pandemic. *Journal of Population Economics*, *34*, 691–738. https://doi.org/10.1007/s00148-020-00818-x

Popova, M., & Valkov, I. (2022). Media Representations and the Politics of the COVID-19 Pandemic in Bulgaria. *Journal of Media Ethics*, 1–4. https://doi.org/10.1080/23736992.2022.2057313

Salvi, C., Iannello, P., Cancer, A., McClay, M., Rago, S., Dunsmoor, J. E., & Antonietti, A. (2021). Going viral: How fear, socio-cognitive polarization and problem-solving influence fake news detection and proliferation during COVID-19 pandemic. *Frontiers in Communication*, *5*, 562588. https://doi.org/10.3389/fcomm.2020.562588

Sellnow, D. D., Lane, D. R., Sellnow, T. L., & Littlefield, R. S. (2017). The IDEA model as a best practice for effective instructional risk and crisis communication. *Communication Studies*, *68*(5), 552–567. https://doi.org/10.1080/10510974.2017.1375535

Stankutė, I., Stankūnas, M., & Czabanowska, K. (2021). Leadership and crisis management of COVID-19 pandemic in Lithuania–a survey among public health professionals. *Sztuka Leczenia. Kraków: Uniwersytet Jagielloński Collegium Medicum, 2021, nr. 2, 2*, 9–24. https://doi.org/10.34938/1whm-er33

Sun, Y., Chia, S. C., Lu, F., & Oktavianus, J. (2020). The battle is on: Factors that motivate people to combat anti-vaccine misinformation. *Health communication*. https://doi.org/10.1080/10410236.2020.1838108

Szabó, L. P., & Szabó, G. (2022). Attack of the critics: Metaphorical delegitimisation in Viktor Orbán's discourse during the Covid-19 pandemic. *Journal of Language and Politics*, *21*(2), 255–276. https://doi.org/10.1075/jlp.21068.sza

te Poel, F., Linn, A. J., Baumgartner, S. E., van Dijk, L., & Smit, E. S. (2021). Sick for information?: Information needs and media use of the Dutch public during the Covid-19 pandemic. *European Journal of Health Communication*, *2*(3), 24–43. https://doi.org/10.47368/ejhc.2021.302

Todorova, B., & Padareva-Ilieva, G. (2021). Nostalgia as a device for dealing with traumatic experiences during the COVID-19 crisis. *East European Journal of Psycholinguistics*, *8*(1), 110–124. https://doi.org/10.29038/eejpl.2021.8.1.tod

Varghese, N. E., Sabat, I., Neumann-Böhme, S., Schreyögg, J., Stargardt, T., Torbica, A., van Exel, J., Barros, P. P., & Brouwer, W. (2021). Risk communication during COVID-19: A descriptive study on familiarity with, adherence to and trust in the WHO preventive measures. *PloS one*, *16*(4), e0250872. https://doi.org/10.1371/journal.pone.0250872

WHO. (2022). *Risk communication and community engagement*. https://www.who.int/europe/publications/i/item/WHO-EURO-2022-6186-45951-66353

Appendix A: References for Table 10.1

1 Džakula, A., Banadinović, M., Lovrenčić, I. L., Vajagić, M., Dimova, A., Rohova, M., Minev, M., Scintee, S. G., Vladescu, C., & Farcasanu, D. (2022). A comparison of health system responses to COVID-19 in Bulgaria, Croatia and Romania in 2020. *Health Policy*, *126*, 456–464. https://doi.org/10.1016/j.healthpol.2022.02.003

2 Kamburova, M., & Georgieva, S. (2021). The impact of the COVID-19 epidemic and anti-epidemic measures in the Roma neighborhood in Bulgaria. *European Journal of Public Health*, *31*(Supplement_3), ckab164. 244

3 Popova, J., Koev, K., & Popova, A. (2021). The COVID 19 pandemic lessons in the area of security, social policy and culture: The case with Bulgaria. *Journal of Danubian Studies and Research*, *11*(2), 18–28

4 Popova, M., & Valkov, I. (2022). Media representations and the politics of the COVID-19 pandemic in Bulgaria. *Journal of Media Ethics*, 1–4. https://doi.org/10.1080/23736992.2022.2057313

5 Commission, E. (2020). *Crisis management, coordination and capacities*. EU. Retrieved from: https://ec.europa.eu/info/sites/default/files/ht0921295enn.en_.pdf

6 Gagneux-Brunon, A., Botelho-Nevers, E., Bonneton, M., Peretti-Watel, P., Verger, P., Launay, O., & Ward, J. K. (2022). Public opinion on a mandatory COVID-19 vaccination policy in France: A cross-sectional survey. *Clinical Microbiology and Infection*, *28*(3), 433–439. https://doi.org/10.1016/j.cmi.2021.10.016

7 Ghanchi, A. (2020). Adaptation of the national plan for the prevention and fight against pandemic influenza to the 2020 COVID-19 epidemic in France. *Disaster Medicine and Public Health Preparedness*, *14*(6), 805–807. https://doi.org/10.1017/dmp.2020.82

8 Glenn, J., Chaumont, C., & Dintrans, P. V. (2020). Public health leadership in the times of COVID-19: A comparative case study of three countries. *International Journal of Public Leadership*, *17*(1), 81–94. https://doi.org/10.1108/IJPL-08-2020-0082

9 Hansson, S., Orru, K., Torpan, S., Bäck, A., Kazemekaityte, A., Meyer, S. F., Ludvigsen, J., Savadori, L., Galvagni, A., & Pigrée, A. (2021). COVID-19 information disorder: Six types of harmful information during the pandemic in Europe. *Journal of Risk Research*, *24*(3–4), 380–393. https://doi.org/10.1080/13669877.2020.1871058

10 Jørgensen, F., Bor, A., & Petersen, M. B. (2020). *Compliance without fear: Predictors of protective behavior during the first wave of the Covid-19 pandemic* (PsyArXiv, Issue)

11 Lindholt, M. F., Jørgensen, F., Bor, A., & Petersen, M. B. (2021). Public acceptance of COVID-19 vaccines: Cross-national evidence on levels and individual-level predictors using observational data. *BMJ Open*, *11*(6), e048172. http://dx.doi.org/10.1136/bmjopen-2020-048172

12 Margraf, J., Brailovskaia, J., & Schneider, S. (2021). Adherence to behavioral Covid-19 mitigation measures strongly predicts mortality. *PloS One*, *16*(3), e0249392. https://doi.org/10.1371/journal.pone.0249392

13 OECD. (2021). *First lessons from government evaluations of COVID-19 responses: A synthesis* (Tackling Coronavirus (COVID-19)): Contributing to a global effort, issue. https://www.oecd.org/coronavirus/policy-responses/first-lessons-from-government-evaluations-of-covid-19-responses-a-synthesis-483507d6/

14 Schwarzinger, M., Watson, V., Arwidson, P., Alla, F., & Luchini, S. (2021). COVID-19 vaccine hesitancy in a representative working-age population in France: a survey experiment based on vaccine characteristics. *The Lancet Public Health*, *6*(4), e210–e221. https://doi.org/10.1016/S2468-2667(21)00012-8
15 Singhal, A., & Kim, D. K. D. (2021). The role of the communication discipline to tackle COVID-19: Interrogating positive deviations and critical discourses. In (Vol. *16*, pp. 135–138): SAGE Publications
16 Vardavas, C., Odani, S., Nikitara, K., El Banhawi, H., Kyriakos, C., Taylor, L., & Becuwe, N. (2021). Public perspective on the governmental response, communication and trust in the governmental decisions in mitigating COVID-19 early in the pandemic across the G7 countries. *Preventive Medicine Reports*, *21*, 101252. https://doi.org/10.1016/j.pmedr.2020.101252
17 Varghese, N. E., Sabat, I., Neumann-Böhme, S., Schreyögg, J., Stargardt, T., Torbica, A., van Exel, J., Barros, P. P., & Brouwer, W. (2021). Risk communication during COVID-19: A descriptive study on familiarity with, adherence to and trust in the WHO preventive measures. *PloS One*, *16*(4), e0250872. https://doi.org/10.1371/journal.pone.0250872
18 Warren, G. W., & Lofstedt, R. (2021). COVID-19 vaccine rollout risk communication strategies in Europe: A rapid response. *Journal of Risk Research*, *24*(3-4), 369–379. https://doi.org/10.1080/13669877.2020.1870533
19 Warren, G. W., & Lofstedt, R. (2022). Risk communication and COVID-19 in Europe: Lessons for future public health crises. *Journal of Risk Research*, *25*(10), 1161–1175. https://doi.org/10.1080/13669877.2021.1947874
20 Warren, G. W., Lofstedt, R., & Wardman, J. K. (2021). COVID-19: the winter lockdown strategy in five European nations. *Journal of Risk Research*, *24*(3–4), 267–293. https://doi.org/10.1080/13669877.2021.1891802
21 Wodak, R. (2021). Crisis communication and crisis management during COVID-19. *Global Discourse*, *11*(3), 329–353. https://doi.org/10.1332/204378921X16100431230102
22 Bendau, A., Plag, J., Petzold, M. B., & Ströhle, A. (2021). COVID-19 vaccine hesitancy and related fears and anxiety. *International Immunopharmacology*, *97*, 1–5. https://doi.org/10.1016/j.intimp.2021.107724
23 Berg, M. (2022). Information-precarity for refugee women in Hamburg, Germany, during the COVID-19 pandemic. *Information, Communication & Society*, 1–17. https://doi.org/10.1080/1369118X.2022.2129271
24 Betsch, C., Korn, L., Sprengholz, P., Felgendreff, L., Eitze, S., Schmid, P., & Bohm, R. (2020). Social and behavioral consequences of mask policies during the COVID-19 pandemic. *Proceedings of the National Academy of Sciences*, *117*(36), 21851–21853. https://doi.org/10.1073/pnas.2011674117
25 Dadaczynski, K., Okan, O., Messer, M., Leung, A. Y., Rosário, R., Darlington, E., & Rathmann, K. (2021). Digital health literacy and web-based information-seeking behaviors of university students in Germany during the COVID-19 pandemic: cross-sectional survey study. *Journal of Medical Internet Research*, *23*(1), e24097. https://doi.org/10.2196/24097
26 El-Far Cardo, A., Kraus, T., & Kaifie, A. (2021). Factors that shape people's attitudes towards the COVID-19 pandemic in Germany—The influence of MEDIA, politics

and personal characteristics. *International Journal of Environmental Research and Public Health, 18*(15), 7772. https://doi.org/10.3390/ijerph18157772

27 Gehrau, V., Fujarski, S., Lorenz, H., Schieb, C., & Blöbaum, B. (2021). The impact of health information exposure and source credibility on COVID-19 vaccination intention in Germany. *International Journal of Environmental Research and Public Health, 18*(9), 4678. https://doi.org/10.3390/ijerph18094678

28 Hanson, C., Luedtke, S., Spicer, N., Sörensen, J. S., Mayhew, S., & Mounier-Jack, S. (2021). National health governance, science and the media: Drivers of COVID-19 responses in Germany, Sweden and the UK in 2020. *BMJ Global Health, 6*(12), e006691. http://dx.doi.org/10.1136/bmjgh-2021-006691

29 Kieweg, P. H., Schöberl, S., & Palozzi, G. (2021). The role of communication in COVID-19 crisis management: findings about information behavior of German and Italian young people. *International Journal of Business Research and Management (IJBRM), 12*(5), 263–288. https://www.cscjournals.org/journals/IJBRM/description.php

30 Kojan, L., Burbach, L., Ziefle, M., & Calero Valdez, A. (2022). Perceptions of behavior efficacy, not perceptions of threat, are drivers of COVID-19 protective behavior in Germany. *Humanities and Social Sciences Communications, 9*(1), 1–15. https://doi.org/10.1057/s41599-022-01098-4

31 Kristensen, K., Lorenz, E., May, J., & Strauss, R. (2021). Exploring the use of web searches for risk communication during COVID-19 in Germany. *Scientific Reports, 11*(1), 1–10. https://doi.org/10.1038/s41598-021-85873-4

32 Leder, J., Pastukhov, A., & Schütz, A. (2020). Social value orientation, subjective effectiveness, perceived cost, and the use of protective measures during the COVID-19 pandemic in Germany. *Comprehensive Results in Social Psychology*, 1–23. https://doi.org/10.1080/23743603.2020.1828850

33 Meier, K., Glatz, T., Guijt, M. C., Piccininni, M., van der Meulen, M., Atmar, K., Jolink, A.-T. C., Kurth, T., Rohmann, J. L., & Najafabadi, A. H. Z. (2020). Public perspectives in social distancing and other protective measures in Europe: A cross-sectional survey study during the Covid-19 pandemic. *medRxiv*. https://doi.org/10.1101/2020.04.02.20049676

34 Meier, K., Glatz, T., Guijt, M. C., Piccininni, M., van der Meulen, M., Atmar, K., Jolink, A. C., Kurth, T., Rohmann, J. L., Zamanipoor Najafabadi, A. H., & Group, C.-S. S. (2020). Public perspectives on protective measures during the COVID-19 pandemic in the Netherlands, Germany and Italy: A survey study. *PloS One, 15*(8), e0236917. https://doi.org/10.1371/journal.pone.0236917

35 Meier, K., Glatz, T., Guijt, M. C., Piccininni, M., van der Meulen, M., Atmar, K., Jolink, A.-T. C., Kurth, T., Rohmann, J. L., & Najafabadi, A. H. Z. (2020). Public perspectives in social distancing and other protective measures in Europe: A cross-sectional survey study during the Covid-19 pandemic. *medRxiv*. https://doi.org/10.1101/2020.04.02.20049676

36 Rerimassie, V., Roedema, T., Augustijn, L., Schirmer, A., & Kupper, F. (2021). *Making sense of the COVID-19 pandemic: An analysis of the dynamics of citizen sensemaking practices across Europe* (Report of an analysis of the dynamics of sensemaking practices). RETHINK SciComm.eu, Issue. R. SciComm

37 Rivas-De-roca, R., García-Gordillo, M., & Rojas-Torrijos, J. L. (2021). Communication strategies on Twitter and institutional websites in the Covid-19 second wave:

Analysis of the governments of Germany, Spain, Portugal, and the United Kingdom. *Revista Latina de Comunicacion Social, 79*, 49–72. https://doi.org/10.4185/RLCS-2021-1517

38 Rybnikova, I., Juknevičienė, V., Toleikienė, R., Leach, N., Āboliņa, I., Reinholde, I., & Sillamäe, J. (2022). *Digitalisation and e-leadership in local government before COVID-19: Results of an exploratory study*. Forum Scientiae Oeconomia

39 Utz, S., Gaiser, F., & Wolfers, L. N. (2022). Guidance in the chaos: Effects of science communication by virologists during the COVID-19 crisis in Germany and the role of parasocial phenomena. *Public Understanding of Science*, *31*(6), 799–817. https://doi.org/10.1177/09636625221093194

40 Völkel, G., Fürstberger, A., Schwab, J. D., Werle, S. D., Ikonomi, N., Gscheidmeier, T., Kraus, J. M., Groß, A., Holderried, M., & Balig, J. (2021). Patient empowerment during the COVID-19 pandemic by ensuring safe and fast communication of test results: Implementation and performance of a tracking system. *Journal of Medical Internet Research*, *23*(6), e27348. https://www.jmir.org/2021/6/e31253/

41 Ziegele, M., Resing, M., Frehmann, K., Jackob, N., Jakobs, I., Quiring, O., Schemer, C., Schultz, T., & Viehmann, C. (2022). Deprived, radical, alternatively informed: factors associated with people's belief in Covid-19 related conspiracy theories and their vaccination intentions in Germany. *European Journal of Health Communication*, *3*(2), 97–130. https://doi.org/10.47368/ejhc.2022.205

42 Bene, M., & Boda, Z. (2021). Hungary: Crisis as usual—Populist governance and the pandemic. In *Populism and the Politicization of the COVID-19 crisis in Europe* (pp. 87–100). Springer. https://doi.org/10.1007/978-3-030-66011-6_7

43 Bíró-Nagy, A., & Szászi, Á. J. (2022). The roots of COVID-19 vaccine hesitancy: evidence from Hungary. *Journal of Behavioral Medicine*, 1–16. https://doi.org/10.1007/s10865-022-00314-5

44 Bleyer-Simon, K. (2021). Government repression disguised as anti-disinformation action: Digital journalists' perception of covid-19 policies in hungary. *Journal of Digital Media & Policy*, *12*(1), 159–176. https://doi.org/10.1386/jdmp_00053_1

45 Gabay, G., Gere, A., Fehér, O., Bellissimo, N., & Moskowitz, H. (2021). Rapid discovery of optimal messages for behavioral intervention: the case of Hungary and Covid-19. *Heliyon*, *7*(12), e08535. https://doi.org/10.1016/j.heliyon.2021.e08535

46 Mihelj, S., Kondor, K., & Štětka, V. (2022). Establishing trust in experts during a crisis: Expert trustworthiness and media use during the COVID-19 pandemic. *Science Communication*, *44*(3), 292–319. https://doi.org/10.1177/10755470221100558

47 Szabó, L. P., & Szabó, G. (2022). Attack of the critics: Metaphorical delegitimisation in Viktor Orbán's discourse during the Covid-19 pandemic. *Journal of Language and Politics*, *21*(2), 255–276. https://doi.org/10.1075/jlp.21068.sza

48 Bastoni, S., Wrede, C., Ammar, A., Braakman-Jansen, A., Sanderman, R., Gaggioli, A., Trabelsi, K., Masmoudi, L., Boukhris, O., & Glenn, J. M. (2021). Psychosocial effects and use of communication technologies during home confinement in the first wave of the COVID-19 pandemic in Italy and The Netherlands. *International Journal of Environmental Research and Public Health*, *18*(5), 2619. https://doi.org/10.3390/ijerph18052619

49 Bosa, I., Castelli, A., Castelli, M., Ciani, O., Compagni, A., Galizzi, M. M., Garofano, M., Ghislandi, S., Giannoni, M., & Marini, G. (2021). Corona-regionalism?

Differences in regional responses to COVID-19 in Italy. *Health Policy*, *125*(9), 1179–1187. https://doi.org/10.1016/j.healthpol.2021.07.012
50 Casalegno, C., Civera, C., & Cortese, D. (2021). COVID-19 in Italy and issues in the communication of politics: Bridging the knowledge-behavior gap. *Knowledge Management Research & Practice*, *19*(4), 459–467. https://doi.org/10.1080/14778238.2020.1860664
51 Croucher, S. M., Nguyen, T., Pearson, E., Murray, N., Feekery, A., Spencer, A., Gomez, O., Girardelli, D., & Kelly, S. (2021). A comparative analysis of Covid-19-related prejudice: the United States, Spain, Italy, and New Zealand. *Communication Research Reports*, *38*(2), 79–89. https://doi.org/10.1080/08824096.2021.1885371
52 Cucchiarini, V., Caravona, L., Macchi, L., Perlino, F. L., & Viale, R. (2021). Behavioral changes after the COVID-19 lockdown in Italy. *Frontiers in Psychology*, *12*, 617315. https://doi.org/10.3389/fpsyg.2021.617315
53 Moreira, A., Léon, M., Coda Moscarola, F., & Roumpakis, A. (2021). In the eye of the storm… again! Social policy responses to COVID-19 in Southern Europe. *Social Policy & Administration*, *55*(2), 339–357. https://doi.org/10.1111/spol.12681
54 Mori, E., Barabaschi, B., Cantoni, F., & Virtuani, R. (2021). Local governments' communication through Facebook. Evidences from COVID-19 pandemic in Italy. *Journal of Public Affairs*, *21*(4), e2551. https://doi.org/10.1002/pa.2551
55 Muselli, M., Cofini, V., Desideri, G., & Necozione, S. (2021). Coronavirus (Covid-19) pandemic: How may communication strategies influence our behaviors? *International Journal of Disaster Risk Reduction*, *53*, 101982. https://doi.org/10.1016/j.ijdrr.2020.101982
56 Palamenghi, L., Barello, S., Boccia, S., & Graffigna, G. (2020). Mistrust in biomedical research and vaccine hesitancy: The forefront challenge in the battle against COVID-19 in Italy. *European Journal of Epidemiology*, *35*(8), 785–788. https://doi.org/10.1007/s10654-020-00675-8
57 Reno, C., Maietti, E., Fantini, M. P., Savoia, E., Manzoli, L., Montalti, M., & Gori, D. (2021). Enhancing COVID-19 vaccines acceptance: Results from a survey on vaccine hesitancy in Northern Italy. *Vaccines*, *9*(4), 378. https://doi.org/10.3390/vaccines9040378
58 Rullo, L. (2021). The COVID-19 pandemic crisis and the personalization of the government in Italy. *International Journal of Public Leadership*. https://doi.org/10.1108/IJPL-08-2020-0083
59 Tagliacozzo, S., Albrecht, F., & Ganapati, N. E. (2021). International perspectives on COVID-19 communication ecologies: public health agencies' online communication in Italy, Sweden, and the United States. *American Behavioral Scientist*, *65*(7), 934–955. https://doi.org/10.1177%2F0002764221992832
60 Vacondio, M., Priolo, G., Dickert, S., & Bonini, N. (2021). Worry, perceived threat and media communication as predictors of self-protective behaviors during the COVID-19 outbreak in Europe. *Frontiers in Psychology*, *12*, 577992. https://doi.org/10.3389/fpsyg.2021.577992
61 Buneviciene, I., Bunevicius, R., Bagdonas, S., & Bunevicius, A. (2021). COVID-19 media fatigue: Predictors of decreasing interest and avoidance of COVID-19–related news. *Public Health*, *196*, 124–128. https://doi.org/10.1016/j.puhe.2021.05.024

62 Černikovaitė, M. E. (2022). Manifestation of panic in mass media: Covid 19 case in Lithuania. In *6th World Conference on Media and Mass Communication MEDCOM 2020+ 1*, 17–19 June 2021, Cagliari, Italy, Online Conference: Book of Abstract

63 Dobryninas, A. (2022). Pandemic and infodemic in Lithuania. In D. Siegel, A. Dobryninas, & S. Becucci (Eds.), *Covid-19, society and crime in Europe* (pp. 43–62). Springer. https://doi.org/10.1007/978-3-031-13562-0_3

64 Stankutė, I., Stankūnas, M., & Czabanowska, K. (2021). Leadership and crisis management of COVID-19 pandemic in Lithuania–a survey among public health professionals. *Sztuka Leczenia. Kraków: Uniwersytet Jagielloński Collegium Medicum, 2021, nr. 2, 2*, 9–24. https://doi.org/10.34938/1whm-er33

65 Unikaitė-Jakuntavičienė, I., & Rakutienė, S. (2022). MEPs political communication online: A case study of MEPs elected in Lithuania. *Studies of Transition States and Societies, 14*(1). http://publications.tlu.ee/index.php/stss/article/view/1000

66 Žemaitienė, N., Kukulskienė, M., Miglinė, V., Kubilienė, L., Urbonaitė, G., Digrytė-Šertvytienė, L., Norė, A., & Šmigelskas, K. (2021). *Psychological aspects of media communication during the COVID-19 pandemic: Insights from healthcare and pharmacy specialists in Lithuania*. Healthcare

67 Ashraf, A. (2021). Lessons learned from COVID-19 response for disaster risk management. *Natural Hazards, 107*(2), 2027–2032. https://doi.org/10.1007/s11069-021-04658-0

68 Buijzen, M., Anschütz, D., de Leeuw, R. N., Bleize, D. N., Sadza, A. J., de Droog, S. M., & Rozendaal, E. (2021). Behind the policy frontline in the Netherlands during the Corona crisis. *Journal of Children and Media, 15*(1), 49–54. https://doi.org/10.1080/17482798.2020.1858899

69 deVries, H., Verputten, W., Preissner, C., & Kok, G. (2022). COVID-19 Vaccine hesitancy: The role of information sources and beliefs in Dutch adults. *International Journal of Environmental Research and Public Health, 19*(6), 3205. https://doi.org/10.3390/ijerph19063205

70 DeVries, M., Claassen, L., Te Wierik, M. J., van den Hof, S., Brabers, A. E., de Jong, J. D., Timmermans, D. R., & Timen, A. (2021). Dynamic public perceptions of the coronavirus disease crisis, the Netherlands, 2020. *Emerging Infectious Diseases, 27*(4), 1098–1109. https://doi.org/10.3201%2Feid2704.203328

71 GrootKormelink, T., & Klein Gunnewiek, A. (2022). From "far away" to "shock" to "fatigue" to "back to normal": How young people experienced news during the first wave of the COVID-19 pandemic. *Journalism Studies, 23*(5–6), 669–686. https://doi.org/10.1080/1461670X.2021.1932560

72 Minderhout, R. N., Baksteen, M. C., Numans, M. E., Bruijnzeels, M. A., & Vos, H. M. (2021). Effect of COVID-19 on health system integration in the Netherlands: a mixed-methods study. *Journal of the American College of Emergency Physicians Open, 2*(3), e12433. https://doi.org/10.1002/emp2.12433

73 Mouter, N., de Ruijter, A., de Wit, G. A., Lambooij, M. S., van Wijhe, M., van Exel, J., & Kessels, R. (2022). "Please, you go first!" preferences for a COVID-19 vaccine among adults in the Netherlands. *Social Science & Medicine, 292*, 114626. https://doi.org/10.1016/j.socscimed.2021.114626

74 tePoel, F., Linn, A. J., Baumgartner, S. E., van Dijk, L., & Smit, E. S. (2021). Sick for Information?: Information needs and media use of the Dutch public during the

Covid-19 pandemic. *European Journal of Health Communication*, *2*(3), 24–43. https://doi.org/10.47368/ejhc.2021.302

75 vanden Broek-Altenburg, E., & Atherly, A. (2021). Adherence to COVID-19 policy measures: Behavioral insights from The Netherlands and Belgium. *PloS One*, *16*(5), e0250302. https://doi.org/10.1371/journal.pone.0250302

76 Aparicio, J. T., de Sequeira, J. S., & Costa, C. J. (2021). Emotion analysis of Portuguese political parties communication over the covid-19 Pandemic. In *2021 16th Iberian Conference on Information Systems and Technologies (CISTI)*

77 Araújo, R., Lopes, F., Magalhães, O., Sá, A., & Aguiar, A. (2021). Behavior guidance during the Covid-19 pandemic: Health literacy as a weapon against the virus. *Health communication*, 1–9. https://doi.org/10.1080/10410236.2021.1956070

78 Belim, C. (2022). Communicating COVID-19 on Twitter at supranational and national levels: The European Union and Portugal with "the ball in their court". *KOME*, *0*(0), 0–22. https://doi.org/10.17646/KOME.75672.89

79 CastroSeixas, E. (2021). War metaphors in political communication on COVID-19. *Frontiers in Sociology*, *5*(583680), 112. https://doi.org/10.3389/fsoc.2020.583680

80 Delicado, A., & Rowland, J. (2021). Visual representations of science in a pandemic: COVID-19 in images. *Frontiers in Communication*, 59. https://doi.org/10.3389/fcomm.2021.645725

81 Fernandes, N., Costa, D., Costa, D., Keating, J., & Arantes, J. (2021). Predicting COVID-19 vaccination intention: The determinants of vaccine hesitancy. *Vaccines*, *9*(10), 1161. https://doi.org/10.3390/vaccines9101161

82 Gonçalves, G., Piñeiro-Naval, V., & de Sá, S. (2022). Risk communication and disinformation in Portugal: How media consumption affects the understanding of COVID-19 health-protective messages. In R. Tench, J. Meng, & A. Moreno (Eds.), *Strategic communication in a global crisis* (pp. 112–131). Routledge. https://doi.org/10.4324/9781003184669

83 Jiménez-Sánchez, Á., Margalina, V.-M., & Vayas-Ruiz, E. (2020). Governmental communication and brand advertising during the COVID-19 pandemic. *Tripodos*, *2*(47), 29–46. https://doi.org/10.51698/tripodos.2020.47p29-46

84 Leão, T., Amorim, M., Fraga, S., & Barros, H. (2021). What doubts, concerns and fears about COVID-19 emerged during the first wave of the pandemic? *Patient Education and Counseling*, *104*(2), 235–241. https://doi.org/10.1016/j.pec.2020.11.002

85 Mont'Alvão, C. R., Duarte, E., & Teles, J. (2021). Perceptions about the design of informational materials used in the fight against COVID-19 in Portugal and Brazil. *Information Design Journal*, *26*(2), 105–123. https://doi.org/10.1075/idj.20027.mon

86 Padeiro, M., Bueno-Larraz, B., & Freitas, Â. (2021). Local governments' use of social media during the COVID-19 pandemic: The case of Portugal. *Government Information Quarterly*, *38*(4), 1–20. https://doi.org/10.1016/j.giq.2021.101620

87 Pasion, R., Paiva, T. O., Fernandes, C., & Barbosa, F. (2020). The AGE effect on protective behaviors during the COVID-19 outbreak: Sociodemographic, perceptions and psychological accounts. *Front Psychol*, *11*, 561785. https://doi.org/10.3389/fpsyg.2020.561785

88 Saraiva, I., & Ferreira, C. (2020). *The impact of visual communication in COVID-19's prevention and risk mitigation*. International Conference on Design and Digital Communication

89 Silva, P., Costa, E., & Moniz, J. (2021). A Portuguese miracle: the politics of the first phase of Covid-19 in Portugal. *South European Society and Politics*, 1–29. https://doi.org/10.1080/13608746.2021.1979741
90 Soares, P., Rocha, J. V., Moniz, M., Gama, A., Laires, P. A., Pedro, A. R., Dias, S., Leite, A., & Nunes, C. (2021). Factors associated with COVID-19 vaccine hesitancy. *Vaccines*, *9*(3), 300. https://doi.org/10.3390/vaccines9030300
91 Strzelecki, A., Azevedo, A., & Albuquerque, A. (2020). *Correlation between the spread of COVID-19 and the interest in personal protective measures in Poland and Portugal*. Healthcare
92 Bjørkdahl, K., Kjeldsen, J. E., Villadsen, L., & Vigsø, O. (2021). Argumentum ad solidaritatem: Rhetorical Leadership Strategies in Scandinavia during COVID-19. In *Communicating COVID-19* (pp. 163–184). Springer. https://doi.org/10.1007/978-3-030-79735-5_9
93 Esaiasson, P., Sohlberg, J., Ghersetti, M., & Johansson, B. (2021). How the coronavirus crisis affects citizen trust in institutions and in unknown others: Evidence from 'the Swedish experiment'. *European Journal of Political Research*, *60*(3), 748–760. https://doi.org/10.1111/1475-6765.12419
94 Habib, H. (2020). Covid-19: What Sweden taught Scandinavia for the second wave. *BMJ*, *371*, 1–3. https://doi.org/10.1136/bmj.m4456
95 Helsingen, L. M., Refsum, E., Gjøstein, D. K., Løberg, M., Bretthauer, M., Kalager, M., & Emilsson, L. (2020). The COVID-19 pandemic in Norway and Sweden–threats, trust, and impact on daily life: A comparative survey. *BMC Public Health*, *20*(1), 1–10. https://doi.org/10.1186/s12889-020-09615-3
96 Ihlen, Ø., Johansson, B., & Blach-Ørsten, M. (2022). Experiencing COVID-19 in Denmark, Norway and Sweden: The role of the Nordic model. In R. Tench, J. Meng, & A. Moreno (Eds.), *Strategic communication in a global crisis* (pp. 184–198). Routledge. https://doi.org/10.4324/9781003184669
97 Ihlen, Ø., Just, S. N., Kjeldsen, J. E., Mølster, R., Offerdal, T. S., Rasmussen, J., & Skogerbø, E. (2022). Transparency beyond information disclosure: Strategies of the Scandinavian public health authorities during the COVID-19 pandemic. *Journal of Risk Research*, 1–14. https://doi.org/10.1080/13669877.2022.2077416
98 Johansson, B., Hopmann, D. N., & Shehata, A. (2021). When the rally-around-the-flag effect disappears, or: When the COVID-19 pandemic becomes "normalized". *Journal of Elections, Public Opinion and Parties*, *31*(sup1), 321–334. https://doi.org/10.1080/17457289.2021.1924742
99 Johansson, B., Sohlberg, J., Esaiasson, P., & Ghersetti, M. (2021). Why Swedes don't wear face masks during the pandemic-a consequence of blindly trusting the government. *Journal of International Crisis and Risk Communication Research*, *4*(2), 335–358. https://doi.org/10.30658/jicrcr.4.2.6
100 Johansson, B., & Vigsø, O. (2021). Sweden: Lone hero or stubborn outlier? In D. Lilleker, I. A. Coman, M. Gregor, & E. Novelli (Eds.), *Political communication and COVID-19* (pp. 155–164). Routledge. https://doi.org/10.4324/9781003120254

Appendix B References for Table 10.2

1 Berg, M. (2022). Information-precarity for refugee women in Hamburg, Germany, during the COVID-19 pandemic. *Information, Communication & Society*, 1–17. https://doi.org/10.1080/1369118X.2022.2129271

2 Bruinede Bruin, W., & Bennett, D. (2020). Relationships between Initial COVID-19 risk perceptions and protective health behaviors: A national survey. *American Journal of Preventative Medicine*, *59*(2), 157–167. https://doi.org/10.1016/j.amepre.2020.05.001

3 Buijzen, M., Anschütz, D., de Leeuw, R. N., Bleize, D. N., Sadza, A. J., de Droog, S. M., & Rozendaal, E. (2021). Behind the policy frontline in the Netherlands during the Corona crisis. *Journal of Children and Media*, *15*(1), 49–54. https://doi.org/10.1080/17482798.2020.1858899

4 Buneviciene, I., Bunevicius, R., Bagdonas, S., & Bunevicius, A. (2021). COVID-19 media Fatigue: predictors of decreasing interest and avoidance of COVID-19–related news. *Public Health*, *196*, 124–128. https://doi.org/10.1016/j.puhe.2021.05.024

5 CastroSeixas, E. (2021). War metaphors in political communication on COVID-19. *Frontiers in Sociology*, *5*(583680), 112. https://doi.org/10.3389/fsoc.2020.583680

6 Cucchiarini, V., Caravona, L., Macchi, L., Perlino, F. L., & Viale, R. (2021). Behavioral changes after the COVID-19 lockdown in Italy. *Frontiers in Psychology*, *12*, 617315. https://doi.org/10.3389/fpsyg.2021.617315

7 deNoronha, N., Moniz, M., Gama, A., Laires, P. A., Goes, A. R., Pedro, A. R., Dias, S., Soares, P., & Nunes, C. (2022). Non-adherence to COVID-19 lockdown: who are they? A cross-sectional study in Portugal. *Public Health*, *211*, 5–13. https://doi.org/10.1016/j.puhe.2022.07.001

8 DeVries, M., Claassen, L., Te Wierik, M. J., van den Hof, S., Brabers, A. E., de Jong, J. D., Timmermans, D. R., & Timen, A. (2021). Dynamic public perceptions of the coronavirus disease crisis, the Netherlands, 2020. *Emerging Infectious Diseases*, *27*(4), 1098–1109. https://doi.org/10.3201%2Feid2704.203328

9 Diers-Lawson, A., Omondi, G., & Hillier, S. (2022). Shooting from the hip or taking careful aim? Developing the VISTA analytic framework comparing the English and Scottish visual campaigns for self-protective behavior throughout the COVID-19 pandemic. *Journal of Visual Political Communication, TBA (TBA)*, TBA. https://doi.org/TBA

10 Gabay, G., Gere, A., Fehér, O., Bellissimo, N., & Moskowitz, H. (2021). Rapid discovery of optimal messages for behavioral intervention: The case of Hungary and Covid-19. *Heliyon*, *7*(12), e08535. https://doi.org/10.1016/j.heliyon.2021.e08535

11 Gehrau, V., Fujarski, S., Lorenz, H., Schieb, C., & Blöbaum, B. (2021). The impact of health information exposure and source credibility on COVID-19 vaccination intention in Germany. *International Journal of Environmental Research and Public Health*, *18*(9), 1–12. https://doi.org/10.3390/ijerph18094678

12 Genys, D., & Krikštolaitis, R. (2021). Interrelation among COVID-19 situation, evaluation of government actions and subjective well-being in Lithuania. *Filosofija Sociologija*, *32*(4), 335–345. https://doi.org/10.6001/fil-soc.v32i4.4617

13 Gonçalves, G., Piñeiro-Naval, V., & de Sá, S. (2022). Risk communication and disinformation in Portugal: How media consumption affects the understanding of

COVID-19 health-protective messages. In R. Tench, J. Meng, & A. Moreno (Eds.), *Strategic communication in a global crisis* (pp. 112–131). Routledge. https://doi.org/10.4324/9781003184669

14 Hansson, S., Orru, K., Torpan, S., Bäck, A., Kazemekaityte, A., Meyer, S. F., Ludvigsen, J., Savadori, L., Galvagni, A., & Pigrée, A. (2021). COVID-19 information disorder: Six types of harmful information during the pandemic in Europe. *Journal of Risk Research, 24*(3-4), 380–393. https://doi.org/10.1080/13669877.2020.1871058

15 Johansson, B., Sohlberg, J., Esaiasson, P., & Ghersetti, M. (2021). Why swedes don't wear face masks during the pandemic-a consequence of blindly trusting the government. *Journal of International Crisis and Risk Communication Research, 4*(2), 335–358. https://doi.org/10.30658/jicrcr.4.2.6

16 Jørgensen, F., Bor, A., & Petersen, M. B. (2020). *Compliance without fear: Predictors of protective behavior during the first wave of the Covid-19 pandemic* (PsyArXiv, Issue)

17 Kieweg, P. H., Schöberl, S., & Palozzi, G. (2021). The role of communication in COVID-19 crisis management: findings about information behavior of German and Italian young people. *International Journal of Business Research and Management (IJBRM), 12*(5), 263–288. https://www.cscjournals.org/journals/IJBRM/description.php

18 Kojan, L., Burbach, L., Ziefle, M., & Calero Valdez, A. (2022). Perceptions of behavior efficacy, not perceptions of threat, are drivers of COVID-19 protective behavior in Germany. *Humanities and Social Sciences Communications, 9*(1), 1–15. https://doi.org/10.1057/s41599-022-01098-4

19 Leder, J., Pastukhov, A., & Schütz, A. (2020). Social value orientation, subjective effectiveness, perceived cost, and the use of protective measures during the COVID-19 pandemic in Germany. *Comprehensive Results in Social Psychology*, 1–23. https://doi.org/10.1080/23743603.2020.1828850

20 Lee, Y., & Li, J. Y. Q. (2021). The role of communication transparency and organizational trust in publics' perceptions, attitudes and social distancing behavior: A case study of the COVID-19 outbreak. *Journal of Contingencies and Crisis Management, 29*(4), 368–384. https://doi.org/10.1111/1468-5973.12354

21 Margraf, J., Brailovskaia, J., & Schneider, S. (2021). Adherence to behavioral Covid-19 mitigation measures strongly predicts mortality. *PloS One, 16*(3), e0249392. https://doi.org/10.1371/journal.pone.0249392

22 Muselli, M., Cofini, V., Desideri, G., & Necozione, S. (2021). Coronavirus (Covid-19) pandemic: How may communication strategies influence our behaviors? *International Journal of Disaster Risk Reduction, 53*, 101982. https://doi.org/10.1016/j.ijdrr.2020.101982

23 Papageorge, N. W., Zahn, M. V., Belot, M., van den Broek-Altenburg, E., Choi, S., Jamison, J. C., & Tripodi, E. (2021). Socio-demographic factors associated with self-protecting behavior during the Covid-19 pandemic. *Journal of Population Economics, 34*, 691–738. https://doi.org/10.1007/s00148-020-00818-x

24 Petrocchi, S., Iannello, P., Ongaro, G., Antonietti, A., & Pravettoni, G. (2022). The interplay between risk and protective factors during the initial height of the COVID-19 crisis in Italy: The role of risk aversion and intolerance of ambiguity on distress. *Current Psychology, 41*(1), 437–448. https://doi.org/10.1007/s12144-021-01601-1

25 Sheridan, A., Andersen, A. L., Hansen, E. T., & Johannesen, N. (2020). Social distancing laws cause only small losses of economic activity during the COVID-19 pandemic in Scandinavia. *Proceedings of the National Academy of Sciences*, *117*(34), 20468–20473. https://doi.org/10.1073/pnas.2010068117

26 Strzelecki, A., Azevedo, A., & Albuquerque, A. (2020). *Correlation between the spread of COVID-19 and the interest in personal protective measures in Poland and Portugal*. Healthcare

27 Vacondio, M., Priolo, G., Dickert, S., & Bonini, N. (2021). Worry, perceived threat and media communication as predictors of self-protective behaviors during the COVID-19 outbreak in Europe. *Frontiers in Psychology*, *12*, 577992. https://doi.org/10.3389/fpsyg.2021.577992

28 vanden Broek-Altenburg, E., & Atherly, A. (2021). Adherence to COVID-19 policy measures: Behavioral insights from The Netherlands and Belgium. *PloS One*, *16*(5), e0250302. https://doi.org/10.1371/journal.pone.0250302

29 Varghese, N. E., Sabat, I., Neumann-Böhme, S., Schreyögg, J., Stargardt, T., Torbica, A., van Exel, J., Barros, P. P., & Brouwer, W. (2021). Risk communication during COVID-19: A descriptive study on familiarity with, adherence to and trust in the WHO preventive measures. *PloS One*, *16*(4), e0250872. https://doi.org/10.1371/journal.pone.0250872

30 Kamburova, M., & Georgieva, S. (2021). The impact of the COVID-19 epidemic and anti-epidemic measures in the Roma neighborhood in Bulgaria. *European Journal of Public Health*, *31*(Supplement_3), ckab164. 244

31 Džakula, A., Banadinović, M., Lovrenčić, I. L., Vajagić, M., Dimova, A., Rohova, M., Minev, M., Scintee, S. G., Vladescu, C., & Farcasanu, D. (2022). A comparison of health system responses to COVID-19 in Bulgaria, Croatia and Romania in 2020. *Health Policy*, *126*, 456–464. https://doi.org/10.1016/j.healthpol.2022.02.003

32 Popova, M., & Valkov, I. (2022). Media representations and the politics of the COVID-19 pandemic in Bulgaria. *Journal of Media Ethics*, 1–4. https://doi.org/10.1080/23736992.2022.2057313

33 Todorova, B., & Padareva-Ilieva, G. (2021). Nostalgia as a device for dealing with traumatic experiences during the COVID-19 crisis. *East European Journal of Psycholinguistics*, *8*(1), 110–124. https://doi.org/10.29038/eejpl.2021.8.1.tod

11 Communication Inequality of Ethnic Groups in Public Health Crisis

State of the Art and Model of Community-Based Crisis Response

Hui Zhao and Jesper Falkheimer

Pandemic-related health disparities among social groups have attracted attention from researchers, the media, and the public in many countries. One might think this was not so relevant to countries like Sweden, a developed Nordic welfare society with a long history of social equality. But the statistics from the Public Health Agency in Sweden showed that during the early COVID-19-pandemic, people born in Turkey, Ethiopia, Somalia, Chile, and Iraq represented the five highest incident rates of the COVID-19 in Sweden, despite the valiant national efforts to fight the pandemic (Folkhälsomyndigheten, 2020). Furthermore, Sweden is far from the only country where people from ethnic groups have been disproportionately affected by COVID-19. Ethnic groups in this chapter refers to communities that have foreign background, namely, people from ethnic groups at least have one parent born abroad. According to public health experts from the neighboring country Norway, people born in Somalia had infection rates more than ten times above the national average in the early stage of the pandemic outbreak (Cookson & Milne, 2020). The same pattern is shown in other countries in Europe. In the U.K., different ethnic groups were disproportionately affected, and black people were more than four times likely to die from COVID-19 than white people, according to stark official figures that expose a dramatic divergence in the impact of the coronavirus pandemic in England and Wales.

These statistical reports demonstrate that the COVID-19 pandemic has not only posed unprecedented threats to global health but has also raised significant concerns about equality and inclusiveness. To public health experts and researchers, the fact that people from ethnic groups have been disproportionately affected by COVID-19 (e.g., CDC, 2021) is not a surprise. Previous research has addressed how social conditions, such as social class and socioeconomic status (SES), determine which social groups are more vulnerable than others in crises (Maguire & Hagan, 2007). Kalocsányiová et al. (2022) conclude:

> … there was a consensus before the pandemic among communication scholars and practitioners that groups with less social power such as minority

DOI: 10.4324/9781003375296-14

> language speakers, (forced) migrants and those living in poverty, may require targeted and tailored messaging to ensure that they have equal access to health and risk information and are capable to act upon it.

There is also a correlation between SES and ethnic groups' vulnerability to COVID-19, and several explanatory factors (Bhala et al., 2020).

> Socioeconomic factors have had an effect on the distribution and outcome of the COVID-19 pandemic, both in Sweden and in other countries, and such factors can explain a significant part of the differences between foreign-born and Swedish-born. When adjusting for socioeconomic factors and living conditions, the relative risk of needing ICU [intensive care] care is significantly reduced for certain groups of foreign-born. There is an effect of both income and education, where lower income and shorter education is associated with an increased risk of needing ICU care. The same is true for the mortality risk.
>
> (Folkhälsomyndigheten, 2020, p. 8)

While acknowledging the work done so far in studying disparities of public health outcomes among ethnic minorities, this chapter argues that we also need to consider communication inequality as a cause of vulnerability that could hinder some social groups from resilience to crises. Needless to say, strategic communication (in the form of risk, crisis and public health communication) is not the overall solution to the problem addressed. This is not only a communication problem. But there are undoubtedly reasons to investigate the role that public health risk and crisis communication have, especially regarding access to information, trust, and the formation of knowledge, attitudes, and behavior.

To this end, this conceptual paper sets up two main research goals: (1) to understand which communication inequalities exist in the context of COVID-19 concerning ethnic groups, and (2) to explore how strategic health communication could be implemented to reach, engage, and communicate effectively with ethnic groups in the context of the pandemic. The following section reviews the body of work that addresses communication inequality of ethnic groups during public health crises, interrogates the literature, and raises pertinent points for consideration from the perspectives of the public and organizations. It then proposes a community-based crisis response model in strategic health communication. Finally, this chapter returns to a case of neighborhood mums during a vaccine campaign in Sweden to illustrate the explanatory power of the proposed community-based crisis response model.

Literature Review

This section presents a literature review of existing studies of the manifestation of communication inequality among ethnic groups during public health crises.

Public Health Disparities and Communication Inequality

Despite some positive signs toward reducing inequality in many dimensions in society, inequality still persists, and the COVID-19 pandemic has unfortunately deepened existing disparities, which are, in turn, amplifying the impacts of the pandemic (Ahmed et al., 2020; Blundell et al., 2022). Studies show that the COVID-19 pandemic has raised significant concerns about equality in societies, including economic, social, health sectors, etc. (e.g., Kim, 2020; Kwan et al., 2021; Mejía-Dorantes et al., 2021). Many studies have addressed the social determinants of public health, which may lead to health inequities in large vulnerable populations in societies. Some current studies pointed out that COVID-19 pandemic-driven inequalities in different sectors of society also find a parallel in communication (Viswanath et al., 2020).

Existing studies have identified many social determinants that lead to disparities in public health outcomes, such as demographics, personal health beliefs, and health insurance status (Derose et al., 2011). Among them, communication plays a crucial role in determining public health outcomes. Previous research on public health crises has pointed out the key role of communication in disseminating public health information, raising public awareness, increasing public knowledge, and influencing the public to adopt protective behaviors (Viswanath & Emmons, 2006). Nevertheless, existing literature also notes that individuals and social groups do not have the same communication literacy and competence (e.g., Andrulis et al., 2007; Taylor-Clark et al., 2010), which is characterized as communication inequality among social groups in a society. Hence, Pareek et al. (2020) call for more studies to examine communication-related inequality during the pandemic. Addressing communication inequality could reduce ethnic groups' vulnerability and improve adaptive capacity in the realm of health outcomes.

Communication inequality in this chapter refers to "differences in the generation, manipulation, and distribution of information among social groups; and differences in (a) access and use, (b) attention, (c) retention, and (d) capacity to act on relevant information among individuals" (Viswanath & Emmons, 2006, p. 242). In the context of public health crises, communication inequality can be understood as "the differences in exposure to public health communication messages and capacity to access, process, and act upon the information received" (Lin, Savoia, et al., 2014, p. 484). Thus, communication inequality in the context of public health crisis leads to heterogeneity in exposure to public health communication messages and hence disparities in health-related knowledge, behavior choices, health outcome, and, ultimately, the resilience of particular social groups to cope with the crisis in even a same society (Lin, Jung, et al., 2014). Communication inequalities may not only hamper the resilience of certain social groups subject to a disproportionate burden of adversity, but also reduce the resilience of public health authorities and societal systems to prevent and respond to a public health crisis effectively.

Ethnicity and Communication Inequality in Public Health Crisis

Existing studies have identified various elements as mediating factors that moderate communication inequality, such as SES, social capital, socioecological factors, and media use. Nevertheless, fewer studies explore ethnicity as a mediating factor in shaping communication inequality, even though ethnicity has been identified with an enduring connection to both health and communication inequality (Lee, 2009). According to Pareek et al. (2020), ethnic groups are at increased risk of disease acquisition, disease severity, and poor health outcomes during the COVID-19 pandemic for several reasons. Among them, communication is one of the reasons linked to both health and social behaviors and, more specifically, one connected to "education and understanding about COVID-19", "English literacy and proficiency", and "health-seeking behavior" (Pareek et al., 2020, p. 1421).

Ethnicity is a complex entity composed of social constructs, cultural identity, and behavioral patterns. Ethnic classification systems have limitations yet still been used to explore genetic and other population differences. Therefore, ethnicity as a concept, fully or accurately, captures the environmental, cultural, behavioral, or socio-political experiences that health communication faces during a public health crisis. Hence, this chapter takes ethnicity as "macrosocial units" (Ragin, 1987, p. 7) to scrutinize and compare communication inequality among different ethnic groups in a multicultural society (Falkheimer & Heide, 2009). As Viswanath and Emmons (2006) observe, most studies have centered attention on the individual level of analysis, leaving the community-level phenomenon underexplored. The community's characteristics would determine, in part, local access to goods and services, social norms, and the ability of residents to maintain social control over individual behavior, to mention a few.

The Manifestation of Communication Inequality among Ethnic Groups

Communication inequality exacerbates health outcomes through mechanisms in which access to information, literacy (in relation to a language, media, or health literacy), and trust play vital roles.

Media Literacy

Studies particularly demonstrate that ethnic communities are less likely to have the necessary media literacy and skills to access and use information resources for health-related purposes (Ritzhaupt et al., 2013). Prior research in the US demonstrates a significant disparity in internet access and digital literacy among ethnic groups, especially for those over the age of 65 (Eruchalu et al., 2021).

Before the pandemic, studies have shown differences in media access, skills, literacy, and consumption between ethnic groups and the rest of society (e.g., Nguyen et al., 2020; 2021; Viswanath et al., 2020). Taking Sweden as an example, prior studies show that ethnic groups' media consumption behaviors are distinct from those of native Swedes, including (1) the use of mainstream media is relatively low in ethnic communities (Andersson, 2005), while (2) the consumption of media content from their native countries retains large (Falkheimer, 2008).

The COVID-19 pandemic has deepened the media issue among ethnic groups as societies increasingly rely on digital technology for social connection and support (Germain & Yong, 2020). Even in 2020 the access to the internet and digital skills is not universal; studies show that ethnic communities have worse internet access than the rest of society. Helsper and Reisdorf (2017)s study draws attention to the link between digital exclusion, social isolation, and poor mental health during the COVID-19 pandemic. More specifically, Fancourt and colleagues pointed out that the lack of internet access and sufficient media literacy among ethnic groups has led to a higher likelihood of isolation and being less able to access crucial public health guidance and key services such as online food ordering (2021).

Language Barrier

Studies show the COVID-19 pandemic is characterized by the large-scale exclusion of linguistic minorities from timely high-quality information (e.g., Chong & Druckman, 2007; Grey, 2020; Hopkyns, 2020; Piller et al., 2020). The language barrier has created significant challenges for some ethnic communities, recent migrants or culturally and linguistically diverse communities, who are overrepresented in the COVID-19 infectivity and mortality (Grey, 2020; Knights et al., 2021). These studies also demonstrated that the inadequacy of multilingual messaging stems from the longstanding neglect of minority languages and the lack of investment in multilingual capabilities. Furthermore, the enforced isolation from the lockdown disconnected individuals in the ethnic groups from their communicative infrastructures, which created more difficulties for ethnic groups to receive timely, high-quality information. For example, Elers et al. (2021) show that, due to the lockdown, many individuals, especially older people, have trouble receiving relevant health information in an understandable language as the lockdown has cut their access to translators and communal collectives.

In addition, the existence of multilingual messages alone does not guarantee that these messages are of sufficient quality. O'Brien and his colleagues (O'Brien et al., 2018; O'Brien & Federici, 2019) raised questions regarding multilingual health information: (1) *availability* or whether multilingual health information is recognized as an essential service and is available to society; (2) *accessibility* or whether multilingual health information is freely accessible on multiple platforms with multiple modes (spoken, written, signed, digital, etc.); (3) *acceptability* or whether multilingual health information is accurate and appropriate; and/or (4) *adaptability* or whether multilingual health can be adapted to various technological demands and mobile populations.

The Model: Toward a Community-Based Crisis Response

Communication inequality, including media literacy and language barrier, has led to public health disparities among ethnic groups during public health crises. Based on participatory communication, the chapter introduces a community-based crisis response model to address communication inequality induced public health disparities.

Participatory Communication and Public Health Crisis

Participatory communication is a concept that has been used mainly in health communication (Schiavo, 2013). Participatory communication in the context of health communication considers community members as part of meaning construction and development efforts (Basu & Dutta, 2009; Schiavo, 2013). In this sense, participatory communication generates a communicative effort that enables community members to weave together individual and collective discourses on health and living (Frey et al., 2000). Participatory communication has been used in communication campaigns (Rogers & Singhal, 2009).

Participatory communication resonates well with strategic communication as it aims to understand the clutter in the information environment (audience perspective) and communication strategically to reach one's intended target audience with effective messages (organizational perspective). Strategic communication, defined initially as "the purposeful use of communication by an organization to fulfil its mission" (Hallahan et al., 2007, p. 3), denotes goal-oriented communicativeness. Recent developments of a participatory approach to strategic communication (Falkheimer & Heide, 2017) emphasize the importance of engaging the concerned communities in implementing strategic communication at the local level. In this sense, participatory strategic communication views strategic communication as a social phenomenon (Ihlen & Verhoeven, 2017) that occurs in discrete societal contexts with implications for how people (and organizations) purposefully affect and relate to one another (Falkheimer & Heide, 2018; Heath & Gregory, 2014).

Participatory strategic communication underscores that the public perspective is equally important to the organization's perspective in achieving organizational missions. In the context of public health communication, participatory strategic communication entails two aspects. First, strategic communication could be used to enhance the participation of marginalized communities during public health campaigns. For instance, configuring participatory communication platforms in designed campaigns to diffuse the intervention to local communities. Second, strategic communication could also contribute to enacting agencies of local communities in the process of meaning-making during public campaigns. In this sense, participatory communication involves community members as participants in the process of meaning construction. It constitutes a communicative effort that enables community members to weave together individual and collective discourses on health and living (Frey et al., 2000).

A Model of Community-Based Crisis Response: Macro, Meso, and Micro Practices

Applying participatory strategic communication in public health facilitates community dialog and participation to empower local communities to find and solve their solutions during a public health crisis. A community could be understood as a variety of social, ethnic, cultural, or geographical associations, for example, a school, workplace, city, neighborhood, organized patient or professional group, or association of peer leaders (Schiavo, 2013). Hence, communities always tend to share similar values, beliefs, and overall objectives and priorities. Participatory strategic communication helps local communities to frame the health issue in a way that will respond to their needs and effectively address them. This chapter proposes a community-based crisis response framework to address communication inequality issues during a public health crisis. The three dimensions of the framework are depicted in Table 11.1.

Macro Level

The macro level of the community-based crisis response model examines the broader systemic and structural factors that contribute to enhance long-term social inclusion of all, irrespective of ethnicity. Therefore, the society as a whole need to work on large-scale systematic change such as crafting laws and molding social policy to develop a more equal, inclusive, sustainable communication system to meet challenges of the immigration flow. Even if the model we propose identifies the micro level as the most crucial when it comes to impact and value-creation, there is need of laws, frameworks, policies and knowledge diffusion at macro levels, from national to international actors. Communication inequality not only undermines people's well-being, but, more broadly, prevents diverse contributions of ethnic groups to social cohesion. In this regard, we need to further advance our knowledge about ethnic relations, in particular during public health crises. Furthermore, the inclusive approach to

Table 11.1 Three levels of the community-based crisis response model

Level	*Crisis response*
Macro Level	Working toward large-scale systematic change such as crafting laws and molding social policy.
Meso Level	Working with groups and organizations such as neighborhoods, nonprofits, and churches.
Micro level	Working directly with individuals by providing health information.

public health crisis communication would address international migration and ethnic relations and contributes to the solidarity and sustainable development of refugee-hosting countries.

Meso Level

The meso level of the community-based crisis response model focuses on actively working with existing organizations with ethnic communities in the co-creation of effective communication strategies. First, it is vital to understand the community's key characteristics, structure, values, needs, attitudes, social norms, health behaviors, and priorities. The meso level of the community-based model aims to leverage the existing infrastructure to facilitate rapid dissemination of culturally relevant resources and materials to economically and socially marginalized communities whose socioeconomic challenges are exacerbated by a public health crisis. To this end, the meso level of the community-based model could focus on developing partnerships and ownership of local communities during public health crises. One of the main strategies is to facilitate and maintain partnerships with organizations within ethnic communities to rapidly engage with ethnic minority populations (Costas-Bradstreet, 2004). Studies show that the partnership with organizations within ethnic groups could forge authentic communication with the ethnic population to diminish health disparities (Brewer et al., 2020). The community-based model also needs to create the ownership of local communities of the public health communication process. The ownership acknowledges the participatory nature of well-designed health communication interventions in which communities and other key groups are the lead architects of the communication process.

Micro Level

The micro level of the community-based crisis response framework is to work directly with individuals by providing health information to an individual in ethnic communities. The aim of participatory strategic communication is to increase interactions with individuals in ethnic communities and to involve them throughout the crisis communication campaign cycle. To this end, on the one hand, we need to identify and map out the communication challenges of the individuals within ethnic groups during the crisis. From the participatory view (Falkheimer & Heide, 2018) of strategic communication, we must first acknowledge and understand the ethnically diverse public reactions to critical information or their interests in public health crises. Therefore, we need to examine participants' communication behavior, including attention to information, sources of information, diffusion of information, trust of information, and acting on the information.

On the other hand, it is crucial to identify and motivate trusted messengers, such as public opinion leaders within ethnic communities. For example, engagement with leaders of faith-based organizations on infectious disease prevention initiatives led to successes during the Ebola outbreak in West Africa and increases in influenza immunization rates during the H1N1 pandemic (Ali et al., 2022). Therefore, we emphasize the importance of interpersonal communication in managing ethnic relations during public health communication. Previous studies have found that interpersonal communication is a channel or a parallel source to mass communication that is important to create behavior changes during campaigns (Cartwright, 1949).

Neighborhood Mums during Vaccine Campaign in Sweden: An Illustrated Case

Pandemic-Related Health Disparities in Sweden

This chapter takes ethnic groups in Sweden as a case to explore communication inequality and its impact on public health crises in the context of the COVID-19 pandemic. Pandemic-related health disparities among social groups in Sweden have attracted attention from both the media and the public. The recent statistics from Folkhälsomyndigheten have proved that the incidence rates (the number of confirmed cases during the given period) are higher in some ethnic groups. According to Folkhälsomyndigheten (2020), the incidence of COVID-19 was highest among people born in Turkey, followed by Ethiopia, Somalia, Chile, and Iraq between 13 March and 7 May 2020. In this chapter, health outcome (e.g., reported incidence) is considered an indicator of resilience during a public health crisis. In this regard, the above-mentioned ethnic groups are less resilient to the ongoing public health crisis. In a special report focusing on differences between Swedish-born and Foreign-born inhabitants, Folkhälsomyndigheten shows the differences between different groups. The statistics show that inhabitants born in Africa and the Middle East have been the most vulnerable. Besides high age, the background factor that has the most impact there is, as mentioned in the introduction, a strong effect of SES factors, especially low income and lower education.

Among many studies that explore different sociodemographic factors and their influence on communication inequality, race/ethnicity/minority has been recognized as one of the key factors that shape communication competencies (e.g., Lin, Jung, et al., 2014). In the context of Sweden, some studies (e.g., Andersson, 2005; Camauër, 2005) depict the different communication behaviors of ethnic groups to native Swedes: (1) the role of mainstream media is relatively low in ethnicity groups (Andersson, 2005); (2) ethnicity groups have more significant consumption of media content from their native countries (Falkheimer, 2008); (3) ethnicity groups rely more on new media to gain information (Falkheimer & Heide, 2009). In other words, ethnic groups "have not been socialized into a certain and national media tradition the way native Swedes have" (Falkheimer &

Heide, 2009, p. 60). This was concluded several years ago; and considering the development of new media technologies and new media use patterns since then, this has become even clearer. Meanwhile, few studies have so far investigated communication inequality among ethnic groups and its influence on knowledge and misconceptions about a perceived threat in these communities, as well as their subsequent behavioral compliances.

Neighborhood Mums during Vaccine Campaign in Sweden

An example of the critical role that women may have in public health crises can be found in the city of Helsingborg, Sweden, during the COVID-19 pandemic. The case described below is based on two interviews with communication managers in the municipality (May 2022) and an internal analysis of evaluation made by the municipality.

When the public officials in charge of risk and crisis communication were bewildered at the difficulty of reaching immigrants and inhabitants with differing foreign backgrounds in the municipality, a grassroots initiative got in touch – the neighborhood mums (in Swedish "stadsdelsmammorna") – a volunteer network of women in areas with a multicultural population. The original idea of working through the neighborhood mums was not from inside the city government but started as a voluntary initiative in the winter of 2020 by the mothers themselves. Representatives from the network proposed to a social welfare department in the city, which, in turn, contacted the communications department to act as voluntary communicators raising attention and knowledge about the need for vaccination. The group of neighborhood mums had existed for some time. It had earlier mainly worked to strengthen integration in vulnerable areas, often with a focus on integrating women (initially inspired by a model from Norway).

According to the interviewed communication managers, the primary communication obstacle was not only the language but also that the trust in government was low and that "(…) these people are not in the channels that the city has or that the majority society consists of". The neighborhood mums were supported with instructions and handbooks (basic information, Q&A, so that the women knew what to convey – and this was done mainly verbally in telephone conversations) and access to a couple of mobile phones. The communication tactic was primary and interpersonal – the neighborhood mums called people in the districts, told them about the pandemic, recommended vaccination, and answered questions. The municipality city also did an information campaign focusing on awareness where one of the neighborhood mums participated as an opinion leader. The quantitative effect of the neighborhood mums' efforts is hard to measure, but they made around 1,400 calls and reached probably several times more people indirectly in the families. The evaluation and experience from the municipality was very positive.

The Application of the Community-Based Crisis Response Model to Neighborhood Mums Case Elaboration

The following part elaborates on how the case of the neighborhood mums in during the vaccine campaign exemplified the meso and micro levels of the community-based crisis response model. The macro level is not in focus, but there are obviously several possible actions – such as policies, laws, and national support systems – that may be taken it next steps.

The community-based crisis response model pointed to the importance of identifying and making connections to existing organizations with ethnic communities before the crisis. In this case, Helsingborg municipality had already established a relationship with the network of neighborhood mums before the vaccine campaign. So, launching a campaign to disseminate vaccine information during a crisis, Helsingborg municipality reactivated the existing partnership and rapidly motivated the network of neighborhood mums to join the vaccine campaign. The network of neighborhood mums also demonstrated its ownership of their local ethnic communities. The network voluntarily joined the vaccine campaign and took the lead to raise their communities' attention about the need for vaccination.

The neighborhood mum's case highlighted the importance of interpersonal communication in reaching individuals within ethnic communities. As one communication manager at Helsingborg municipality mentioned in the interview, ethnic communities have different communication behaviors than native Swedes. Therefore, the vaccination information disseminated via mainstream media channels or other new media platforms such as webpages or social media platforms has difficulty reaching individuals in ethnic communities. By identifying the communication behaviors, the vaccine campaign adopted a more direct way of communication, using phone calls to get individuals within ethnic communities. The phone call contact also effectively distributed reliable vaccine-related information to ethnic communities.

Neighborhood mums are opinion leaders, making the vaccine information more credible and assessable. For one thing, neighborhood mums worked as "interpreters" who received the information from the municipality and "translated" the information in a more assessable way for ethnic communities. For another, neighborhood mums bridged the municipality with ethnic communities. The message delivered by neighborhood mums was credible to ethnic communities who have lower trust in the government.

To sum up, Helsingborg municipality relied on an existing partnership with a local volunteer network to disseminate accurate COVID-19 information to individuals in ethnic communities. In this regard, the role of neighborhood mums in the vaccine campaign in Sweden provides an example of how to use the community-based crisis response model to address communication inequality during public health crises.

Implications

This chapter has important theoretical, practical, and social implications. Theoretically, this chapter develops an inclusive approach to public health crisis communication and addresses communication inequality among ethnic groups. Practically, this chapter helps practitioners to increase interactions with ethnic groups and involves them throughout the crisis communication campaign cycle. More specifically, we (1) identify the obstacles that hampered the efforts and effectiveness of public health communication during the pandemic, (2) explore efficient approaches to produce awareness-raising, behavior change and information campaigns during public health crises, (3) strengthen the design, delivery, and evaluation of public communication during crises, and (4) improve medium- and long-term strategies and crisis communication leadership in public sectors. As for social implications, this chapter addresses international migration and ethnic relations and explores how to develop more equal, inclusive, sustainable communication systems during crises to promote the long-term social inclusion of all, irrespective of ethnicity. In this regard, this chapter contributes to the solidarity and sustainable development of refugee-hosting countries such as Sweden.

Conclusion

This chapter explores the role of strategic communication in eliminating communication inequality and sequentially enhancing the social resilience of the whole society during a public health crisis. Hence, this chapter advances strategic communication in the following two specific ways. First, this chapter draws on goal-oriented communication, the main theme in strategic communication, to propose a theoretical framework to canvas how organizations (e.g., public health authorities) could communicate strategically about health-related information to enhance the social resilience of the whole society during public health crises. Second, this chapter resonates with the participatory view (Falkheimer & Heide, 2017) of strategic communication. This chapter argues that understanding how ethnically diverse publics react to critical information or their interests in a public health crisis is essential in public health communication. Third, this chapter advances the societal approach to strategic communication. The use of strategic communication to eliminate communication inequality for social resilience during public health crises will broaden the scope of strategic communication research by anchoring its value in serving not only specific organizational interests but also the interests of society. Furthermore, by highlighting communication inequalities as one of the crucial factors that has amplified the impacts of the pandemic, this chapter argues that reducing communication inequality services is a part of a comprehensive crisis response that aims at long-term sustainability from the social point of view. Utilizing strategic health communication to address the communication inequality issue of ethnic groups contributes to the resilience of the whole society during public health crises. The societal approach to strategic communication broadens the scope of crisis communication research and strategic communication research by confirming its value in serving not only organizational interests but also the interests of society.

References

Ahmed, F., Ahmed, N. e., Pissarides, C., & Stiglitz, J. (2020). Why inequality could spread COVID-19. *The Lancet Public Health*, *5*(5), e240.

Ali, S. H., Fallah, M. P., McCarthy, J. M., Keil, R., & Connolly, C. (2022). Mobilizing the social infrastructure of informal settlements in infectious disease response–the case of ebola virus disease in West Africa. *Landscape and Urban Planning*, *217*, 104256.

Andersson, U. (2005). *Nya svenskar och svenska medier. Arbetsrapport nr. 34.*

Andrulis, D. P., Siddiqui, N. J., & Gantner, J. L. (2007). Preparing racially and ethnically diverse communities for public health emergencies. *Health Affairs*, *26*(5), 1269–1279.

Basu, A., & Dutta, M. J. (2009). Sex workers and HIV/AIDS: Analyzing participatory culture-centered health communication strategies. *Human Communication Research*, *35*(1), 86–114. https://doi.org/10.1111/j.1468-2958.2008.01339.x

Bhala, N., Curry, G., Martineau, A. R., Agyemang, C., & Bhopal, R. (2020). Sharpening the global focus on ethnicity and race in the time of COVID-19. *The Lancet*, *395*(10238), 1673–1676.

Blundell, R., Costa Dias, M., Cribb, J., Joyce, R., Waters, T., Wernham, T., & Xu, X. (2022). Inequality and the COVID-19 crisis in the United Kingdom. *Annual Review of Economics*, *14*, 607–636.

Brewer, L. C., Asiedu, G. B., Jones, C., Richard, M., Erickson, J., Weis, J., Abbenyi, A., Brockman, T. A., Sia, I. G., & Wieland, M. L. (2020). Emergency preparedness and risk communication among African American churches: Leveraging a community-based participatory research partnership COVID-19 initiative. *Preventing Chronic Disease*, *17*, E158.

Camauër, L. (2005). *Minoritetsmedier och minoritetsmediepolitik i Sverige: En kartläggning*. Styrelsen för psykologiskt försvar.

Cartwright, D. (1949). Some principles of mass persuasion: Selected findings of research on the sale of United States war bonds. *Human Relations*, *2*(3), 253–267. https://doi.org/10.1177/001872674900200303

CDC. (2021). *Health equity considerations and racial and ethnic minority groups*. https://www.cdc.gov/coronavirus/2019-ncov/community/health-equity/race-ethnicity.html

Chong, D., & Druckman, J. N. (2007). Framing public opinion in competitive democracies [Article]. *American Political Science Review*, *101*(4), 637–655. https://doi.org/10.1017/S0003055407070554

Cookson, C., & Milne, R. (2020). Nations look into why coronavirus hits ethnic minorities so hard. *Fanancial Times*. https://www.ft.com/content/5fd6ab18-be4a-48de-b887-8478a391dd72

Costas-Bradstreet, C. (2004). Spreading the message through community mobilization, education and leadership: A magnanimouse task. *Canadian Journal of Public Health/Revue Canadienne de Sante'e Publique*, *95*, S25–S29.

Derose, K. P., Gresenz, C. R., & Ringel, J. S. (2011). Understanding disparities in health care access—and reducing them—through a focus on public health. *Health Affairs, 30*(10), 1844–1851.

Elers, C., Jayan, P., Elers, P., & Dutta, M. J. (2021). Negotiating health amidst COVID-19 lockdown in low-income communities in Aotearoa New Zealand. *Health communication, 36*(1), 109–115.

Eruchalu, C. N., Pichardo, M. S., Bharadwaj, M., Rodriguez, C. B., Rodriguez, J. A., Bergmark, R. W., Bates, D. W., & Ortega, G. (2021). The expanding digital divide: Digital health access inequities during the COVID-19 pandemic in New York City. *Journal of Urban Health, 98*(2), 183–186.

Falkheimer, J. (2008). Glocalising public relations and crisis communication: Bridging gaps of trust in multicultural societies. In A. Zerfass, B. van Ruler, & K. Sriramesh (Eds.), *Public relations research: European and international perspectives and innovations* (pp. 293–304). VS Verlag für Sozialwissenschaften. https://doi.org/10.1007/978-3-531-90918-9_19

Falkheimer, J., & Heide, M. (2009). Crisis communication in a new world: Reaching multicultural ublics through old and new media. *Nordicom Review, 30*(1), 55–65.

Falkheimer, J., & Heide, M. (2017). Strategic communication in participatory culture: From one- and two-way communication to participatory communication through social media. In D. Holtzhausen & A. Zerfass (Eds.), *The Routledge handbook of strategic communication* (pp. 337–349). Routledge.

Falkheimer, J., & Heide, M. (2018). *Strategic communication: An introduction [Nonfiction]*. Routledge. http://ludwig.lub.lu.se/login?url=http://search.ebscohost.com/login.aspx?direct=true&db=cat07147a&AN=lub.5069349&site=eds-live&scope=site

Fancourt, D., Steptoe, A., & Bu, F. (2021). Trajectories of anxiety and depressive symptoms during enforced isolation due to COVID-19 in England: A longitudinal observational study. *The Lancet Psychiatry, 8*(2), 141–149.

Folkhälsomyndigheten. (2020). *Demografisk beskrivning av bekräftade covid-19 fall i Sverige 13 mars-7 maj 2020*. https://www.folkhalsomyndigheten.se/contentassets/d6538f6c359e448ba39993a41e1116e7/covid-19-demografisk-beskrivning-bekraftade-covid-19-fall.pdf

Frey, L. R., Adelman, M. B., Flint, L. J., Query, J., Jim L, & Terry Wang, D. (2000). Weaving meanings together in an AIDS residence: Communicative practices, perceived health outcomes, and the symbolic construction of community. *Journal of Health Communication, 5*(1), 53–72.

Germain, S., & Yong, A. (2020). COVID-19 highlighting inequalities in access to health-care in England: A case study of ethnic minority and migrant women. *Feminist Legal Studies, 28*(3), 301–310.

Grey, A. (2020). Multilingual Australia is missing out on vital COVID-19 information. No wonder local councils and businesses are stepping in. *The Conversation*. https://theconversation.com/multilingual-australia-is-missing-out-on-vital-covid-19-information-no-wonder-local-councils-and-businesses-are-stepping-in-141362

Hallahan, K., Holtzhausen, D., Van Ruler, B., Verčič, D., & Sriramesh, K. (2007). Defining strategic communication. *International Journal of Strategic Communication, 1*(1), 3–35.

Heath, R. L., & Gregory, A. (2014). Editors' introduction: Strategic communication. In R. L. Heath & A. Gregory (Eds.), *Strategic communication*. Sage. https://doi.org/10.4135/9781473915497

Helsper, E. J., & Reisdorf, B. C. (2017). The emergence of a "digital underclass" in Great Britain and Sweden: Changing reasons for digital exclusion. *New Media & Society, 19*(8), 1253–1270.

Hopkyns, S. (2020). Linguistic diversity and inclusion in the era of COVID-19. *Language on the Move*, 07–08. https://www.languageonthemove.com/linguistic-diversity-and-inclusion-in-the-era-of-covid-19/

Ihlen, Ø., & Verhoeven, P. (2017). Social theories for strategic communication. In D. Holtzhausen & A. Zerfass (Eds.), *The Routledge handbook of strategic communication* (pp. 337–349). Routledge.

Kalocsányiová, E., Essex, R., & Fortune, V. (2022). Inequalities in Covid-19 messaging: A systematic scoping review. *Health Communication, 38*(12), 2549–2558. https://doi.org/10.1080/10410236.2022.2088022

Kim, J. (2020). Equality, inclusion, and diversity in healthcare during the COVID-19 pandemic. *International Neurourology Journal, 24*(2), 180.

Knights, F., Carter, J., Deal, A., Crawshaw, A. F., Hayward, S. E., Jones, L., & Hargreaves, S. (2021). Impact of COVID-19 on migrants' access to primary care and implications for vaccine roll-out: A national qualitative study. *British Journal of General Practice, 71*(709), e583–e595.

Kwan, C.-K., Ling, H. W.-H., Cheung, J. C.-S., & Chui, E. W.-T. (2021). Safeguarding health equality for the disadvantaged during the COVID-19 pandemic: Lessons learned for the social work profession. *Qualitative Social Work, 20*(1–2), 463–469.

Lee, C. (2009). "Race" and "ethnicity" in biomedical research: How do scientists construct and explain differences in health? *Social Science & Medicine, 68*(6), 1183–1190.

Lin, L., Jung, M., McCloud, R. F., & Viswanath, K. (2014). Media use and communication inequalities in a public health emergency: A case study of 2009–2010 pandemic influenza a virus subtype H1N1. *Public Health Reports, 129*(6), 49–60.

Lin, L., Savoia, E., Agboola, F., & Viswanath, K. (2014). What have we learned about communication inequalities during the H1N1 pandemic: A systematic review of the literature. *BMC Public Health, 14*(1), 484. https://doi.org/10.1186/1471-2458-14-484

Maguire, B., & Hagan, P. (2007). Disasters and communities: Understanding social resilience. *The Australian Journal of Emergency Management, 22*(2), 16–20.

Mejía-Dorantes, L., Montero, L., & Barceló, J. (2021). Mobility Trends before and after the pandemic outbreak: Analyzing the Metropolitan area of Barcelona through the lens of equality and sustainability. *Sustainability, 13*(14), 7908.

Nguyen, M. H., Gruber, J., Fuchs, J., Marler, W., Hunsaker, A., & Hargittai, E. (2020). <? covid19?> Changes in Digital communication during the COVID-19 global pandemic: Implications for digital inequality and future research. *Social Media+ Society, 6*(3), 2056305120948255.

Nguyen, M. H., Hargittai, E., & Marler, W. (2021). Digital inequality in communication during a time of physical distancing: The case of COVID-19. *Computers in Human Behavior, 120*, 106717.

O'Brien, S., Federici, F., Cadwell, P., Marlowe, J., & Gerber, B. (2018). Language translation during disaster: A comparative analysis of five national approaches. *International Journal of Disaster Risk Reduction, 31*, 627–636.

O'Brien, S., & Federici, F. M. (2019). Crisis translation: Considering language needs in multilingual disaster settings. *Disaster Prevention and Management: An International Journal, 29*(2), 129–143.

Pareek, M., Bangash, M. N., Pareek, N., Pan, D., Sze, S., Minhas, J. S., Hanif, W., & Khunti, K. (2020). Ethnicity and COVID-19: An urgent public health research priority. *The Lancet*, *395*(10234), 1421–1422.

Piller, I., Zhang, J., & Li, J. (2020). Linguistic diversity in a time of crisis: Language challenges of the COVID-19 pandemic. *Multilingua*, *39*(5), 503–515.

Ragin, C. C. (1987). *The comparative method: Moving beyond qualitative and quantitative strategies*. JSTOR.

Ritzhaupt, A. D., Liu, F., Dawson, K., & Barron, A. E. (2013). Differences in student information and communication technology literacy based on socio-economic status, ethnicity, and gender: Evidence of a digital divide in Florida schools. *Journal of Research on Technology in Education*, *45*(4), 291–307.

Rogers, E., & Singhal, A. (2009). Empowerment and communication: Lessons learned from organizing for social change. In P. J. Kalbfleisch (Ed.), *Communication Yearbook* (Vol. 27, pp. 67–85). Routledge.

Schiavo, R. (2013). *Health communication: From theory to practice* (Vol. *217*). John Wiley & Sons.

Taylor-Clark, K. A., Viswanath, K., & Blendon, R. J. (2010). Communication inequalities during public health disasters: Katrina's wake. *Health Communication*, *25*(3), 221–229.

Viswanath, K., & Emmons, K. M. (2006). Message effects and social determinants of health: Its application to cancer disparities. *Journal of Communication*, *56*(1), S238–S264. https://doi.org/10.1111/j.1460-2466.2006.00292.x

Viswanath, K., Lee, E. W., & Pinnamaneni, R. (2020). We need the lens of equity in COVID-19 communication. *Health Communication*, *35*(14), 1743–1746.

12 How to Do Evidence-Informed Risk Communication during an Emergency

Experiences from a Pandemic

Ben Duncan

It used to be the case that epidemiologist and public health doctors responded to disease outbreaks then the communicators came to tell the grateful public what the response team had done. A key insight of the World Health Organization (WHO) following the 2003 SARS epidemic (and various subsequent emergencies) is that, done properly, risk communication is part of the response: if risk communication gives the communities as risk the information they need to protect themselves, then it is a highly effective public health intervention (WHO, 2005, 2018). But even though risk communicators have been part of health emergency response teams in WHO and other health authorities since the 2000s they often still feel like outsiders – or even imposters.

A particular source of anxiety and frustration for many risk communicators during a health emergency might be described as "evidence-envy". The epidemiology lead will come to the emergency response team meeting armed with graphs and tables analyzing reams of data on the outbreak. Their reams of evidence have come from a variety of disease surveillance systems – long standing programs that gather standardized data on infectious disease cases from hospitals, clinics, and individual doctors. The microbiology lead will make a presentation analyzing the pathogen's genome. This has come from a team of scientists using the latest high-tech equipment at some gleaming national laboratory. The medical lead will share initial (unpublished) results from clinical trials on some new treatment or therapy. In contrast, the risk communication lead has a list of that latest questions being asked by journalists and maybe, if they are lucky, an analysis of the latest chatter from social media. It is enough to make even the most intellectually secure person feel lightweight.

The start of the COVID-19 pandemic in 2020 presented an opportunity for these risk communicators to show they could "play with the big boys and girls" on the emergency response team. Unprecedented amounts of money and human resources rapidly became available to respond to this once-in-a-century sized emergency. From a communication professional's perspective, surely some of this could be used for rapid studies and data generation to guide risk communication interventions. And surely then we could establish risk communication

DOI: 10.4324/9781003375296-15

as an evidence-based – or at least evidence informed – discipline alongside epidemiology, microbiology, and medicine? This chapter reflects a frontline risk communication practitioner's perspective on how this scenario played out and the importance of evidence-based risk communication.

Evidence-Based Risk Communication during COVID-19

The COVID-19 response of the Netherland's National Institute for Public Health and the Environment (RIVM) provides a template for what an evidence-based approach to risk communication can look like. Early in 2020, RIVM established a Corona Behavioral Unit with both in-house social scientists and external academics to run a program of mixed methods research. Its initial remit was to analyze public support for public health and social measures (PHSMs) such as lockdowns, distancing and mask wearing and advise how this could be maximized (De Vries et al., 2021; Kolner et al., 2022; RIVM, 2023). From 2021 onwards, as COVID-19 vaccines became available, the RIVM team – in common with counterparts in France, Spain, Sweden and UK produced studies and advice on drivers of, and barriers to, vaccine uptake (de Bruin et al., 2022; Duncan & Salvi, 2022). In their case studies for WHO, Duncan and Salvi (2022) cite a practical example from Sweden of personae of vaccine hesitant community members being developed using insights from studies on vaccine demand and acceptance. These helped health workers carrying out vaccine outreach to engage more effectively with patients who had concerns about being vaccinated.

Duncan and Salvi (2022) also describe the system of expert committees that advised the UK government in London and the Scottish government in Edinburgh on all aspects of the COVID-19 response, including risk communication. As early as March and April 2020 the UK-level Independent Scientific Pandemic Insights Group (SPI-B) gave advice, based on a rapid synthesis of its members' social science knowledge, on how to communicate in a way that maximizes adherence to protective behaviors (SAGE, 2020).

At an international level, WHO significantly increased it in-house social science expertise relevant to RCCE from 2020 onwards. Programs applying social and behavioral research to improve public health interventions were boosted both WHO's headquarters in Geneva and in WHO's Regional Offices. These programs, at international level and in the WHO European Region for example, were already written into multi-annual plans developed ahead of the pandemic (WHO, 2023c). Though conceived as programs to apply social and behavioral research across a range of public health issues (WHO, 2023a) during 2020 and 2021 they focused most of their effort on supporting the response to the COVID-19 pandemic – and in particular the RCCE component of the response. For example, in October 2020 the first ever report produced by the global-level WHO technical advisory group on behavioral insights and sciences for health focused on considerations for acceptance and uptake of COVID-19 vaccines (WHO, 2020a) while in 2021 it produced a policy brief on behavioral considerations for promoting safe behaviors to young people (WHO, 2021b). In the European Region, the Behavioral and Cultural Insights team, working in partnership with the University of Erfurt, developed a toolkit of standardized, validated survey questions and advice on how to run qualitative surveys. This was published by WHO Regional Office for Europe in July 2020 (WHO, 2020b). The Regional Office then followed up with a program of hand-on technical assistance, which even extended to finding and funding research organizations to conduct fieldwork on behalf of national ministries of health. This helped many of WHO's priority countries and areas in the European Region run qualitative surveys and use the results to inform their public health response to COVID-19. Findings from this program also helped inform Europe-wide guidance on risk communication for contact tracers, which was then used as the basis for a WHO-led program of training for contact tracers (WHO, 2021a).

Another initiative led by WHO global headquarters, at least partly relevant to evidence informed RCCE, has been the development of a research agenda and program of work on the emerging discipline of *infodemiology* (Calleja et al., 2021). In February 2020, in a speech to the Munich Security Conference about the new disease that had emerged in China, the Director-General of WHO, Dr Tedros Adhanom Ghebreyesus (2020) stated "*we're not just fighting an epidemic; we're fighting an infodemic. Fake news spreads faster and more easily than this virus, and is just as dangerous*". WHO subsequently came up with a technical definition of an *infodemic* as being "*too much information including false or misleading information in digital and physical environments during a disease outbreak*" (WHO, 2023b). During June and July 2020, the High Impact Event Unit in WHO global organized a first global *infodemiology* conference, entirely online, with a follow-up process from August to October 2020, to review current multidisciplinary evidence, interventions, and practices that could be applied to the response to the COVID-19 *infodemic*. This produced important insights into the modern information environment. In particular, the dramatic rise of social media platforms and an equally dramatic decline of traditional mass media in many countries, tends to promote misinformation with sensational, polarizing messages more effectively than accurate, science-based messages from health authorities (Calleja et al., 2021). An important practical application promoted by the *infodemic management* movement has been increased attention to monitoring and analyzing online conversations about COVID-19 and other emerging health threats such as Monkeypox (mpox) from 2022 onward. In some parts of WHO and UNICEF and in some well-resourced national health authorities, this monitoring and analysis is being done using sophisticated "Big Data" tools originally developed for private sector marketeers and corporate communicators, such as Meltwater, CrowdTangle, BrandWatch and Talkwaker. In less well-resourced health authorities, particularly in low- and middle-income countries, it is done by manual monitoring and qualitative analysis of comments made online in response to the health authority's social media posts or news stories about major developments. The International Federation of Red Cross and Red Crescent developed guidance and a toolkit for national societies on gathering rapid offline feedback from communities to guide the response to COVID-19 and other emergencies (Cross, 2023). Meanwhile, some countries set-up COVID-19 telephone hotlines and gathered information on the questions being asked to guide their national response to the pandemic (Duncan & Salvi, 2022).

Challenges and Barriers to Pursuing Evidence-Led RCCE and How to Address Them

Despite all the progress outlined above, significant challenges remain for health authorities wanting to take an evidence informed approach to RCCE. Running a program of high-quality rapid social-science studies during an emergency requires:

1. A dedicated team of social scientists to design the studies
2. System(s) for rapid validation of the study design
3. System(s) for rapid ethical clearance of study protocols
4. System(s) for rapid recruitment of study participants
5. Capacity to do rapid fieldwork
6. Capacity to do rapid analysis of results and
7. Capacity to translate results into evidence informed options for action to present to emergency decision-makers.

These capacities only exist in a minority of national health authorities in the world, mainly in rich countries with strong social science capacity in their universities. My experience working for WHO in low- and middle-income countries (LMICs) in 2020 is that it was prohibitively expensive to retroactively create this level of capacity in health authorities in LMICs at the start of the pandemic.

Even though many hundreds of thousands of US dollars of emergency funding to support the pandemic response became available to WHO Country Offices in many LMICs in early 2020, risk communication was competing for funds against requests for hospital equipment and supplies, equipment and supplies to expand laboratory testing capacity and support to expand COVID-19 contact tracing capacity. In this context in most LMICs, proposals to spend upwards of USD 100,000 per year on a program of regular, rapid social science studies were not credible.

That said, WHO and partners such as UNICEF and the RCCE Collective Service (an international collaboration started in June 2020 to reinforce RCCE capacities in Africa and the Middle East), ***did*** support numerous social science studies in LMICs during the pandemic. Typically, this support enabled countries run two or three studies per year. This was not enough to run the RCCE component of the emergency response based on real-time data and evidence, but it did gather insights to guide their strategies and actions. For example, Duncan and Salvi's (2022) case studies show how insights from survey questions on public attitudes to, and perceptions of, COVID-19 contact tracing in various WHO European Region countries was used to develop guidance and training for contact tracers. Duncan and Salvi (2022) also give examples of data from surveys being used to guide COVID-19 vaccination programs. Results from a significant number of studies conducted by LMICs with support from international have been published (Service, 2023). But a significant number of study results were never made public; anecdotal evidence from talking to health officials in various countries suggests that some survey results (for example, showing low trust in government or low intention to comply with prevention measures) were not published to avoid causing embarrassment to political leaders and senior officials. Other reasons often cited by colleagues at national level for not publishing are lack of time and incentives. Even more fundamental a barrier is that very often "*the data do not speak for themselves*" (Duncan & Salvi, 2022). Interpreting study results and constructing an analysis that forms the basis of a peer-reviewed journal article, or even a report on a health authority website, requires a highly specific skill set. Indeed, this is also true for taking the results of a study and constructing an analysis that can inform and improve strategy and actions in during an emergency response also requires a highly specific skill set. It requires either a senior emergency response professional with a deep understanding of how to interpret social science results, or a social science scholar with a deep understanding of the context and strategies underpinning health emergency response. In most countries, there is a shortage of people with such skill set.

From the perspective of the academic world, it may be something of a loss that so many applied studies are run by, or are commissioned for, emergency response practitioners and are never written up and published. From the point of view of health emergency responders, the loss is that if results are not interpreted and put into the correct context, they do not seem relevant. It means they lose the opportunity to take evidence informed action to improve their response to the emergency. Closer collaboration between public health authorities and academic researchers seems like an obvious solution to this skills and knowledge gap, but this is not as easy as it may first seems. There are barriers to collaboration on both sides.

For the risk communicators working in emergency response, the key barriers are trust and time. Public health authorities handle a lot of confidential data (e.g. clinical data about identifiable individuals) and will be in the media and political spotlight during an emergency. Before they engage with an academic researcher, the risk communicators and their managers need to feel they can trust them to respect confidentiality and not do anything to embarrass them. Time may be an even bigger issue than trust. In an emergency, the risk communicators are under pressure and short of time. The emergency responder needs to believe the academic researcher will deliver useful insights to inform their work within a short period and without absorbing large amounts of the responder's time (they are busy with so many other things...). If they feel a research project will be slow and burdensome for them, then the emergency responder will not engage.

Time and trust (that their work will produce a publication...) are also the key barriers that prevent scholars and their academic institutions from engaging with emergency responders in public health authorities. The pacing and prioritization of academic work is often incompatible with engaging in a project for an emergency responder. Scholars working in academic institutions typically work on projects on timescales between three months to four years. Most work around their teaching obligations, institutional demands for "service" work, and research revision processes that will often last from three months to two years to get a single piece of research out – and that is after the research is conducted, data analyzed, and the results written. All of this makes it nearly impossible for most academics, and particularly those in the early stages of their careers, to suddenly suspend their long-planned research and teaching commitments to go work with a health emergency response team.

Even if the unpredictable timing and the "*drop all your other work*" demand for rapid results when doing applied emergency research for responders do not put off the scholar, or their academic institution, there are then issues around publication to contend with. "*Publish or perish*" has long been the advice given to new scholars by their more experienced peers. Increasingly, academic institutes also strongly encourage scholars to produce large, funded research projects. Working on applied studies for emergency responders usually does not help scholars meet either of these imperatives. Emergency research, when done for responders, needs to produce rapid results. This tends to limit the size, complexity – and therefore the budget – of these studies. It also means, due to limited sample size and "quick and dirty" methods, that emergency study results have tended to be much less attractive to peer-reviewed journals than results from larger, more sophisticated studies conducted over a longer time span. Finally, the emergency responders who commission the study will typically be too busy responding to the emergency to help write up the results. And they may actively block publication if they perceive the results might embarrass the senior officials or politicians they report to.

Even sitting on scientific advisory groups for national governments or international bodies such as WHO can be regarded as "lost time" by some scholars and their academic institutions since it produces neither a peer-reviewed publication nor research funding. The attitudes described above have started to change in recent years, with significant progress made since 2020. Some academic institutions are taking a broader view of what constitutes impact when looking at their scholar's work; they are willing to take account of impact on professional practice (where relevant) and on society more widely along-side contributing to peer reviewed literature. The COVID-19 pandemic significantly increased the number of scholars interested in researching topics linked to emergency risk communication, while the demand for social science evidence and advice has also expanded significantly among emergency responders.

A final challenge that has emerged for health authorities since 2020 has been the large and increasingly diverse range of academics and academic disciplines publishing articles and offering advice intended to inform RCCE intervention. Already in 2019, a survey of social scientists led by scholars that had worked with WHO in responding to Ebola and Zika characterized epidemics as "*complex biosocial events*" where knowledge from a range of social sciences – from anthropology and geography through to political science and social psychology – can usefully inform response strategies and actions (Bardosh et al., 2020). With the emergence of *infodemic management* as a priority area promoted by WHO globally since 2020, information science, computer science and indeed the emerging area of *infodemiology* (WHO, 2021a) are now added to the list of disciplines emergency responders are asked to engage with. The diversity of methods and approaches now available is exciting in terms of improvements to RCCE and other public health interventions enabled by using emerging techniques for rapid "social listening" (Posada et al., 2023). Nonetheless, protocols and methods for emerging social listening techniques are not yet standardized (Posada et al., 2023) and further thought is needed on how best to combine these with the various social science knowledge and methods (Bardosh et al., 2020).

Conclusions

We have seen that cooperation between scholars and emergency responders on RCCE, and more widely the use of evidence including social listening data to inform this area of work, increased significantly from 2020 onwards. Major developments at international level included the establishment of the RCCE Collective Service by WHO, UNICEF and IFRC to make applied social science expertise available in low-and-middle income countries, along with significant new investments by WHO in the areas of behavioral insights and the emerging field of infodemiology. In 2023, WHO's Regional Office for Europe formalized its cooperation with scholars and expert practitioners and established WHO's first ever official technical advisory group looking specifically at RCCE. Despite this, significant practical and structural barriers remain for collaboration between social science scholars and emergency responders, as was seen during the COVID-19 pandemic. These range from the difficulties obtaining funding or getting rapid ethical clearance to incompatibilities between the work schedules of scholars and the demands of emergency response. New collaborations emerged during the pandemic that overcome these barriers. For example, the appointment of social scientists to government advisory groups at national and international level (SAGE, 2020). Also, the society-wide impact of the COVID-19 pandemic combined with the relative ease of harvesting samples of public opinion from social media saw the growth of social listing by emergency response teams including in low resource setting. Though methods and protocols for social listening have not yet been standardized, there is some evidence of this having a positive impact on RCCE and other public health interventions (Posada et al., 2023). A truly evidence-led model of RCCE would go beyond social listening, to having a systematic approach for incorporate knowledge and data from a wide range of disciplines into emergency response. Various groups have proposed agendas to achieve this, but they have yet to be meaningfully enacted (Bardosh et al., 2020; Posada et al., 2023). It will be interesting to follow over the coming years whether, and to what extent, these agendas are implemented.

References

Bardosh, K. L., de Vries, D. H., Abramowitz, S., Thorlie, A., Cremers, L., Kinsman, J., & Stellmach, D. (2020). Integrating the social sciences in epidemic preparedness and response: A strategic framework to strengthen capacities and improve global health security. *Globalization and Health, 16*, 1–18. https://doi.org/https://doi.org/10.1186/s12992-020-00652-6

Calleja, N., AbdAllah, A., Abad, N., Ahmed, N., Albarracin, D., Altieri, E., Anoko, J. N., Arcos, R., Azlan, A. A., & Bayer, J. (2021). A public health research agenda for managing infodemics: methods and results of the first WHO infodemiology conference. *JMIR Infodemiology, 1*(1), e30979. https://doi.org/https://doi.org/10.2196/30979

Cross, B. R. (2023). *CEA Guide and Toolkit*. British Red Cross. Retrieved 10 April from https://communityengagementhub.org/cea-guide-and-toolkit/

de Bruin, M., Suk, J. E., Baggio, M., Blomquist, S. E., Falcon, M., Forjaz, M. J., Godoy-Ramirez, K., Leurs, M., Rodriguez-Blazquez, C., & Romay-Barja, M. (2022). Behavioural insights and the evolving COVID-19 pandemic. *Eurosurveillance, 27*(18), 2100615. https://doi.org/https://doi.org/10.2807/1560-7917.ES.2022.27.18.2100615

De Vries, M., Claassen, L., Te Wierik, M. J., van den Hof, S., Brabers, A. E., de Jong, J. D., Timmermans, D. R., & Timen, A. (2021). Dynamic public perceptions of the coronavirus disease crisis, the Netherlands, 2020. *Emerging Infectious Diseases, 27*(4), 1098. https://doi.org/https://doi.org/10.3201%2Feid2704.203328

Duncan, B., & Salvi, C. (2022). *Risk communication and community engagement: A compendium of case studies in times of COVID-19*. R. O. f. E. World Health Organization. https://www.who.int/europe/publications/i/item/WHO-EURO-2022-6186-45951-66353

Ghebreyesus, D. T. (2020). *Director general speeches detail Munich security conference*. World Health Organization. Retrieved July 30, 2021 from https://www.who.int/director-general/speeches/detail/munich-security-conference

Kolner, C., van der Borg, W., Sanders, J., Keijsers, J., Joosten, M., & de Bruin, M. (2022). Public health measures during the COVID-19 pandemic through the lens of community organisations and networks in the Netherlands: Five lessons for pandemic decision-making. *European Surveillance*, *27*(42), 2200242. https://doi.org/https://doi.org/10.2807/1560-7917.ES.2022.27.42.2200242

Posada, A., Inigo, R. L., & Sport, J. (2023). *Turning social listening data into action: Barriers and recommendations observed through a COVID-19 rumor response*. Resources, Issue. Internews. https://www.alnap.org/help-library/turning-social-listening-data-into-action-barriers-and-recommendations-observed-through

RIVM. (2023). *Applying behavioural science to COVID-19*. Ministry of Health, Welfare and sport. Retrieved 12 August, 2023 from https://www.rivm.nl/en/coronavirus-covid-19/research/behaviour

SAGE. (2020). *The role of behavioural science in the coronavirus outbreak*. COVID-19 Research and Analysis, Issue. https://www.gov.uk/government/publications/spi-b-the-role-of-behavioural-science-in-the-coronavirus-outbreak-14-march-2020

Service, C. (2023). *Social data tracker*. Collective Service Retrieved 31 March from https://www.rcce-collective.net/data/data-tracker/

WHO. (2005). *WHO outbreak communication guidelines*. Emergency Preparedness, Issue. W. H. Organization. https://www.who.int/publications/i/item/who-outbreak-communication-guidelines

WHO. (2018). *Communicating risk in public health emergencies: A WHO guidelines for Emergency Risk Communication (ERC) policy and practice*. Emergencies Preparedness, Guidelines Review Committee, Issue.

WHO. (2020a). *Behavioural considerations for acceptance and uptake of COVID-19 vaccines*. COVID-19: Critical Preparedness, Readiness and Response, Issue. WHO. https://www.who.int/publications/i/item/9789240016927

WHO. (2020b). *Survey tool and guidance: Rapid, simple, flexible behavioural insights on COVID-'19*. Meeting Report, Issue. WHO. https://www.who.int/europe/publications/i/item/WHO-EURO-2020-696-40431-54222

WHO. (2021a). *Risk communication and community engagement for COVID-19 contact tracing: Interim guidance*. Technical Documents, Issue. WHO. https://apps.who.int/iris/handle/10665/339100

WHO. (2021b). *Young people and COVID-19: Behavioural considerations for promoting safe behaviours*. COVID-19: Risk communication and community engagment, Issue. https://www.who.int/publications/i/item/978-92-4-002831-9

WHO. (2023a). *Behavioural sciences for better health*. WHO. Retrieved 13 August from https://www.who.int/initiatives/behavioural-sciences

WHO. (2023b). *Infodemic*. WHO. Retrieved 31 March from https://www.who.int/health-topics/infodemic#tab=tab_1

WHO. (2023c). *Thirteenth general programme of work 2019–2023*. WHO. Retrieved 13 August from https://www.who.int/about/what-we-do/thirteenth-general-programme-of-work-2019---2023

13 The Role of Culture in Risk and Crisis Communication Management

The Case of Switzerland and the Governmental Communication during the COVID-19 Pandemic

Albena Björck and Fabienne Farner

The COVID-19 pandemic has presented unprecedented challenges for risk and crisis communication on a global scale. In Switzerland, the government has taken numerous measures to control the spread of the virus and protect the population, including imposing lockdowns, implementing mask mandates, and closing borders. As elsewhere in the world, these measures considered suitable for the situation (Bjørkdahl and Carlsen, 2019) have been met with both support and criticism by the public.

One key factor that has influenced the way that COVID-19 has been managed in Switzerland is the country's national cultural values. Switzerland is known for its strong tradition of individualism and self-responsibility, which has shaped the way the government has approached the crisis. For example, rather than imposing strict rules and regulations, the government has largely relied on the voluntary compliance of the population to follow recommended guidelines. This approach has been met with mixed results, as some members of the public have been more compliant than others. By examining how cultural values and beliefs influence the way that information is received and acted upon, as well as the communication strategies employed by the government and other organizations, this book chapter offers a better understanding of the interplay between national culture and risk and crisis communication. The current case study has been conducted during the first year of the pandemic, covering the time of March to December, 2020. This study includes a rich base of secondary data of publicly available information and internal documentation of the Swiss authorities at national and regional levels. Furthermore, the case builds upon unique primary data from semi-structured interviews with representatives of the different language regions, national authorities, and communication experts directly involved in the COVID-19 communication.

Dimensions of National Culture

Culture is a complex concept that has been studied by scholars in a wide range of disciplines. Culture, in general, has been defined as "both a dynamic

DOI: 10.4324/9781003375296-16

phenomenon that surrounds us at all times, being constantly enacted and created by our interactions with others and shaped by leadership behavior, and a set of structures, routines, rules, and norms that guide and constrain behavior" (Schein, 2010, p. 1). Through constant interactions with others, people continuously shape and reshape culture and at the same time culture creates stability and rigidity in a group of people regarding how they should perceive, feel and act in a given situation (Schein, 2010). Or we could say that: "We live and breathe through it" (Trompenaars & Hampden-Turner, 2012, p. 20). As diverse as culture itself, there are a myriad of different definitions and models which aim to describe the term culture.

Hofstede et al. (2010) and Trompenaars and Hampden-Turner (2012) offer two frameworks to analyze culture: six and seven (respectively) cultural dimensions help identify and organize value preferences so that the resulting patterns can be categorized along cultural divide. Hofstede's cultural dimensions model is a widely used and cited framework for cross-cultural communication that describes the impact of a society's culture on the values of its members, and how these values relate to behavior (Hofstede et al., 2010). Furthermore, the model is used to understand and predict differences in communication styles, business practices, and social norms across cultures. His six dimensions of culture are used to describe differences between societies. However, they are not exhaustive and should not be used to stereotype or oversimplify cultural differences. Trompenaars and Hampden-Turner developed another cultural model in the 1990s that identifies seven dimensions that represent different "layers" of culture, with each layer influencing and interacting with the others (Trompenaars & Hampden-Turner, 2012). They argue these layers can help to explain why people from different cultures may have different values, behaviors, and communication styles, and that understanding these layers can be useful for improving cross-cultural communication and understanding cultural differences. The seven dimensions are dichotomies of value orientations (see Table 13.1). Cultures very often reveal a certain level of coherence when it comes to value orientation, either staying within the first or the second group of the seven cultural dimension pairs (Björck & Barthelmess, 2020).

Cultural Influences on Risk and Crisis Communication

Different cultures have distinct norms and values that shape how information is perceived. However, there are many barriers to mutual understanding when people from different cultural backgrounds communicate, due to differences in language and context (Falkheimer & Heide, 2006). This can lead to misunderstandings and miscommunication, which can amplify the challenges and complexities of a crisis, making the resolution and recovery more arduous (Hyland-Wood et al., 2021). The resulting misinformation among the different

Table 13.1 Seven Dimensions of Culture According to Trompenaars and Hampden-Turner (2012)

Value Orientations Group 1	*Value Orientations Group 2*
Universalism: Everyone is considered the same and treated the same. The law relates to everyone equally.	**Particularism**: People get treated differently, depending on what relationship they have with a person.
Individualism stands for the individual wants and needs of people.	**Communitarianism** support solidarity and importance of community and family.
Specific implies a clear separation of public and private life.	**Diffuse**: go from general to specific, establishing a personal relationship as a foundation for a business one.
Neutral: feelings are controlled.	**Emotional**: people show their true emotions and express how they feel.
Achievement: is celebrated, the winner gets the credits, not the loser.	**Ascription:** it focuses on a person's background and family connections.
Sequential time: is seen as a series of passing events.	**Synchronous time**: is seen as a cycle.
Internal direction gives importance to what is inside of a person, what values and morale someone has.	**Outer direction** trust in the power of nature and thus, in the surroundings of an individual.

cultural groups can hinder effective collaboration. Additionally, the ignorance of different cultural settings may result in insensitive or inappropriate communication, which hinders trust-building efforts as individuals may feel marginalized or excluded.

It is therefore crucial to have in-depth knowledge of the culture and language of the target audience to communicate effectively. In addition, practitioners should be cautious of translation and linguistic misinterpretations to avoid cultural differences and cultural misunderstanding. Although the topic of culture is considered extremely important in the context of crisis communication by various scholars around the world, it is still rather under-researched and seldom integrated in the known frameworks (Björck, 2016, Sellnow et al., 2017, Hamidovic, 2012).

A notable exception is the CERC Model. According to CERC, culture can play a significant role in shaping how individuals and organizations perceive and respond to risk and crisis situations (Reynolds et al., 2014). It may influence the way that people assess and evaluate risks, and moreover, it can shape the way that they cope with and recover from crisis events. Specific aspects of culture, such as language distribution, perception of risk and trust, credibility and forms of acceptable communication, and individualistic versus collectivistic cultures, can impact crisis communication (Reynolds et al., 2014). First, translation and linguistic misinterpretations are key areas to pay attention to, especially in multilingual countries or areas with multicultural and emigrant population (Vetsch, 2017). Second, the perception of risk and trust and belief in institutions such as governments may vary across cultural settings (Falkheimer & Heide, 2006; Reynolds et al., 2014). Furthermore, distinct cultural settings may feature distinct sources of credibility and forms of acceptable communication (Reynolds & Quinn, 2008). Understandings of family or rituals for grieving may also differ. Lastly, individualistic cultures and collectivistic cultures diverge. In the case of vaccination, the emphasis may lie on the vaccination of an individual on the one side, and the vaccination of a group (e.g., a family) on the other side (Reynolds et al., 2014). Ignorance of cultural differences in general should be avoided at all costs (Rani, 2013).

According to Björck and Barthelmess (2020) the different levels of culture also influence different crisis communication core themes. The first level of artifacts and behavior is visible in the employed communication channels, the direction of communication, and responsibilities. The second level of espoused values influences the objectives and messaging as well as organizational values implemented in existing plans. The last, invisible, level of the basic assumptions forms the implicit expectations, implicit communication rituals and routines, and informal responsibilities during a crisis. Analog to the already mentioned two opposing and consistent groups of value orientations Björck and Barthelmess (2020) identified dichotomies in the culturally affected crisis communication themes (Figure 13.1). The first cultural pattern is built upon prepared communication based on pre-defined guidelines and centralized processes, confidential and selective information provision and reception, slow reaction due to detailed and accurate situation analysis preceding crisis communication aiming for distributing only correct information, mistake avoidance because of shame and zero-error culture, divided responsibility between communication experts and leadership. The opposite and second cultural pattern represents a flexible and spontaneous communication and missing pre-defined processes, open and transparent provision of information, instantaneous information delivery aiming for

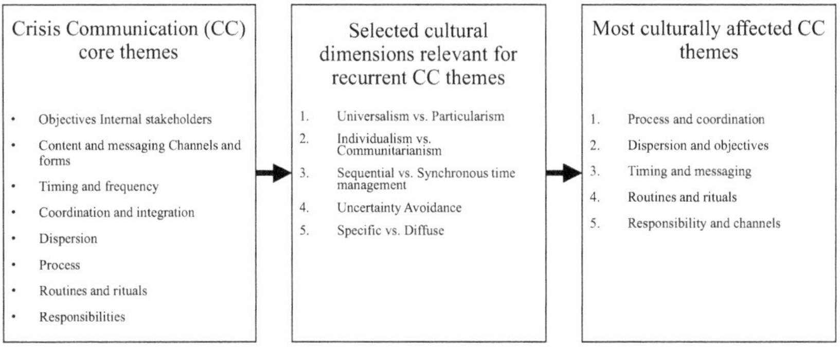

Figure 13.1 Crisis Communication core themes, relevant cultural dimensions and culturally affected themes (Björck & Barthelmess, 2020).

avoiding anxiety among staff, solution oriented approach with mistake and risk tolerance, top management responsibility, and direct communication channels.

Risk and Crisis Communication in a Multi-Cultural Context: The Case of Switzerland

To delve deeper insight into the complexities of crisis communication within a multi-cultural context we next analyze the case study of the Swiss authorities' crisis communication during the COVID-19 pandemic. This case presents a plethora of distinct cultural and contextual challenges and offers additional insights for both crisis communication researchers and practitioners to consider.

Switzerland's Context for Crisis Communication

Various factors form the unique and complex communication context of Switzerland. Switzerland is interesting not only because of its political system of direct democracy but also because of its culturally diverse landscape. Switzerland is a neutral federal state with 8.6 million inhabitants, 26 cantons, 2,172 municipalities, and four national languages (Bundeskanzlei, 2021). The Swiss have one of the highest life expectancies in the world: on average, it is 82 years for men and 86 years for women. This is also evident in the age distribution. According to BK.admin, the proportion of people over 64 has increased over the course of the last 60 years, while that of people under 20 and the proportion of people aged 20–64 has decreased.

Switzerland's national official languages include German (62%), French (23%), Italian (8%), and Rhaeto-Romanic (0.5%). At the federal level, all official texts must be published in German, French, and Italian. Multilingualism is defined by the Language Act so that equal consideration is granted to all language regions. The four national languages are actively promoted by the Federal Office of Culture. In addition, the Swiss learn at least one other national language at school.

Switzerland is divided, not only by the many rivers and mountains but by the so-called "Röstigraben". Political and behavioral differences between the three main language regions (German, French, and Italian) are evident (Eichenberger, 2014). The word "Röstigraben" is composed of the Swiss-German potato dish "Rösti" and the German word for "ditch". The "Röstigraben" has its origins in World War I, when the German-speaking Swiss supported the Germans and the French-speaking Swiss sympathized with the French (Eichenberger, 2014). Currently, the term is predominately used to explain the different voting behavior of the Swiss. Eugster et al. described the phenomenon of the "Röstigraben" as following: "In the Swiss context, cultural differences arise among social groups that speak different languages but face very similar institutions and economic opportunities" (Eugster et al., 2017, p. 1090). The application of Hofstede's six cultural dimensions model on Switzerland to elaborate the cultural differences between the German-speaking part and the French-speaking part is shown in Figure 13.2.

According to Hofstede Insights (2021), examples for strong cultural differences between German and French-speaking Switzerland are in the dimensions of "power distance" and "uncertainty avoidance" which have a direct impact on the organization and effectiveness of crisis communication. Power Distance reflects the importance of hierarchies and centralization resulting in directive communication styles in French-speaking Switzerland respectively a collaborative, more informal, and decentralized communication style in German-Speaking Switzerland. Uncertainty avoidance regulates how a culture is dealing with risk, thereby assigning lower risk awareness in German than in the French part of the country.

Additionally, the Swiss population is becoming more diverse: while the population is steadily getting older there is also an increasing number of people coming from different cultural backgrounds (Bundeskanzlei, 2021). This diversity of the Swiss population is further reflected in a small but differentiated media landscape (Publicom, 2020b). Furthermore, the media outlets of neighboring nations (Germany, France and Italy) exert a significant impact on the shaping of public opinion in Switzerland, due to the linguistic proximity (Publicom, 2020a, 2020b). There is no state medium in Switzerland, only a subsidized association, which by law has the mission to provide information on politics, economy, sport, society, and culture at a national level in all four national languages (SRG SSR, n.d.).

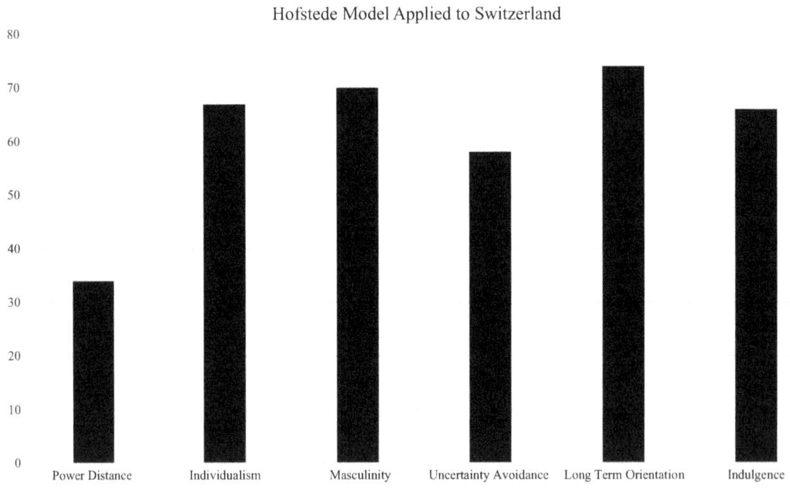

Figure 13.2 Cultural Dimensions according to Hofstede (Hofstede Insights, 2021).

Furthermore, it is stated that the shift of influence from mass media toward social media, interpersonal communication channels, and sources of information is hardly conducive to maintaining a balanced formation of opinion in the country. Another important aspect is **media consumption** that differs from generation to generation (Publicom, 2020a). Printed newspapers and television are more likely to reach the older generation than the younger one. Radio consumption is also higher among the older generation, while social media is most frequently used by the younger generation.

Cultural Aspects of Governmental Communication During the COVID-19 Pandemic

On 16 March 2020, in Switzerland, the Federal Council declared the "extraordinary situation" due to the COVID-19 pandemic. In Switzerland, the definition of roles and responsibilities in a pandemic is based on the law EpidA (Federal Office of Public Health, 2020). Moreover, the division of responsibilities between the Confederation and the cantons depends on the crisis phases defined in this law. A three-stage model was adopted by the Swiss according to EpidA, distinguishing between *normal*, *particular*, and *extraordinary* situations. Although the cantons in Switzerland possess a high degree of independence, this law provides the confederation with a stronger and thus more active role in crisis management once a specific situation has been declared a crisis. Therefore, responsibility has changed several times during the COVID crisis, which has led to different regulations applying in the meantime depending on the canton, resulting in confusion and uncertainty among the population. Figure 13.3 shows the crisis communication channels used by the Swiss authorities.

Throughout the duration of the pandemic, Switzerland did not enforce a curfew. Despite the implementation of recommendations for individuals to stay at home and work remotely, only a limited number of restrictions and guidelines were implemented. Such restrictions included border closure, the mandatory wearing of masks in public spaces, and, subsequently, the requirement for certain areas to obtain a health pass, which stated the vaccination status, recovery, or a negative COVID test to minimize the risk of a potential infection. Additionally, Switzerland did not mandate vaccination at any point in time. This emphasis on individual accountability was not uniformly well-received across all regions. Specifically, while individuals in the German-speaking regions emphasized personal responsibility, those in the French-speaking regions advocated for more stringent regulations.

For example, the crisis communication of the Swiss authorities was based on the legal framework of the Epidemics Act and did not follow a specific strategy. The strategic approach to crisis communication was missed, as the focus of the Swiss authorities was on "learning organizations" and ad hoc reactions throughout the crisis. This led to ambiguities regarding the leadership in crisis

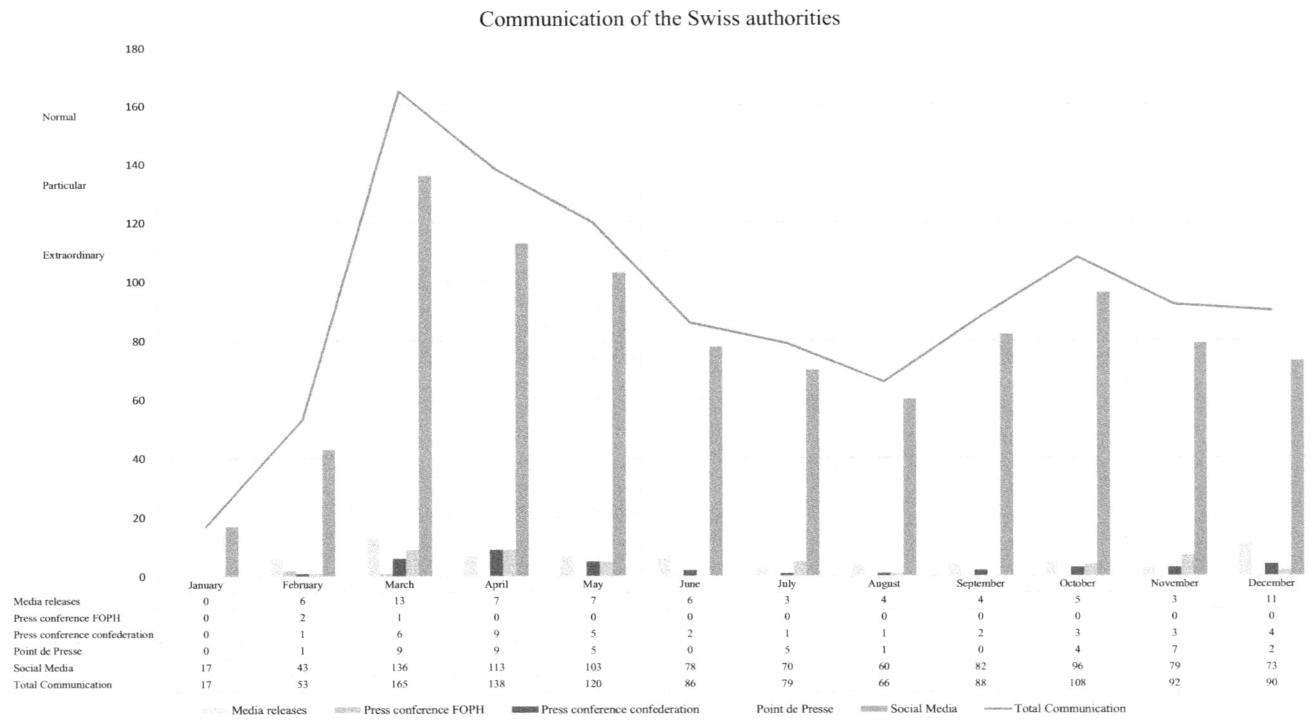

	January	February	March	April	May	June	July	August	September	October	November	December
Media releases	0	6	13	7	7	6	3	4	4	5	3	11
Press conference FOPH	0	2	1	0	0	0	0	0	0	0	0	0
Press conference confederation	0	1	6	9	5	2	1	1	2	3	3	4
Point de Presse	0	1	9	9	5	0	5	1	0	4	7	2
Social Media	17	43	136	113	103	78	70	60	82	96	79	73
Total Communication	17	53	165	138	120	86	79	66	88	108	92	90

Figure 13.3 Communication channels used in the first year of the Covid-10 pandemics in Switzerland.

management as well as crisis communication. Although a crisis spokesperson was identified as a crucial confidence-building measure, it was not possible for the Swiss authorities to establish a spokesperson after the initial spokesperson's retirement.

Surveys conducted on behalf the Swiss government have shown that the hygiene and behavioral rules have become firmly established in the minds of the Swiss (Hermann, 2020). This is no coincidence, but the result of a successful and ubiquitous information campaign by the Federal Office of Public Health (FOPH). The campaign translated scientific information into a simple language that could be understood by everyone by communicating on two different levels at the same time: emotional and informative. The campaign was then disseminated through various communication channels: social media, traditional media, posters, flyers and with the help of influencers. But the longer the pandemic lasted, the more messages, pictograms and colors were added. The campaign became confusing.

Simple, credible, and consistent messages from trusted sources minimize the risk of misinterpretation in a crisis. However, not all the messages communicated by the authorities were consistent in their implementation. Mandatory masks were introduced despite repeated statements that masks do not provide protection against the virus. Measures were relaxed even though the communicated criteria were not yet met. The judgmental interviews of the COVID-19 task force members were another disruptive factor of the one-voice principle of crisis communication. Nevertheless, there were factors such as inconsistent messages as well as missing and incorrect translations of documents which negatively impacted the one voice principle and subsequently the crisis communication of the Swiss authorities during the COVID pandemic. Duc to the delayed launch of the campaign in Romansh, the missing and incorrect translations, as well as the imbalance of social media posts in only one language, the unique cultural and linguistic backdrop of Switzerland was identified as a stumbling block for the crisis communication of the authorities.

Crisis Communication Strategies in Different Swiss Cultural Regions

In expert interviews from the German-speaking region (Zurich Canton), no such thing as an official crisis communication strategy of the Swiss authorities existed; the division of tasks and the subsequent communications were completed according to the EpidA. This statement is further consistent with the statement that no strategy paper regarding crisis communication existed at the FOPH. Further, the French-speaking region (canton of Valais) was not directly involved in a crisis communication strategy but identified its role in the crisis communication according to EpidA (interview with Waeber-Kalbermatten, 2021).

When the extraordinary situation was announced, the lead of the communication was with the Federal Chancellery and the FOPH. The Confederation ensured communication and "dictated the course of action" with the support of the cantons (Konferenz der Kantonsregierungen, 2020, p. 16). The role of the cantons in crisis communication, therefore, concerned the communication of the tasks within their responsibility and the support of the messages and rules of conduct communicated by the FOPH and the Federal Council (BAG, 2018). Providing information to the population on how the measures and restrictions affect life in the canton was also an important part of the cantons' crisis communication. Therefore, the role of the cantons was mostly an operative, supportive, and informative one during the extraordinary situation (Interviews with the representatives of the Zürich and Valais Cantons, 2021, Waeber-Kalbermatten, 2021). When the situation's classification was reverted to *particular*, more responsibilities, including those relating to communication, were returned to the cantons, such that less stringent restrictions could not be imposed by the various cantons (Waeber-Kalbermatten, 2021). However, the governments of individual cantons could tighten measures based on the particular epidemiological situation.

At first glance, the two cantons chosen for comparison of their implementation of crisis communication could not be more different. The bilingual Valais Canton is a tourism canton with 10% of its population being employed in the tourism sector, while the canton of Zurich is the economic engine of Switzerland (Kanton Zürich, n.d.; Staatsrat, 2020). The size of the populations also diverges. While 345,525 people lived in the canton of Valais in 2019, 1,536,400 lived in the canton of Zurich in the same year (Kanton Zürich, 2020; Kantonale Finanzverwaltung, 2020). Despite their differences, they have not acted entirely different in their implementation of crisis communication. Both cantons used the channels of social media, media releases, and press conferences to inform not only the public but also the media. Furthermore, both set up information hotlines and homepages on which to publish daily numbers of coronavirus cases.

While the Valais Canton mentioned sound, comprehensive, and regular communication as the measures taken to increase and establish trust, the Zurich Canton used the words "transparent", "continuous", and "comprehensible" (interviews with the representatives of the Cantons, 2021; interview with Waeber-Kalbermatten, 2021). The cantons tried to include the media in their crisis communication strategy by inviting them to press conferences and sending them media releases. However, the Valais Canton first had to establish and define a team to handle the media inquiries of the health department (Waeber-Kalbermatten, 2021). Furthermore, the Zurich Canton (2021) mentioned that due to the size of the canton, it must contribute disproportionately to crisis management. Nearly every fifth Swiss person lives in the Zurich Canton, and it is also home to most of the country's large media companies. Therefore, Zurich Canton must tackle around 30 media inquiries daily, which is not only time-consuming but also taxing the employees, as it is almost impossible to answer this number of inquiries. While in the Valais Canton the media work was praised and described as successful, the Zurich Canton were less euphoric. The work with the media was complicated by coronavirus-related measures, and in the interim one was forced to switch to media releases and telephone information for the media. In addition, the zero-error tolerance makes communication more difficult, as the focus is only on the negative, and the positive results achieved are somewhat lost.

However, one significant difference between the two cantons was the number of press conferences and media releases. In Valais Canton, there were a total of 80 media releases and 13 press conferences, compared to 130 media releases and 30 press conferences in the canton of Zurich during the same period. In addition, the interviewee in Valais mentioned that all communication was completed in two languages to account for the different languages in the canton (interview with Waeber-Kalbermatten, 2021). However, the communication was geared more toward the touristic regions, and less toward cultural differences. For example, during the Christmas season, the protection measures were communicated more often in these touristic places.

During the period in which the cantons had more responsibility, communication was insufficient and diminished credibility and trust as the lead in the communication was not clearly defined. "The communication processes and competencies must be clearly defined to ensure that the cantons' most important demands are communicated comprehensively in real time" (Konferenz der Kantonsregierungen, 2020, p. 16). The cantonal representatives further expressed the wish to be included in the strategic communication of the Federal Chancellery and the FOPH – for example, the collaborative creation of messages – and they mentioned the need to receive the informative material early on (Konferenz der Kantonsregierungen, 2020). Moreover, they noted that a coherent flow of information can be ensured only if the cantons are informed continuously and on time about planned decisions and expressed the wish to be informed at least two hours before decisions are communicated by the Federal Council or the FOPH (Bundeskanzlei, 2021; Konferenz der Kantonsregierungen, 2020).

Cultural Influences on the Perception of Effectiveness

Trust has been identified as an important pillar of successful crisis communication (Hyland-Wood et al., 2021). Measures taken to strengthen and build the trust of the population toward the government and the authorities, include accurate, continuous, credible, and comprehensible communication (Hyland-Wood et al., 2021; Reynolds et al., 2014). Equal treatment of the media as a multiplier of trust, with equity according to the guidelines of the Federal Chancellery. Moreover, listening to the population's needs and the explanation of why certain things are done a certain way were mentioned as among the important trust-building measures taken by Swiss authorities (interview with Lüthy, 2021).

However, not only was the style of communication mentioned as a trust-building factor, but also the intervals of communication and the presence of

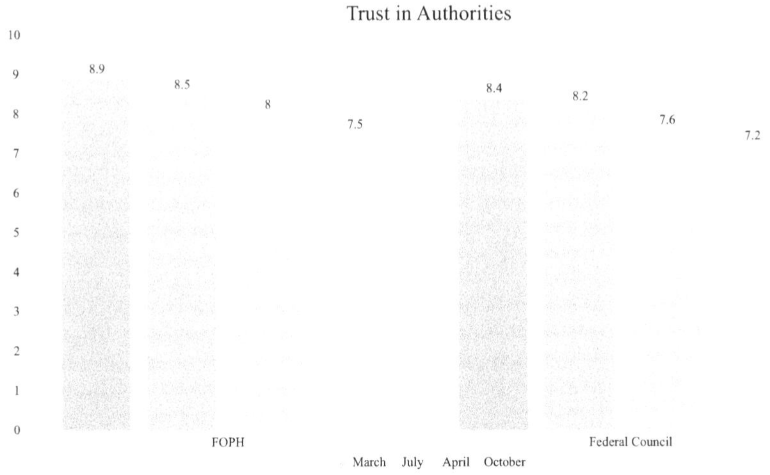

Figure 13.4 Trust in the Swiss authorities (Hermann, 2020).

mostly multiple Federal Councils at the press conferences. The spokesperson Daniel Koch and Federal Council Alain Berset further bolstered the trust of the population. These two figures were praised for their calm and unagitated communication at the beginning of the pandemic. However, the two communication experts interviewed mentioned that no pre-crisis trust-building measures could be identified, as issue management was neglected. Further, all interviewees agreed that the back and forth with the masks undermined the trust of the population, as did the faulty testing strategy, the unclear advice on mass testing, and the relaxation of the lockdown despite that the predefined criteria were only partially met.

The surveys on trust of the FOPH demonstrate that the confidence in information providers regarding the coronavirus declined in Switzerland following a peak in mid-March as displayed in Figure 13.4. The analysis of the SRG even identified differences between the different language regions regarding trust toward the Federal Council, exhibited in Figure 13.5. Initially, trust was highest in German-speaking Switzerland and skepticism was highest in French-speaking Switzerland. However, trust in the Federal Council declined most in the German-speaking part of Switzerland. In Italian-speaking Switzerland, trust declined most after an initial boost in April, it increased in June, but declined steeply between June and October (see Figures 13.4 and 13.5).

Regarding the campaign, the colors and pictographic approaches reached their limits at some point, as the extent of the crisis could not really be assessed at the beginning (interview with Koerfer, 2021). Due to the many color changes, the concept of the colors became confusing regarding which color was currently valid. The launch of the COVID tracing app was also described as rather bumpy, although it now works well and is contributing to crisis management (interview with Koerfer, 2021). Moreover, the principles governing the campaign were

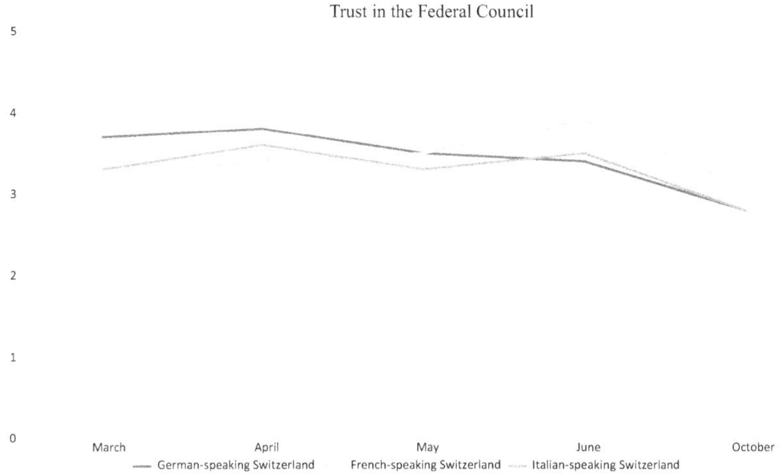

Figure 13.5 Trust in the Federal Council (Bosshard, et al., 2021).

praised: maximum simplicity and comprehensibility on different levels. The pictograms were neutral and informative, and with the communication on an emotional level, the whole population could be addressed.

Strategic communication in the sense of a systematic stakeholder orientation and targeted communication strategies, by definition was missed. The interviewees of both the FOPH and the cantons stated the room for strategic communication was limited, moreover, because one was driven by "daily business". Critics consistently noted the management failure on the part of the authorities to streamline and lead the public conversation. This was particularly true regarding wearing masks or face coverings. The interviewed experts believed that an apology strategy would have fostered the population's trust. The government statement, "We can Corona", was also described as highly unhelpful and not conducive to the implementation of crisis communication and fostering trust. It was further emphasized that the content of the communication should be distinguished from the communication process. The most important lessons of the FOPH regarding communication were that many personal resources are needed and that a more explanatory method of communication was appreciated by the population. Moreover, it was realized that notes on even seemingly minor matters can influence content. Nevertheless, the fast set-up of the *point de presse* was mentioned as effective. By contrast, media interviews with certain task force members were regarded as distracting from general crisis communication.

Nevertheless, public satisfaction with communication from authorities was high until June, 2020. Throughout the language regions in Switzerland, a slump in the satisfaction curve can be observed. However, satisfaction with the campaign remained high, as seen in Figure 13.6, despite a small reduction in overall satisfaction in July and October, 2020.

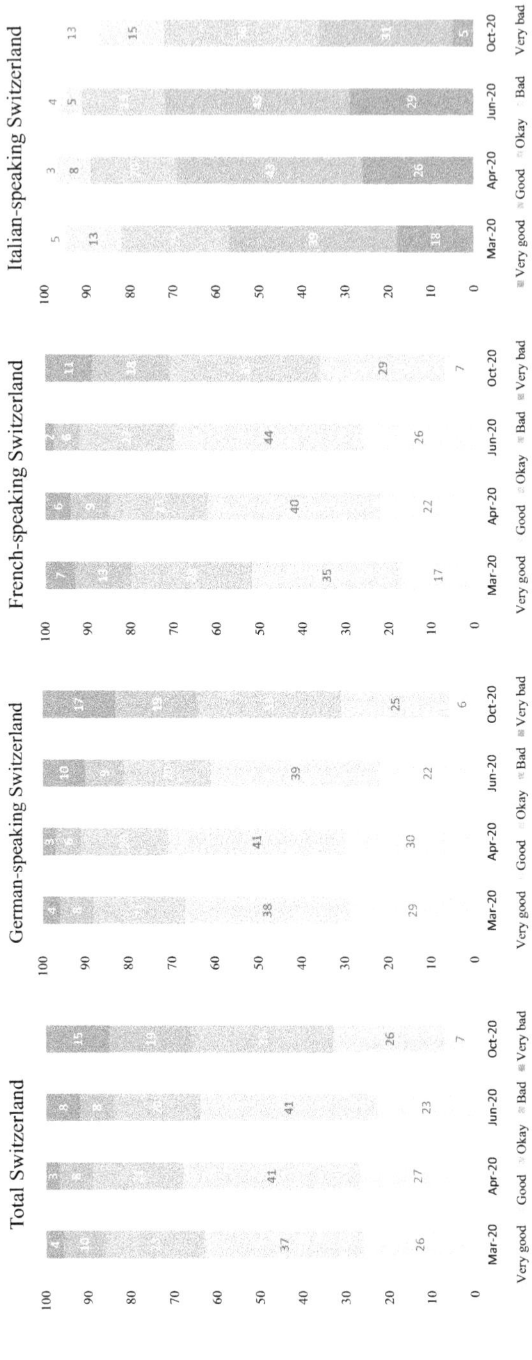

Figure 13.6 Assessment of the communication of the decision-makers. (Bühler, et al., 2020).

Cultural Diversity in Switzerland: How the Swiss Authorities Accounted for the Röstigraben

According to the interviews with Lüthy and Koefer (2021), all the FOPH's communication was conducted in at least three national languages – sometimes four – and sporadically also in English. For this translation work, the FOPH relied on an "in-house" translation service. Furthermore, the FOPH has French-speaking staff in the media team and staff in Ticino to attempt to discern how the FOPH is perceived by the target population. Moreover, it was explained that the cultural differences were mainly addressed through the campaigns.

Furthermore, for different social media challenges, influencers were chosen according to the respective national language to ensure an equal distribution of challenges – and subsequently, messages – in all language regions in Switzerland. Moreover, it was identified by the FOPH that the French-speaking regions of the country have higher expectations toward the government and government authorities, while the Swiss- Germans emphasize individual responsibility. This is also in line with Hofstede's findings on power distance in Switzerland.

However, criticism was voiced that not every language region received the same amount of attention, which impacted trust. "The authorities must ensure equal treatment of Switzerland's linguistic minorities, and all the more so in an exceptional situation where delayed implementation of measures may have serious consequences" (Konferenz der Kantonsregierungen, 2020, p. 27). The quoted report of the regional governments identifies various examples demonstrating that national authorities struggled to provide documents in the different national languages (Konferenz der Kantonsregierungen, 2020). The evaluation mentions the publication of ordinances and explanations, translation errors, and certain information and communication available only in German. Due to time constraints, certain information was first published in only one language, after which the translations followed.

This inequality was also evident in the campaign, which was initially only sporadically translated into Rhaeto-Romanic. The social media posts exhibit that translation and consideration of national language has not always been precise, with dominating communication in German, followed by French and Italian.

Conclusion and Lessons Learned

In conclusion, the case illustrates that culture transported via two different national languages in the same country can influence the risk and crisis perception and the effectiveness of communication strategies. The cultural differences and strong traditions within the different language areas in Switzerland have both supported and challenged the government's response to the COVID-19 pandemic. On the one side, culturally and language adapted themes, unified channels and messaging, as well as dedicated influencers fostered trust. On the other side, insufficient information available in the respective languages, changing responsibility and multiple spokepersons, as well as uncoordinated messaging between central and culturally different regional governments undermined the credibility of the authorities.

Effective risk and crisis communication is crucial in mitigating uncertainty and anxiety during a crisis. Based on the case, the authors identified several elements as key to ensuring effective communication in a multi-cultural context during a public health crisis. First, communication is characterized by simple, credible, and consistent messages to minimize the potential for misinterpretation in the respective language. Second, crisis communication must be adaptable and innovative to combat information overload and proactively and timely communicate risks and events, missing or late information can reduce trust. Third, all affected individuals must be reached quickly through various channels to persuade and motivate them to support crisis management. To achieve that, communication has to be available in the languages spoken by the targeted public and be distributed via its preferred communication channels. Fourth, the communication should be also conveyed by spokespersons enjoying the trust of the respective cultural community, who demonstrate strong cultural and geographical proximity. Fifth, an empathic and emotional strategy should recognize the "hidden" preferred cultural tonality of the communication, taking the audiences' national cultural attitudes into account, such as for example directive or consultative, motivating on the individual or collective level. Lastly, in order to implement these elements, a systematic and consistent, and not "ad hoc" approach to crisis communication is needed. Cultural beliefs and value orientations of stakeholders and crisis managers must be an integral part of every strategic communication plan.

References

BAG. (2018). *Influenza-Pandemieplan Schweiz* (5th ed.). Bundesamt für Gesundheit BAG

Björck, A. (2016). Crisis typologies revisited: An interdisciplinary approach. *Central European Business Review*, *5*(3), 25–37. https://doi.org/10.18267/j.cebr.156

Björck A., & Barthelmess P. (2020). The role of organizational culture for creating understanding and trust through internal crisis communication. *Proceedings of the International Crisis and Risk Communication Conference*, *Volume 3* (pp. 17–20). Orlando FL: Nicholson School of Communication and Media. https://www.doi.org/10.30658/icrcc.2020.4

Bjørkdahl, K., & Carlsen, B. (Eds.). (2019). *Pandemics, publics, and politics: Staging responses to public health crises* (1st ed.). Imprint: Palgrave Pivot. https://doi.org/10.1007/978-981-13-2802-2

Bosshard C., Bühler G., Craviolini J., Hermann M., Krähenbühl D. (2021). 6. SRG Corona-Monitor. SRG. https://sotomo.ch/site/wp-content/uploads/2021/01/6.-SRG-Corona-Monitor.pdf

Bühler, G., Craviolini, J., Hermann, M., Krähenbühl, D., & Wenger, V. (2020). 5. SRG Corona-Monitor [Studienbericht]. SRG. https://sotomo.ch/site/wpcontent/uploads/2020/10/5.-SRG-Corona-Monitor_small.pdf

Bundeskanzlei. (2021). *Der Bund kurz erklärt. Der Bund kurz erklärt.* https://www.bk.admin.ch/bk/de/home/dokumentation/der-bund-kurz-erklaert.html

Coombs, W. T. (2007). Protecting organization reputations during a crisis: The development and application of situational crisis communication theory. *Corporate Reputation Review*, *10*(3), 163–176. https://doi.org/10.1057/palgrave.crr.1550049

Coombs, W. T., & Holladay, S. J. (Eds.). (2010). *The handbook of crisis communication.* Wiley-Blackwell. https://1lib.ch/book/983970/697391

Eichenberger, I. (2014). Der 'Röstigraben', die verbindende Kluft der Helvetier. *SWI swissinfo.ch.* https://www.swissinfo.ch/ger/deutsch-vs--franzoesisch_der—roestigraben—die-verbindende-kluft-der-helvetier/41177160

Eugster, B., Lalive, R., Steinhauer, A., & Zweimüller, J. (2017). Culture, work attitudes, and job search: Evidence from the Swiss language border. *Journal of the European Economic Association*, *15*(5), 1056–1100. https://doi.org/10.1093/jeea/jvw024

Falkheimer, J., & Heide, M. (2006). Multicultural crisis communication: Towards a social constructionist perspective. *Journal of Contingencies and Crisis Management*, *14*(4), 180–189. https://doi.org/10.1111/j.1468-5973.2006.00494.x

Federal Office of Public Health. (2020). Communicable diseases legislation – Epidemics act, (EpidA). https://www.bag.admin.ch/bag/en/home/gesetze-und-bewilligungen/gesetzgebung/gesetzgebung-mensch-gesundheit/epidemiengesetz.html

Hamidovic, H. (2012). An introduction to crisis management. *ISACA Journal*, *15*, 1−4.

Hermann, M. (2020). *Bevölkerungsbefragung Oktober 2020—BAG* (pp. 1–22). Sotomo. https://www.bag.admin.ch › k-und-i › 2019-nCoV

Hofstede, G. (2021). What about Switzerland? *Hofstede Insights.* https://www.hofstede-insights.com/country/switzerland/

Hofstede, G., Hofstede, G. J., & Minkov, M. (2010). *Cultures and organizations: Software of the mind* (3rd ed.). McGraw-Hill Education.

Hofstede Insights. (2021). National culture. https://hi.hofstede-insights.com/national-culture

Hyland-Wood, B., Gardner, J., Leask, J., & Ecker, U. K. H. (2021). Toward effective government communication strategies in the era of COVID-19. *Humanities and Social Sciences Communications*, *8*(1). https://doi.org/10.1057/s41599-020-00701-w

Kanton Zürich. (2020, February 7). *Zürcher Bevölkerung erneut stark gewachsen.* Kanton Zürich. https://www.zh.ch/de/news-uebersicht/medienmitteilungen/2020/02/bevoelkerung.html

Konferenz der Kantonsregierungen. (2020). *Covid-19-Pandemie: Das Krisenmanagement in der ersten Welle aus Sicht der Kantone* (p. 29). Haus der Kantone. https://kdk.ch/uploads/media/AN_4310-5-20201221-Zwischenbericht__Covid-DE_final.pdf

Predikon. (n.d.). Wahlverhalten. *Predikon.* http://archive.predikon.ch/de/wahlverhalten/sprache

Publicom. (2020a). *Medienmonitor Schweiz—Medienmarken.* Medienmarken Und Meinungsmacht.https://www.medienmonitor-schweiz.ch/medien/medienmarken/italienische-schweiz/gesamt/2019

Publicom. (2020b). *Medienmonitor Schweiz—Medienmonitor Schweiz.* Medien Und Meinungsbildung. https://www.medienmonitor-schweiz.ch/

Rani, M. (2013). Cross-culture: A hurdle in communication. *Global Institute for Research & Education*, *2*, 1–4.

Reynolds, B., & Quinn, S. C. (2008). Effective communication during an influenza pandemic: The value of using a crisis and emergency risk communication framework. *Health Promotion Practice*, 9(4). https://www.jstor.org/stable/26736825

Reynolds, B., Seeger, M., Palenchar, M., Gable, L., Holsinger, R., Neuberger, B., & Christoffel, T. (2014). Crisis emergency risk communication (J. Cox, M. Gaines-McCollom, N. Grimsley, A. Herbert, J. Lynch, N. M. Maiden, D. Olivares, T. Sinks, V. Siegel, C. Shockey, L. Berryman, L. E. Pechta, & P. O. Williams, Eds.). *CDC*. https://emergency.cdc.gov/cerc/ppt/cerc_2014edition_Copy.pdf

Schein, E. H. (2010). *Organizational culture and leadership* (4th ed.). Jossey-Bass.

Sellnow, D. D., Lane, D. R., Sellnow, T. L., & Littlefield, R. S. (2017). The IDEA model as a best practice for effective instructional risk and crisis communication. *Communication Studies*, *68*(5), 552–567. https://doi.org/10.1080/10510974.2017.1375535

SRG SSR. (n.d.). Politischer Rahmen und Auftrag | *SRG SSR*. Politischer Rahmen Und Auftrag. https://www.srgssr.ch/de/wer-wir-sind/auftrag-politik-werte-und-strategie/politischer-rahmen-und-auftrag

Trompenaars, F., & Hampden-Turner, C. (2012). *Riding the waves of culture: Understanding diversity in global business* (3rd ed.). McGraw-Hill Education.

Vetsch, C. (2017). *Internationale Krisen-Public Relations*. Springer Fachmedien Wiesbaden. https://doi.org/10.1007/978-3-658-15581-0

Vos, M., Lund, R., Harro-Loit, H., & Reich, Z. (2011). Developing a crisis communication scorecard. https://www.researchgate.net/publication/256545248_Developing_a_crisis_communication_scorecard

14 The Finnish Government's Strategic Ambiguity in COVID-19 Pandemic Communication

A Case Study

Matias Lievonen, Chiara Valentini and Mark Badham

During pandemics national governments and their agencies are perceived to be responsible for containment and management measures and to oversee dissemination of vital information concerning the pandemic (Quinn et al., 2013; van der Meer & Jin, 2020). The preparation and dissemination of this information and its reception by the public are extremely important health management steps that authorities must undertake to reduce the spread of an infectious disease and safeguard public health.

Research on health and risk communication has primarily argued for the importance of clear, accurate, consistent, and prompt communication to help individuals and communities protect themselves from risks of different natures (Hyland-Wood et al., 2021; Nivette et al., 2021). However, when facing diverse, conflicting, and changing stakeholder concerns and demands during a major crisis such as a pandemic, clear communication can sometimes pose critical challenges for governments responsible for pandemic management.

The COVID-19 pandemic resulted in a prolonged crisis for governments across the world, lasting over several years, and producing many negative social, human, and economic consequences due to governments' decisions regarding pandemic measures as well as the communication of those decisions. Some of these measures severely impacted businesses' revenues, undermined national economic growth, and increased public expenditures. The human cost also was severe as governments' measures mentally and physically affected large groups of individuals in society (OECD, 2021).

When a novel infectious disease such as COVID-19 begins to spread within a population, communicating clear, consistent, and accurate containment and protection measures may be difficult as not much is known about the disease, such as where it comes from, how it spreads, and its effects (Hung & Lin, 2022). The conundrum for health authorities is that while novel diseases such as COVID-19 spread fast, scientific knowledge about the disease requires time to be validated and communication plans need time to be formulated. While facing this high-pressure environment, authorities are often called on

DOI: 10.4324/9781003375296-17

to act and communicate about elements that may be later disconfirmed or not completely supported. Within these knowledge uncertainty situations, national governments', and health authorities' communications, whether intentional or not, can be inconsistent, lack clarity, and may not sufficiently engage the local community (Lowe et al., 2022). Thus, ambiguous communication emerges in some situations.

The strategic use of ambiguous organizational communication has gained recent attention in strategic communication research (e.g., Hoffjann, 2022). Knowledge about the opportunities and drawbacks of using ambiguous communication is important, especially for the public sector facing major crises which would typically demand very clear instructions for the public to understand and follow. Furthermore, it can even affect how the public perceives their authorities' capacity to manage a crisis such as a pandemic, which impacts public trust in authorities and subsequently the level of public compliance toward authorities' recommended actions. Despite extant research on strategic ambiguity in communication situations, there is limited strategic communication research into concrete practices of strategic ambiguity (Hoffjann, 2022).

Accordingly, in this chapter we seek to identify, examine, and illustrate practices of strategic ambiguity as they emerged in public communications of the Finnish Government and public sector authorities during the pandemic and how this ambiguity may have been useful to addressing diverse stakeholders' demands over COVID-19 pandemic actions. Acknowledging that early research has identified intentional and emergent approaches in strategic ambiguity, in this study we adopt the emergent approach (Lowe & Jones, 2004; Mintzberg, 1972, 1978) that views strategic ambiguity as emerging from meso-level communication in which a polyphony of organizational voices representing government simultaneously convey a range of divergent-unified messages to accommodate multiple stakeholders' diverse concerns surrounding a highly contentious situation (Hoffjann, 2022; Mintzberg, 1972, 1978). Hence, drawing on the concept of "emergent strategy" (Mintzberg, 1972, 1978), this study intends to investigate strategic ambiguity as a social and relational phenomenon making sense of adaptive (i.e., agile), cross-organizational and polyphonic communications involving spokespeople representing the national government, the national health authority and its independent expert agency, various government ministries, and diverse regional and municipal governments. We studied how all these entities simultaneously, collectively, and yet loosely communicated policies and actions concerning the management of COVID-19. In line with Lowe and Jones' (2004) thinking, we are interested in "seeking to explain the manner in which" the "explicit intentions" of an organization "are adapted to provide new understandings in a dynamic environment", (ibid, p. 1317) which is the environment of a society under an emergency.

This study utilized multiple data sets collected during early 2022. Data was collected from oral and written Finnish Government public communications, including press conferences, news articles from the most popular Finnish online newspapers, and material from official government institutions' websites describing the COVID-19 situation in the country. Key facts, policy decisions, and the main government spokespeople were identified to map out a chronological evolution of how the Government's pandemic management actions developed. This data set was used to build the storyline of the events that led to the Government's use of ambiguous communication. Based on our analysis, five rhetorical strategies were identified characterizing strategic ambiguity: *postponement, deniability/structural duality, content expansiveness, equivocality, preservation of rights,* and *protective silence.*

Our study's findings suggest that government and public sector communicators in Finland used ambiguity in their public communications in the described situations and this use was strategic because they had to address the public's knowledge uncertainty about the nature and status of the pandemic and the implications on individuals and society overall. Based on these findings we contend that government and public sector communicators' use of ambiguity can provide strategic advantages during crisis and risk situations addressing diverse and contradictory stakeholder concerns.

Overall, this study advances our understanding of how governments and public sector organizations communicate during pandemics to maintain their legitimacy and reputation while managing diverse and conflicting stakeholder demands in times of high uncertainty. It does so by illustrating and discussing the use of strategic ambiguity in pandemic communications toward the general public. The chapter concludes with some managerial reflections on the benefits and drawbacks of strategic ambiguity during a pandemic.

Situation Analysis

As one of the Nordic countries, Finland experienced 118 fatalities per 100,000 citizens due to the COVID-19 pandemic as of November 2022 (Johns Hopkins University & Medicine, 2022). Early tracking and ad doc containment measures, coupled with a general high trust toward the government, which translated into higher public acceptance of COVID-19 measures and preventive behaviors than other regions, helped Finland to lower some of the "social toll" of the pandemic. As in many countries, several public sector organizations were involved in health crisis management (Valentini & Badham, 2023). The Finnish Government, led by the (former) Prime Minister Sanna Marin, worked closely with and supported the efforts of multiple state agencies to prevent the spread of the coronavirus. The Ministry of Social Affairs and Health (STM) was responsible for the general planning, guidance, and monitoring of the prevention of infectious diseases. The Finnish Government also relied on the Finnish Institute for Health and Welfare (THL), an independent expert agency working under the STM. THL serves the national, municipal, and provincial government decision-makers, as well as the research community and the public. THL was heavily involved in communicating about the pandemic alongside the Finnish Government.

The critical situation addressed in this study constitutes two events involving the Government decision over whether to keep schools closed for safety reasons and the other was about face mask recommendations. The first event began during the fourth wave of COVID-19 infections in Finland in December 2021 when the Finnish Government started discussing whether reopening schools after the Christmas break was safe. This event started on January 5th 2022, when news stories broke out about THL and OKM (Ministry of Education and Culture) recommending that schools continue operating as normal despite the increasing number of people getting infected and despite the general recommendations by STM and OAJ (Trade Union of Education) to keep them closed. On January 7th, as this public discussion in news and social media began to end, STM changed its approach and allowed schools to reopen.

The public discourse continued in the second event in Spring 2022 concerning recommendations to use face masks in public places. It started on April 14th 2022 when THL disseminated a press release announcing the end of mask recommendations in Finland. Six days later, on April 20, the local government in the capital city Helsinki finally dropped the mask recommendations. During almost a week, divergent discourses on the pros and cons of wearing face masks (especially in public transport) emerged and these were highly veiled with ambiguous references between the local authorities and the expert organization THL.

In both events, THL wanted to ease the recommendations whereas STM in event 1 and the local authorities in event 2 wanted to maintain them. These polarized political positions sparked a vivid conversation in Finnish public arenas, mostly in traditional news media and social media, bringing to public attention the lack of clear, accurate, and consistent pandemic communication by the Finnish Government and its various ministries. These two events, as we elaborate later in this chapter, constitute the settings of the Finnish Government's use of strategic ambiguity and are used in this chapter to illustrate the use of strategic ambiguity in the context of a national government attempting to communicate while facing diverse stakeholder concerns during a national and global health crisis.

In the following section we briefly review the core literature on strategic ambiguity to offer the reader some theoretical understanding of strategic ambiguity as a communication strategy as well as the contexts and situations in which it has been studied. This is followed by a description of how the data concerning the two events outlined here was collected and analyzed.

Literature Review

The concept of ambiguity has been studied in different disciplines from organizational studies (e.g., Alvesson & Sveningsson, 2003; Daft & Weick, 1984) to communication studies (e.g., Eisenberg, 1984; Hoffjann, 2022; Johansen, 2018), including political science and international relations (e.g., Black et al., 1999; Herman et al. 2010). Ambiguity has been described as a form of indirectness, vagueness, unclarity (i.e., lack of transparency), and disqualification (Eisenberg, 1984), and it has mostly been perceived as a negative element of communication. Yet, a more nuanced view of ambiguity has recently emerged among organizational, managerial, and communication scholars who view leaders' and organizations' ambiguous communication as strategies appropriate for addressing diverse opinions and complex and critical situations, including the possibility to protect a corporate image from critique and increase opportunities for changing management approaches.

As the concept of communication ambiguity is intrinsic to a source's intention, a receiver's interpretation, and the message itself (Eisenberg, 1984), different approaches to the study of strategic ambiguity have been used in research. When ambiguity is considered a property of the communication message itself based on the source's intention, messages have been examined for evidence of a lack of a clear connection between the signifier (i.e., the textual, oral, or figurative element of the message) and the signified, and the message's meanings as interpreted by the receivers (Christensen et al., 2015). For instance, Guthey and Morsing (2014) used content analysis to investigate strategic ambiguity communication in news media coverage of CSR by examining messages in news articles and their level of clarity, consistency, and discursive closure. Their analyses recorded information on the motives, the significant actors addressed in the news, and the issues through a grounded-theory approach with results indicating that strategic ambiguity serves the interest of the CSR community and even society at large (Guthey & Morsing, 2014).

A similar approach to strategic ambiguity communication was used by Sumelius et al. (2020) when analyzing interview data on employee communication related to talent management systems to identify instances of secrecy and information asymmetry. They concluded that some unambiguous signals may be useful and false signaling should be avoided when using strategic ambiguity communication (Sumelius et al., 2020). Chen and Lawless (2018) utilized thematic analysis to study female immigrant discourses on their integration into a university faculty and found the use of strategic ambiguity to reorient or resist expectations embedded in a university work context. Suzuki et al. (2021) reviewed 159 documents submitted by stakeholders during a multi-stakeholder consultation and used an open coding scheme to identify issues, stakeholder positions, and frames. In their analysis ambiguity was also identified in the use of equivocal language, in defining the roles of different stakeholders, and in attempts to downplay conflicting interests. Recognizing differences in intentional and emergent approaches in strategic ambiguity research, this study adopts the emergent approach (Lowe & Jones, 2004; Mintzberg, 1972, 1978) that views organizational ambiguous communication as flowing from a collective relational decision-making process involving multiple agencies responding simultaneously to diverse stakeholder concerns in highly uncertain situations such as a pandemic.

In this study, we particularly draw on the literature examining strategic ambiguity through rhetorical strategies that emerged in communications. Jarzabkowski et al. (2010) found four types of rhetorical strategies when studying business schools' ambiguous written communications about their internationalization strategy. These strategies varied according to two dimensions: breadth (narrow or broad interpretations) and accommodativeness (emphasis on personal or broader interests). Denis et al. (2011) added more micro level elements to rhetorical strategies, identifying five main rhetorical strategies characterizing strategic ambiguity: *equivocal language* (through vague words or the removal of certain details), *inflection* (by slightly exaggerating and promoting proposals), *postponement* (by essentially not deliberating on a solution), *preservation of rights* (where the rhetor essentially keeps the discussion open for future collaborations with diverse partners), and *equivocal commitment* (avoiding binding and clear commitment for actions). Abdallah and Langley (2014) also analyzed strategic ambiguity through written texts by focusing on three rhetorical strategies which they called *duality, equivocality*, and *expansiveness* and which in part overlap with those identified by Denis et al. (2011).

Four major benefits of ambiguity use by organizations have been identified in previous research. These relate to the possibility of (a) promoting unified diversity, (b) protecting an organization's or individual's existence and legitimacy, (c) fostering deniability, and (d) facilitating organizational change (Eisenberg & Witten, 1987). In some studies, the strategic use of ambiguity has been praised for impeding intense examinations by competitors and regulators (Ozcan & Gurses, 2018), shifting blame of responsibility (Mena et al., 2016), and repositioning public interpretation of a critical event and thus diminishing negative consequences (Reuter & Ueberbacher, 2019), for instance in cases of organizational crises (Sellnow & Ulmer, 1995; Smith et al., 2006; Vergne, 2012). In other studies, it has been criticized for increasing confusion, indirectness and used to strategically maintain existing power dynamics (Eisenberg, 1984).

In this study, we specifically focus on ambiguity as a protective function, and how it can foster future opportunities for expressions of deniability. This choice was made because ambiguity in its protective function enables managers to rhetorically link different stakeholder interests through ambiguous appeals to protect interests, such as to rescue an organization's image from public scrutiny (Cappellaro et al., 2021; Sillince et al., 2012). Strategic ambiguity enables opportunities for future denial while maintaining organizational credibility. Although all communications can be denied, it is more difficult to do without losing face if the communication is clear and non-contradictory. Strategic ambiguity may become particularly relevant when leaders need to communicate about something yet unknown or linked to limited scientific knowledge, such as the COVID-19 disease.

Methodology

To analyze the Finnish Government's external communications in the above-mentioned critical events, we adopted a qualitative research method approach and predominantly drew from the literature on strategic ambiguity through rhetorical strategies.

Data Collection Approach

For each of these two events, we identified the timeline and main spokespersons and/or communicators (both individuals and organizations, see Table 14.1). These sources were chosen because (a) they were central players in the public management of the pandemic, and (b) they were officially cooperating in finding pandemic solutions. In event 1 (school closures/openings for student safety reasons), the sources were THL, STM, and OKM. In event 2 (face mask recommendations), the sources were THL, City of Helsinki, and City of Jyväskylä. Surprisingly, there was no official communication by STM during event 2 and two public sector organizations at city municipality level were included instead. We chose Helsinki because it is the capital and largest city in Finland, with a population around one million in the metropolitan area. Jyväskylä is a mid-size city and represents a somewhat different local administrative area in the middle of the country. These two city public sector organizations were included as they also discussed the pros and cons of the two possible decisions in relation to event 2.

All communicative instances related to these two exemplary events were then identified and retrieved from the official websites of STM and THL (events 1 and 2), official websites of the city of Helsinki and Jyväskylä (event 2), online news stories written by the main Finnish newspapers *Helsingin Sanomat, Ilta-Sanomat,* and *Iltalehti* (both events), and news stories published by the Finnish public broadcaster YLE (both events). These news media are among the

Table 14.1 Overview of the data collected for events 1 and 2

Events	*Timeframe*	*Data collected*	*Sources of communication*
1 School closures/ openings	January 5–7, 2022	4 online news stories 1 press conference 1 Twitter feed discussion	• THL (Mika Salminen) • STM (Krista Kiuru, Kirsti Varhila, Taneli Puumalainen) • External experts (Risto O. Roine, Mika Rämet) • OKM (Li Andersson)
2 Mask recommendation	April 14–20, 2022	4 press releases 3 online news stories	• THL (specifically, Otto Helve, Piritta Rautavuori) • City of Helsinki (specifically) • City of Jyväskylä (specifically)

most popular and important news outlets in Finland and are considered credible sources of news information (Media Metrics Finland, 2022). We also screened social media posts, specifically the official Twitter accounts of the identified sources and included only those social media posts published in the two periods and with content directly discussing topics related to the two events. We excluded data that did not fit in with the chosen timeframe or were otherwise not applicable to the analysis. Table 14.1 offers an overview of our data set.

Analytic Procedures

The data set was first transcribed from the audio of video files and/or copied from online texts into an MS Word file and analyzed with NVivo 12 software. A coding scheme was developed from the strategic ambiguity literature (see Table 14.2) and used to analyze textual and spoken communication and messages aimed at the public. We adopted a range of strategic ambiguity indicators used by scholars across disparate studies investigating rhetorical strategies in ambiguous settings and, combined, these guided our analysis and coding of the collected data. Specifically, six indicators of strategic ambiguity were compiled from studies by Abdallah and Langley (2014), Cappellaro et al. (2021), Denis et al. (2011), and Scandelius and Cohen (2016). The texts were read multiple times and coded in native Finnish language to be able to capture linguistic nuances used in natural language settings.

First, we identified discursive elements that represented illustrative examples of one or multiple strategic ambiguity indicators. Next, we recorded opposing and contradictory views made by other Finnish authorities in their key arguments in both events and coded them in the qualitative analysis tool NVivo 12. For event 1, the main contradictory views were either for or against closing of the schools and resuming distant teaching. For event 2, the main contradictory views were either for or against dropping the face mask recommendations. Having these contradictory views in mind, we then highlighted the comments of the main communicators and included them in the analysis.

Analysis

In the following we present a summary of the main findings related to event 1 and then those of event 2.

Event 1: School Closures/Openings

The discussion about schools remaining open or closed included multiple and diverse communicative exchanges between three main communicators representing the Finnish Government. It evolved quickly as the time span from when it started and when it ended was about three days. All key players shared their

Table 14.2 Strategic ambiguity indicators

Indicators	*Deniability/ Structural Duality* (1)	*Equivocality* (1–4)	*Postponement* (2) (4)	*Preservation of rights* (3) (4)	*Content expansiveness* (1)	*Protective Silence* (2)
Explanation	The co-presence of both continuity and change within a source's statement.	The use of equivocal words with various diverse meanings while avoiding precise definitions and numerical targets.	Usually refers to decision making in the future and could include statements where an authority indicates a decision on something but does not say when the decision will be made.	Preserving the right to participate in future actions and decisions as a safeguard to ensure the ability to intervene (and change a decision) later.	Usually consists of statements that list multiple sources, a broad range of potential actions and/ or a wide variety of mission-related action proposals. These are often evidenced without consideration of resource limitations.	Instances of silence when clear communication is expected.
Examples from data set	Statements from THL declaring both "You don't have to wear a mask" and "Wearing a mask is still recommended" in the same press release. (THL, 2022).	Contradictory statements and interpretation of data between the government and experts at the same press conference.	Recommendations given during press conference but no concrete schedule on when the recommendations will take place.	THL instructed the public not to follow its own guidance in a news story:	STM listed a variety of options on possible restrictions concerning public meetings without disclosing whether they are legally valid or not under current legislation:	A THL expert was invited to an STM press conference, but the expert stayed silent the whole time. Instead, external experts had a chance to give their statements. (Finnish Government, 2022).

(*Continued*)

Table 14.2 (Continued)

Indicators	*Deniability/ Structural Duality* [(1)]	*Equivocality* [(1–4)]	*Postponement* [(2) (4)]	*Preservation of rights* [(3) (4)]	*Content expansiveness* [(1)]	*Protective Silence* [(2)]
		STM: "Data shows that 15000 kids can get long-covid symptoms" vs. External experts: "We don't have specific data yet available but less than 1% of the kids could generate long-covid symptoms". (Finnish Government, 2022).	STM: "We recommend that the schools should continue in remote teaching (after the Christmas break) but we don't comment on this before the next meeting" (Finnish Government, 2022).	"The instructions from the Finnish railway company should override THL's recommendations regarding public transport" (Karhu, 2022)	"The decision to close all indoor activities in the whole country will be given as soon as possible" (Luotonen et al., 2022)	

(1) Abdallah and Langley (2014).
(2) Cappellaro et al. (2021).
(3) Denis et al. (2011).
(4) Scandelius and Cohen (2016).

opinions during the debating process, and all of them eventually used some form of strategic ambiguity and contributed to ambiguity in their arguments for or against the decision. Eventually, STM dropped the recommendation for distance schooling on January 7th but left the door open for decentralizing the decision-making responsibility to local authorities (Luotonen et al., 2022).

Specifically, the analysis of discourses shows the presence of five main ambiguity indicators:

Postponement was identified in many instances (especially on January 5th) (see e.g. Näveri et al., 2022) to give a sense of openness toward alternative solutions. Statements about the decision-making process, all the formalities, and individuals involved in the decision making were all convoluted with vagueness and a general sense of delaying decisions. The issue of reopening schools also was the starting point for discussing other related issues, many of which sidetracked the major concern of safety. The inclusion of other issues can be seen as a rhetorical strategy to increase content expansiveness, another indicator of strategic ambiguity.

Deniability / structural duality emerged as another highly visible rhetorical strategy used for strategic ambiguity purposes by all communicators while discussing the pros and cons of reopening schools. For example, a press conference was held by STM on January 7th to inform the public about long-term COVID-19 effects to argue for tighter recommendations such as closing the schools. Yet, the same discourse was used to confute the tighter recommendations during later stages of the same press conference (see Finnish Government, 2022).

Content expansiveness was also apparent during the same press conference on January 7th (Finnish Government, 2022) held by the key individuals representing STM, including Krista Kiuru (Minister of Family Affairs and Social Services in Finland), Kirsti Varhila (Permanent Secretary), and Taneli Puumalainen (Director General). They all gave their own statements about long-term COVID-19 and, in relation to that, whether it was safe or not to return to normal classroom teaching. Moreover, external experts outside STM such as Risto O. Roine (Professor of Neurology) and Mika Rämet (Professor of Immunology) also gave their own somewhat distinctive views on the potential risk for children to get long-term COVID-19 symptoms. The experts warned about the potential risk but stated that statistics and evidence-based data are still lacking. In fact, the referred levels of risk were debated in different occasions, with different cited numbers. These sources' discourses dealing with quantifying the level of risk show that at that point of time, the authorities had no clear idea of the impact of school reopening on long COVID infections among the young population.

To make the situation more ambiguous, these communicators employed *equivocality* when they tried to back up their arguments for or against reopening schools. Data, facts, and statistics were extrapolated from different situations and contexts and applied to justify the Finnish situation. For example, Krista

Kiuru used illustrative examples based on statistics that were used quite differently by STM's external experts during the same press conference (see Finnish Government, 2022). Even though THL is the main expert source for STM in health-related issues (and as such the public sector organization with the most updated fact-based information) STM chose not to invite THL spokespeople to a press conference and instead invited other external experts to discuss the risks of long-term COVID-19 effects on children and the safety of school reopening. Specifically, the external expert, University of Turku professor of neurology Risto O. Roine, noted that there were no statistics available on children's long-term COVID-19 effects in Finland. This contradicted the argument made by Krista Kiuru earlier in the same press conference.

Moreover, STM used strategic ambiguity to limit public attention toward the authority's capacity to control the infection spread which had been growing during the period leading up to this event. In addition, on January 7th Kirsi Varhila, Permanent Secretary of STM, shifted the focus to multiple other issues (Finnish Government, 2022), indicating use of a *content expansiveness* strategy. Varhila discursively offered multiple interpretations of measures that gave alternative options to protect key stakeholders, but none of which was realistically and thoroughly analyzed and explained.

Notably, during the press conference held on January 7th to explain the event and situation, one of the key players of the pandemic management was completely silent. Markus Perola (Research Professor at THL) did not say a single word during the meeting, which eventually made it impossible to hear THL's viewpoint in relation to STM's position and the external experts the Ministry had invited to support its own political decision (Finnish Government, 2022). This *protective silence* strategy refers to instances of silence when clear communication is expected.

To keep open the involvement of other social actors in the decision making on whether schools should open and thus to create a sense of ambiguity, *preservation of rights* emerged as a rhetorical strategy in combination with *postponement.* This was apparent when STM eventually decided after three days of discussion to act against its original plan which was about keeping remote schooling (Luotonen et al., 2022). Despite the decision to reopen schools, the Minister of Family Affairs and Social Services, Krista Kiuru, did not want to take a clear stance on this measure and discursively constructed the idea of preserving the rights of local authorities in deciding whether to reopen schools, thus paving the way for a localized, decentralized approach on in-person versus distance teaching.

Event 2: Recommendations for Face Masks

The Finnish Government's communication about the dropping of mask recommendations was characterized by a high level of strategic ambiguity and a lot of vagueness about whose health instructions citizens should follow to prevent the spread of infections. There were a lot of diverse and somewhat conflicting recommendations by different communicators. In the end, the recommendations among the key pandemic management players were somewhat in line, even though ambiguity was still clearly visible in their public statements.

Event 2 started on April 14th when THL disseminated a press release announcing the end of mask recommendations in Finland. In this press release THL clearly indicated this institute's role in the decision-making process. Other institutions were also mentioned by THL as key actors that can make local decisions on mask wearing recommendations (see THL, 2022). Moreover, THL indicated its intention to leave to others the option to choose what to do in respect of mask wearing; THL stated that masks should still be used at people's own discretion or if individuals consider themselves to be in a risk group. This can be considered a rhetorical strategy of *preservation of rights* for the purpose of ambiguity. Yet, THL added that widespread use of masks is ineffective to prevent the spread of COVID-19, thus indicating some form of *deniability / structural duality* as strategic ambiguity. Furthermore, THL also expanded the rights of those involved in the decisions of mask recommendations when it allowed the National Institute of Occupational Health to be involved in the discussion. This highly resonates with the findings of Jackall (1988) who noted that when managers wish to avoid making decisions, they tend to make their responsibility more ambiguous by involving many others in the decision process.

Finnish authorities utilized *deniability/structural duality* in several instances to justify their changes of opinions and positions and multiple understandings of the issue at stake. For example, in a press release, THL recommended that Finns no longer needed to wear masks, but they also gave a lot of different examples of occasions when they should wear a mask (THL, 2022). This indicates the co-presence of statements about continuity yet about changes at the same time.

When THL instructed that from now on people should also follow the guidelines of their local authorities more often, the rhetorical strategy of *postponement* was observed, as local authorities may or may not follow up with THL recommendations and the timing for instructive information was unspecified (THL, 2022). The decisions made by local administrations offer evidence of *deniability* and *structural duality* throughout the mask debate. For example, immediately following THL's press release, the City of Helsinki gave its own guidelines in a press release (see City of Helsinki, 2022). Even though THL instructed that local administrations can provide their own recommendations and guidelines, it was still evident that the City of Helsinki was clearly against the argument that "*widespread use (of masks) as a single measure does not significantly prevent the spread of the virus*". They even made the recommendations somewhat tighter than expected due to the recommendation to use face masks, for example in school facilities. However, a sense of discursive *postponement* was also apparent as the authorities indirectly revealed that face mask recommendations were about to change (at the time of their statement, these recommendations were under review).

Just one day after the less populated city of Jyväskylä in Central Finland (see City of Jyväskylä, 2022) dropped its mask recommendation, the city of Helsinki also changed its direction concerning the recommendations and moved closer toward THL's recommendations (Karhu, 2022). Despite the clear action to drop mandatory wearing of face masks, the rhetoric in the press release indicated the use of strategic ambiguity when denying the possible implications of such a decision as the city authorities argued that the risk of getting the COVID-19 virus was still high (City of Helsinki, 2022). At the same time, the press release indicated the use of *content expansiveness* as a strategy as the city listed a wide range of potential situations where face masks should still be used, albeit not enforced.

On April 20th, THL's communications manager Piritta Rautavuori gave a statement to Finnish Broadcasting company YLE (Karhu, 2022). In the statement a strong indication of the strategy of *preservation of rights* was visible as THL highly recommended following individual guidelines provided by (private sector) organizations such as Finnish railway company VR, and even encouraged people that those instructions should override THL's guidelines. This demonstrates a paradox, given that this official THL spokesperson suggesting that people not follow THL's guidelines, thus advising citizens to go against the organization she represents. At the same time, as Rautavuori played down the role of THL on this matter, she also acted against the City of Helsinki recommendations to drop the mask recommendations, which indicates *deniability* and *structural duality* as well. Interestingly, STM, which had previously been very vocal in event 1 and was expected to participate in the communication process in event 2, remained silent during this event, which suggests it adopted *protective silence* for the purpose of ambiguity.

Discussion and Conclusions

The purpose of this chapter was to identify, examine, and illustrate communicative practices of strategic ambiguity to protect an organization's image and to increase opportunities to mitigate otherwise contrasting stakeholder demands. Accordingly, this chapter examined two events as examples of the use of strategic ambiguity by the Finnish Government during the COVID-19 pandemic in the face of wide-ranging public opinions over the governments' pandemic decisions. Specifically, the chapter presented the findings of a study investigating how the Finnish authorities handled diverse demands while trying to control the spread of the virus in the country. The two events dealt with (1) whether schools should be reopened after the Christmas holidays despite the fourth wave of infections still going on and (2) whether people should continue to wear face masks in Spring 2022. The findings demonstrate how the Finnish Government and its authorities intentionally or unintentionally used the following five rhetorical strategies to convey ambiguity while discussing health recommendations in public arenas: *postponement, deniability/structural duality, content expansiveness, equivocality, preservation of rights,* and *protective silence.*

These events centered around highly debated topics in multiple Finnish public arenas and increased public attention toward the cross-organizational, polyphonic, and strategically ambiguous communication of the Finnish Government and its various authorities in situations when people expected accurate, clear, consistent and prompt information on what to do and what not to do in highly uncertain times. This study shows how multiple government authorities and health-related experts held contrasting opinions on these measures' efficacy in preventing new infections and did not shy away from engaging in public conversations to address their different views. It also demonstrates emergent use of strategic ambiguity by the national government, the national health authority and its independent expert agency, various government ministries, and diverse regional and municipal governments. Crisis and risk communication literature primarily stresses the importance of clear instructive information in times of crisis, as the most important organizational duty is to save people's lives. Maintaining that the primary goal of crisis management is public safety, it is also important to consider the ramifications of communicating assumptions and thereby instructions transparently and too early when facts and data about the situation are not available. In such situations, balancing instructive information with other communications, including the use of ambiguous communication, that serves the purpose of aligning divergent opinions is recommended. This is not just because in this manner organizations can protect their own image in turbulent and unclear times, but because ambiguous communication can keep open opportunities for different interpretations that can promote unified diversity, collaborations, and interactions among social actors. Since in critical situations individuals tend to exhibit a tendency to seek and accept information congruent with their emotional state and mental pre-assumptions (Nabi, 2003), ambiguous communication could allow organizations to reach out to a wider range of individuals with conflicting views on the situation who otherwise would not be reached. Thus, ambiguity could increase opportunities for an organizational message to be received, understood, and processed by all the diverse set of stakeholders.

Some managerial lessons can be drawn from this study as food for thought for communication professionals working in pandemic management and public sector organizations who may one day face diverse and conflicting stakeholder demands in times of high uncertainty. First, ambiguous communication should be considered in cross-organizational and polyphonic communication contexts, which public sector organizations tend to face in risk and crisis events. It is often difficult to manage one voice across multiple agencies in a crisis. Accordingly, while navigating information uncertainty and contradictory knowledge, ambiguous communication, including silence, can gain time for all entities to gather vital information and come to agreement while maintaining some level of public trust in the public institutions, which maintains organization's legitimacy and reputation. Second, effective use of strategic communication ambiguity can be useful to promote unified diversity for a limited time when diversity of opinion is unavoidable, and to foster later opportunities to deny the meaning of a message conveyed earlier (Eisenberg & Witten, 1987). Third, it also demands the ability to adapt to a fluid communication strategy in dynamic and fast-changing situations. If strategic ambiguity is not employed properly, there is a risk of losing public and stakeholder confidence in your ability to manage a major crisis, which negatively impacts organizational legitimacy. This is especially harmful for governmental organizations.

Finally, strategic ambiguity in communication should only be used when it benefits organizational stakeholders and the wider public (Guthey & Morsing, 2014). In the two events analyzed in this study, one could argue that it was the public authorities and Government that benefitted most from strategic ambiguity; their use of communication ambiguity was for the protection of their own image and legitimacy rather for the public good. The public would have benefitted far more if the Government and its authorities had instead communicated in a more clear, integrated, and coherent way. Abuse of strategic ambiguity in communication can lead to a vacuum of clear public knowledge (such as how to stay safe) which may be quickly filled by misinformation and disinformation.

Bearing in mind the limits of a single case study based on two critical events, this chapter offers the reader some insights on the complexity of managing pandemic communications when scientific knowledge (e.g., about a disease) is continuously evolving and challenging previous assumptions on the best course of actions, such as to prevent the diffusion of a highly deadly disease. The analysis of the main public statements by the Finnish Government illustrates how governments and public sector organizations through strategic ambiguity tread a fine line between taking concrete actions to reduce the spread of infection and meeting the public need to return to normal life.

Overall, this chapter contributes to the advancement of our understanding of communication strategies in crisis communication research by showing how strategic ambiguity was used by a national government during a global pandemic. It also calls for further research addressing the complexity of crisis messaging strategies under uncertain situations when clear and instructive messages are not possible. There is also further need to increase our understanding of the effects of public polarization and how preventive and protective behavioral measures are received, perceived, and internalized. Polyphony (see Hoffjann, 2022) is not only inside organizations, but externally among stakeholders and publics, and this polyphony can be challenging and dangerous in times of health and emergency crises.

References

Abdallah, C., & Langley, A. (2014). The double edge of ambiguity in strategic planning. *Journal of Management Studies, 51*(2), 235–264. https://doi.org/10.1111/joms.12002

Alvesson, M., & Sveningsson, S. (2003). Good visions, bad micro-management and ugly ambiguity: Contradictions of (non-) leadership in a knowledge-intensive organization. *Organization Studies, 24*(6), 961–988.

Black, J. S., Morrison, A. J., & Gregersen, H. B. (1999). *Global explorers: The next generation of leaders*. London: Routledge.

Cappellaro, G., Compagni, A., & Vaara, E. (2021). Maintaining strategic ambiguity for protection: Struggles over opacity, equivocality and absurdity around the Sicilian mafia. *Academy of Management Journal, 64*(1). https://doi.org/10.5465/amj.2017.1086

Chen, Y. W., & Lawless, B. (2018). 'Oh my god! You have become so Americanizised': Paradozes of adaptation and strategic ambiguity among female immigrant faculty. *Journal of International and Intercultural Communication, 11*(1), 1–20.

Christensen, L. T., Morsing, M., & Thyssen, O. (2015). The polyphony of values and the value of polyphony". *ESSACHESS: Journal for Communication Studies, 8*(1), 9–25.

City of Helsinki. (2022). *Pääkaupunkiseudun maskisuositukseen muutoksia*. https://www.hel.fi/uutiset/fi/kaupunginkanslia/muutoksia-maskisuositukseen

City of Jyväskylä. (2022). *Maskisuositus päättyi myös Jyväskylässä – kaupungin omassa toiminnassa maskien käyttö jatkuu sosiaali- ja terveyspalveluissa*. https://www.jyvaskyla.fi/uutinen/2022-04-19_maskisuositus-paattyi-myos-jyvaskylassa-kaupungin-omassa-toiminnassa-maskien

Daft, R. L., & Weick, K. E. (1984). Toward a model of organizations as interpretation systems. *Academy of Management Review, 9*(2), 284–295.

Denis, J.-L., Dompierre, G., Langley, A., & Rouleau, L. (2011). Escalating indecision: Be-tween reification and Strategic ambiguity. *Organization Science, 22*(1), 225–244.

Eisenberg, E. M. (1984). Ambiguity as strategy in organizational communication. *Communication Monographs, 51*, 227–242.

Eisenberg, E., & Witten, M. (1987). Reconsidering openness in organizational communication. *Academy of Management Review, 12*, 418–426.

Finnish Government. (2022). Tiedotustilaisuus pitkäkestoisesta koronasta (long covid) 7.1.2022 [Video]. *YouTube*. https://www.youtube.com/watch?v=b6UnEFR3ijc

Guthey, E., & Morsing, M. (2014). CSR and the mediated emergence of strategic ambiguity. *Journal of Business Ethics, 120*(4), 555–569.

Herman, J. L., Stevens, M. J., Bird, A., Mendenhall, M., & Oddou, G. (2010). The tolerance for ambiguity scale: Towards a more refined measure for international management research. *International Journal of Intercultural Relations, 34*, 58–65.

Hoffjann, O. (2022). Between strategic clarity and strategic ambiguity – oscillating strategic communication. *Corporate Communications: An International Journal*, 27(2), 284–303.

Hung, L, & Lin, M. (2022). Clear, consistent and credible messages are needed for promoting compliance with COVID-19 public health measures. *Evidence-Based Nursing, 25*(22). http://doi.org/10.1136/ebnurs-2020–103358

Hyland-Wood, B., Gardner, J., Leask, J., & Ecker, U. (2021). Toward effective government communication strategies in the era of COVID-19. *Humanities & Social Sciences Communications, 8*(1), 1–11. http://doi.org/10.1057/s41599-020-00701-w

Jarzabkowski, P., Sillince, J. A., & Shaw, D. (2010). Strategic ambiguity as a rhetorical resource for enabling multiple interests. *Human Relations*, *63*(2), 219–248.

Johansen, W. (2018). Strategic ambiguity. In R. Heath & W. Johansen (Eds.), *International encyclopedia of strategic communication* (pp. 1454–1457). Wiley & Son.

Johns Hopkins University & Medicine. (2022). Mortality analyses. https://coronavirus.jhu.edu/data/mortality

Karhu, O. (2022). Yleinen maskisuositus päättyi pääkaupunkiseudulla – vastaisuudessa maskia on käytettävä oman harkinnan mukaan. *YLE*. https://yle.fi/uutiset/3-12410542

Lowe, A., & Jones, A. (2004). Emergent strategy and the measurement of performance: The formulation of performance indicators at the microlevel. *Organization Studies*, *25*(8), 1313–1337.

Lowe, M., Harmon, S. H. E., Kholina, K., Parker, R., & Graham, J. E. (2022). Public health communication in Canada during the COVID-19 pandemic. *Canadian Journal of Public Health*. https://doi.org/10.17269/s41997-022-00702-z

Luotonen, A, Stenroos, M., Hassinen, H., Martikainen, A., Gertsch, M., Kuukkanen, T., & Haukka, I. (2022). Kiuru: Kansallista etäopetussuositusta kouluille ei anneta – kaikki sisätilat suljetaan ja ravintoloiden aukioloa rajoitetaan koko maassa. *YLE*. https://yle.fi/uutiset/3-12261947

Mena, S., Rintamäki, J., Fleming, P., & Spicer, A. (2016). On the forgetting of corporate irresponsibility. *Academy of Management Review*, *41*(4), 720–738.

Mintzberg, H. (1972). Research on strategy-making. In *Proceedings of the 32nd Annual Meeting of the Academy of Management*, Minneapolis.

Mintzberg, H. (1978). Patterns in strategy formulation. *Management Science*, *24*(3), 934–948.

Nabi, R. L. (2003). Exploring the framing effects of emotion: Do discrete emotions differently influence information accessibility, information seeking, and policy preference. *Communication Research*, *30*, 224–247.

Näveri, A., Keränen, T., Tikkala, H., & Stenroos, M. (2022). STM esittää koulujen siirtymistä etäopetukseen – opetusministeri Andersson: "Asiasta pitää keskustella koko hallituksen sisällä".

OECD. (2021). The territorial impact of COVID-19: Managing the crisis and recovery across levels of government. https://read.oecd.org/10.1787/a2c6abaf-en?format=pdf

Ozcan, P., & Gurses, K. (2018). Playing cat and mouse: Contests over regulatory categorization of dietary supplements in the United States. *Academy of Management Journal*, *61*(5), 1789–1820.

Quinn, S. C., Parmer, J., Freimuth, V. S., Hilyard, K. M., Musa, D., & Kim, K. H. (2013). Exploring communication, trust in government, and vaccination intention later in the 2009 H1N1 pandemic: Results of a national survey. *Biosecurity and Bioterrorism*, *11*, 96–106. http://dx.doi.org/10.1089/bsp.2012.0048

Media Metrics Finland. (2022). *Public media site toplist*. https://datastudio.google.com/reporting/445ac769-037b-408e-b383-9014d561cee5/page/QCkcB

Nivette, A., Ribeaud, D., Murray, A., Steinhoff, A., Bechtiger, L., Hepp, U., Shanahan, L., & Eisner, M. (2021). Non-compliance with COVID-19-related public health measures among young adults in Switzerland: Insights from a longitudinal cohort study. *Social Science & Medicine*, *268*, 113370. https://doi.org/10.1016/j.socscimed.2020.113370

Reuter, E., & Ueberbacher, F. (2019). Corporate strategies to defend social irresponsibility: A typology of symbolic and substantive tactics. In A. Sales (Ed.), *Corporate social responsibility and corporate change* (pp. 221–239). Springer.

Scandelius, C., & Cohen, G. (2016). Achieving collaboration with diverse stakeholders—The role of strategic ambiguity in CSR communication. *Journal of Business Research, 69*(9), 3487–3499. https://doi.org/10.1016/j.jbusres.2016.01.037

Sellnow, T. L., & Ulmer, R. R. (1995). Ambiguous argument as advocacy in organizational crisis communication. *Argumentation and Advocacy, 31*(3), 138–150.

Sillince, J., Jarzabkowski, P., & Shaw, D. (2012). Shaping strategic action through the rhetorical construction and exploitation of ambiguity. *Organization Science, 23*(3): 630–650.

Smith, S. W., Atkin, C. A., & Roznowski, J. A. (2006). Are "drink responsibility" alcohol campaign strategically ambiguous? *Health Communication, 20*(1), 1–11.

Sumelius, J., Smale, A., & Yamao, S. (2020). Mixed signals: Employee reactions to talent status communication amidst strategic ambiguity. *International Journal of Human Resource Management, 31*(4), 511–538. https://doi.org/10.1080/09585192.2018.1500388

Suzuki, M., Webb, D., & Small, R. (2021). Competing frames in global health governance: An analysis of stakeholder influence on the political declaration on non-communicable diseases. *International Journal of Health Policy Management.* https://dx.doi.org/10.34172/ijhpm.2020.257

THL. (2022). THL:n yleinen maskisuositus poistuu, mutta maskia voi edelleen käyttää. https://thl.fi/fi/-/thl-n-yleinen-maskisuositus-poistuu-mutta-maskia-voi-oman-harkinnan-mukaan-edelleen-kayttaa

Valentini, C., & Badham, M. (2023). Public trust in governments communicating with intermediaries: Finnish and Swedish Governments during COVID-19 pandemic in 2020. In R. Tench, J. Meng, & A. Moreno (Eds.), *Strategic Communication in a Global Crisis* (pp. 165–183). Routledge.

van der Meer, T. G. L. A., & Jin, Y. (2020). Seeking formula for misinformation treatment in public health crises: The effects of corrective information type and source. *Health Communication, 35*, 560–575. https://doi.org/10.1080/10410236.2019.1573295

Vergne, J.-P. 2012. Stigmatized categories and public disapproval of organizations: A mixed-methods study of the global arms industry, 1996–2007. *Academy of Management Journal, 55*(5), 1027–1052.

15 The COVID-19 Pandemic in the Polish and British Media

A Content Analysis

Stanisław Jędrzejewski, Krzysztof Kuźmicz and Gavin Rae

After the first COVID-19 case was detected in Wuhan China in December 2019, the virus spread quickly around the world, with the World Health Organization (WHO) declaring a global pandemic by March 2020. By late August, there had been more than 211 million reported cases and 4.43 million officially recorded deaths, with the actual human cost of the pandemic (measured in excess mortality) significantly higher (Ians, 2021; *Economist*, 2022). This pandemic also negatively affected economies around the world, forcing businesses to temporarily shut and trade to be halted.

The COVID-19 pandemic forced governments to react and introduce extraordinary policy measures to attempt to restrict the spread of the virus. Furthermore, public health systems had to respond to an unprecedented health emergency, placing a huge strain on public health services (Lal et al., 2021). The roll-out of a vaccination program also raised new issues of (un)equal access to the vaccines, the abilities of national health systems to administer them; and the willingness of populations to be vaccinated (Witter, 2021).

Countries applied a range of different strategies when trying to deal with the COVID-19 pandemic. These have ranged a "zero-COVID" policy of trying to eliminate the virus; to those that have pursued a policy of "herd immunity," based on the belief that the virus can be controlled once the infection has spread throughout society (Aschwanden, 2020). This myriad of differing strategies, and ongoing spread of the virus, has helped sow social divisions and even unrest (such as protesting lockdowns or vaccinations) and helped lay the ground for new "conspiracy theories" to grow (Douglas, 2021).

This paper carries out a content analysis of the media in Poland and the United Kingdom during the first "wave" of the pandemic, from March to June 2020. In this paper we deploy the working definition of "wave" put forward by Zhang et al (2021), which has two main characteristics: (1) an epidemic wave constitutes some upward and/or downward periods and (2) the increase in an upward period or the decrease in a downward period has to be substantial and sustained over a period of time.

DOI: 10.4324/9781003375296-18

In the initial phase of the pandemic, Poland focused on the rapid introduction of strict restrictions, including closing borders, limiting the number of people congregating and making it mandatory to wear masks in public spaces. In the UK, less stringent measures were initially taken, based on the theory that achieving adequate levels of infection can lead to natural immunity. However, when the number of infections and deaths began to rise, the British government introduced stricter restrictions, including lockdowns.

Ultimately, in the later phases of the pandemic, both countries focused on vaccination programs and other preventive measures to limit the impact of the pandemic on their populations.

The conducted research has three objectives: (1) to analyze media content during the first wave of the COVID-19 pandemic in Poland and the UK in order to understand the media's approach to managing the crisis and implementing preventive measures; (2) to examine what topics attracted the most media attention, such as lockdown, remote work, remote education, government information policy, and the impact of the pandemic on the economy; and (3) to identify differences in media approaches in Poland and the UK, including differences in perspective, coverage tone, and publicized issues.

The researchers also posed the following research questions:

1 What topics attracted the most media attention in Poland and the UK during the first wave of the COVID-19 pandemic?
2 What were the most common tones of coverage in the Polish and British media during the COVID-19 pandemic?
3 What were the most important contexts that influenced the media's approach to the COVID-19 pandemic in Poland and the UK, such as social, cultural, and political contexts?
4 What were the most common sources of information relied on by the media in Poland and the UK during the first wave of the COVID-19 pandemic?
5 What were the most important differences between the media's approach to the COVID-19 pandemic in Poland and the UK, and what were their consequences for society and the preventive measures taken?

Because remote work and online education were two areas of economic and social life that were particularly affected by the COVID-19 pandemic and related restrictions, this study only focuses on these contexts. For example, remote work became one of the most important topics during the pandemic, as many companies and organizations had to switch to this form of work in response to the introduction of pandemic-related restrictions. Remote work also affected many aspects of social life, including the way work is organized, employee relations, work efficiency, and work-life balance.

Moreover, education is the other area of social life that was affected by the pandemic, as many institutions moved to online teaching. This affected the learning process, the relationship between teachers and students, as well as students' families and private lives. All these changes have affected the quality of teaching and the emotional health of students and teachers.

COVID-19 First Wave in Poland and the United Kingdom

The first COVID-19 wave in Poland was much milder than that in the UK. The first case of the virus was detected on 19 March (i.e., nearly 2 months after that in the UK). Cases peaked at 376 (71 per million people) on April 9, with hospitalizations reaching 3,099 (82 per million people) on April 23; and deaths equaled a high of 28 (0.74 per million people) on April 29. Meanwhile excess mortality rates in Poland did not exceed 7.6% until August, although it remained above the average much longer than in the UK.

In Poland, the public debate at the beginning of the pandemic focused on support for the government in introducing harsh restrictions, such as closing borders, limiting the number of people congregating and making it mandatory to wear masks in public spaces. As more restrictions were introduced, some Poles began to question their effectiveness and express dissatisfaction with the government (see Figure 15.1). Public debate in Poland also focused on issues related to testing, vaccination, and the government's handling of the crisis. In the UK, the public debate about the pandemic focused initially on criticism of the government's approach to the pandemic, particularly in the context of the herd immunity theory. With the introduction of stricter restrictions and lockdowns, public opinion began to change, and the vaccination campaign was met with strong support. However, public debate in the UK also focused on issues related to the health care system, the availability of tests and problems with the supply of drugs. In both countries, the public debate also touched on issues related to the economy, the impact of the pandemic on people's private and professional lives, and issues related to the mental effects of the pandemic.

Poland managed to keep the number of cases, hospitalizations, and deaths at a much lower level than in the UK during the first COVID-19 wave (see Figures 15.2 and 15.3). This was partly due to the Polish government introducing containment measures earlier than in the UK, despite the virus arriving weeks later.[1] In March 2020, the government first introduced policies of closing schools, universities, restaurants and non-essential trade and service outlets. They also banned mass gatherings and introduced border controls. These measures stayed in place until April 20, when a staged opening of economic and social life began.

Meanwhile the British government initially toyed with the idea of allowing the virus to spread freely in society, hoping that this would allow natural herd immunity to be achieved. However, the sharp growth of cases in March, hand predictions of the health service being overrun, led to the UK government introducing restrictions from March 23.[2] Restrictions were gradually eased from the middle of May, ending in the opening of schools and universities in September.

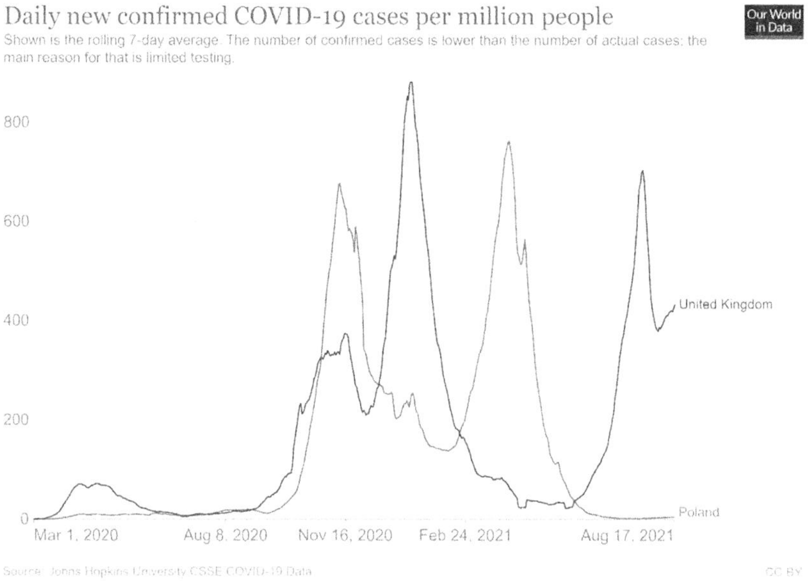

Figure 15.1 Comparison in Confirmed Cases of COVID-19: Poland vs. the UK.

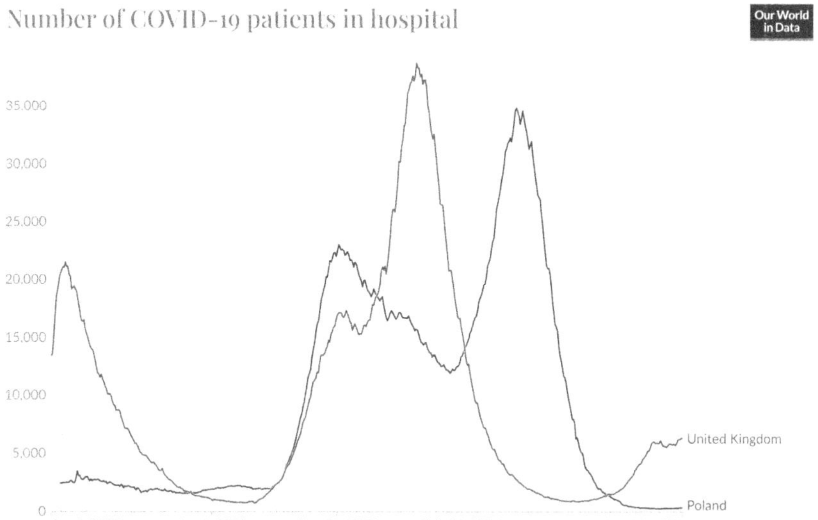

Figure 15.2 Comparison in Hospitalization from COVID-19: Poland vs. the UK.

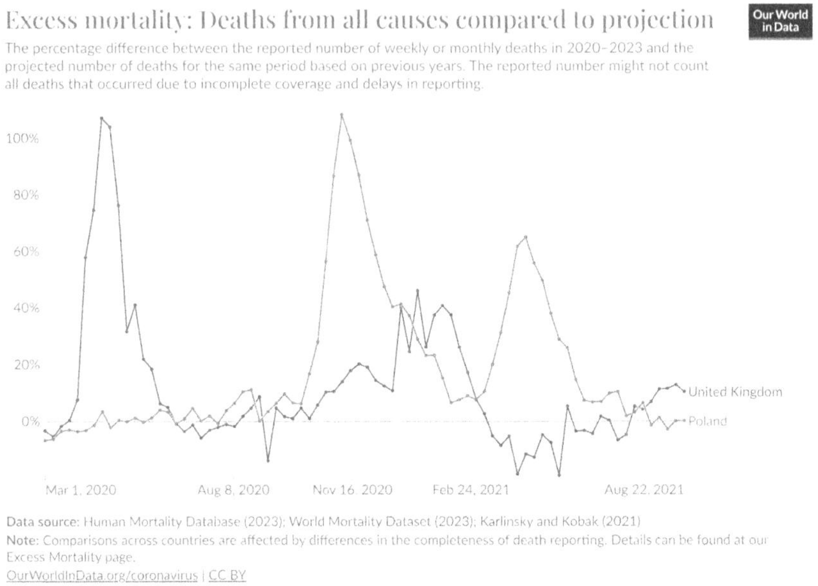

Figure 15.3 Comparison in Deaths from COVID-19: Poland vs. the UK.

Methodology

In this chapter we present both quantitative and qualitative data, to analyze the different media content in Poland and the UK during the first wave of the pandemic. The quantitative data refers to the frequency of specific words, phrases, the number of statements assigned to a category, etc. appearing in media content, which allows for further statistical processing (Babbie, 1978, p. 386; Silverman, 2005, pp. 40, 64, 148–149). The data were collected in a rolling model from 01.03.2020 to 30.06.2020 (Phase I/wave of the COVID-19 pandemic), for the generic keyword phrase "COVID" and the complementary keywords "sars cov 2," "koronavirus*" for Polish media and the generic keyword phrase "COVID" and the variants "sars cov 2," "coronavirus" for UK media. The data corpus for analysis included 45,886 journalistic materials from Polish media and 47,090 journalistic materials from British media. The database provider was Newspoint, a professional media monitoring company.

The qualitative approach has been deployed to analyze "naturally occurring" data, which does not require the intervention of the researcher in the object of study. The textual material we obtained through the keyword search method allowed us to extract the hidden meanings in media publications about remote working and distance education practiced during the first wave of the pandemic. In line with grounded theory, we based the creation of categories solely on what emerges directly from the content of the publications themselves, without adopting any preconceived notions (Charmaz, 2009, pp. 60–69; Konecki, 2000, p. 58).

In this paper, we have analyzed how the media portrayed the course of the pandemic in two areas: work and education. Within these two areas, we focus on remote working and distance learning.

Remote work is made possible by technologies such as virtual private networks (VPNs), internet voice protocols (VoIP), virtual meetings, cloud technology, and even facial recognition technologies. Of course, in addition to helping prevent the spread of viruses, remote work also saves commuting time and provides greater work flexibility.

However, remote work also presents challenges for employers and employees. Information security, privacy, and technical support can raise serious issues, as evidenced by recent class action lawsuits filed against Zoom Video Communications, Inc. Remote work can also complicate labor law issues regarding the provision of a safe work environment and income tax issues. If remote work continues to be widespread after the COVID-19 pandemic, it is likely that employers will choose to reduce office space and hire people from regions with lower labor costs. Moreover, not every job can be done from home. According to the US Bureau of Labor Statistics, around 25% of the employed already worked from home, at least occasionally, in 2017–2018. Workers with a college education are at least five times more likely to work from home than those with a high school education. Naturally, some professions, such as medical services or manufacturing, cannot take advantage of this opportunity at all.

In mid-April 2020, 191 countries closed schools and colleges. To avoid the perturbations associated with the effects of the pandemic, many educational institutions have offered online courses. Distance learning technologies are like those used for distance work and also include virtual reality, augmented reality, 3D printing, and robots using artificial intelligence.

One concern with distance learning is that these technologies can create a new "digital divide" An important disadvantage of distance learning is also that this type of teaching counteracts the formation of so-called soft skills acquired mainly through cooperation with others, observing the behavior of teachers, presenting one's own judgments and beliefs. Distance learning can also put economic pressure on parents (most often women) who must stay at home to look after and help their children, risking a reduction in wages and professional degradation.

Results: Media in Poland and UK – Quantitative Perspective

The data collected for the configured keywords in the period covered by the media monitoring included 3.5 million publications from Polish Internet portals and 2.5 million from UK portals. The detailed distribution, along with the number of journalistic materials published each day, is illustrated in Figure 15.4.

During the research period, between 4224 and 51507 journalistic materials and mentions of the COVID-19 pandemic were published each day on Polish portals and between 4494 and 32653 on UK portals. Most articles were published

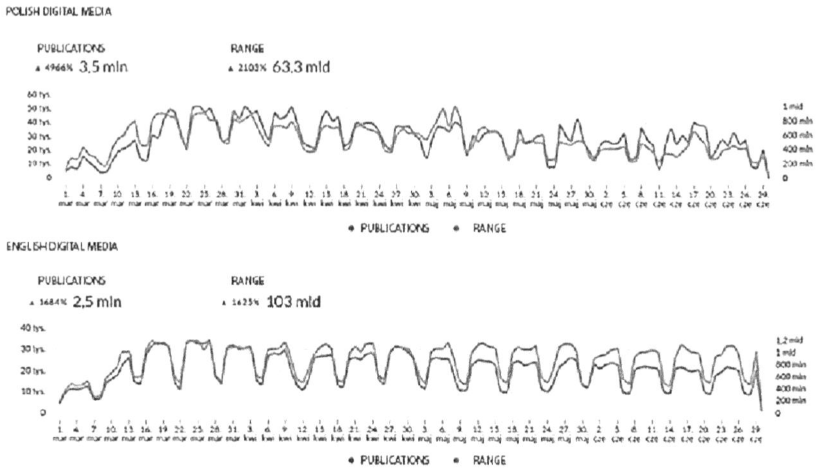

Figure 15.4 Publications on COVID-19 and their coverage in Polish and English digital media (portals) in the period 01.03.202–30.06.2020.

between 19 March and 15 April 2020 (Poland) and between 17 March and 28 April (UK). Among the most active content producers, it was evident that news portals and sites aggregating content from different media, as well as websites belonging to the mainstream media, dominated.

Tone of Media Content

Most of the analyzed articles can be considered neutral in overtone (see Figure 15.5 where the top line denotes neutral coverage). This was the case for 3.3 million publications in the Polish media and 2.4 million in the English media. Only in the case of 10.8 thousand publications in Poland and 1.8 thousand in the United Kingdom, were the overtones of journalistic materials classified as positive. In the cases analyzed, there were also texts with negative overtones. This group included 118.4 thousand Polish publications and 10.2 thousand UK publications. Detailed analyses of selected publications will be presented in the qualitative part of the publication.

Results: Education and Work during a Pandemic – Qualitative Analysis of Media Messages

A qualitative analysis of the media coverage of remote work and education during the first wave of the COVID-19 pandemic identified important themes and issues faced by both Poland and the UK. The analysis considered context and

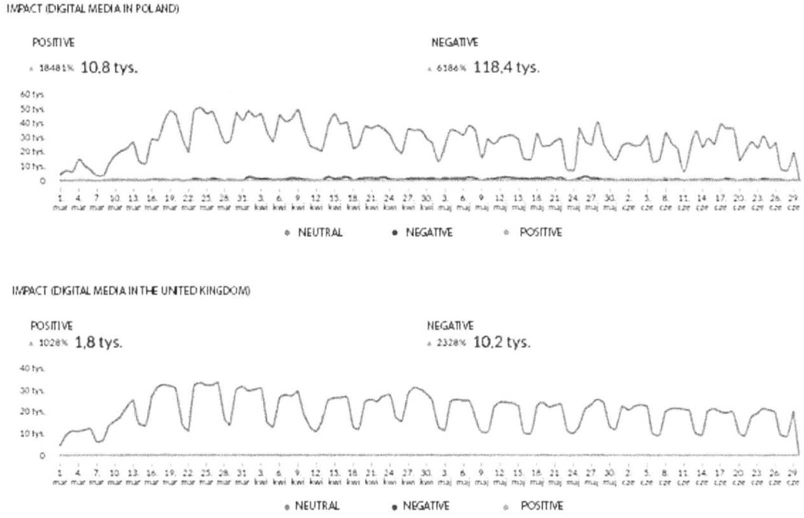

Figure 15.5 The impact of articles published in digital media in Poland and The United Kingdom with a quantitative distribution per day during the survey period.

perspective, which allows for a better understanding of the differences between the relationships in Poland and the UK.

A clear difference between coverage in Poland and the UK was the social perspective. In Poland, media coverage focused on the impact of the pandemic on daily life and the difficulties of working remotely and teaching remotely for average people. In the UK, coverage focused more on the impact of the pandemic on the economy and the business sector and the challenges of adapting to new forms of work and learning.

In a qualitative analysis of randomly selected media reports, we first show how TV or newspaper journalists described the situation, following a certain established pattern and how they characterized the attitudes of the main actors involved in the e-learning processes: teachers and pupils, as well as parents, school management, educational authorities, teachers' trade unions, and administrative and political authorities.

By focusing on media statements in selected TV channels (TVN24,SkyNews), an Internet portal (Onet) and an opinion-forming daily newspaper (Guardian), we necessarily fail to take into account the reactions to these statements by the public, which together with the broadcasters and publishers form a community of discourse. In other words, we take into account the produced texts, while leaving "aside" the issues of their perception (enrichment of knowledge, understanding, assessment of credibility, remembering, etc.).

Technology, Equipment (Infrastructure) for Distance Learning

The Ministry of Education (MEN) in Poland is working on improving the government's education platform. As described by the newspaper "Gazeta Wyborcza," the MEN had already organized a tender in 2018 for a PLN 16 million platform for remote lessons, a communicator and – in the future – videoconferencing. However, the functional ministerial communicator only appeared on 11 May, and the conferencing tool was still absent. Meanwhile, Minister Dariusz Piontkowski assured that the Ministry of Education would try to launch it before the new school year. (TVN24,19.06.2020)

British Education Minister Gavin Williamson said on 13 May 2020 that while he "*knows how hard schools, grammar schools, nurseries and parents are working to ensure that children and young people can continue to learn at home Nothing can replace face-to-face participation in lessons in the school classroom*" (SkyNews, 13.05.2020).

Remote Learning, Parents and Family

Parents of those children who stay at home hoped that school and care facilities would continue to provide remote education. "*And after all, we are not splitting up,*" – said Ms Marta, a kindergarten teacher from Gorzów. And she explained: "*These children often do not return to kindergartens because parents are afraid for their families' health. Meanwhile, the Minister of Health has said that if parents do not have to send their children to kindergartens, it would be fine if they stayed at home.*" And she added: "*And it is the parents, unlike those in power, who apparently remember thata kindergarten not only provides care, but also education and this education is what they expect from us*"(TVN24 08.05.2020).

Distance Learning as a Factor in the Emergence of Social Inequalities

Remote learning has had the unexpected effect of exacerbating social, due to a lack of equipment or Internet access and also as parents cannot equally support their children.

For many children in Poland, school is the place where, in addition to being educated, they have the chance to eat their only hot meal of the day. What happens to them now? Local governments have introduced a new form of assistance for needy families. There is also "Pajacyk," a nationwide feeding campaign financed by voluntary contributions. In Poland, in 2018, there were 417,000 or 6 % of all children living in extreme poverty. According to CSO calculations, its limit is the amount of PLN 503 per family member per month (TVN24, 28.04.2020).

"Many students do not have internet access at home, or an adequate broadband connection to participate in remote school activities. The turn to remote learning has revealed inequalities that, while present, were not apparent during traditional classroom teaching" (Guardian, 24.04.2020).

Six months of lockdown has been a disaster for everyone, but especially for those who have the least. For those whose education will continue until the age of 21 or later, three months is less of a loss than for students who leave school at 18. Rising unemployment and a dysfunctional housing market mean that dropping out of school is just one of many serious problems facing millions of low-income households.

Education policy alone cannot solve many of the problems associated with poverty, especially when the latter is on the rise. However, targeted support for pupils deemed to be excluded, combined with an emphasis on high-quality teaching, should help to minimize the damage done to the "COVID generation." The increase in the number of teachers that always accompanies a recession should bring new colleagues to ministers, head teachers, teaching unions and everyone else involved in the recovery effort. Their work is extremely important (Guardian, 06.09.2020)

Technology and Media Supporting Remote Learning

Pupils could gain access to teaching aid in various ways. Sky Kids channels, for example, feature a range of programs for preschool children, including Numberblocks, which helps with numeracy, Labuntina teaches educational songs and Rusty Rivets shows how to use technology to solve problems. Ryan's Mystery Playdate, meanwhile, involves physical challenges and puzzle solving, and with Octonauts children can learn about sea creatures and their habitats. Plus, on Netflix you can take a ride with Ms Frizzle and her students on The Magic School Bus, exploring everything from the cosmos to the human body, or choose StoryBots to get answers to all the important questions, such as how computers work or why I can't eat dessert all the time. (SkyNews, 25.03.2020)

Meanwhile, in Poland, the public television station TVP1 ran a much-criticized program "School with TVP." In one episode, a teacher confused the definition of diameter and circle when she wanted to show a nest of storks. The program was intended to help pupils who only have access to television and do not have a computer. These are students who live in smaller towns, who are brought up not by their parents but, for example, by their grandparents, who have no knowledge of modern technologies. (Onet, 01.04.2020)

While technologies specifically designed for remote learning, such as Seesaw, are in high demand, the use of traditionally workplace-based technologies is also widespread. The huge popularity of Zoom is one example, but Trello, a project management tool, also saw a 73% increase in registrations in March compared to last year. The company attributes much of this growth to its decision to provide free access to a premium package for teachers to help combat the challenges of school closures. (Guardian, 24.04.2020)

Keeping Children Safe When They Return to School

In the UK, unions have been critical of the need for and delivery of distance learning, fearing whether teachers, school support staff and pupils will be safe. According to a survey carried out by Unison, only 2% of school staff said they felt safe following the Prime Minister's speech and the Government's guidance on reopening education and care facilities. Dr Mary Bousted, General Secretary of the National Education Union, told Sky News that "*plans to reopen schools are leading to chaos. The union believes there is no evidence that reopening schools will be safe*" (SkyNews, 26.05.2020).

As in other European countries, younger children will be a priority in the first phases of reopening schools. SAGE recommendations indicate that there is a lower risk associated with opening schools and kindergartens to younger children, and they are less likely to deteriorate in the event of coronavirus infection compared to adults. Some of the main victims of this concern are children, in whom the medical risk of serious infection is virtually zero:

"*For goodness sake, 47% of Brits were recently surveyed as wanting home schooling to continue indefinitely. This is tantamount to the end of public education.*"

Another aspect of ensuring health security relies on a specific "hygiene" rhetoric that people do not understand:

"People are told about making different behavioral changes – from social distancing to extra hand washing – and many may struggle to understand why," – says Professor Dave Hodgson of the University of Exeter. "*Instead of explanations, children learn by heart dilemmas about handwashing, twist their arms to make sure no one comes near them, stand alone in isolated 'chalk circles' and drop toys and materials every five minutes that cannot be disinfected*" (SkyNews 04.06.2020).

Remote Learning and Women

A study carried out by the University of Valencia show that women take on the burden of children's homeschooling responsibilities. They are the ones who contact teachers and help with homework. During the pandemic, Spanish women, for example, spent an average of 2.5 hours a day longer on housework and caring for loved ones. Another problem has become the need to exclude grandparents from childcare. The increase in women's domestic responsibilities as a result of the need for children to be taught remotely is reported by feminist organizations in France such as Osez le Féminisme, who estimate that remote education, and the forced closure of schools and kindergartens, has tripled women's domestic and family responsibilities.

Marlène Schiappa, French Secretary of State for Gender Equality, commissioned research on the subject. Almost 60% of the women surveyed admitted that more domestic responsibilities fall on them during the shutdown. According to around 20% of men, it is women who do more at home during a pandemic. What does this look like in practice? It is estimated that French women spend an average of 2 hours and 34 minutes per day on housework, 24 minutes longer than French men. Although the difference does not seem that big, as many as 63% of French women surveyed said that they are the ones who take care of preparing all the meals for the household. (Guardian, 29.05.2020)

Work – Qualitative Data

In this section we present a qualitative analysis of selected journalistic materials, focused on the general problems emerging in media discourse about work. Due to the thematic diversity of issues related to labor, we have decided to present two dimensions: work in health care and remote working.

Working in the Health Sector

The media reported on the heroic actions of medical professionals and described the emotions of the staff working in difficult, sometimes extreme conditions. In TVN24 footage, we could hear what attitudes prevailed among doctors and nurses:

> "*There is fear, because only the stupid are not afraid, there is a will to fight, because it is normal to work in extreme conditions in this environment.*"
>
> (TVN24, 12.05.2020)

The media statements were complemented by information on the need to create working conditions adapted to the emergency, as well as on legal regulations that would prevent the growing number of cases of nurses working 24 hours a day. Information was also broadcast on the position of the Sejm and the Senate of the Republic of Poland on salary supplements, respite leave and weekly testing of medical staff for the SARS-CoV-2 virus. In addition, the station presented profiles of health professionals who gave their lives saving patients:

> "*They knew they were risking their health and lives. Despite this, they did not hesitate, they did not walk away from their patients' beds, because for them it was more than a job and earning money.*"
>
> (TVN24, 27.06.2020)

Among the problems described in the media were ethical dilemmas, creating a sense of internal tension among doctors and nurses, stemming from: "*the need to fulfil professional responsibilities, to help patients – and responsibilities to themselves and their own families*" (ONET, 11.06.2020, 08:58). Deciding to choose between work and family in a crisis is a huge psychological burden for many medical professionals. Analogous problems have been experienced by doctors in the UK: "*It's hard because my kids are everything to me. They are my world and I miss them so much.," said NHS doctor Adele Holland.* (SkyNews, 01.04.2022)

In the UK, retired doctors and nurses have been actively involved in the fight against the COVID-19 pandemic. In information published by SkyNews, we could read that "*The health secretary says he is "delighted" thousands of nurses and doctors have signed up to the NHS – but many more are needed*" (SKYNEWS, 22.03.2020, 01:36). In total, more than 4,500 retired health professionals joined the fight against the pandemic during this period. This involvement fully corresponded with the strain on the medical system: "*NHS is "already working at full capacity" and that a rise in COVID-19 cases in the UK would "put a huge strain on the system"* (SkyNews, 11.03.2020).

The Guardian, presented complex forms of journalism, often drawing on survey data as well as describing situations from an international perspective. For example, the publication selected for qualitative analysis featured information on the situation of US nurses, who: "*have not been tested for COVID-19, are reusing personal protective equipment (PPE), or have exposed skin or clothing while caring for COVID-19 patients*" (Guardian, 20.05.2020).

There were also statements about the ethos of the medical profession and the commitment of workers to health care. Among the articles describing the situations of European medical workers, readers of The Guardian were able to hear the account of Professor Massimo Galli, director of the Infectious Diseases Department at Milan's Sacco Hospital, who said that coronavirus was: "*the equivalent of a tsunami for the number of patients with major diseases being hospitalised all together*" (Guardian, 01.03.2020).

Remote Working

The first wave of the COVID -19 pandemic triggered significant transformations in existing work patterns. Looking at a sample of publications drawn for qualitative analysis, we notice that on TVN 24 they concentrated on the issue of sportspeople and remote work. In material published on 12 June, TV viewers were able to learn about the story of Norwegian ski jumper Marius Lindvik: "*He used the break in training due to the COVID-19 pandemic usefully, employed himself at roadworks. The jumper worked on laying grass and asphalt. He also secured the area where heavy equipment was working*" (TVN24, 12.06.2020). Also, Swedish pole vaulter Angelica Bengtsson, was forced to temporarily change jobs for financial reasons: "The *season is what it is, which means there is no season. Without competition for an athlete there is no income (...). I need an income. I have found an interesting job outdoors doing road repairs*" (TVN24, 21.04.2020).

Problems of remote working also include the infrastructure and ergonomics of the working environment. Readers of the Onet.pl portal could find articles of a tutorial nature, which described in a simple way how best to reorganize home space to fulfill office functions: "*Working at the computer is much more comfortable when we have a monitor at our disposal. Setting it up on a kitchen table or desk can be problematic, mainly due to lack of space*" (Onet, 18.03.2020). Part of the focus was on apps that allow monitoring of remote working staff:

> *Working from home will enable a clever boss to have even stronger control than in the office, because there are already conferencing apps that let him know if you're listening in all the time, and he can also keep track of whether you're simultaneously sitting on some messenger or other app.*
>
> (Onet, 23.03.2020)

The transfer of professional activity from the office to the home brought to light social problems related to domestic violence, most frequently against women and children: "*So far we have provided some form of help to more than 50 people*" (Onet, 17.04.2020). The confinement at home of parents with children, who could not always take childcare leave, working remotely caused cases of growing frustration: "*What do I have to say to my employer? That I can't reply to an email because I'm cooking soup and in a minute I have to do maths with my daughter and teach her prayers?*" (Onet, 17.03.2020). Journalists tried to look for prescriptions that would provide ad hoc solutions to help parents working in the home office model during the quarantine period. The problem was becoming more acute for families with many children: "*Let's face it – we can handle one child, but what about when we have three children and one computer to work on?*" (Onet, 24.03.2020).

Businesspeople sometimes expressed their opinion in the media that isolation was an effective weapon in the fight against the virus: "*Many companies suggest that employees who can work at home do just that*" (SkyNews, 03.06.2020). The first few months of the global pandemic have driven the use of ICT on an unprecedented scale. Major technology companies have been quick to take advantage of the situation: "*Google announced (...) that it would be giving away free access to its advanced video conferencing capabilities (...) a move quickly followed by Microsoft*" (SkyNews, 03.06.2020).

Large tech companies were among the leading businesses to recommend a remote working model for their employees in the early stages of the pandemic:

> *In Seattle, Amazon, LinkedIn, Microsoft and Google advised employees to stop coming into the office at the end of February. In early March, Twitter strongly advised all its employees worldwide to do the same, and on Wednesday made it mandatory.*
>
> (Guardian, 13.03.2020)

At the end of April, regulations came in to reduce the sanitation regime, but for businesses the changes were not immediate. In The Guardian, Joanna Daly, vice president of human resources at IBM, spoke on the issue, saying: *"About 95% of employees now work from home. Countries may start to lift stay-at-home orders, but that does not mean we will immediately return to workplaces*" (Guardian, 29.04.2020).

Though there was an initial enthusiasm for remote working, later there grew a longing for the "old normal" office culture where people meet in the real world. This was shown through the words of Satya Nadella, CEO of Microsoft, who said that: "*any perceived productivity gains of remote working should not be overly celebrated. What I miss is when you walk into a physical meeting, you're talking to the person next to you*" (Guardian, 11.06.2020).

The collapse of the UK labor market due to the COVID-19 pandemic, was reported in The Guardian publications, which, citing statements by the Deputy National Economic Statistician Jonathan Athow, presenting the employment report, stated that: "*The decline in employment is highest among the youngest and oldest workers, as well as those in lower-skilled jobs*" (Guardian, 11.04.2020).

Conclusions

The COVID-19 pandemic changed people's behavior and revolutionized the functioning of many institutions. These changes were starkly visible in the spheres of work and education, where millions of people were compelled to work and study at home. This created new issues of social inequality and exclusion, with the digital divide in society exposed by the demands of remote work and learning.

Inevitably, the media had to react to all these changes. In this chapter, we tried to portray the reactions of the Polish and British media. The Polish and British media differed during the first wave of the pandemic in their approach to reporting on the COVID-19 pandemic. The Polish media tended to focus on emotional and dramatic issues, publicizing the problems associated with the pandemic and sometimes being critical of the government's actions. The British media, on the other hand, presented issues in a calmer way, within an international context. There is a need for further analyses of the media during the pandemic. The global nature of the pandemic provides the ground for future comparative research of the media in different countries during this time.

Notes

1 Unless otherwise stated, the information on government policies in this paper is taken from: https://www.imf.org/en/Topics/imf-and-covid19/Policy-Responses-to-COVID-19#P. Although it will not be covered in this paper, it should be noted that the timings and details of government policies sometimes differed in the United Kingdom between England, Scotland, Wales and Northern Ireland.

2 Research carried out at Imperial College predicted in March 2020 that if the government's strategy at that time would lead to 260,000 deaths (https://www.theguardian.com/world/2020/mar/16/new-data-new-policy-why-uks-coronavirus-strategy-has-changed).

References

Aschwanden, C. (2020). *The false promise of herd immunity for COVID-19, Nature News*. Nature Publishing Group. Available at: https://www.nature.com/articles/d41586-020-02948-4 (Accessed: December 18, 2022).

Babbie, E. (1978). *Practising social research: Guided activities to accompany the practice of social research*. Cengage

Charmaz, K. (2009). *Constructing grounded theory*. Sage Publications Ltd.

Douglas, K. M. (2021). COVID-19 conspiracy theories. *Group Processes & Intergroup Relations*, *24*(2), 270–275. https://doi.org/10.1177/1368430220982068

Gates, M. B. (2020). COVID – 19 global perspetive 2020 goalkeepers report. https://www.gatesfoundation.org/goalkeepers/report/2020-report/#CollaborativeResponse

IANS (Indo-Asian News Service). (2021). *Global COVID-19 caseload TOPS 211.7 Gmn, deaths surged to 4.43 mn, Business Standard News*. Business-Standard. https://www.business-standard.com/article/current-affairs/global-COVID-19-caseload-tops-211-7-mn-deaths-surged-to-4-43-mn-121082300074_1.html. Accessed: December 18, 2022.

Konecki, K. (2000) *Studia z metodologii badań jakościowych. Teoria ugruntowana*. Warszawa PWN U.S. Bureau of Labor Statistics.

Lal, A. et al. (2021). Fragmented health systems in COVID-19: Rectifying the misalignment between global health security and Universal Health Coverage. *The Lancet*, *397*(10268), 61–67. https://doi.org/10.1016/s0140-6736(20)32228-5

Silverman, D. (2005). *Doing qualitative research. A practical handbook*. Sage Publication.

Tracking COVID-19 Excess Deaths across Countries. (no date). The Economist. *The Economist Newspaper*. https://www.economist.com/graphic-detail/coronavirus-excess-deaths-tracker Accessed: December 18, 2022.

Witter, A. (2021). *How unequal COVID-19 vaccine distribution is exacerbating global inequalities*, *ONE*. Available at: https://www.one.org/international/blog/covid19-vaccine-inequity/ Accessed: December 18, 2022.

16 Information Seeking Repertoires in Migrant-Dense Swedish Suburbs during the COVID-19 Pandemic

Bengt Johansson, Sofia Johansson and Marina Ghersetti

As in many countries, migrant residents in Sweden were more severely affected by the COVID-19 virus than the population in general (cf. Hargraves et al., 2021; Migration Data Portal, 2022; SOU, 2021). Both the infection and the mortality were higher compared to the rest of society (Folkhälsomyndigheten, 2021). Further, the share of vaccinated individuals was lower among residents with foreign backgrounds, which prompted targeted governmental communication efforts (Ekman, 2022; Folkhälsomyndigheten, 2022).

Among other factors, information gaps have been pointed out as a potential explanation. Health and crisis communication campaigns are mainly designed for majority populations, creating information deficits in migrant populations (Backholm & Nordberg, 2023; Brekke, 2021; Yoon et al. 2017). Thus, understanding how residents use different channels to inform themselves, and especially how they combine different information sources to make sense of a potentially dangerous situation, is essential for effective crisis communication. In addition, we need to acknowledge different information needs during different stages of a prolonged crisis, such as a pandemic, as well as pandemic fatigue, making individuals inclined to change their information seeking behavior or avoid information about the situation (Broersma & Swart, 2022; Ford et al., 2022). Further, an increased understanding of the heterogeneity of migrant populations is needed. In migrant-dense communities, residents from different parts of the world live side by side and levels of integration differ extensively, not at least in terms of language skills (Esaiasson, 2020). As such, they are prone to combine information sources differently.

Against this backdrop, this chapter analyzes how individuals combine information sources in migrant-dense suburbs at two different phases of the COVID-19 pandemic, using a panel survey conducted in two migrant-dense suburbs in Sweden in the years 2020 and 2021.

DOI: 10.4324/9781003375296-19

Information Seeking, Migrants, and Effective Crisis Communication

The overriding goal in the most acute phase of a crisis is to provide motivation for self-protection (Sellnow & Seeger, 2021) which cannot be accomplished without knowledge about how individuals seek information. To better align theories of crisis management and public information campaigns with individuals' information seeking practices, crisis communication research has, in recent years, accentuated the importance of audience perspectives (Fraustino & Liu, 2018). Audience perspectives on crisis communication are found in different traditions, and at least three strands of audience-based perspectives can be detected in crisis communication research (Fraustino & Liu, 2018). The first one focuses on the relationship between an organization and its public when deciding on an appropriate crisis response. The second perspective aims to understand and segment audiences' information seeking practices. Finally, the third strand of research emphasizes the public's emotions and coping strategies. Although the second strand specifically focuses on information seeking, all three perspectives involve knowledge on how citizens seek information. Understanding individuals' information seeking practices is not only a prerequisite for segmenting audiences, building relationships, and effective crisis management (Frandsen & Johansen, 2020; Ulmer et al., 2019), it is also important for understanding self-protective behavior and emotions generated by the crisis (Dillard et al., 2020; Fraustino & Liu, 2018; Guo & Bai, 2022; Li & Zheng, 2020).

The growing interest in information seeking patterns is partly related to the high-choice media environment, in which legacy news media live side by side with social media and alternative sources (Andersen et al., 2022). In the contemporary media system, individuals can combine a wide variety of sources during a crisis, which might provide conflicting or false information. Still, previous research on information seeking during crises generally focuses on one source or compares different types of sources (Liu et al., 2011, 2016). Although this body of research has provided important insights to information-seeking habits, it tends to be channel-centric and therefore fails to capture how individuals combine different sources to make sense of a threatening situation. Recent research has made different attempts to overcome this deficit. As an example, Houston (2021) proposes communication ecology network (CEN) to explain the relationship between the use of different crisis communication sources during COVID-19. Similarly, Zhao et al. (2022) use the convergence framework and apply a cluster analysis to identify simultaneous use of information from a plethora of sources and channels during COVID-19. The repertoire approach is yet another way to understand the combination of different information sources used. Following this approach, the mix of different sources builds an individual information seeking repertoire (Sommerfeldt, 2015). Broadly speaking, such studies have identified a range of different types of information seekers, including groups who mainly seek information in traditional sources, groups who rarely seek information in any source and heavy information seekers who use a wide variety of sources (Houston, 2021; Johansson et al., 2023b; Sommerfeldt, 2015; Zhao et al., 2022).

As is noticeable, previous research has mainly identified different types of information seekers among the general public. Studies have not yet looked at how different subgroups combine sources during a crisis. However, contemporary societies are multi-public, meaning information seeking as well as media habits vary between groups of citizens depending on socio-demographic factors as well as personal interests (Andersen et al., 2022). The lack of studies of information seeking among various subgroups of the population is problematic since subgroups which tend to be more severely affected by a crisis also tend to have different information seeking strategies. This is especially relevant considering that information-seeking has shown to influence self-protective behaviors (Li & Zheng, 2020).

Focusing on migrant-dense communities, we know that the share of vaccinated individuals was lower and the number of infected individuals was higher during the COVID-19 pandemic. At the same time, we know that migrant-dense suburbs entail a higher degree of news avoiders compared to other parts of society and that residents in these areas to a lesser extent rely on Swedish news media to inform themselves. In addition, research from the onset pandemic shows that individuals living in migrant-dense areas tend to use social and foreign news media more frequently for information seeking purposes (Esaiasson et al., 2020). Finally, previous research indicates that interpersonal communication may be of bigger importance to minority populations during a crisis (Spence et al., 2007). However, to what degree individuals in migrant-dense suburbs avoid Swedish news media and rely on other sources is likely to depend on individual level factors. Specifically, previous studies indicate that cultural identity (i.e., how strongly individuals identify with their cultural background), language skills, societal trust, and social capital impact information seeking behavior (Backholm & Nordberg, 2023; Esaiasson et al., 2020; Kim et al., 2022; Sellnow & Veil, 2016). Such factors are thus likely to impact which sources individuals include in their information seeking repertoires, giving rise to a large variety of information seeking practices within migrant-dense communities.

How individuals combine sources is additionally likely to change during a prolonged societal crisis, such as a pandemic. An increased need to take precaution at the onset of a crisis tends to give rise to an increased search for crisis related information (Sellnow & Seeger, 2021). This need might, however, not only make individuals prone to increase their frequency of information seeking but include additional sources in their repertoire. During the COVID-19 pandemic, the acuteness of the crisis resurfaced in various phases, potentially causing individuals to search more frequently for information or include other information sources in their mix during times of higher infection rates. During the final (less acute) stages of a crisis, however, there is a need to understand how society can be rebuilt and who is considered responsible (Johansson et al., 2023a; Sellnow & Seeger, 2021), which also might cause individuals to transform their information seeking repertoires. Finally, previous research shows that some individuals reach a "tipping point" at which they start to decrease their consumption of crisis-related information, despite the fact that the threat level remains high. This phenomenon has been explained by a heightened level of pandemic fatigue, making individuals less inclined to search for information about the situation (Broersma & Swart, 2022; Chen et al., 2022; Ford et al., 2022; Vandenplas et al., 2021).

Based on previous research, it can be assumed that residents in migrant-dense communities combine information sources during a crisis in different ways and that the combination of sources they use varies in different phases of the crisis due to changing information needs. However, there is a lack of studies analyzing how subgroups, and especially residents in migrant-dense communities, combine sources during such events, making our knowledge of these practices scarce or even non-existent. By identifying different types of information seekers in these communities, however, crisis communication practitioners are better equipped to communicate effectively with groups that tend to be difficult to reach during a crisis. The aim of this chapter is therefore to (1) identify different information seeking repertoires during the COVID-19 pandemic in two migrant-dense communities in Sweden and (2) analyze the stability of such repertoires in two different phases of the crisis (September/October 2020 and April 2021).

The Swedish Case

Sweden is the most multi-ethnic society among the Nordic countries (Nordic Statistics Database, 2019). In 2021, 26% of the residents had non-Swedish background and 20% were foreign-born. Of the seven largest ethnic minorities living in Sweden in 2021, only two came from other European countries, Finland (no.3) and Poland (no.4). The other five came from Syria (no.1), Iraq (no.2), Iran (no.5), Somalia (no.6), and Afghanistan (no.7).

Sweden of today is also a highly segregated society (Delmos, 2021). Since the first immigration wave from southern Europe in the 1950s, foreign-born residents have formed and settled in their own communities, mostly in suburbs outside major cities (Esaiasson, 2020). In the three largest cities, Stockholm, Gothenburg, and Malmoe, 22–27% of the residents are foreign-born (SCB, 2022). Often, ethnic segregation occurs in parallel with socio-economic segregation (Hedman & Andersson, 2015). The fact that foreign-born people are over-represented in neighborhoods where many low-income people live, is a

Table 16.1 Socio-demographics in two migrant-dense suburbs in Gothenburg, Sweden, 2021

	Östra Bergsjön	*Hjällbo*	*Gothenburg City, total*
Born in other country	63.3%	59.8%	28.3%
Foreign background[a]	88.6 %	90.5%	38.1 %
Average annual income, personal (2020)	193,000 SEK	197,500 SEK	332,400 SEK
Unemployment	17.6 %	18.0 %	6.6 %
Sickness rate[b]	24.7	25.5	19.5
Household w. 4 persons or more	29.6 %	33.7 %	16.1 %
Post college education, 3 yrs or more	16.1 %	14.2 %	37.9 %
Ownership/tenancy of apartment/house	9.9 %	8.6 %	46.3 %

Sources: Göteborg Stad (https://goteborg.se/wps/portal/enhetssida/statistik-och-analys/goteborgsbladet/hamta-statistik).

[a] Born in another country oneself, or with mother and/or father born in another country.
[b] Number of days per person in the population receiving public benefits in the form of sickness benefit, rehabilitation allowance and sickness and activity compensation.

sign that the primary reason for settlement patterns is income and not whether the person is native or foreign born. In areas with a high proportion of foreign-born with low-income, native-born people with low income also live (Malmberg & Clark, 2020).

Two such neighborhoods included in this study are Hjällbo and Östra Bergsjön in the outskirts of Gothenburg, the second largest city in Sweden. Most residents have a foreign background, and compared to the average Gothenburg resident, their income and level of education is significantly lower. Unemployment is higher, a larger majority live in rented apartments and households generally have more members than the average Gothenburg household (Goteborg City, 2022). The sickness rate, measured by the number of days of public benefits per resident, is also higher than the average rate in Gothenburg (see Table 16.1).

Methods and Sample

The Resident Panel, collected by the SOM-institute at the University of Gothenburg, was used for the analysis. The panel included individuals living in Hjällbo and Östra Bergsjön, had a net sample size of 3,757 and was conducted between 2018 and 2021 (a total of four survey waves). The panel was created to overcome problems with recruiting individuals living in migrant-dense suburbs with low socioeconomic status (Tourangeau et al., 2014) by establishing local contacts, being on site, asking questions that were relevant to residents, offering monetary incentives, and making it easy to participate. Participants were recruited using different methods, such as approaching individuals who visited the centrally located square, the local hospital, as well as local events, but also by knocking on doors to randomly selected addresses in the neighborhood (Esaiasson, 2020).

The final sample was skewed toward middle aged and younger individuals and contained a higher number of women compared to men. The analyses are based on individuals who answered the indicator variables. Therefore, the final number of respondents varied across the survey waves (239 in survey 1, 210 in survey 2). In both surveys, the sample size was smaller than the suggested size of 300 participants for the chosen analytical approach (see below). However, smaller samples might be adequate with simpler models and well separated classes (Nylund-Gibson & Choi, 2018), which will be discussed further under analytical strategy.

The two surveys that were sent out during the COVID-19 pandemic were used for the analysis. The first survey was sent out in September/October 2020, and the second one in April 2021. During September/October 2020 (survey 1), the infection and mortality rates were relatively low. Notably, the spread was even lower in Hjällbo and Östra Bergsjön compared to many other parts of Gothenburg at the time (Folkhälsomyndigheten, 2022). In November 2020, the second wave hit and the number of infected increased rapidly. The Delta variant of the virus reached Sweden in February 2021, and there was consequently no gap between wave two and three, causing high infection rates throughout spring 2021. Although it seemed like there was no end to the rising infection rates, there was a light at the end of the tunnel. During spring 2021, the vaccine program was rolled out, resulting in significantly lower mortality rate in April 2021 (survey 2). Although infection rates were high during the spring of 2021, vulnerable groups were protected from serious illness and death when being infected.

Measurement

Information seeking was measured by asking participants *"How often have you searched for information about* COVID-*19 in/from the following sources?"*. The question was accompanied by a 5-point scale, ranging from 1 (Several times a day) to 5 (Never), for the following items: Swedish news media, foreign news media, social media, government agency web pages, family/friends, and alternative media. No example outlets were specified for the items, meaning the indicators were measured on a general level. A low number of indicators is suitable considering the sample size. It is, however, also likely to increase measurement error. This is especially relevant concerning the items "family/friends" and "social media", where differences between the categories are not clear.

Analytic Strategy

To identify information seeking repertoires at both time points, a cross-sectional latent class analysis (LCA) was applied in each wave. LCA is a latent variable mixture modeling approach which aims to identify subgroups that share certain characteristics within larger populations. By analyzing individual's response patterns to specific indicators, the LCA probabilistically assigns individuals to different groups. This, in turn, results in different subgroups, called latent classes, in which individuals are similar to each other but differ from those assigned to other classes (Petersen et al., 2019; Weller et al., 2020).

A maximum solution of five classes were tested in each wave[1]. When testing the solutions, different estimation approaches were applied, such as listwise deletion of cases and FIML estimation of missing at random. The best solution was chosen by examining the Bayesian information criteria (BIC), sample size adjusted Bayesian information criteria (aBIC), Consistent Akaike criterion (CAIC), and Bootstrap Likelihood Ratio test (BLRT). To be precise, the information criteria were used to determine whether increasing the number of classes improved the overall model fit (Nylund et al., 2007). Since the CAIC is less reliable on skewed data (Morgan et al., 2016) and the sample size was small (Nylund-Gibson & Choi, 2018), the aBIC was primarily used to identify the best model fit.

Traditionalists, Pluralists, Frequent Pluralists, and Information Junkies

The aBIC suggested four classes as the best fitting model in the two suburbs in September/October 2020 (survey 1) and five classes as the best fitting model in April 2021 (survey 2). While the aBIC value decreased sharply from one to two classes, the four-class solution in survey 1 and the five-class solution in survey 2 had the absolute lowest aBIC values (see Appendix). However, the five-class solution did not generate any cAIC or Entropy-value, indicating that the sample size might have been too small to conduct the calculations. On this basis, and since the four-class solution made theoretical sense in both surveys, it was chosen as the best fitting model. The Entropy-value for the four-class solution was over eight in each survey, indicating well-separated classes (Celeux & Soromenho, 1996).

The four types of information seekers identified by the model include: *traditionalists, pluralists, frequent pluralists,* and *information junkies* (see also, Andersen et al., 2022; Castro et al., 2021; Johansson et al., 2023b; Zhao et al., 2022). These repertoires were identified in both surveys, with only slight changes between the two-time points[2]. Although the frequency of information seeking was lower for almost all classes in April 2021, the general structure (i.e., which sources were included in the repertoires) was similar. As such, it can be argued that the information seeking repertoires were rather stable, at least between the two chosen time points (September/October 2020 and April 2021). Although similar information seeking types were discovered, it should be noted that the sizes of the repertoires changed from time point one to time point two, indicating that individuals moved between different classes by transforming their repertoires. It is likely that individuals moved between similar types, such as the *Pluralists* and the *Frequent pluralists.* While the same repertoires were identified, they might, in other words, include different individuals.

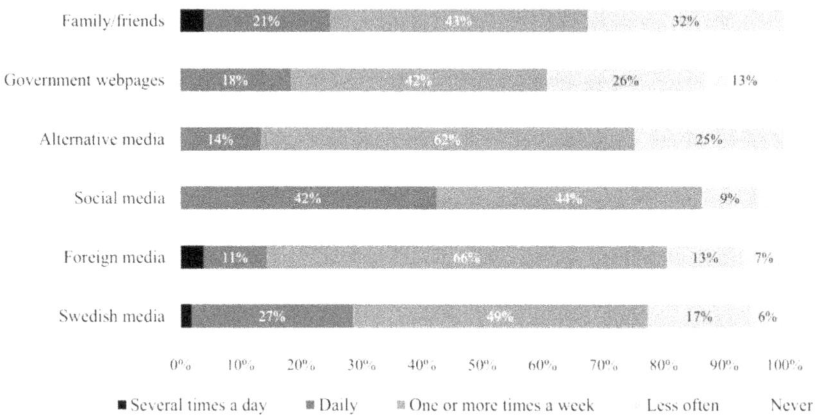

Figure 16.1 Item response probabilities survey 1, Pluralists.

Three of the repertoires largely resemble each other in relation to which channels and sources they are likely to use for information seeking purposes. Specifically, the *Pluralists*, the *Frequent pluralists* and the *Information junkies* all share the characteristic of not excluding any channels or sources for information seeking purposes. However, one aspect separates the three types of repertoires from each other: the *frequency* of information seeking. As an example, the *Pluralists* are likely to use all channels and sources for seeking information purposes, but less frequently than the *Frequent pluralists*. To be precise, the *Pluralists* are likely to search for information about COVID-19 one or more times a week, while the *Frequent pluralists* are likely to search for information about COVID-19 daily. The item response probabilities for the *Pluralists* and *Frequent pluralists* are visualized in Figures 16.1 and 16.2 (item probabilities from survey 1, representing a general pattern).

The *Information junkies* search for information about COVID-19 even more frequently. Compared to the *Frequent pluralists'* daily use, the *Information junkies* are likely to use all channels and sources for information seeking purposes several times a day. Interestingly, the probability that the *Information junkies* use alternative media is equally as high as the probability of them using Swedish news media several times a day in survey 1. The item response probabilities for the *Information junkies* are visualized in Figure 16.3 (item probabilities from survey 1, representing a general pattern).

The *Traditionalists*, however, differ significantly from previous types. They have a higher probability of using Swedish news media, family and friends, and government web pages for information seeking purposes, but are more likely to exclude social, alternative, and foreign media. In other words, the *Traditionalists* are more selective in relation to which channels and sources they include in their

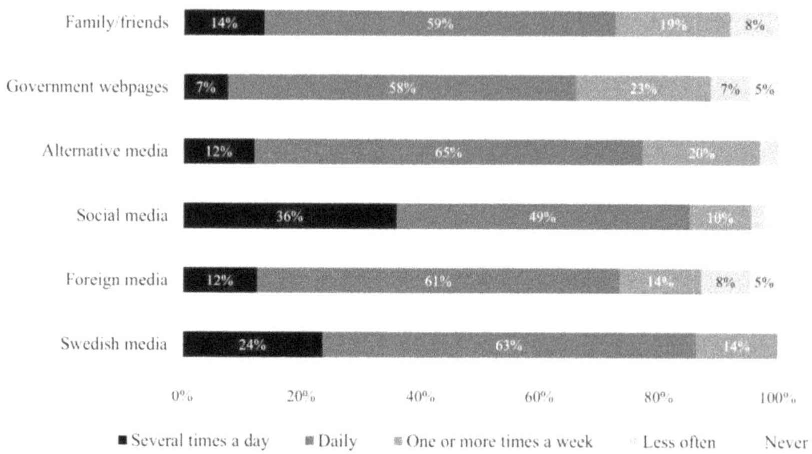

Figure 16.2 Item response probabilities survey 1, Frequent pluralists.

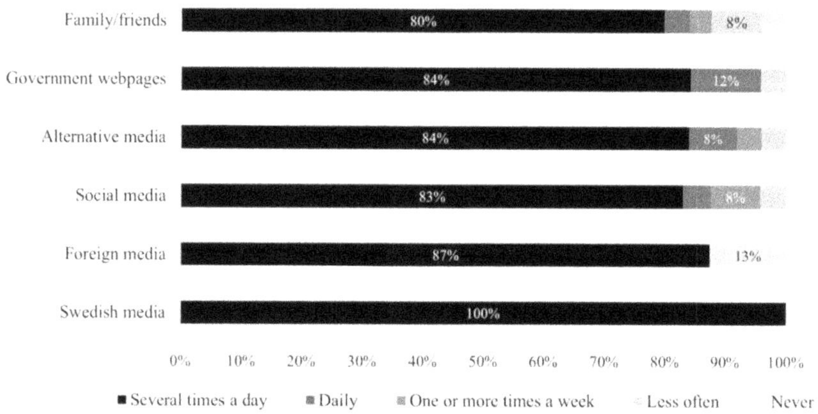

Figure 16.3 Item response probabilities survey 1, Information junkies.

information seeking repertoire compared to the other types. The item response probabilities for the *Traditionalists* are visualized in Figure 16.4 (item probabilities from survey 1, representing a general pattern).

Conclusion

Understanding how different subgroups in society combine sources during a crisis, and the heterogeneity among such practices, is vital to perform effective

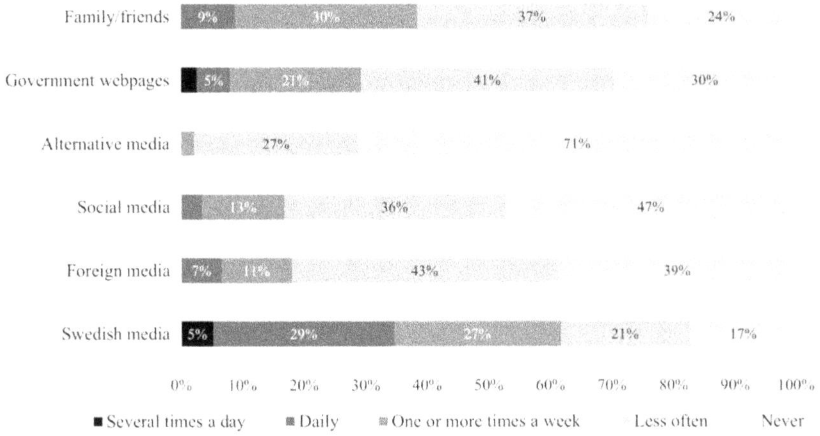

Figure 16.4 Item response probabilities survey 1, Traditionalists.

crisis communication. By applying a repertoire approach, four types of information seekers were identified in two migrant-dense suburbs in Sweden during the COVID-19 pandemic: *Traditionalist*, *Pluralists*, *Frequent pluralists*, and *Information junkies*. In contrast to what was expected based on previous research, none of the identified repertoires excludes Swedish news media for information seeking purposes. In fact, all identified repertoires tend to use Swedish news media to search for information about COVID-19. While three of the repertoires highly resembled each other, one of the information seeking repertoires differed significantly: the *Traditionalist*. Compared to the other groups of information seekers, the *Traditionalists* tend to exclude social, alternative, and foreign media for information seeking purposes. The other three repertoires did not exclude any sources for information seeking purposes, and mainly differ in their frequency of use. Put differently, all of the identified types of information seekers, besides the *Traditionalists*, used all channels and sources to search for information about COVID-19. Although the information seeking frequency decreased for almost all classes in April 2021, the types remained the same, indicating that the information seeking repertoires are rather stable between the two chosen time points.

On a positive note, the findings suggest that crisis communication practitioners do not need to worry about not reaching individuals in migrant-dense areas with crisis messages. We did not identify any group who did not search for information about COVID-19 or did so very rarely. As aforementioned, this stands in contrast to previous results showing a larger share of news avoiders in migrant-dense communities (Esaiasson et al., 2020), and is probably related to the magnitude of the COVID-19 pandemic. During a highly impactful crisis, even news avoiders tend to follow the news to inform themselves (Broersma & Swart, 2022). The results therefore stress the importance of looking at information seeking repertoires in specific subgroups of the population, as information seeking during a crisis might significantly differ from everyday media consumption.

However, from a practitioner's point of view, the frequent use of a large variety of channels might be problematic. Individuals who combine many sources, including Swedish news media as well as social, foreign, and alternative media, might receive a higher number of conflicting messages. This is especially relevant for the *Information junkies*, *Frequent pluralists* and *Pluralists*. While they are likely to receive relevant crisis information in Swedish news media or on government web pages, they are also likely to be exposed to conflicting information in alternative media or on social media platforms. Moreover, the quality of the information might vary greatly depending on which source is used, meaning they might be exposed to a higher degree of incorrect or misleading information. All in all, broader information seeking repertoires might result in confusion regarding which information to trust and which guidelines and recommendations to follow. Practitioners therefore need to find strategies to deal with the conflicting or misleading information that these individuals might receive.

Finally, even though the threat level was significantly higher in the spring of 2021 (the third wave of the pandemic) compared to the fall of 2020, almost all groups searched for information less frequently in April 2021. This lack of correlation between threat and information-seeking during prolonged crises can be interpreted as a sign of pandemic fatigue (Ford et al., 2022), causing individuals to seek less information about the situation. This is of course troublesome news for practitioners as information dissemination seems to become harder and harder the longer the crisis prevails. Future research should therefore include more waves to see whether this trend accumulates at later stages of a prolonged health crisis, potentially causing some individuals to refrain from information seeking entirely.

Turning to limitations, it should be noted that the categories of information seeking were rather broad. As a result, we do not know which specific source individuals are using when they seek information on, for instance, social media. It also increases the likelihood of measurement error. Adding to this, we do not know which source they trust the most or which source influences them the most. Future research should therefore analyze the specific sources individuals use on, for instance, social media platforms as well as which sources individuals trust the most. Moreover, the sample was small, posing limitations regarding the generalizability of the repertoires to migrant-dense communities in Sweden in general. Finally, the analyses only included two waves, making generalization about potential stability of the information seeking repertoires limited. In addition, we did not analyze movements between repertoires, meaning that the repertoires might be relatively stable but include different individuals. Future studies should consequently add additional waves and analyze movements between repertoires to see how stable the repertoires are throughout a prolonged crisis.

Acknowledgments

This chapter is based on research conducted in the context of the KRISAMS project by Grant #2017-2860 from the Swedish Civil Contingencies Agency and the COVINFORM project, funded by the European Union's H2020 research and innovation program under Grant Agreement No. 101016247.

References

Andersen, K., Johansson, J., Shehata, A., & Johansson, B. (2022). Maintenance and reformation of news repertoires: A Latent transition analysis. *Journalism & Mass Communication Quarterly*, *99*(1), 237–261. https://doi.org/10.1177/10776990211019750

Backholm, K., & Nordberg, C. (2023). Efficient authority communication in times of crisis: Examining how vulnerable language minorities experienced Covid-19 communication strategies in Finland, Norway, and Sweden. In B. Johansson, Ø. Ihlen, J. Lindholm, & M. Blach-Ørsten (Eds.), *Communicating a pandemic: Crisis management and Covid-19 in the Nordic countries* (pp. 325–346). Nordicom, University of Gothenburg. https://doi.org/10.48335/9789188855688-15

Brekke, J. (2021). Informing hard-to-reach immigrant groups about Covid-19 – Reaching the Somali population in Oslo. *Journal of Refugee Studies*, *35*(1), 641–661. https://doi.org/10.1093/jrs/feab053

Broersma, M., & Swart, J. (2022). Do Novel routines stick after the pandemic? The formation of news habits during COVID-19. *Journalism Studies*, *23*(5–6), 551–568. https://doi.org/10.1080/1461670X.2021.1932561

Castro, L., Strömbäck, J., Esser, F., et al. (2021). Navigating high-choice European political information environments: A comparative analysis of news user profiles and political knowledge. *The International Journal of Press/Politics*, *27*(4), 827–859. https://doi.org/10.1177/19401612211012572

Celeux, G., & Soromenho, G. (1996). An entropy criterion for assessing the number of clusters in a mixture model. *Journal of Classification*, *13*(2), 195–212. https://doi.org/10.1007/BF01246098

Chen, M., Yu, W., & Cao, X. (2022). Experience pandemic fatigue? Social media use may play a role: Testing a model of pandemic fatigue development from a social media perspective. *Health Communication*. https://doi.org/10.1080/10410236.2022.2149095

Delmos. (2021). *Segregation i Sverige. Årsrapport 2021 om den socioekonomiska boendesegregationens utveckling [Segregation in Sweden. Annual Report 2021 about the development of socio-economic housing segregation]*, DELMOS 2021/334. Delegationen mot segregation.

Dillard, J. P., Li, R., & Yang, C. (2020). Fear of Zika: Information seeking as cause and consequence. *Health Communication*, 1–11. https://doi.org/10.1080/10410236.2020.1794554

Ekman, J. (2022). *Bridging the gap. Analysing the vaccination guide project in Gothenburg during the Covid-19 pandemic: A case of interpersonal risk and crisis communication targeted towards ethnic minority communities*. MA-thesis, University of Gothenburg, Department of Journalism, Media and Communication.

Esaiasson, P. (2020). *Förorten – ett samhällsvetenskapligt reportage [The Hood. A social science report]*. Timbro.

Esaiasson, P., Johansson, B., Ghersetti, M., & Sohlberg, J. (2020). *Kriskommunikation och segregation i en pandemi. Hur boende i utsatta områden informerade sig om coronaviruset våren 2020 [Crisis communication and segregation in a pandemic: How residents in vulnerable areas informed themselves about the corona virus in the spring of 2020]*. JMG-report no. 84. Dept. of Journalism, Media and Communication, University of Gothenburg.

Folkhälsomyndigheten (2021). *Utrikesfödda och covid-19 Konstaterade fall, IVA-vård och avlidna bland utrikesfödda i Sverige 13 mars 2020 – 15 februari 2021 [Foreign-born and COVID-19 Confirmed cases, ICU admissions, and deaths among foreign-born individuals in Sweden March 13, 2020 – February 15, 2021]*. Folkhälsomyndigheten.

Folkhälsomyndigheten (2022). *Vaccinationstäckning per födelseland, inkomst och utbildningsgrad [Vaccination coverage by country of birth, income, and level of education]*. Folkhälsomyndigheten.

Ford, J. L., Douglas, M., & Barrett, A. K. (2022). The role of pandemic fatigue in seeking and avoiding information on COVID-19 among young adults. *Health Communication*, 1–14. https://doi-org.ezproxy.ub.gu.se/10.1080/10410236.2022.2069211

Frandsen, F., & Johansen, W. (2020). Reframing the field: Public crisis management, political crisis management, and corporate crisis management. In F. Frandsen, & W. Johansen (Eds.), *Crisis communication* (pp. 59–102). De Gruyter Mouton.

Goteborg City. (2022). *Statistik och analys [Statistics and Analysi]*. https://goteborg.se/wps/portal/enhetssida/statistik-och-analys/goteborgsbladet/hamta-statistik. Accessed 21.11.22.

Fraustino, J. D., & Liu, B. F. (2018). Toward more audience-oriented approaches to crisis communication and social media research. In L. Austin, & Y. Jin (Eds.), *Social media and crisis communication* (pp. 129–140). Routledge.

Guo, W., & Bai, Q. (2022). How risk information seeking influences media trust and emotions: The mediating role of media beliefs and the moderating role of information processing methods. *Computers in Human Behavior*, 107522. https://doi.org/10.1016/j.chb.2022.107522

Hargraves, S., Hayward, S., Noori, T., McKee, M., & Kumar, B. (2021). COVID-19: Counting migrants in. *The Lancet*, *398*(10296), 211–212. https://doi.org/10.1016/S0140-6736(21)01339-8

Hedman, L., & Andersson, R. (2015). Etnisk segregation och inkomstsegregation i Sveriges tio största arbetsmarknadsregioner 1990–2010. In R. Andersson, B. Bengtsson, & G. Myrberg (Eds.), *Mångfaldens dilemman: Boendesegregation och områdespolitik [Dilemmas of diversity: Housing segregation and community policy]* (pp. 15–38). Gleerups Utbildning AB.

Houston, J. B. (2021). Covid-19 communication ecologies: Using interpersonal, organizational, and mediated communication resources to cope with a pandemic. *American Behavioral Scientist*, *65*(7), 887–892. https://doi.org/10.1177/0002764221992837

Johansson, B., Ihlen, Ø., Lindholm, J., & Blach-Ørsten, M. (2023a). Introduction: Communicating a pandemic in the Nordic countries. In B. Johansson, Ø. Ihlen, J. Lindholm, & M. Blach-Ørsten (Eds.), *Communicating a pandemic: Crisis management and Covid-19 in the Nordic countries* (pp. 11–30). Nordicom, University of Gothenburg.

Johansson, S., Johansson, B., & Johansson, J., (2023b). The dynamics of information-seeking repertoires: A cross-sectional latent class analysis of information-seeking during the COVID-19 pandemic. *Mass Communication and Society*. https://doi.org/10.1080/15205436.2023.2258863.

Kim, H., Chan-Olmsted, S. & Chen, H. (2022). COVID-19 information seeking behavior versus value perception among U.S. ethnic/racial minorities: differences and vaccination implications, *Information Technology & People*, Vol. ahead-of-print No. ahead-of-print. https://doi.org/10.1108/ITP-02-2022-0107

Li, J., & Zheng, H. (2020). Online information seeking and disease prevention intent during COVID-19 outbreak. *Journalism & Mass Communication Quarterly*, *99*(1), 69–88. https://doi.org/10.1177/1077699020961518

Liu, B. F., Austin, L. L., & Jin, Y. (2011). How publics respond to crisis communication strategies: The interplay of information form and source. *Public Relations Review*, *37*(4), 345–353. https://doi.org/10.1016/j.pubrev.2011.08.004

Liu, B. F., Fraustino, J. D., & Jin, Y. (2016). Social media use during disasters: How information form and source influence intended behavioral responses. *Communication Research*, *43*(5), 626–646. https://doi.org/10.1177/0093650214565917

Malmberg, B., & Clark, W. A. (2020). Migration and neighborhood change in Sweden: The interaction of ethnic choice and income constraints. *Geographical Analysis*, *53*(2), 1–24. https://doi.org/10.1111/gean.12250

Migration Data Portal. (2022). *Migration data relevant for the COVID-19 pandemic*. https://www.migrationdataportal.org/themes/migration-data-relevant-covid-19-pandemic. Accessed: 28.11.2022.

Morgan, G., Hodge, K., & Baggett, A. (2016). Latent profile analysis with non normal mixtures: A Monte Carlo examination of model selection using fit indices. *Computational Statistics & Data Analysis*, *93*, 146–161. https://doi.org/10.1016/j.csda.2015.02.019

Nordic Statistics. (2019). *Nordic statistics*. https://www.nordicstatistics.org/areas/integration-and-migration/, retrieved 27.10.2022

Nylund, K., Asparouhov, T., & Muthén, B. (2007). Deciding on the number of classes in Latent class analysis and growth mixture modeling: A Monte Carlo simulation study. *Structural Equation Modeling: A Multidisciplinary Journal*, *14*(4), 535–569. https://doi.org/10.1080/10705510701575396

Nylund-Gibson, K., & Choi, A. Y. (2018). Ten frequently asked questions about latent class analysis. *Translational Issues in Psychological Science*, *4*(4), 440. https://doi.org/10.1037/tps0000176

Petersen, K. J., Qualter, P., & Humphrey, N. (2019). The application of latent class analysis for investigating population child mental health: A systematic review. *Frontiers in Psychology*, *10*, 1214. https://doi.org/10.3389/fpsyg.2019.01214

SCB. (2022). *SCB*. https://www.scb.se/hitta-statistik/sverige-i-siffror/manniskorna-i-sverige/utrikes-fodda/, retrieved 21.11.2022.

Sellnow, T. L., & Seeger, M. L. (2021). *Theorizing crisis communication*. Johns Wiley & Sons.

Sellnow, T. L., & Veil, S. R. (2016). Preparing for international and cross-cultural crises: The role of competing voices, inclusivity, and the interplay of responsibility in global organizations. In A. Schwarz, M. W. Seeger, & C. Auer (Eds.), *The handbook of international crisis communication research* (pp. 489–498). Wiley-Blackwell.

Sommerfeldt, E. J. (2015). Disasters and information source repertoires: Information seeking and information sufficiency in postearthquake Haiti. *Journal of Applied Communication Research, 43*(1), 1–22. https://doi.org/10.1080/00909882.2014.982682

SOU (Swedish Government Official Reports). (2021). *Delbetänkande 2 _ Sverige under pandemin [Interim Report2_Sweden during the pandemic].* SOU 2021:89.

Spence, P. R., Lachlan, K. A., & Griffin, D. R. (2007). Crisis communication, race, and natural disasters. *Journal of Black Studies, 37*(4), 539–554. https://doi.org/10.1177/0021934706296192

Tourangeau, R., Edwards, B., Johnson, T. P., Wolter, K. M., & Bates, N. (Eds.) (2014). *Hard-to-survey populations.* Cambridge University Press.

Ulmer, R., Sellnow, T., & Seeger, M. (2019). *Effective crisis communication. Moving from crisis to ppportunity.* SAGE.

Vandenplas, R., Truyens, P., Vis, S., & Picone, I. (2021). Tuning out the news. A cross-media perspective on news avoidance practices of young news users in Flanders during the COVID-19 pandemic. *Journalism Studies, 22*(16), 2197–2217. https://doi.org/10.1080/1461670X.2021.1990788

Weller, B. E., Bowen, N. K., & Faubert, S. J. (2020). Latent class analysis: A guide to best practice. *Journal of Black Psychology, 46*(4), 287–311. https://doi.org/10.1177/0095798420930932

Zhao, X., Xu, S., & Austin, L. L. (2022). Medium and source convergence in crisis information acquisition: Patterns, antecedents, and outcomes. *New Media & Society, 0*(0). https://doi.org/10.1177/14614448221088866

Yoon, J., Huang, H., & Kim, S. (2017). Trends in health information-seeking behaviour in the US foreign-born population based on the health information national trends survey, 2005–2014. *Information Research: An International Electronic Journal, 22*(3), n3. https://doi.org/10.1177/0093650208315958

Appendix: Information Seeking Repertoires Among Ethnic Minorities in Sweden

The Consistent Akaike information criterion (CAIC), Bayesian Information Criteria (BIC), and the aBIC (Adjusted Bayesian Information Criteria) are information criteria that are used to evaluate the best model fit. The BIC is computed by imposing a penalty for the number of parameters estimated. In addition to penalizing for the number of parameters estimated, the aBIC additionally adjusts for sample size. The BIC value tends to decrease when classes are added to the model. The model with the lowest cAIC, BIC, and aBIC statistics can be perceived as the optimal solution (Morgan et al., 2016).

The CAIC pointed at two (survey 2) and three (survey 1) classes as the best model. However, since the CAIC performs worse on skewed data (Morgan et al., 2016) and the sample size was small, the aBIC was primarily used to choose best model fit. The aBIC suggested four classes as the best model fit in survey 1 and five classes as the best fitting model in survey 2. The five-class solution, however, did not generate any cAIC or Entropy-value, indicating that the sample size might have been too small to conduct the calculations.

Entropy measures the model's ability to "provide well separated" classes (Celeux & Soromenho, 1996, p. 200). In other words, it is a measure of classification accuracy, but not used for determining which solution/model is the best fit. Values can range between 0 and 1. The Entropy-value for the four-class solution was over .8 in each wave, indicating well-separated classes (Celeux & Soromenho, 1996).

17 Understanding What Is at Stake

Challenges and Opportunities for Corporate Communication during the COVID-19 Crisis

Christine Buse, Florian Meissner and Holger Sievert

Companies across the globe have been affected by the pandemic economically and/or epidemiologically, causing countless organizational crises. It is without question that the ongoing COVID-19 pandemic posed significant challenges for the corporate communication sector. Depending on whether these challenges were met successfully, the crisis has strained or strengthened relations with stakeholders. As Francis Ingham, Director General of the Public Relations and Communications Association, asserted: "These recent months have seen corporate reputations made. And corporate reputations wrecked" (PRCA, 2020, p. 13).

In the context of the pandemic, stakeholders have developed new communication expectations and information demands of businesses and brands. In times of such crises, businesses need to develop persuasive corporate narratives and crisis response strategies to protect their reputation and mitigate negative reactions from key stakeholders inside and outside the organization. This paper explores to what degree companies across the United Kingdom (UK), the United States (US), and Germany (GER) have met this challenge. The study is based on qualitative case analyses. Some of the case studies have already been published in a previous version of this paper (Sievert et al., 2021). Early literature on this issue relies mostly on anecdotal evidence regarding corporate crisis responses and their effect on reputation. Several researchers point out how corporate communication and marketing have been strongly influenced by the COVID-19 pandemic and how it provides both challenges and opportunities for corporate social responsibility (CSR) communication (e.g., Crane & Matten, 2021; He & Harris, 2020).

More recently, Han (2021) found that excellent CSR companies communicated more proactively on social media during the crisis. They prioritized addressing external publics and focused more on information dissemination than on persuasive communication. However, companies with lower CSR ratings communicated more actively and showed a stronger online presence (Han, 2021). Analyzing corporate emails, Urban and Tefertiller (2021) observed that many companies employed a corrective action approach. National businesses were more likely to

DOI: 10.4324/9781003375296-20

employ CSR than local companies, and anticipatory responses constituted most of the corporate email responses (Urban & Tefertiller, 2021). Leonidou et al. (2020) examined different internal and external CSR communication initiatives taken by American international business firms. In terms of internal CSR activities, their study showed that companies like AT&T suspended fees for home usage and overage caps of certain products and refrained from canceling services or charging late fees (Leonidou et al., 2020). Furthermore, their analysis demonstrated that it is important for international companies to select CSR response strategies that meet stakeholder expectations and crisis requirements, and to share information about the results of their CSR activities with various stakeholders to maintain or build a positive reputation (Leonidou et al., 2020).

Additionally, there are also some studies that focus on consumers' reactions to crisis communication responses. For instance, Wang et al. (2021) focused on the influence of defensive and offensive response strategies as well as emotional and rational response framing on consumer sentiment and trust recovery. Their study revealed that using a defensive, emotionally framed response led to a more positive consumer sentiment, while consumer trust recovered significantly when crisis responses were framed in an emotional manner (Wang et al., 2021).

There is a growing body of studies with a crisis communication perspective in relation to the pandemic. The findings described in this chapter show that a substantial amount of research on corporate communication related to the COVID-19 crisis has so far focused on CSR communication. However, a perspective on the internal management structure required for the communication function during crises is largely absent.

Theoretical Foundations

As a first step to close the described research gap, we use excellence theory and situational crisis communication theory (SCCT) to identify necessary internal management structures as well as appropriate communication strategies based on a series of case studies. These are not only two of the most influential theories in crisis communication and public relations research; if combined, they also offer a lot of explanatory power to investigate why a megacrisis such as the pandemic can turn into a reputation crisis for an affected organization. This is because excellence theory provides a lens to analyze the internal structural conditions of the crisis response. Meanwhile, situational crisis communication theory contributes a procedural view on the crisis response focusing on external communication for image protection and image repair.

Structural Dimension of Crisis Response: Excellence Theory in Public Relations

Excellence theory is a general theory that explains the value of public relations and identifies characteristics that are correlated with managerial and organizational effectiveness (Grunig et al., 2002; Grunig & Grunig, 2008). Excellence in public relations can be defined as a set of attributes that help to "build quality, long-term relationships with strategic constituencies" (Grunig & Grunig, 2008, p. 328). The general theory stems from a longitudinal study of best practices in public relations and communication management and incorporates middle-range theories, including concepts of publics, organizational theory and decision-making, models of public relations, and evaluation of public relations. Thanks to the study, several generic principles of excellent public relations could be formulated that can be categorized into four distinct groups. Grunig and Grunig's (2008, p. 337) findings suggest

> that excellent departments design more of their communication programs on the two-way symmetrical model of collaboration and public participation than on three other typical models: press agentry (emphasizing only favorable publicity), public information (disclosing accurate information but engaging in no research or other form of two-way communication), or two-way asymmetrical (emphasizing only the interests of the organization and not the interests of publics).

According to excellence theory, to generate organizational value, the company should empower the public relations function as a strategic management function. Furthermore, characteristics of excellent public relations are the involvement of the senior public relations executive in strategic management decisions, the identification of strategic publics, the development of specific and strategically managed communication programs, the senior public relations executive's membership in the organization's dominant coalition, and the empowerment of public relations practitioners with diverse backgrounds. Regarding the communicator roles, excellence theory postulates that a strategic manager rather than a technician or an administrative manager should head the public relations unit, members of the public relations unit should have the knowledge needed to carry out the managerial role, and people of all genders should have equal opportunities to occupy the manager role. Concerning the organization of the communication function and its relationship to other management functions, excellence theory also postulates that public relations should be an integrated communication function and a specialized management function separate from other management functions, e.g., human resources or marketing (Grunig & Grunig, 2008; Grunig et al., 2002).

Only if these basic organizational requirements are fulfilled, a successful crisis communication approach seems to be possible. Institutions where communication is not really understood as a management function, will – due to missing communication alignments and limited stakeholder understanding – be at a higher risk of making mistakes, especially in the particularly challenging discipline of crisis communication (Chon et al., 2022; Erikson, 2012; Marra, 1998).

Procedural Dimension of Crisis Response: Situational Crisis Communication Theory

"A crisis is a sudden and unexpected event that threatens to disrupt an organization's operations and poses both a financial and a reputational threat" (Coombs, 2007, p. 164). The situational crisis communication theory (SCCT) helps to anticipate how stakeholders will react to a crisis and respond to corporate crisis response strategies used to manage a crisis (Coombs, 2020). And if an organization can anticipate reactions, it can more easily build up internal management structures e. g. for the issue of image building or even repair. Therefore, SCCT helps to match the crisis response to the crisis and provides a set of guidelines for communication managers on how to repair or prevent reputational damage (Coombs, 2007).

SCCT is built upon crisis responsibility and attribution theory (Heider, 1958). The premise of attribution theory is that individuals seek to determine the causes of events and have a need to attribute responsibility (Weiner, 2018). Depending on the causes of a crisis and the perceived responsibility, the reputational threat is varied. According to Coombs (2007), the initial threat is based on the crisis type. A crisis type is a frame that emphasizes certain aspects of a crisis (Coombs, 2020). The frame shapes how individuals define a crisis, interpret its causes, attribute responsibility, and evaluate possible crisis solutions (Coombs, 2007). In SCCT, crisis types are grouped into three clusters based on the level of crisis responsibility and public expectations in relation to the response. Coombs differentiates between three different clusters: (1) the victim cluster, (2) the accidental cluster, and (3) the preventable/intentional cluster. If a crisis falls into the victim category, the organization is seen as an unintentional victim of the crisis event, with very low attributions of responsibility and a mild reputational threat. Examples of crises that fall into this category are natural disasters or rumors. If a crisis falls into the accidental cluster, the event is considered unintentional or uncontrollable by the organization, with minimal attributions of responsibility and a moderate reputational threat. The cluster includes, for example, accidents due to technical errors. In case of a preventable/intentional crisis, the crisis event is considered purposeful. The perceived crisis responsibility is high and the resulting reputational threat severe. Faults such as organizational misdeeds or human-error accidents are classified into this category. In addition to the perceived crisis responsibility, contextual modifiers, such as the company's crisis history and prior reputation, can alter the initial crisis assessment and shape the reputational threat posed by a crisis (Coombs, 2007, 2020).

Depending on the crisis type, communication managers can choose from a variety of response strategies that can be used to shape crisis attributions, change perceptions of the organization in crisis, and reduce reputational damage generated by the crisis (Coombs, 2007). According to SCCT, communication professionals should assess the potential crisis responsibility a crisis event will generate

Table 17.1 Crisis response strategies

Primary crisis response strategies	*Management action*
Denial	Claim that there is no crisis
Attack accuser	Confront the person or group claiming something is wrong
Scapegoat	Blame some person or group outside of the organization
Excuse	Deny intent to do harm/claim inability to control events
Justification	Minimize the perceived damage caused
Compensation	Offer money or other gifts to victims
Apology	Accept responsibility and ask stakeholders for forgiveness
Secondary crisis response strategies	Management action
Reminder	Tell stakeholders about past good works
Ingratiation	Praise stakeholders and/or remind them of past good works
Victimage	Remind stakeholders that the organization is also a victim

Note. Adapted from Coombs (2007, p. 170).

and select a response that fits the anticipated level of responsibility. Coombs proposes different crisis response strategies that vary in their acceptance of responsibility for the crisis. Furthermore, he differentiates between primary and secondary response strategies (see Table 17.1). Some strategies are considered secondary because they seem to be most effective when being used in combination with primary response strategies (Coombs, 2020). According to Coombs, primary crisis response strategies are attack the accuser, denial, scapegoat, excuse, justification, compensation, and apology. Secondary crisis response strategies include reminder, ingratiation, and victimage (Coombs, 2007).

Based on Coombs' elaborations, communication professionals should focus on reputation-oriented crisis response strategies only after effectively addressing the physical and physiological concerns of their stakeholders by providing instructing and adjusting information as part of their initial ethical base response (Coombs, 2007, 2020). Furthermore, Coombs argues that highly accommodative crisis response strategies, such as compensation or apology, are optimal crisis response strategies when attributions of crisis responsibility are high, whereas the ethical base response serves as the optimal strategy when attributions of crisis responsibility are low (Coombs, 2020).

SCCT has already been applied to the analysis of crisis communication in the context of the pandemic (Macnamara, 2021; Scheiwiller & Siska, 2021). In his ethnographic case study of an Australian university, Macnamara (2021) found that the crisis types did not fully align with the situation. Furthermore, his analysis showed that primary crisis response strategies were mostly irrelevant to the organization (Macnamara, 2021). In their analysis of European airlines' crisis responses in social media and press releases, Scheiwiller and

Siska (2021) observed that the most used SCCT communication strategy was instructing and adjusting.

In this context, it is important to investigate the connections between crisis communication and corporate social responsibility (CSR), which has increasingly attracted scholarly attention (e.g., Sievert et al., 2021; Tu et al., 2023). According to Coombs and Holladay (2015), CSR can be considered not only as a reputational resource during crisis but also must be considered as crisis risk. This is because, for instance based on prior CSR communication, consumers or the public might have specific expectations toward the demeanor of a company. When companies fail to live up to these expectations, the result can be an organizational crisis with severe reputational damage (Hoffmann & Russ-Mohl, 2023). Hegner et al. (2016), however, found mixed results in the sense that while institutional CSR initiatives do provide a buffer for potential reputational damage, moral-harm crises have a detrimental effect on integrity-based trust in the organization.

There are also a few studies on corporate communication related to the COVID-19 crisis could be found that included excellence theory as their analytical framework. However, most of them focus on very specific geographical or thematic contexts (e.g., Islam & Luqman, 2022; Shimawua & Ternenge, 2022; Sukandar et al., 2022) or try to adopt very special theoretical perspectives (e.g., Meyer, 2021). Some authors even state that "the excellence theory was no longer a viable framework to answer questions about the evolving field because internationalization and technologies, like the Internet, changed how organizations communicate with publics" (Taylor, 2023).

Yet, from our point of view, it is meaningful to combine especially the internal organizational perspective of the excellence theory and SCCT for the purpose of this study because they are complementary in that they allow us to understand the success or failure of corporate crisis responses from different angles. SCCT provides an analytical toolkit for identifying crisis types and suitable response strategies. Meanwhile, excellence theory refers to the organizational structure of corporate (crisis) communication. It allows us to understand to what degree internal structures (the position of the communication department within a company) help to anticipate and prevent reputational damage. This can be the case for instance because of controversial managerial decisions, especially in the heated environment of a crisis where corporate actions quickly become the object of public scrutiny, but also very "independent" CEO communication via social media that might be considered as authentic but did not use the critical multi-stakeholder competence of the corporate communication department and therefore sometimes leads to communication crises.

Based on the insights of both theories outlined in this paper, the aim is to understand why some companies were able to make reputational gains during the pandemic while others stumbled into a reputational crisis, considering both procedural and structural levels of analysis.

Methods

To achieve the objective of this paper, the study follows an exploratory, qualitative approach, allowing for an in-depth analysis of a series of cases and a reconstruction of needed context. It combines a series of case studies based on publicly available data with in-depth interviews to reconstruct both external and internal perspectives on the selected cases.

Data Collection and Analysis

In a first step, contrasting examples based on some of the most prominently discussed "positive" and "negative" cases of corporate crisis communication were collected. This is a rather general categorization and practical solution that was chosen despite its limitations to provide exploratory insights into particularly diverse cases. As a heuristic for the selection of positive cases, we chose companies who won renowned communication awards for their crisis communication during the pandemic. Worst practice cases were selected based on reputational crises of companies that became the object of social media "shitstorms" and/or negative media coverage and reached at least national news.

To be able to draw comparisons and include international perspectives, after an initial check of the material, six cases in Germany, two in the UK and two in the US, including five best practice and five worst practice examples. The five best practice cases were selected based on communication award winners, especially in the category "crisis communication." The country choices were made because they represent the three strongest Western economies which also have a strong impact on other markets (especially the US), also in terms of communication practices.

In a next step, all related press releases and selected social media posts that were published by the companies and their communication managers between March and December 2020 were collected and analyzed using a theoretical qualitative coding approach. SCCT's crisis types and response strategies were used as coding categories for the content analysis. As mentioned above, a qualitative approach was chosen because the analysis was aimed at a deeper understanding of the cases and their given contexts and not at a quantitative measurement of the companies' communication.

Additionally, six high-level communication professionals from the selected cases were interviewed to reconstruct decision-making and learnings related to communication practices during the pandemic. In addition, the interviews were used to reconstruct the extent to which crisis communication and crisis management corresponded to the principles of excellence theory.

Individual semi-structured interviews were conducted with two of the respondents. A group discussion based on a semi-structured interview guide was held with four communication professionals. Questions were asked about when COVID-19 became relevant for the company and how they reacted to it.

The interview also focused on how the companies positioned themselves internally to deal with the crisis in terms of communication. Furthermore, it was addressed whether the companies would do anything differently in retrospect, what lessons they took away from the situation and what they could recommend to other companies in a crisis such as the COVID-19 pandemic.

Case Summaries

The five selected "negative" cases in this explorative study were Adidas AG (Germany), Douglas (Germany), Tönnies (Germany), Frasers Group (UK) and Tyson Foods (US). The five selected "positive" cases were Webasto (Germany), Lufthansa (Germany), Deutsche Post DHL Group (Germany), Tesco (UK), and AT&T (US).

Adidas is a German multinational corporation and the second largest sportswear manufacturer in Europe. During Germany's first lockdown in March 2020, Adidas announced that it would withhold rent payment for its stores in Germany, citing a pandemic aid agreement issued by the German Federal Ministry of Justice that was made to protect tenants who were unable to pay their rent as a result of the COVID-19 pandemic (Bauchmüller et al., 2020). The second "negative" example is Douglas – the largest perfumery chain in Europe. During the second German lockdown, Douglas tried to present some of their stores as drugstores to keep them open (Bialek, 2020). Tönnies – the third selected "negative" case – is Germany's largest meat manufacturer. Their slaughterhouse and manufacturing site situated in Gütersloh was at the center of one of the largest single outbreaks of COVID-19 in the world (Lee, 2020). The fourth "negative" example is Frasers Group. Frasers Group is a British retail company that owns Sports Direct – the largest sports goods retailer in the UK. During the first UK lockdown, Frasers tried to keep its Sports Direct stores open, despite lockdown rules. Several company statements stated that Sport Direct stores should have been deemed essential retail because selling fitness equipment made them a vital asset to keep the UK healthy (Sweney & Goodley, 2020). The last selected "negative" case is Tyson Foods, an American multinational corporation and the second largest processor and marketer of chicken, beef, and pork in the world. According to a lawsuit filed by an employee's family, company managers at Tyson's Waterloo plant bet on how many workers would get infected with COVID-19 (Shepherd, 2020).

The first selected best practice case is Webasto, a German manufacturing company and one of the 100 largest automotive suppliers in the world. In January 2020, Webasto confirmed that a worker at its headquarters had been infected with COVID-19 following the visit of an employee from China, becoming the first known COVID-19 case in Germany (Boseley, 2020). Webasto reacted quickly and transparently. Webasto's head of corporate communications won the PR Report Award 2020 for the company's successful crisis communication (Schasche, 2020). The second "positive" example is Lufthansa. Lufthansa is the largest airline in Germany and, when combined with its subsidiaries, also the second largest airline in Europe. The company's business almost collapsed due to the travel restrictions. Lufthansa was praised for its reliable communication about the billion-dollar government loans and large-scale job cuts prompted by the crisis. The German publication PR-Magazin named the head of group communications at Lufthansa "PR Manager of the Year 2021" (Dillmann, 2021). Deutsche Post DHL Group – the third selected "positive" case – is Europe's largest postal company. Logistics and supply chains play a critical role during crises like the COVID-19 pandemic while at the same time being challenged by the crises. In the face of the growing challenges, Deutsche Post DHL Group established a task force led by the CEO to ensure that all stakeholders were provided with crucial information, while upholding supply chains. As part of the German Stevie Awards, the company's campaign "The only choice left is to do what's right" was named the best COVID-19-related information campaign of the year 2021 (Stevie Awards, n.d.). Another "positive" case included in the study is Tesco. Tesco is the largest supermarket chain in the UK. Following the outbreak of COVID-19, Tesco launched the campaigns "Keeping you safe" and "Some little helps for safer shopping" to inform customers about the implemented social distancing measures and to trigger positive emotions and reduce fear among consumers (Rogers, 2020). For its widely praised corporate response to the coronavirus crisis, Tesco won "Brand of the Year" at the 2020 Marketing Week Masters Awards (Marketing Week, 2020). The last selected "positive" case is AT&T, the world's largest telecommunications company and the second largest provider of mobile telephone services. During the first lockdown, AT&T established a COVID-19 team to be able to respond quickly to communications needs throughout the pandemic. As a result, AT&T won an award for "Best Global Crisis Communications/Crisis Management" at the 2020 Platinum PR Awards (PR News, 2020).

Results

The aim of this paper is to understand why some companies were able to make reputational gains during the pandemic while others stumbled into a reputational crisis, considering both procedural and structural levels of analysis. The following case analysis investigates the procedural dimension, investigating how the selected companies chose to respond to the crisis and to what effect. The subsequent interview analysis reconstructs the wider context for these decisions and explores the structural factors influencing the crisis response.

Case Analysis

Our analysis shows that despite the pandemic being a natural disaster in the first place, all five "negative" examples faced a preventable crisis accompanied by high attributions of responsibility and a severe reputational threat. In four cases,

Table 17.2 Crisis type and selected response strategies

Case		*Crisis type*	*Primary response strategy*	*Secondary response strategy*
"Negative"	Adidas (GER)	Preventable crisis	Apology	Victimage
	Douglas (GER)	Preventable crisis	Apology	Victimage
	Tönnies (GER)	Preventable crisis	Excuse, compensation	Victimage
	Frasers Group (UK)	Preventable crisis	Compensation, justification	Victimage
	Tyson Foods (US)	Preventable crisis	Excuse, (internal) scapegoat	Ingratiation
"Positive"	Webasto (GER)	Victim crisis	Excuse, compensation	Victimage, reminder
	Lufthansa (GER)	Victim crisis	Justification	Victimage, ingratiation
	Deutsche Post DHL Group (GER)	Victim crisis	Justification	Victimage, reminder
	Tesco (UK)	Victim crisis	Justification	Victimage, ingratiation
	AT&T (US)	Victim crisis	Justification	Reminder

Note: Assessment and categorization by the research team.

the crisis was caused by organizational misdeed or management misconduct. In the case of Tönnies, the crisis was prompted by injuries due to organizational misdeeds. Additionally, it needs to be taken into consideration that Adidas is a special case. Investigations by the *Financial Times* showed that the tabloid *Bild* possibly scandalized the Adidas case, concealing in its news coverage that Axel Springer's chief executive in charge of *Bild* was the landlord of an Adidas store and therefore would have been affected by withheld rent payment (Storbeck, 2022). Meanwhile, all selected "positive" cases were faced with a victim crisis caused by the natural disaster and therefore confronted with very low attributions of crisis responsibility and a mild reputational threat (see Table 17.2).

Negative Cases

Additionally, the qualitative content analysis shows that between the best practice and worst practice examples the selected response strategies varied quite a lot. As their primary response strategy, the German sportswear manufacturer Adidas and Douglas accepted their responsibility, apologized for their statements, and asked key stakeholders for forgiveness. In addition to this very accommodating primary response strategy, the companies reminded the public that they, too, were a victim of the crisis. In contrast to Adidas and Douglas, Tönnies made use of the excuse strategy, denying the intent to harm, stressing that the events that triggered the crisis were out of the company's control. Tönnies also offered compensation to the victims. In addition to these primary response strategies, the meat manufacturer presented itself as a victim of the crisis. Frasers Group made use of the compensation strategy and the justification strategy by offering the victims compensation and minimizing the perceived reputational damage caused by the crisis. Like Adidas, Douglas and Tönnies, presented themselves as victims. Tyson Foods tried to minimize the reputational damage by denying the intent to do harm and distancing itself from specific persons inside the organization. Furthermore, the company praised its stakeholders and reminded them of past good works. All in all, in the five "negative" cases, the companies chose rather diverse primary response strategies, while four of the five cases chose victimage as their second response strategy, reminding their stakeholders that they were a victim too.

Positive Cases

In the context of the "positive" cases, the German automotive manufacturer Webasto made use of the excuse strategy with elements of compensation, denying the intent to harm, claiming that the events that triggered the crisis were out of its control and trying to minimize the damage through quick and transparent actions. In addition to these primary response strategies, Webasto presented itself as a victim of the crisis and informed its stakeholders of past good works. This has worked well for Webasto, which for a long time after being affected by the COVID-19 cases was repeatedly cited as a crisis management and communication role model in the news media. Lufthansa made use of the justification strategy by minimizing the perceived reputational damage caused by the crisis. As a secondary response strategy, the airline presented itself as a victim rather than the cause of the crisis. Furthermore, the company made use of the ingratiation strategy by praising stakeholders and reminding them of past achievements.

Like Webasto and Lufthansa, the postal company Deutsche Post DHL Group made use of the justification strategy by minimizing the perceived reputational damage caused by the crisis. In addition to this primary response strategy, the company presented itself as a victim of the crisis and informed its stakeholders about past good performances. Additionally, Lufthansa and Deutsche Post DHL Group, Tesco also made use of the justification strategy. In this regard, the company sought to minimize the perceived reputational threat by focusing on customer safety. On top of that, Tesco presented itself as a victim of the crisis, praised its stakeholders and reminded them of former efforts and accomplishments. Like Tesco, AT&T made use of the justification strategy and tried to minimize reputational damage by supporting online communication. Furthermore, AT&T focused on communicating past good deeds. All in all, four out of the five "positive" examples chose justification as their primary response strategy.

Furthermore, four out of the five cases chose victimage as their second response strategy, reminding their stakeholders that they, too, were a victim of the crisis.

Contrastingly, the sporting goods manufacturer Adidas was faced with a preventable crisis with high attributions of responsibility by deferring the rent for some of its German stores. Only when there was already a rapidly rising amount of criticism in both journalistic and social media, the CEO gave an interview trying to justify Adidas' decision. However, it was too late to make an impact. In the end, the CEO decided to continue the payment and issue an apology to limit further negative reputational damage (Boehmer & Harrison, 2022).

Interview Analysis

In the next step, we conducted a group discussion and two direct interviews with a total of six high-ranking communication officials of the companies included in our study. Five major themes evolved in the qualitative analysis: (1) the *initial impact* (when did the pandemic become relevant for the company and what were the initial challenges?); (2) *internal positioning of the communications division* (in what constellation did the corporate comms team interact with other divisions in the company in response to the crisis?); (3) *considerations for crafting the response* (what were the key factors and reasons for the chosen response); (4) *critical reflection* (in hindsight, what should have been done differently?); (5) *lessons learned* (what are the insights and recommendations resulting from your experience?). The five themes roughly correspond with the theoretical foundations of this study: 1, 3 and 4 can be related to SCCT's crisis types and response strategies, while 2 and 5 can be linked to excellence theory.

Initial Impact

Overall, the interviewees unanimously highlighted the fundamental uncertainty in the beginning of the crisis. According to several interviewees, the vast effects of the pandemic and the sheer speed of events caught them by surprise and led to a situation where both management and communication officials were struggling to keep up with the situational development. Regarding the first lockdown in Germany, one interviewee asserted that within three days, almost the entire world was closed and with it most of the stores.

The initial challenge for communication departments was to address the general uncertainty and the lack of knowledge about the effects of the pandemic, both on the internal and the external communication level. The most important stakeholders during the initial impact phase were employees and clients, focusing on safety and service-related issues.

Only when the organization respectively its management was deemed to behave in a way that was actively violating stakeholders' concerns or a general sense of appropriate and solidary behavior in a crisis, reputational damage occurred. Examples are the Tyson Food managers who betted on staff getting sick or the Douglas CEO tweeting about trying to keep some stores open despite lockdown regulations.

Internal Positioning of the Communications Department

Most of the interviewees stated that their communications department quickly became part of a task force, with communication playing a key strategic role for the organizational response to the crisis, in some cases even about two months before COVID-19 was declared a pandemic by the World Health Organization. Several interview partners highlighted how the inclusion of the communications department in the crisis management process helped in crafting responses that would address the needs of their various stakeholders and to link communications efforts to corporate decision-making.

However, in some cases that resulted in (preventable) reputational crises for the company, the management apparently took decisions before consulting the communications department according to the respective interviewees. It is of course hypothetical that an earlier inclusion of the communications officials in the crisis response would have influenced managerial decisions and prevented the reputational damage that occurred. However, it seemed that reputational risks could not be anticipated by the management alone. On the other hand, another case illustrates that the prominent inclusion of the communication department in the crisis response also does not guarantee avoidance of a reputational crisis. The interviewed spokesperson reflected on a spontaneous (and much criticized) media statement by his CEO: "That was not a written speech. It was pure emotionality." Furthermore, the interviewee pointed out that the communication department can only influence the communication of managers to a certain extent and that one must accept that people want to speak authentically and in their own words.

Considerations for Crafting the Response

Two of the negative cases described how they were confronted with an "avalanche," as one spokesperson put it, of negative reactions while they felt they had actually done nothing wrong. This created not only cognitive dissonance but a struggle to effectively convey the company's perspective: "[When] this avalanche of criticism comes towards you as a company, then you won't stop it by trying to put a positive story against it." One of the interviewees emphasized that organizations must be patient and wait until it is time to rebuild.

In this case, the company published an apology to limit reputational damage and put an end to the ongoing scandalization both on social media and in the yellow press. However, as the interviewee asserted, because the case had a strong, long-term impact on the company's reputation, it triggered critical reflection on how to better anticipate reputational risks of managerial decisions.

On the other hand, the connecting element between the more "positive" cases was not only a high priority for the communicative response, but also a pronounced focus on stakeholders' needs and concerns. In that sense, the following statement shows that effective corporate crisis communication during the pandemic did not have media relations as a priority: "We had to protect our employees… And we had to communicate with all the target groups… We have to communicate with neighbors."

The interviews conducted with the positive cases did not include any instance where the public reaction to their companies' crisis response would turn more critical, indicating the preventive effect of stakeholder-oriented communication during a crisis. However, some interviewees did mention room for improvement despite the recognition they received for their crisis response.

Critical Reflection

Several interviewees stated that in retrospect, they would have taken some decisions differently. One of the clear messages communicated was that organizations must be better prepared for such situations and already aware of possible negative reactions and challenges that their decisions may trigger. For example, two spokespersons (both from a negative and a positive case) saw it as a mistake that they had not communicated earlier and better with political stakeholders as well as authorities. The reasons are that such stakeholders can be crucial not only in providing support to the company, but that they are also important partners in framing crisis responsibility. For instance, according to one interviewee, local authorities publicly declared they had lost all trust in his company because it would not communicate quickly and openly enough, shattering its efforts to mitigate reputational damage.

Finally, the interview analysis revealed that emotional CEO communication can easily cause a preventable crisis for the company. For instance, this was true in one case where a CEO had publicly made demands vis-à-vis the government that were perceived as outrageous by the public.

> … it totally blew up in our face. So, I think it was simply an attempt to stand up for our employees… to make sure that they can continue to be employed. The attempt backfired because the communication was not at all successful.

Lessons Learned

The interviews revealed several lessons to be learned in corporate responses to future large-scale crises. As one interviewee asserted, among the most important recommendations for crisis communication in general are "transparency, openness, speed, and empathy. And if you take these criteria into account in communication, then a lot of things go well." Another spokesperson supported this conclusion noting that because of the open, transparent, and fast communication via social media from their company the follow-up communication regulated itself and the recipients communicated and discussed among themselves and provided each other with information and answers to questions.

In cases where the public reaction was more negative toward the company, the main challenge was to find a way to reduce the ongoing media criticism, and the "shitstorms" on social media. Several interviewees described how they found it difficult to effectively justify their company's decisions for the public because of the heated debate. In such a case, apologizing can be a painful, yet effective way to go forward, especially when the apology is given quickly after the criticism evolved.

Finally, an important lesson learned for one interviewee was that while it is important to prepare for crises, companies can never anticipate every scenario, especially in a large-scale crisis such as the COVID-19 pandemic because it was "an exceptional situation for corporate communication."

Conclusion

All in all, COVID-19 had a strong impact on stakeholder relations and corporate crisis communication. The qualitative analysis illustrates that for affected companies, the pandemic can be both an opportunity to build and enhance a positive reputation or a significant threat to reputation. In a preventable crisis with a severe reputational threat, an apology was more successful than less defensive stances such as justification or excuse, which were more effective in crisis situations with low attributions of responsibility. Furthermore, our case studies as well as the interview analysis revealed that a strictly stakeholder-oriented crisis response can protect a company from being perceived as bearing responsibility for the crisis.

On the theoretical level, we conclude that a combined application of SCCT and excellence theory seems to be very effective in large-scale crises. Regarding the selected case studies, a strong empowerment of the public relations function helped to navigate communication pitfalls. Moreover, excellence theory can be deemed suitable for evaluating a company's response strategy. Regarding the application of SCCT, slight modifications of the crisis types and a broader understanding of responsibility are needed. For example, in some sense, all companies are victims of this global disaster, but not all fit into the classical "victimage" pattern. However, it depends on their crisis response whether they remain in the victim cluster or whether they risk a reputational crisis. Also, some response strategies seem to be too narrow for the cases under investigation. For instance, according to Coombs (2007), the scapegoating strategy seeks an external guilty party, but this study suggests that internal scapegoating is likely also to be used by organizations working to minimize blame. All in all, SCCT has proven helpful as a theoretical lens for our study, but for a global crisis like COVID-19, we found it necessary to use it in a more flexible manner.

Of course, this study has limitations. Most importantly, the sampling strategy is highly dependent on the visibility of cases thanks to awards (best cases, mainly based on self-nomination) or in the context of media criticism (worst cases, mainly based on external coverage). Also, the analysis includes only cases from Western countries, excluding cases from the non-Western world where crisis (communication) mechanisms might be different.

Furthermore, the dichotomous classification of examples into good and bad cases is a simplification that leaves little room for the consideration of specific characteristics and contextual conditions of the companies included in the analysis. For instance, there were self-critical statements by "positive" cases (like communicating with political stakeholders more proactively) and later developments in "preventable" crisis cases that seem to reduce the degree of responsibility the organization had for the crisis (like strategic scandalization by the yellow press). To learn more about effective corporate crisis communication strategies in the face of the pandemic, a broader study on the subject is needed, including companies from non-Western countries.

Practical and Social Implications

The analysis shows that the main factors for a successful crisis communication are defined a long time ahead of a crisis. In the long run, the underlying threat of another pandemic crisis remains a concern for companies worldwide. In the future, corporate communications must be prepared to handle long-term public health crises, strengthen its crisis communication strategies, and perhaps dominant theories should identify a broader set of crisis response. That said, the combination of SCCT and excellence theory provides a powerful tool to improve crisis responses and preparedness.

Especially for those working in communication professions, these findings can be helpful in at least two directions: On one hand, they can be used as an argument for a greater empowerment of PR and similar functions within their own institutions, e.g., to their board of directors; only a really empowered communication professional can help to reduce or even avoid the negative consequences of communicative crisis situations. On the other hand, the exemplary findings regarding crisis types, response strategies and their effects may even help well established communication managers to choose their responses with even more care. Nevertheless, there is still much research needed on this topic. When we consider other large-scale or even global crises such as the Ukraine War and the climate crisis, companies face similar challenges when they are perceived as not behaving in a responsible way or as failing to adhere to ethical standards. Therefore, we suggest that future studies specifically investigate the increasing social expectations companies are faced with, especially in the context of crises.

References

Bauchmüller, M., Fromm, T., & Ritzer, U. (2020). Mietfrei im Schuhladen. *Süddeutsche Zeitung*. https://www.sueddeutsche.de/wirtschaft/corona-adidas-deichmann-miete-1.4860662

Bialek, C. (2020). Marketingexpertin Tina Müller erleidet mit Douglas eine PR-Bruchlandung. *Handelsblatt*. https://www.handelsblatt.com/unternehmen/handel-konsumgueter/parfuembranche-marketingexpertin-tina-mueller-erleidet-mit-douglas-eine-pr-bruchlandung/26728250.html

Boehmer, J., & Harrison, V. S. (2022). No long-term consequences for social irresponsibility? Adidas' rent incident during the COVID-19 pandemic in Germany. *European Sport Management Quarterly*, *22*(1), 12–34. https://doi.org/10.1080/16184742.2021.1926526

Boseley, S. (2020). Germany confirms first human coronavirus transmission in Europe. *The Guardian*. https://www.theguardian.com/science/2020/jan/28/germany-confirms-first-human-coronavirus-transmission-in-europe

Chon, M. G., Kim, J. N., & Tam, L. (2022). From messaging to behavioral strategy: constructing a model of relationship-and action-focused crisis communication principles. *International Journal of Communication*, *16*(23). https://ijoc.org/index.php/ijoc/article/view/18185/3751

Coombs, W. T. (2007). Protecting organization reputations during a crisis: The development and application of situational crisis communication theory. *Corporate Reputation Review*, *10*(3), 163–176. https://doi.org/10.1057/palgrave.crr.1550049

Coombs, W. T. (2020). Situational crisis communication theory: Influences, provenance, evolution, and prospects. In F. Frandsen & W. Johansen (Eds.), *Crisis communication* (pp. 121–140). De Gruyter Mouton. https://doi.org/10.1515/9783110554236-005

Coombs, W. T., & Holladay, S. (2015). CSR as crisis risk: expanding how we conceptualize the relationship. *Corporate Communications: An International Journal*, *20*(2), 144–162. https://doi.org/10.1108/CCIJ-10-2013-0078

Crane, A., & Matten, D. (2021). COVID-19 and the future of CSR research. *Journal of Management Studies*, *58*(1), 280–284. https://doi.org/10.1111/joms.12642

Dillmann, T. (2021). "prmagazin" kürt Lufthansa Kommunikationschef Bartels zum "PR-Manager des Jahres 2021". *PR-Journal*. https://www.pr-journal.de/lese-tipps/preise-und-awards/27842-prmagazin-kuert-lufthansa-kommunikationschef-bartels-zum-pr-manager-des-jahres-2021.html

Grunig, J. E., & Grunig, L. A. (2008). Excellence theory in public relations: Past, present, and future. In A. Zerfass, B. van Ruler, & K. Sriramesh (Eds.), *Public relations research: European and international perspectives and innovations* (pp. 327–347). VS Verlag für Sozialwissenschaften. https://doi.org/10.1007/978-3-531-90918-9_22

Grunig, J. E., & Hunt, T. (1984). *Managing public relations*. Holt, Rinehart and Winston.

Grunig, L. A., Grunig, J. E., & Dozier, D. M. (2002). *Excellent public relations and effective organizations: A study of communication management in three countries*. Erlbaum.

Han, K. J. (2021). Examining the excellent CSR companies' CSR communication. In *71st Annual International Communication Conference (ICA)*, Washington, DC, USA.

He, H., & Harris, L. (2020). The impact of Covid-19 pandemic on corporate social responsibility and marketing philosophy. *Journal of Business Research*, *116*, 176–182. https://doi.org/10.1016/j.jbusres.2020.05.030

Hegner, S. M., Beldad, A. D. & Kraesgenberg, A.-L. (2016). The impact of crisis response strategy, crisis type, and corporate social responsibility on post-crisis consumer trust and purchase intention. *Corporate Reputation Review*, *19*, 357–370. https://doi.org/10.1057/s41299-016-0007-y

Heider, F (1958). *The psychology of interpersonal relations*. John Wiley & Sons.

Hoffmann, C. P., & Russ-Mohl, S. (2023). Crisis communication and corporate responsibility in media companies. In F. Weder, L. Rademacher, & R. Schmidpeter (Eds.), *CSR communication in the media. CSR, sustainability, ethics & governance* (pp. 59–73). Springer. https://doi.org/10.1007/978-3-031-18976-0_6

Islam, K. R., & Luqman, Y. (2022). Public relations in Diponegro national hospital from the excellence theory perspective. *Journal of Humanities and Social Studies*, *6*(3), 305–312. https://doi.org/10.33751/jhss.v6i3.6384

Lee, G. (2020). Coronavirus: What went wrong at Germany's Gütersloh meat factory? *BBC*. https://www.bbc.com/news/world-europe-53177628

Leonidou, L. C., Aykol, B., Eteokleous, P., & Voskou, A. (2020). Corporate social responsibility response strategies to COVID-19. In M. A. Marinov & S. T. Marinova (Eds.), *COVID-19 and international business: Change of era* (pp. 237–256). Routledge. https://doi.org/10.4324/9781003108924-20

Macnamara, J. (2021). New insights into crisis communication from an "inside" emic perspective during COVID-19. *Public Relations Inquiry*, *10*(2), 237–262. https://doi.org/10.1177/2046147X21999972

Marketing Week. (2020). Tesco, ITV and BT sport win top prizes at the Marketing Week Masters awards. *Marketing Week*. https://www.marketingweek.com/marketing-week-masters-awards-winners-2020/

Marra, F. J. (1998). Crisis communication plans: Poor predictors of excellent crisis public relations. *Public Relations Review*, *24*(4), 461–474. https://doi.org/10.1016/S0363-8111(99)80111-8

Meyer, I. (2021). The resurrection of modernistic public relations–a metamodern perspective. *ESSACHESS – Journal for Communication Studies*, *14*(1[27]), 15–36. https://doi.org/10.21409/essachess.1775-352x

PRCA. (2020). How to recover fast from the pandemic: Lessons from communications leaders. https://news.prca.org.uk/prca-covid-19-taskforce-publishes-gobally-crowdsources-report-of-communications-lessons

PR News. (2020). *Platinum PR awards*. https://www.prnewsonline.com/go/2020-platinum-pr-awards/

Rogers, C. (2020). 'Keeping you safe': Tesco campaign urges shoppers to social distance. *Marketing Week*. https://www.marketingweek.com/tesco-social-distance-coronavirus/

Schasche, S. (2020). Nadine Schian ist die Kommunikatorin des Jahres. *Werben & Verkaufen*. https://www.wuv.de/marketing/nadine_schian_ist_die_kommunikatorin_des_jahres

Scheiwiller, S., & Siska, L. (2021). Strategic responses by European airlines to the Covid-19 pandemic: A soft landing or a turbulent ride? *Journal of Air Transport Management*, *95*, Article 102103. https://doi.org/10.1016/j.jairtraman.2021.102103

Shepherd, K. (2020). Tyson foods managers had a 'winner-take-all' bet on how many workers would get covid-19, lawsuit alleges. *The Washington Post*. https://www.washingtonpost.com/nation/2020/11/19/tyson-foods-waterloo-bets-covid/

Shimawua, D., & Ternenge, K. (2022). Public relations strategies in the management of tertiary institutions in post COVID-19 Nigeria. *Asian Research Journal of Arts & Social Sciences*, *18*(4), 97–107. https://doi.org/10.9734/arjass/2022/v18i4407

Sievert, H., Meißner, F., & Buse, C. (2021). #adidasgate and Crisis Award winners: Excellence within corporate communication during the Covid-19 crisis. In *Proceedings of the 28th International Public Relations Research Symposium (Bledcom)* (pp. 338–350). https://e5fea86f-306d-4f86-a60a-3cdba5009bea.filesusr.com/ugd/f6188a_046300a50ffa41338a268d68d5477232.pdf

Sievert, H., Wagner, R., & Weiler, T. (2021). Contributing via Internal Social Media towards a better CSR communication at the top and throughout an organization theoretical foundations and new results from a qualitative case study and an additional quantitative interview survey in Germany. In *Proceedings of the 24th International Public Relations Research Conference*. https://dx.doi.org/10.2139/ssrn.4036563

Stevie Awards. (n.d.). Deutsche Post DHL Group – Beste Nutzung sozialer Medien – COVID-19-bezogene Informationen. https://stevieawards.com/gsa/deutsche-post-dhl-group-beste-nutzung-sozialer-medien-covid-19-bezogene-informationen

Storbeck, O. (2022). Axel Springer boss was landlord to Adidas during campaign against sports brand. *Financial Times*. https://www.ft.com/content/4d65b018-e62d-477d-b5e2-8a02748a4330

Sukandar, R., Nurhajati, L., Oktaviani, R. C., & Wijayanto, X. A. (2022). The public communication of the government of the republic of Indonesia related to Covid-19 pandemic in Indonesia. *PERSPEKTIF*, *11*(2), 771–778. https://doi.org/10.31289/perspektif.v11i2.6281

Sweney, M., & Goodley, S. (2020). Sports direct's Mike Ashley apologises for poor Covid-19 actions. *The Guardian*. https://www.theguardian.com/business/2020/mar/27/sports-direct-mike-ashley-apologises-for-poor-covid-19-actions

Taylor, M. (2023). Public relations and pandemics. In Croucher, S. M., & Diers-Lawson, A. (Eds.), *Pandemic communication* (pp. 79–96). Taylor & Francis.

Tu, C. C., Chang, M. L., & Chiao, Y. C. (2023). Are we all in the same boat? Appropriate response strategies to collective CSR crises. *Asia Pacific Journal of Management*, *40*(2), 483–515. https://doi.org/10.1007/s10490-021-09789-3

Urban, R., & Tefertiller, A. (2021). Company responses in times of crisis: A content analysis of COVID-19 emails. *Southwestern Mass Communication Journal*, *36*(2), 1–10.

Wang, Y., Zhang, M., Li, S., McLeay, F., & Gupta, S. (2021). Corporate responses to the coronavirus crisis and their impact on electronic-word-of-mouth and trust recovery: Evidence from social media. *British Journal of Management*, *32*(4), 1184–1202. https://doi.org/10.1111/1467-8551.12497

Weiner, B. (2018). The legacy of an attribution approach to motivation and emotion: A no-crisis zone. *Motivation Science*, *4*(1), 4–14. https://doi.org/10.1037/mot0000082

18 Internal Crisis Communication and the COVID-19 Pandemic

Heading Towards a New Future?

Silvia Ravazzani, Alessandra Mazzei and Alfonsa Butera

The perceptions and actions of employees are fundamental communication aspects to take care of to overcome an organizational crisis (Mazzei & Ravazzani, 2015, 2022) given employees' complex emotional reactions and specific relational bond to the organization (Frandsen & Johansen, 2017). Internal communication has been variously described as essential for employee crisis preparation, engagement (Mazzei et al., 2021) as well as post-crisis learning (Heide & Simonsson, 2019; Ulmer & Sellnow, 2020). The COVID-19 crisis has represented an unprecedented exogenous crisis challenging organizations' change management and resilience capacities and, more specifically, internal crisis communication (ICC) approaches and role in learning from the crisis and spreading new understandings and practices among employees.

This study adheres to the social constructionist approach promoted by crisis scholars such as Heide and Simonsson (2015) where the emphasis is on crisis as a perceptual phenomenon associated with confusion, ambiguity, feelings of disorientation, and lack of control. It is also based on the perspective of internal crisis communication as a complex process that requires a holistic understanding of the organization, which is made of cultural and psychological elements, multiple voices and often conflicting sensemaking. Part of this social constructionist view on crisis and crisis communication is the consideration of paradoxical tensions as a fundamental characteristic of crisis understanding and discursive management (Pollach et al., 2022). Tensions represent alternatives that seem to be oppositional and are socially constructed, where no simplistic either/or thinking can be adopted, but both-and or more-than thinking is advantageous (Heide & Simonsson, 2015; Lewis, 2000; Stohl & Cheney, 2001).

After reviewing existing literature on ICC and the COVID-19 pandemic, this chapter draws on an empirical qualitative study to examine ICC as performed in the two main stages of the COVID-19 pandemic, that is its outbreak in 2020 followed by its normalization in 2021 when somehow the "new normal" (Manuti et al., 2022) was established in organizations. Results detail key ICC strategy elements (i.e., objectives, contents, tools, initiatives) and challenges as well as contradictory demands (i.e., paradoxical tensions) faced by internal

DOI: 10.4324/9781003375296-21

communicators. The empirical study was carried out in Italy, where all aspects of life were substantially disrupted by the pandemic. Italian authorities undertook serious preventive and containment measures that included lockdowns in 2020 and stringent restrictions throughout 2021. This forced organizations to rapidly change their normal operations and led to a nation-wide adoption of remote working (Mazzei et al., 2021). The chapter ends with highlighting the key study lessons learned and identifying implications and new research avenues.

This chapter contributes a nuanced understanding of how organizations' conceptualization and practice of internal communication can be profoundly changed when faced with sudden and unprecedented crises. It offers insights into the decision-making and learning processes of internal communicators when both adapting and reinventing their communication approaches driven by a crisis and the paradoxical tensions stemming from it.

Overview of Research on ICC and the COVID-19 Pandemic

Because the COVID-19 represented a significant global disruption to organizations, it has been well-studied. For example, Einwiller et al. (2021) investigated the influence of informational and relational internal communication on employees' cognitive and affective responses and job engagement in Austrian organizations. Their survey results highlight the impact of *relational communication* on affective commitment and, in turn, job engagement. Stranzl et al. (2021), again with a quantitative study on employees in Austria, demonstrated the importance of *transparent communication* providing substantial informational resources for job engagement, mediated through organizational trust, while the emotional state of anxiety mediated the relationship between transparency and job disengagement. Ecklebe and Löffler (2021) explored employees' perceptions of the quality of internal communication in German organizations. Results from their survey point to *participatory communication* as one of the antecedents of high-quality ICC, which, in turn, has a positive impact on employee-organization relationships. With a survey among US employees, Sun et al. (2021) provided evidence about how *symmetrical communication* contributes to employees' perceptions of ICC quality, perceptions of organizational support and positive emotions, which, in turn, leads to deeper organizational identification. With another survey among US employees, Lee (2022) highlighted the critical role of *dialogic communication* in fostering employee efficacy and perceived threat of COVID-19, thereby leading employees to engage in safety behaviours in the workplace.

Transparent and participative communication was also emphasized by Haavisto and Linge (2022) in connection to *leadership communication*. Through their qualitative interview study in Finnish and Norwegian organizations, they showed that managerial transparency, dialogue and listening facilitated employees' sensemaking processes and contributed to build trust relationships during the pandemic. Managers' fundamental role in listening and in maintaining links between employees were also among the key results from a study by Horlait and Lambotte (2021) surveying employees from organizations in Belgium. They underlined that an effective ICC strategy considers the diversity of employee communication needs through a refined segmentation of internal publics based on their working reality and perception of different risks. In a similar vein, Neill and Bowen (2021) focused on *organizational listening* during the crisis through an interview study involving US communication management professionals. While recognizing the value of listening, they highlighted a series of barriers such as lack of desire of senior management, time, trust of employees, and remote work. This study also highlights a greater emphasis on *moral sensitivity, empathy,* and *ethical decision-making* in organizations because of this pandemic, which have become essential for effective organizational listening and for building trust and employee-organization relationships.

A final aspect of the dominant research on organizational communication emerging from the COVID-19 pandemic concerns *employee communication behaviour*. In this regard, Chon et al.'s (2021) results from a survey among US employees showed that employees who are active publics on COVID-19 in highly conflict-prone workplaces reported the highest negative megaphoning and turnover intention, and that employees' situational perceptions of COVID-19 would further exacerbate the effects. Based on these findings, they underscored the need for proactive and symmetrical ICC to facilitate employees' coping process and preserve employee-organization relationships. Similarly, Perdana et al. (2021) examined the influence of employee-organization relations and symmetrical internal communication on employee external communication behaviour through a survey on employees of a state-owned company in Indonesia. Results show that when good employee-organization relations exist, employees are more likely to stand up for the organization, recognize the crisis as a serious problem, feel more involved and less constrained in resolving problems, and spread positive information externally.

Taken all together, these studies point to significant challenges as well as unexpected opportunities in the ways organizations performed internal communication for managing employee experiences and bringing positive outcomes for employees and organizations. In the following sections, this study offers a nuanced understanding of these recently emerging paths through a qualitative study in Italy from the perspective of internal communicators.

Methodology

This qualitative study involved internal communication managers and professionals operating in Italy and participating in the activities of the Centre for Employee Relations and Communication based at Università IULM. This purposive sampling strategy was adopted to involve a network of informants possessing specialist knowledge of the research issue and willing to participate in the study with their personal stories (Oliver, 2013). Their companies are mainly large organizations belonging to different sectors, mostly food and beverage, banking and insurance, healthcare and pharmaceutical, energy and infrastructure.

The data are based on interviews and focus groups collected at the beginning of the crisis in 2020 when the changes were set in motion by the COVID-19 outbreak; and following in late 2021 when the "new normal" began to get established in organizations. In the acute stage, two online focus groups were carried out in the first half of April 2020 and ten individual interviews between mid-April and early May 2020 (one video interview and nine email interviews), involving in total 21 internal communication managers and professionals from 15 organizations. In the normalization stage, three online focus groups were carried out between April and July 2021, involving in total 29 internal communication managers and professionals from 15 organizations. Each focus group lasted three hours. This study's findings are not generalizable to all Italian organizations given the small sample and qualitative focus of this research. However, it is worth noting that, out of 15 organizations, 12 participated in both data collections, which helps substantiate the comparative remarks made in relation to the changes occurred in ICC approach across the two crisis stages.

A semi-structured interview guide was employed to collect comparable data from all informants (Daymon & Holloway, 2011). Key topics to cover were developed based on common internal communication strategy elements as well as of insights from ICC research. Questions centred on objectives, contents, tools, initiatives, and challenges of ICC, delving into the detailed descriptions of informants, their viewpoints, and personal experiences (Daymon & Holloway, 2011). All interview material was transcribed, and a qualitative content analysis of this material was performed by the three researchers to find recurrent themes, concepts, and dimensions (Gioia et al., 2013).

The comparative analysis focused on objectives, contents, tools, initiatives, and challenges of ICC in the two crisis stages. Additionally, the analysis of the participants' experiences revealed key paradoxical tensions created by the complexity of this pandemic crisis in terms of contradictory demands internal communicators had to embrace and balance in their communication efforts.

Results: ICC strategy and Paradoxical Tensions

The results section is structured in two main parts. The first part illustrates the key communication strategy elements (i.e., objectives, contents, tools, initiatives) and summarizes the key challenging areas for internal communication in each phase. The second part highlights a series of paradoxical tensions that incorporate the contradictory demands posed to internal communicators by the complexity of this pandemic crisis and that came to light when analysing the empirical material and the overall ICC strategy in the perceptions of internal communicators.

ICC Strategy Elements and Challenges

ICC During the Acute Stage

In terms of ICC *objectives*, internal communicators reported three closely intertwined goals. First, they indicated the objective of *keeping employees constantly informed and updated*, offering guidance on business decisions and hands-on training in the areas of safety measures, social distancing at work, remote working, and virtual collaboration practices. A second objective was related to *reassuring and comforting employees* through empathetic and sensitive communication messages, meant to reduce anxiety and psychological distance as well as to build a larger sense of unity and attachment to the organization. Third, internal communicators pointed out the objective of *listening to the needs and expectations of employees*, through two-way communications also aimed at assessing what to improve in ICC and employee relationship management. Internal communicators described the essence of ICC in this stage as “well-timed”, “specific”, “informative”, “attentive to leveraging ‘team spirit’”, “focused on sensemaking” as well as “empathetic”, “human”, and “focused on listening”.

When considering main ICC *content*, these can be grouped into two areas. First, ICC contents consisted in *pragmatic messages* focused on enabling employees and value generation for the organization. Such messages revolved around health safety measures, in accordance with government indications like: social distancing at work; remote working; digital competencies for effective collaboration; corporate decisions, performance, and plans for the future. Second, ICC contents included *messages addressing emotional and psychological aspects*. These were centred on aspects such as sense of security and solidity; proximity to employees and to their families too; gratitude for their remarkable additional work time and effort, and in particular to those employees still working in physical offices, factories and front-office positions; personal care, including the aspects of physical health, work-life balance, stress management, and resilience; sense of unison and pride in the organization and also in the country at large.

Results also highlight a great variety of *tools*, emphasizing digital tools such as Intranet, internal social media (e.g., Yammer), and digital events (e.g., online town halls). It is worth noting that, because so many employees were working from home – in some cases up to 85% of the workforce – that for the first time in many organizations *digital internal communication* took precedence over more traditional approaches. Intranet and internal social media were widely used in the organizations we studied for internal sensemaking and storytelling. In the words of one internal communication manager, these digital tools quickly transitioned towards a truly “human digital workspace”. Similarly, pages on the external corporate website as well as posts on external social media were employed for engaging stakeholders in direct conversations around the crisis as well as giving resonance to employees’ accounts, selfies, photographs, and positive messages.

Participants revealed a variety of internal communication *initiatives* implemented in this crisis stage. Most organizations solicited employee-generated content (e.g., "our remote working stories") to give visibility to employees' voices and crisis storytelling. Moreover, they strived to create synergy between internal and external communication. On the one hand, external programmes were promoted internally among employees: e.g., organizational projects supporting families, hospitals, and local communities including fundraising and donations. On the other hand, many organizations gave visibility on external media to internal initiatives, such as employees' contributions to emergency management (community service, volunteering). Finally, listening activities represented a particularly challenging activity during the pandemic due to social distancing and remote working. Despite such difficulties, assistance over the phone or specific digital spaces (e.g., on the Intranet) were leveraged to gather employee needs and questions and sustain their well-being and engagement.

Finally, the findings point to some key *challenges* for internal communication in this acute crisis stage. A first challenge was the *sensitive management of psychological aspects and emotions* of employees, such as stress, fear, uncertainty, difficulties in balancing work and family needs. Second, internal communicators were faced with the *harmonization of critical dualisms* that arose because of different risk exposure and work conditions. Such dualisms generated controversies among employees themselves: colleagues working remotely versus those working in factories, logistics centres, front-office positions, and therefore exposed to higher health risks; colleagues still working versus those not working because their areas were temporarily shut down during the lockdowns; colleagues operating in country regions more affected by the virus, and therefore subject to stricter restrictions, versus those working in less affected areas. A third challenge was the *complex management of multiple ICC channels and contents* to reach colleagues with no access to digital devices and those working in offices spread across the country or abroad, and to carefully detect and listen to every individual need. Finally, internal communicators were challenged in *delivering constant information in a global and national scenario characterized by great uncertainty*, with the risk of sending discordant messages if contradicted by the quick development of events. Drawing on the participants' words, internal (and external) communication in this crisis context had to become "multi-channel", "hybrid", "integrated" and "synergic" as ever before.

ICC in the Normalization Stage

The analysis revealed a change in focus in the normalization stage exemplified by different ICC *objectives*. First, the objective of *revitalizing employee engagement in the context of the "new way of working"*, with hybrid work conditions for more than four million employees, and the threat of the great resignation phenomenon. Second, the objective of *accompanying the profound cultural and technological changes* in organizations that the pandemic had started or at least accelerated, including the digital transformation of work instruments and routines, the establishment of new forms of personal relationships, and the emphasis on work-life balance and sustainable workplace practices. Third, the objective of *supporting leadership and key organizational processes* (e.g., newcomer onboarding, diversity and inclusion strategies, innovation) *in collaboration with other functions* such as Human Resources, ICT and Research & Development. Participants highlighted the need to support middle and top managers evolving towards a "new leadership" especially when envisioning the post-pandemic scenario of the "next normal".

To achieve these objectives, most internal communicators focused the *contents* of their ICC on the corporate history and values, for preserving a sense of unity and direction, as well as on the new technological, dialogical, and relational competencies, for empowering employees and especially leaders and people managers. The focus on such competencies was felt as a priority in the light of the establishment of e-relationships and e-collaboration, with the related problems of technostress, social isolation, and the right to disconnect.

In terms of *tools*, the *digital tools and communication spaces were further strengthened* in terms of multimedia formats and apps (e.g., for brainstorming and design thinking). In the words of one interviewee, "the digital workplace has to be imagined as a city, a lively environment, frequented by employees because it is capable of producing professional value". The leading role of internal communication in the digital transformation of the workplace led one organization to change the name of the department into "Internal Communication & Digital Workplace". Some internal communicators were also involved in *redesigning physical workspaces* to facilitate socialization, interaction, and knowledge sharing (e.g., open spaces or "hot desking" with no assigned workstations). Therefore, in this phase ICC tools were geared towards ensuring the effective functioning of both digital and physical communication arenas.

Regarding *initiatives*, it is worth to cite among the most common across the studied organizations the campaigns devoted to *leadership empowerment* to solicit a more humanized approach to manager-employee relationships. Moreover, many organizations decided to launch internal campaigns and events targeted to *employees returning to work on the employer's premise* to increase their engagement (e.g., face-to-face socialization events through breakfasts and aperitifs). Finally, many internal communicators launched formal *employee ambassadorship programs* to disseminate corporate content via external social media, building on the positive experiences during the acute phase when employee crisis storytelling was successfully leveraged.

Taking stock of these findings, it is possible to identify some *key challenges for internal communication* regarding the normalization crisis stage. A first challenge was the *complex management of hybrid ways of working*, with part of the population working fully or partially remotely, and part of the population returned to working on the employer's premise. Hybrid workplaces will likely remain also in the next normal ahead. This implies reconsidering engagement strategies based on a different psychological contract with employees. Accordingly, the communication approach should be adapted in terms of what to communicate on-site, digitally or hybridly (e.g., phygital events), and how (e.g., multimodal formats). In addition, internal communication was faced with *addressing the rising issues of the "right to disconnect", work-life balancing, sustainability at work, and management by objectives.* A final challenge was *bridging the entire organization towards different organizational culture and management models* based on new digital and relational competencies, new values such as shared responsibility, trust, inclusion, and new behaviours like empathetic leadership. One study participant described the key role of internal communication as follows: "The internal communicator should be understood as a sensemaker, the one who connects all the stakeholders of the company and in this way has the opportunity to also influence an evolving corporate culture".

More detailed findings related to key ICC strategy elements and challenges in both stages are visualized in Table 18.1.

Paradoxical Tensions

Tensions Experienced in the Acute Stage

Planning-Improvisation. Internal communicators relied on crisis communication plans and structured initiatives, but also realized the necessity to improvise through the experimentation of new tools, contents, and languages more suitable to capture and adapt to the ever-evolving internal needs and the imposed physical distance. While planned and structured responses were fundamental to react quickly and give employees a compass to navigate uncertainty, participants were challenged in revising priorities on an ongoing basis and implementing ad hoc initiatives. In the words of one interviewee: "You must invent a new internal communication approach completely different from routine (…) that follows necessity and does experiments". Internal communication according to the study participants "broke previous communication canons" to become "less glossy" by employing "artisanal contents and tools" perceived as more significant than more structured communications in that critical moment. In some cases, for instance, the CEO recorded his messages to employees from home through the smartphone, with no or little editing from the IC team, and focused openly on people's concerns and emotional distress. This was described as a revolution in the communication style of these organizations.

Formalization-Spontaneity. Internal communicators employed institutionalized, top-down ICC to ensure a constant, transparent, and complete flow of information from the function and the top management. At the same time, they also acknowledged the importance of embracing bottom-up, employee-generated

Table 18.1 Comparison of key ICC strategy elements and challenges across the two crisis stages

ICC strategy elements	*Phase 1 – Acute stage*	*Phase 2 – Normalization stage*
Objectives	Keeping employees informed and updated Reassuring and comforting employees Listening to employees' needs and fears	Revitalizing employee engagement Accompanying cultural and technological changes Advising leaders and other functions/departments
Contents	Health safety measures, social distancing at work and remote working rules and practices; technological and digital competencies; corporate decisions, business performance, corporate forecasts, and future plans Sense of security and solidity, proximity, gratitude, personal care, sense of unison and pride	Routines and practices related to the "new way of working" and hybrid workplaces Benefits of returning to work in presence Technological, dialogical, and relational competencies for leaders and people managers in particular History and values of the organization, sense of unity Corporate forecasts and future plans
Tools	Intranet, internal social media, mobile apps for employees working on site External corporate website and social media with contents dedicated to employees and to the initiatives taken by the organization to support them Emails, SMS, instant messaging, podcasting Video messages from leaders Digital events Digital newsletters Digital and paper periodicals On-site informational posters, signage, company TV Formal audits as well as informal listening through dedicated telephone numbers, mailboxes, virtual spaces	Strengthening of digital internal communication channels, content, and formats Renovation of physical layouts and internal signage (e.g., posters, wall signs)
Initiatives	Internal contests and projects focused on employee experiences and voices Virtual socialization events and team building (e.g., virtual aperitifs and coffee meetings)	Programmes and training initiatives performed in collaboration with other functions (e.g., projects focused on innovation with "call for ideas", or on socialization and welfare with leisure time engagement initiatives) Leadership empowerment

(*Continued*)

Table 18.1 (Continued)

ICC strategy elements	*Phase 1 – Acute stage*	*Phase 2 – Normalization stage*
	Coaching and training courses (e.g., on e-collaboration and psychological well-being) External communication campaigns and actions promoted internally Internal communication campaigns and actions promoted externally Listening activities (formal and informal) sustained by internal campaigns	Internal engagement campaigns and socialization especially targeted to employees returning to work on the employer's premise Listening activities (formal and informal) focused on employee needs and expectations, e.g. regarding hybrid work Employee ambassadorship programmes via external social media
Challenges	Psychological aspects and emotions of employees Dualisms and controversies among employees Multiple and alternative channels and contents Risk of sending incoherent messages in an ever-evolving scenario	New hybrid ways of working and communicating Rising issues linked to work-life balancing, sustainability at work, management by objectives Evolving organizational culture and management models

communication to respond to employees' needs for crisis sensemaking and storytelling. Participants described the need to make internal communication more "engaging", "bottom-up", "interactive", "familiar", and "less institutional". For example, informal communication was critical for listening and adjusting the crisis response. In addition, digital tools and user-generated content soon became dominant, with spaces dedicated to the sharing of individual stories and content, such as cooking tutorial videos or social challenges created by employees themselves.

Internal-External. Internal communicators focused their efforts on internal stakeholders to keep them constantly informed, reassure them, and listen to their expectations and fears. However, they also opened up to the external environment to share internal initiatives and stories in support of employees' close networks and the whole country living this unprecedented crisis. For example, one organization in the health sector opened a Spotify channel with stories shared by doctors and nurses for both the broader public and employees working remotely: this was "a way to leave a trace, an emotional relief valve (…) and channel of spontaneous communication (…) to the outside world, to the media". As hospitals and other health structures were inaccessible to relatives and friends, the manager explained that "we had to invent new relationship channels to fill a void (…) where the boundaries between internal and external communication definitively fall". Overall, this crisis saw internal communication as actively contributing to external communication with employees as crisis storytellers on stage.

Tensions Experienced in the Normalization Stage

Emergency-Resilience. Internal communicators had to operate in an emergency logic ("change as crisis") focused on this pandemic and on the ongoing effort to cope with a context characterized by high health and legal uncertainty. They also progressively pulled the organization towards a resilience logic ("change as normal"), where any crisis or change should be perceived as a fluid state and be approached with flexibility. This tension reflects the fundamental shift (Smith & Elliott, 2007) from "learning for crisis", which embodies the reaction to the moment a crisis occurs; to "learning as crisis" and "learning from crisis", which entail, respectively, the change of core organizational beliefs and the development of long-lasting organizational resilience. Participants described the novelties introduced during the first phase (e.g., digital tools, employees as external ambassadors, human-centred leadership) as learnings to maintain permanently and as a tangible sign of a strengthened cultural apparatus enabling effective organizational responses to future critical events.

Preserving-Revitalizing. Internal communicators strived to lean on the organization's heritage (history, values, mission, vision) for guiding employees in the never-ending crisis state. They also became active promoters of the evolving cultural and managerial models more sensitive to the newly emerged aspects of work-life balance, inclusion, and human-centred leadership. Corporate culture and values continued to function as an anchor for ICC striving to preserve the cultural cohesion and shared direction of "scattered" employees partially working remotely and partially in presence. At the same time, while revisiting their overall approach and instruments, internal communicators played a critical role in supporting the adjustment of core organizational assumptions and traditional management models based on hierarchy, physical presence in the office, and separation from the outside. For example, they supported leaders to develop people- and dialogue-centred communication, based on what they described as the new values of "perseverance", "transparency", "sustainability", "compassion", and "shared responsibility". It therefore emerges the internal communication's "double role of trainer and enabler" providing all organizational members, and leaders especially, with the communication and relational competencies appropriate for the new normal and the next normal ahead.

Work engagement-Sociality. Internal communicators strived to maintain high employee engagement on work tasks and duties after such a prolonged period of anxiety and of remote and hybrid working, which caused digital burnout and technostress. At the same time they realized the employees' needs for relational and socialization aspects in both work and personal spheres. While protracted physical distancing and digital collaboration raised the need to give new value to work relationships, employees also rediscovered their personal and family dimensions which they did not intend to give up by returning to old work habits based on office work and long hours. Internal communication had to renew work engagement

Table 18.2 Paradoxical tensions experienced by internal communicators in the acute and normalization stages

Paradoxical tensions	
Phase 1 – Acute stage	
Planning-Improvisation	ICC relied on planned and structured responses to react quickly and give employees a compass to navigate uncertainty, but also improvised through the experimentation of new tools, contents and languages, and an ongoing revision of priorities.
Formalization-Spontaneity	ICC employed institutionalized, top-down internal communication to ensure a constant, transparent, complete flow of information, but also embraced bottom-up, employee-generated communication for employee crisis sensemaking and storytelling.
Internal-External	ICC focused on internal stakeholders to keep them informed, comfort them and listen to their expectations and fears, but also opened up to external stakeholders through repurposing internal crisis storytelling in support of employees' close networks and the whole country.
Phase 2 – Normalization stage	
Emergency-Resilience	ICC had to operate in an emergency logic due to a context still characterized by high health and legal uncertainty, but also had to progressively acquire a resilience logic building on the crisis learnings and institutionalizing the novelties experimented in the acute stage.
Preserving-Revitalizing	ICC strived to lean on the organization's heritage as an anchor in the crisis context, but also promoted evolving cultural and managerial models in line with changed conditions and shared internal feelings.
Work engagement-Sociality	ICC strived to maintain high engagement on work tasks and duties, but also took care of a heightened sensitiveness towards relational and socialization aspects in both employees' work and personal spheres.

strategies. This was handled, on the one hand, by focusing more on employee motivation and team spirit to reconstruct social capital and "disconnected relationships" at work and "give sense to returning to the office" (e.g., campaigns revolving around the importance of having lunch with colleagues, or celebration events for organizational achievements). On the other hand, internal communicators extended their reach to the personal sphere to sustain a better balancing of work and family time, the right to disconnect, and the inclusion of diverse needs and lifestyles (e.g., offering resources for personal development and care).

Table 18.2 summarizes the paradoxical tensions with reference to the two crisis stages considered.

Conclusions

Taken all together, this study confirms that the pandemic disruption has triggered a significant renovation of existing internal communication approaches in organizations. Findings align with research stressing the new face of ICC, and internal communication in general, as more *relationship-oriented* (e.g., Einwiller et al., 2021) and *dialogic* (e.g., Lee, 2022), encompassing elements of *improvisation* and *ethical listening* (e.g., Neill & Bowen, 2021), and with a crucial role played by *people-centred and empathetic leaders* (e.g., Haavisto & Linge, 2022) as well as by *employees as crisis sensemakers and communicators* to the outside world too (e.g., Chon et al., 2021). These features are likely to remain in the next normal ahead.

This study also emphasizes the *critical role of internal communication in the newly established hybrid work contexts*, where it is tasked with differentiating employee engagement strategies as well as paying particular attention to avoid the risks of poor digital communication (Fay & Kline, 2011). Moreover, internal communication seems to play a new role in *sustainability* which is increasingly intended in an individual perspective (Kotera & Correa Vione, 2020). This extends internal communication's traditional scope to supporting employees' physical and mental health and addressing their rising concerns around work-life balance and inclusion. What strongly emerges is the *bigger and higher status of the Internal Communication function in the organization*, described by this study's participants with the metaphors of "orchestra conductor", "traffic officer", and "rope that holds everything together" in close synergy with leaders and other functions.

Moreover, the *paradox perspective* allowed delving into a series of tensions that internal communicators felt were embedded in the complexity of this pandemic crisis. They were quite successful in their "synthesis", i.e. the creative combination of coexisting and apparently oppositional aspects (Stohl & Cheney, 2001) while addressing and recombining multiple coexisting demands. It remains to be seen in future studies if, in the next normal ahead, fragmentation of goals and practices and limitations to planning and top-down approaches will be embraced as part of internal communication in both normal and crisis times, also in view of the growing complexity of work contexts made of hybridity, inclusion stances, and fast pace of change. As a concluding remark, an implication of this work for both scholars and practitioners is to recognize the value of the "both-and" and "more-than" paradox perspective (Lewis, 2000). This may help to better understand the messiness of organizational life according to a social constructionism perspective on crisis and crisis communication (Heide & Simonsson, 2015) and to avoid oversimplified solutions where paradox is seen as "a fulcrum for constructive organizational change" (Stohl & Cheney, 2001, pp. 395–396).

Acknowledgements

This study was conducted by the Centre for Employee Relations and Communication (CERC) @ Università IULM. It was supported by the Working Group Employee Communication (WG_EC) @CERC, Università IULM, editions 2018–2020 and 2020–2022, and by the Department of Business LECB "Carlo

A. Ricciardi" @ Università IULM. WG_EC @CERC company partners for 2018–2020 and 2020–2022 are: Campari Group, Coopselios, Cromology Italia, E.ON, Eni, Ferrero, Gruppo Unipol, LFoundry, MM, Sanofi, Saras, Sella, Snam, Takeda, Unicoop Firenze, Vodafone Italia, and Whirlpool EMEA.

References

Chon, M.-G., Tam, L., & Kim, J.-N. (2021). Effects of organizational conflict history and employees' situational perceptions of COVID-19 on negative megaphoning and turnover intention. *Journal of Communication Management*, *25*(3), 298–315. https://doi.org/10.1108/JCOM-10-2020-0114

Daymon, C., & Holloway, I. (2011). *Qualitative research methods in public relations and marketing communications* (2nd ed.). Routledge.

Ecklebe, S., & Löffler, N. (2021). A question of quality: Perceptions of internal communication during the Covid-19 pandemic in Germany. *Journal of Communication Management*, *25*(3), 214–232. https://doi.org/10.1108/JCOM-09-2020-0101

Einwiller, S., Ruppel, C., & Stranzl, J. (2021). Achieving employee support during the COVID-19 pandemic – the role of relational and informational crisis communication in Austrian organizations. *Journal of Communication Management*, *25*(3), 233–255. https://doi.org/10.1108/JCOM-10-2020-0107

Fay, M. J., & Kline, S. L. (2011). Coworker relationships and informal communication in high-intensity telecommuting. *Journal of Applied Communication Research*, *39*(2), 144–163. https://doi.org/10.1080/00909882.2011.556136

Frandsen, F., & Johansen, W. (2017). *Organizational crisis communication: A multivocal approach* (4th ed.). SAGE.

Gioia, D. A., Corley, K. G., & Hamilton, A. L. (2013). Seeking qualitative rigor in inductive research: Notes on the Gioia methodology. *Organizational Research Methods*, *16*(1), 15–31. https://doi.org/10.1177/1094428112452151

Haavisto, V. E., & Linge, T. T. (2022). Internal crisis communication and Nordic leadership: The importance of transparent and participative communication in times of crisis. *Scandinavian Journal of Hospitality and Tourism*. https://doi.org/10.1080/15022250.2022.2123038

Heide, M., & Simonsson, C. (2015). Struggling with internal crisis communication: A balancing act between paradoxical tensions. *Public Relations Inquiry*, *4*(2), 223–255. https://doi.org/10.1177/2046147X15570108

Heide, M., & Simonsson, C. (2019). *Internal crisis communication: Crisis awareness, leadership and coworkership*. Routledge. https://doi.org/10.4324/9780429425042

Horlait, D., & Lambotte, F. (2021). The future of internal communication in the light of the events observed during the Covid-19 crisis. *E S S A C H E S S – Journal for Communication Studies*, *14*(2), 60–80. https://doi.org/10.21409/cme5-wr03

Kotera, Y., & Correa Vione, K. (2020). Psychological impacts of the new ways of working (NWW): A systematic review. *International Journal of Environmental Research and Public Health*, *17*(14), 5080. https://doi.org/10.3390/ijerph17145080

Lee, Y. (2022). How dialogic internal communication fosters employees' safety behavior during the COVID-19 pandemic. *Public Relations Review*, *48*(1). https://doi.org/10.1016/j.pubrev.2022.102156

Lewis, M. W. (2000). Exploring paradox: Toward a more comprehensive guide. *The Academy of Management Review*, *25*, 760–776. https://doi.org/10.2307/259204

Manuti, A., Van der Heijden, B., Kruyen, P., De Vos, A., Zaharie, M., & Lo Presti, A. (2022). Editorial: How normal is the new normal? Individual and organizational implications of the COVID-19 pandemic. *Frontiers in Psychology*, *13*, 931236. doi: 10.3389/fpsyg.2022.931236

Mazzei, A., & Ravazzani, S. (2015). Internal crisis communication strategies to protect trust relationships: A study of Italian companies. *International Journal of Business Communication*, *52*(3), 319–337. https://doi.org/10.1177/2329488414525447

Mazzei, A., & Ravazzani, S. (2022). The strategic role of internal crisis communication. In J. Falckheimer & M. Heide (Eds.), *Research handbook of strategic communication* (pp. 274–289). Edward Elgar Publishing.

Mazzei, A., Quaratino, L., & Ravazzani, S. (2021). *Internal crisis communication in the time of Covid-19 pandemic. Company strategies and working experience of employees*. FrancoAngeli.

Neill, M. S., & Bowen, S. A. (2021), Ethical listening to employees during a pandemic: New approaches, barriers and lessons. *Journal of Communication Management*, *25*(3), 276–297. https://doi.org/10.1108/JCOM-09-2020-0103

Oliver, P. (2013). Purposive sampling. In V. Jupp (Ed.), *The SAGE dictionary of social research methods*. https://methods.sagepub.com/Reference/the-sage-dictionary-of-social-research-methods/n162.xml

Perdana, A. P., Latifunnur, L. & Hendriana, E. (2021). Employee external communication behavior during the COVID-19 pandemic crisis: Case-study of a state-owned company. *Asian Journal of Business Research*, *11*(2), 1–21. https://doi.org/10.14707/ajbr.210104

Pollach, I., Ravazzani, S., & Maier, C. D. (2022). Organizational guilt management: A paradox perspective. *Group & Organization Management*, *47*(3), 487–529. https://doi.org/10.1177/10596011211015 4

Smith, D., & Elliott, D. (2007). Exploring the barriers to learning from crisis: Organizational learning and crisis. *Management Learning*, *38*(5), 519–538. https://doi.org/10.1177/1350507607083

Stohl, C., & Cheney, G. (2001). Participatory processes/paradoxical practices. Communication and dilemmas of organizational democracy. *Management Communication Quarterly*, *14*(3), 349–407. https://doi.org/10.1177/0893318901143 00

Stranzl, J., Ruppel, C., & Einwiller, E. (2021). Examining the role of transparent organizational communication for employees' job engagement and disengagement during the COVID-19 pandemic in Austria. *Journal of International Crisis and Risk Communication Research*, *4*(2), 271–308. https://doi.org/10.30658/jicrcr.4.2.4

Sun, R., Li, J. Y. Q., Lee, Y., & Tao, W. (2021). The role of symmetrical internal communication in improving employee experiences and organizational identification during COVID-19 pandemic-induced organizational change, *International Journal of Business Communication*. https://doi.org/10.1177/23294884211050628

Ulmer, R. R., & Sellnow, T. L., (2020). Discourse of renewal: Understanding the theory's implications for the field of crisis communication. In F. Frandsen & W. Johansen (Eds.), *Crisis communication* (pp. 165–175). De Gruyter Mouton.

19 COVID-19 Communication in Portugal

Exploring the Relationships between Sources of Information and Citizens' Trust in Governmental Risk and Crisis Communication

Gisela Gonçalves, Valeriano Piñeiro-Naval and Bianca Persici Toniolo

International empirical research on risk and crisis communication has increased considerably in recent years (Diers-Lawson, 2020), although this was not the case for public health research (Kuipers & Welsh, 2017) until the COVID-19 outbreak in 2020. The pandemic has presented a unique scenario for the study of risk and crisis communication on health emergencies practiced by governments around the world. Portugal was not a different case, as it is a country that went from being a "good student", tackling the first wave, to the worst country worldwide, in number of deaths and infections per thousand inhabitants, in January 2021 (*Financial Times*, 2021).

Trust in the government has traditionally been found to influence the level of compliance with health regulations during emergencies (Blair et al., 2017). Recent studies on COVID-19 have reflected this point (Bargain & Aminjonov, 2020; Moreno et al., 2020). Therefore, trust is an essential coping mechanism people use when they lack sufficient information or expertise to decide about health recommendations (Valentini et al., 2022). In emergency communication, public institutions and authorities need to disseminate information to alert and protect citizens, but it is also important to use rhetorically effective arguments to persuade people to trust and comply with their guidelines. Governments therefore have a vital role in defining response strategies that elicit an appropriate attitude from the population.

Based on the assumption that (non)compliance with the authorities' recommendations, disseminated by politicians or experts is directly linked to trust in sources of information, in this chapter we analyze the Portuguese case during second wave of the disease. We begin with a brief discussion on the relationships between information sources and citizen trust in government risk and crisis communication, we then reflect upon the theoretical-practical implications of the data within the broader context of the EUPRERA Com-COVID research project.

DOI: 10.4324/9781003375296-22

Information Sources and Spokespersons in Times of Mistrust

The COVID-19 information landscape has been characterized as a massive infodemic, an overabundance of information and disinformation which makes it hard for people to find trustworthy information sources on prevention behaviors. The population's choices regarding sources of information and their corresponding perception information reliability are therefore relevant predictors for the degree of compliance to preventive behaviors in a health crisis (Park et al., 2019). There are several factors that encourage people to seek informational content from different sources (Austin et al., 2012; Lu & Jin, 2020). For example, social media is seen as providing access to unfiltered information (Lu & Jin, 2020; Tai & Sun, 2007) and emotional support (Fraustino et al., 2017). Traditional media are perceived to be more credible than social media (Austin et al., 2012; Moreno et al., 2020). Online news did not replace but instead complemented the consumption of traditional news (Dutta-Bergman, 2004), in the so-called legacy media.

Information Sources and Spokespersons during Health Emergencies

According to the WHO (2011), the capacity to relay information quickly and clearly on different platforms such as TV, radio, print, or the web is an essential strategy to effectively manage a public health emergency. Using a multi-channel strategy is noted as the most suitable to reach different demographics across a given population and also to generate a greater sense of urgency (Sellnow et al., 2019). Risk communication experts likewise emphasize the importance of monitoring the needs and expectations of different segments of the population, providing timely, accurate, specific, sufficient, consistent, and intelligible information (Laajalahti et al., 2016).

At first glance, the news media might be the appropriate channel to educate the public about individual risks. However, studies have revealed that during public health crises, many journalistic messages have not followed best practices in both traditional and digital media (Li Ho et al., 2020). The "COVID-19 Infodemic" showed that citizens access information from both reliable and questionable sources in the digital environment. Moreover, they do not show different patterns of dissemination of this information in digital media (Cinelli et al., 2020). Therefore, public institutions should also rely on direct communication (e.g. social media) to disseminate official information (Liu et al., 2016; Olsson, 2014; Reich et al., 2011).

Citizens' selection of information sources and the perceived reliability of those sources are important factors in predicting preventative behaviors being adopted (Park et al., 2019). Experts in risk and crisis communication establish that any of the institutions involved in public health management can be informative sources, always in accordance with their attributions in crisis management process (Sellnow & Seeger, 2013). Thus, public authorities (e.g., public health agencies) should be responsible for issuing messages related to prevention and treatment, while political sources (e.g., government, ministries, prime minister) should be associated with messages on broader public policies, such as the purchase of vaccines, and the evaluation of the results of the measures implemented (Wukich, 2016).

While the sources of information are important, it is also important to strategically choose the spokesperson(s) communicating directly to the media, as their words will be widely quoted. Moreover, the voices used to endorse informational campaigns can have an impact on citizens' trust. Previous research suggests that scientists are recommended as spokespersons when it comes to preventing and warning about the disease, and health experts are advised as spokespersons on issues related to what to do in case of contagion. Political and government authorities, on the other hand, should be spokespersons for messages that promote confidence in the capacity of public institutions to respond to the crisis (McLean & Ewart, 2015; Seeger et al., 2003; Sellnow & Seeger, 2013).

Trust in the Context of Health Emergencies

As important as it is complex, the concept of trust has received various definitions and approaches in the risk management and communication literature (Earle et al., 2010). Some studies have revealed that the degree of trust in the national health care system has a significant impact on the public's willingness to receive health care instructions (Devos et al., 2002). Research also stressed that low levels of trust can lead the public to distance itself from the health care system which can cause neglect and non-compliance with guidelines, with severe consequences for public health (Meyer et al., 2014).

When making decisions during health crises, individuals need to trust data and guidelines received from institutions and trust the spokespersons communicating that information (Abu-Akel et al., 2021). If a communicator is not deemed trustworthy, the communication strategy will likely fail (Lundgren & McMakin, 2013). That is particularly true when the risk is poorly known or too complex, as it involves relying on expert assessments rather than on one's own judgment (Siegrist & Cvetkovich, 2000).

Credibility, expertise, and transparency are also factors that influence the level of trust in government and public health authorities. While credibility can be defined as the degree of technical expertise attributed to the source and its message (Llewellyn, 2020; Renn & Levine, 1991), expertise is usually established by the speaker's credentials, experience, and institutional affiliation (Lundgren & McMakin, 2013; Seeger et al., 2018). Transparency can stem from one's history, the source's previous behavior in analogous situations (Earle & Siegrist, 2008). If there are reports of data omission or manipulation, subsequent messages are more unlikely to be trusted. The Brazilian case was paradigmatic in this regard, with President Bolsonaro's different narratives of denial of the new virus and its alleged low lethality, when in fact millions of persons were infected and dying (Athaydes et al., 2022).

Governments and public institutions always play a meaningful role in situations of public health emergencies, such as the COVID-19 pandemic. As responsible for managing risk and crisis, they promote a “top-down” communication (Frandsen & Johansen, 2020) that is often mediated by the news media. This was also the case for the daily briefings and press conferences held by public institutions and politicians during the COVID-19 pandemic in Portugal. However, crises are complex processes over which it is impossible to have absolute control. As Frandsen and Johansen note, “when a crisis breaks out, an arena opens up” (p. 240) and then a wide range of actors and voices start determining the crisis agenda.

Although the Portuguese preferred traditional media as a source of information during the second wave of COVID-19 (Gonçalves et al., 2021), citizens’ use of information sources such as influencers, friends, public health professionals, associations, may also have an impact on the population’s level of trust in the authorities’ recommendations and management practices. Aiming to understand the relation between sources of information and citizens trust in government risk and crisis communication in Portugal during the second wave of the pandemic, three research questions (RQ) and five hypotheses derived from previous research guided our study:

RQ1: What sources of information did people trust most in Portugal?
RQ2: What information channels did the Portuguese consult most for information about COVID-19, particularly in the online ecosystem?
RQ3: How did the population assess the management of crisis and risk communication by the government of Portugal?
H1a: The more people use traditional media the more they trust in government sources.
H1b: People who seek more information through scientific and institutional sources have more confidence in health personnel.
H2: The more people use social media for information about COVID-19 the more they trust digital influencers.
H3a: The more positive people perceive the government’s management of crisis communication the more they trust in official government sources.
H3b: People who get more information from traditional media have a more favorable opinion of government communication management.

Methodology: Sample and Questionnaire

In the context of an international investigation of the “EUPRERA Com-COVID” network – a project which aimed to monitor the communication management of the COVID-19 crisis in several countries – a survey was applied to $n = 460$ Portuguese citizens between 7 October and 11 November 2020. The sample, which implies a confidence level of 95% and a margin of error of 4.6% over the country’s population ($N = 10,295,909$ inhabitants), was composed of 65.7% women and 34.3% men, with a mean age of $M = 41.01$ years (SD = 12.09).

This sample was reached using the snowball sampling technique. Invitations with a link to the online survey were sent through email and social networks, in particular WhatsApp and Facebook. The invitation encouraged people to complete and disseminate the questionnaire to their contacts. No compensation for participating in the research was offered. The online questionnaire included questions on information-seeking behavior, trust in different information sources, perception of government communication management, message retention, and demographic questions.

For this chapter, we analyze the three main sections of the survey with questions related to the sources of information that inspire more confidence among the Portuguese population, the frequency of use of different media and information channels, and the opinion of the Portuguese on the management of Government communication, using three scales composed of 13, 14 and 6 items respectively. The response options for each item were operationalized by 7-point Likert-type scales, with 1 being the lowest point and 7 the highest.

To reduce scale dimensions, items were included in three exploratory factor analyses (EFA) to detect associations between them and to create aggregate factors afterwards. As shown in Table 19.1, each of the 13 items relating to trust in information sources (Gonçalves et al., 2021) had a significant factor loading

Table 19.1 Sources of information dimensions trough EFA (varimax rotation and reliability test)

Sources of information	*Influencers and social media (factor 1)*	*Authorities and media (factor 2)*	*Healthcare workers (factor 3)*
1 Influencers of other fields	.877		
2 Alternative medicines influencers	.871		
3 Healthcare influencers	.763		
4 Friends on social media	.695		
5 Healthcare workers disseminating information on social media	.654		
6 Other	.612		
7 Government and Directorate-General of Health		.858	
8 Local authorities		.773	
9 World Health Organization		.730	
10 Media		.602	
11 Professional associations in the healthcare field			.759
12 Personal acquaintances from the healthcare field			.755
13 Prestigious figures in the healthcare field			.657
Eigenvalue	4.345	2.623	1.084
Explained variance	33.42%	20.17%	8.43%
Cronbach's alpha	.84	.77	.71

on some of the 3 factors suggesting the EFA as a latent structure (variance explained = 61.94%, KMO = .83, Bartlett's Test: $p < .001$).

Similarly, an EFA with the 14 items regarding the frequency of use of different media and information channels (Gonçalves et al., 2021) revealed 3 factors suggesting the EFA as a latent structure (explained variance = 58.96%, KMO = .84, Bartlett's Test: $p < .001$) (Table 19.2).

Finally, Table 19.3 shows the variables relating to the opinion of the Portuguese on the management of government communication (Gonçalves et al.,

Table 19.2 Dimensions of the use of different media and information channels through EFA (varimax rotation and reliability test)

Media and channels	*Scientific and institutional sources (factor 1)*	*Media (factor 2)*	*Social media (factor 3)*
1 Scientific websites	.842		
2 Scientific magazines	.789		
3 Healthcare websites	.724		
4 Institutional websites	.658		
5 Alternative treatments websites	.645		
6 Television		.860	
7 Radio		.760	
8 Online news		.670	
9 Print press		.596	
10 Instagram			.835
11 YouTube			.764
12 Twitter			.661
13 WhatsApp			.543
14 Facebook			.436
Eigenvalue	4.924	1.983	1.348
Explained variance	35.17%	14.16%	9.63%
Cronbach's alpha	.85	.75	.71

Table 19.3 Dimensions of the Portuguese opinion on the management of the Government's communication through EFA with varimax rotation and reliability test

Opinion on government's communication management	*Positive (factor 1)*	*Negative (factor 2)*
1 It has always been clear and sufficient	.831	
2 It has been the most reliable	.828	
3 It was disseminated at the appropriate moments	.826	
4 It has been confusing for the population		.827
5 It did not reveal the whole truth		.805
6 It raised social alarm		.767
Eigenvalue	2.469	1.711
Explained variance	41.14%	28.51%
Cronbach's alpha	.78	.73

2021). Each of the six items shows a significant factor loading on some of the two factors suggesting the EFA as a latent structure (explained variance = 69.65%; KMO = .70; Bartlett's test: $p <.001$).

The internal consistency of each factor, measured with the statistical parameter Cronbach's alpha, revealed adequate reliability in all cases (Hair et al., 1999; Robinson et al., 1991).

Analysis and Results

Research Question 1

In response to RQ1 – "In which sources of information has the population shown the greatest confidence in Portugal?" -, it was possible to determine three main types of information sources, presented in Table 19.4 next to the specific items that composed them, ranked according to respondents' average confidence in these sources:

By analyzing each item separately, that is, by source of information, the WHO (M = 5.15, SD = 1.71) is the one that inspired most trust in citizens, followed by personalities with prestige in the health area (M = 5.07, SD = 1.70) and the Government and Directorate General of Health (M = 5.02, SD = 1.71).

After performing a repeated measures analysis of variance, we observed that the differences between the information sources were statistically significant [$\lambda_w = .205$, F (2, 458) = 888.5, $p < .001$, $\eta^2 = .795$], with "health personnel" generating the most trust in the Portuguese population (PI1) above "authorities and media" [t (459) = 3.037, $p < .01$, $d = .144$] and "influencers and social media" [t (459) = 40.227, $p < .001$, $d = 2.115$]. If we compare "authorities and

Table 19.4 Sources of information and the items analysis

Sources of information	*n*	*M*	*SD*	*% high confidence**
Influencers and social media (factor 1)	460	2.19	1.07	
Healthcare workers disseminating information on social media	460	2.65	1.68	15.7
Friends on social media	460	2.43	1.35	7.5
Healthcare influencers	460	2.37	1.51	11.8
Other	460	2.20	1.58	9.1
Alternative medicines influencers	460	1.82	1.28	5.2
Influencers from other fields	460	1.67	1.13	3.5
Authorities and media (factor 2)	**460**	**4.60**	**1.26**	
World Health Organization	460	5.15	1.71	68.9
Government and Directorate-General for Health	460	5.02	1.69	69.1
Local authorities	460	4.31	1.65	51.2
Media	460	3.94	1.56	38.3
Healthcare workers (factor 3)	**460**	**4.79**	**1.37**	
Prestigious figures in the healthcare field	460	5.07	1.70	69.5
Professional associations in the healthcare field	460	4.71	1.67	61
Personal acquaintances from the healthcare field	460	4.60	1.80	56.8

* Joint percentage of respondents who expressed a lot (5), a lot (6) or complete (7) confidence in information sources.

media" with "influencers and social media", there are also significant differences between them [t (459) = 33.509, $p < .001$, d = 2.061].

Research Question 2

To answer RQ2 – "What information channels have the Portuguese consulted most for information about COVID-19, particularly in the online ecosystem?" -, it was also possible to ascertain the average frequency of use of different media and information channels, presented in Table 19.5 together with the specific items that composed them.

After implementing a repeated measures analysis of variance, we observed that the differences between media and channels were statistically significant [λ_w = .294, F (2, 458) = 549.39, $p < .001$, η2 = .706], with "media" being the most used by the Portuguese population (PI1) above "scientific and institutional sources" [t (459) = 29.053, $p < .001$, d = 1.456] and "social media" [t (459) = 31.057, $p < .001$, d = 1.721]. If we compare "scientific and institutional sources" with "social media", there are also significant differences between them [t (459) = 2.73, $p < .01$, d = 0.127], only of smaller effect sizes (Cohen, 1988; Johnson et al., 2008). In isolation, television (M = 5.83, SD = 1.74) was the medium most used by citizens, followed by online news (M = 5.36, SD = 2.01) and radio (M = 4.70, SD = 2.11).

Data also showed that the online medium that the Portuguese consulted more often to obtain information about COVID-19 was the online news (M = 5.36, SD = 2.01), Facebook (M = 4.26, SD = 2.25), and websites of official institutions (M = 3.46, SD = 2.16).

Table 19.5 Frequency of use of means and information channels and constituent items

Frequency of use of media and information channels	*n*	*M*	*SD*	*% high frequency**
Scientific and institutional sources (factor 1)	**460**	**2.73**	**1.54**	
Public institutions websites	460	3.46	2.16	35.2
Healthcare-specialized websites/blogs	460	3.07	2.11	27
Scientific publications	460	2.92	2.07	26.5
Science websites/blogs	460	2.29	1.77	14.7
Alternative therapies websites/blogs	460	1.90	1.58	10.3
Media (factor 2)	**460**	**4.98**	**1.55**	
Television	460	5.83	1.74	80.5
Online news	460	5.36	2.01	73.3
Radio	460	4.70	2.11	59.4
Print press	460	4.03	2.31	46
Social media (factor 3)	**460**	**2.55**	**1.26**	
Facebook	460	4.26	2.25	49.9
WhatsApp	460	2.23	1.80	14.6
Instagram	460	2.20	1.79	13.6
YouTube	460	2.08	1.67	12.2
Twitter	460	1.96	1.75	12.6

* Joint percentage of respondents who expressed a lot (5), a lot (6) or total (7) frequency in the use of media or information channels.

Research Question 3

Regarding the opinion of the Portuguese on the management of government communication (RQ3), it was also possible to establish two clearly distinct opinions, which are shown in Table 19.6 next to the specific items that integrate them.

We can state that there are significant differences between the opinions [t (459) = 2.594, $p < .01$, $d = .183$], although the effect size is small (Cohen, 1988; Johnson et al., 2008). However, the positive opinion is the most widespread among the Portuguese with regard to government communication (RQ3).

Table 19.6 Descriptive statistical data of citizens' opinions regarding the government's communication and constituent items

Opinion on the government's communication management	*n*	*M*	*SD*	*% high concordance**
Positive (factor 1)	**460**	**4.13**	**1.39**	
It was disseminated in the appropriate moments	460	4.33	1.61	45.9
It has been the most reliable	460	4.21	1.69	45.5
It has always been clear and sufficient	460	3.87	1.69	39.3
Negative (factor 2)	**460**	**3.86**	**1.55**	
It has been confusing for the population	460	4.07	1.86	44.6
It did not reveal the whole truth	460	3.93	1.95	40.9
It raised social alarm	460	3.58	1.95	32

* Joint percentage of respondents who expressed strong (5), strong (6) or strong (7) agreement with the statements.

Hypotheses Findings

Finally, the results of testing our five hypotheses are presented in Table 19.7 together with the data supporting them. In this sense, they are verified with statistically significant and positive correlations. According to Cohen (1988), H_{3b} presents a large effect (.500 or higher), H_2 intermediate (.300 to .500), and the rest of them small (.100 to .300).

Table 19.7 Tests of hypotheses (Pearson correlation)

Hypothesis	*Description*	*Result*
H_{1a}	+ use of traditional media (factor 2, table 2) ⇒ + trust on government sources (factor 2, table 1)	r (458) = .263, $p < .001$
H_{1b}	+ use of scientific and institutional sources (factor 1, table 2) ⇒ + trust on health authorities (factor 3, table 1)	r (458) = .279, $p < .001$
H_2	+ use of social media (factor 3, table 2) ⇒ + trust on digital influencers (factor 1, table 1)	r (458) = .356, $p < .001$
H_{3a}	+ positive opinion on government crisis communication management (factor 1, table 3) ⇒ + trust on government sources (factor 2, table 1)	r (458) = .559, $p < .001$
H_{3b}	+ use of traditional media (factor 2, table 2) ⇒ + positive opinion on government crisis communication management (factor 1, table 3)	r (458) = .238, $p < .001$

Discussion and Conclusions

With this study, we analyzed the relationships between information seeking options, trust in information sources and the perception of government communication crisis management in Portugal during the second wave of the pandemic. Overall, we discuss the implications of three main findings that may help improve government and health authorities risk communication in critical times.

First, findings show that three in four of the most used channels to seek information are among the so-called mainstream media: television (80.5%) is the most used medium by citizens, followed by online news (73.3%) and radio (59.4%). This is aligned with previous studies that stress that traditional media are primarily used for information needs, as people perceive them—especially broadcast news and newspapers—to be more credible than social media (Austin et al., 2012; Gonçalves et al., 2021). The leading role of online sources on seeking information was also verified: online news, Facebook (49.9%) and websites of official institutions (35.2%) were the most accessed channels to search COVID information by the participants. However, despite the frequency of information-seeking on news media, it was not considered the most trustful source of information (only 38.3%). Experts and health care personnel were the more reliable sources by the Portuguese: for instance, 68.9% trust WHO and 69.5% health professionals but only 51.2% trust local authorities.

Second, when comparing results about information-seeking behavior with trust in government and health professionals as sources of information, data show that people who often search information on traditional media (particularly, television) trust more in the government. On the other hand, people that often use scientific and institutional sources (particularly, official websites), trust more in health professionals. This result seems in line with previous research. As experts in risk and communication highlight, using different sources to disseminate consistent information are at the core of any successful strategy (Seeger et al., 2003; Sellnow & Seeger, 2013; McLean & Ewart, 2015): scientists and specialists explain preventive measures on how to act in case of disease; government and politicians assure public institutions quality to respond to the crisis. The quantitative nature of our study and the structure of the survey did not allow learning the opinion of the Portuguese on these two levels of messages. It is however an important path for future research regarding the role and importance of intermediaries, as health professionals and experts, in building trust during risk communication processes.

The Portuguese trust healthcare personnel, particularly prestigious personalities, such as doctors, epidemiologists, or the director of the WHO. These sources of information are considered more trustworthy than the media or government authorities, at both the national (government and Directorate-General for Health) and local levels. A similar trend was also identified in the neighboring Spain (Moreno et al., 2020), which underlines the importance of giving more prominence to expert/technical sources than political sources in managing COVID-19 crisis communication.

Third, findings show that the people in Portugal had a primarily positive perception of the government's communication. Many had the impression that the government's information was timely and reliable. Even the most critical people, that is, those who consider that the government's communication has confused the population or has not revealed the whole truth, tend to trust the government and the Directorate-General for Health (69.12%). And clearly, people with positive opinion about government's communication management in Portugal get their information mainly from traditional news media. On the other hand, people that often use social media as sources of information are keener to trust digital influencers: 27% trust influencers from the health sector and health workers that share information on their social media accounts, and almost 20% trust influencers from very different fields, including alternative medicines. These findings pinpoint the importance of digital spokespersons, like YouTubers or Instagramers in contemporary societies. The problem is that online messages about COVID-19 may be instrumentalized for good but also for malicious purposes. Conspiracy theories, for example, have been debated in this context (Evanega, 2020; Fuchs, 2020; Pummerer et al., 2021).

As in many countries, Portugal also tried to fight against fake news and misinformation. The Directorate General of Health published the report "Recommendation for the press", advising on the importance of seeking official institutions as sources of information. Health authorities also designed campaigns with celebrities, both for TV prime time and social media, that alerted the population to the significance of referring to information from reliable sources (Gonçalves, 2013). Different channels and sources of information are of paramount importance to impact different groups of publics. If Instagram and Facebook are the favorite platforms (Data Report, 2022)[1] in Portugal, it is important that health authorities and government plan communication strategies on this digital forum.

All in all, this chapter introduces new empirical knowledge on the relation between sources of information and citizens trust in government crisis communication. As the choice of medium does not only influence the public's sense making of the crisis but also moderates their acceptance of crises messages and trust in the authorities and government, it is important to have a deep understanding of this variable in risk communication processes. Previous studies in the Portuguese context addressed media consumption but not in relation to citizens trust in government communication (Cardoso et al., 2020). We also can find research on health journalism during the pandemic period in Portugal (Lopes et al., 2021) however, it does not analyze news media relationship with citizens' trust in government and authorities. Our findings highlight that a greater use of news media usually correlates with trust in government sources, which, in turn, is also related to a positive opinion about the crisis management process.

In fact, in Portugal, contrary to the case of other countries, as the Netherlands, Belgium, or Austria, there were no major protests anti-lockdown but rather a high degree of respect for government-imposed rules in Portugal. As discussed by De Giorgi and Santana Pereira (2020), government approval ratings in Portugal increased between 2019 and 2020 – possibly aided by more consensus among political parties than in the other countries. Later, the national vaccination process also went smoothly, probably due to the relatively minor presence of anti-vaxxers in Portugal. The forceful leadership of the head of the national vaccination task force, a navy official, may be another fact to explain trust in government risk communication strategies, in a country that only emerged from dictatorship in 1974.

Note

1 Datareport Portugal 2022: https://datareportal.com/reports/digital-2022-portugal?rq=portugal (accessed on 09/06/2022).

References

Abu-Akel, A., Spitz, A., & West, R. (2021). The effect of spokesperson attribution on public health message sharing during the covid-19 pandemic. *PLoS One*, *16*(2), e0245100. https://doi.org/10.1371/journal.pone.0245100

Athaydes, A., Abreu, K., & Jesus, M. (2022). Brazil and the COVID-19 pandemic: Crisis communication management as opposed to public communication. In R. Tench, J. Meng & A. Moreno (Eds.), *Strategic communication in a global crisis* (pp. 220–239). Routledge.

Austin, L., Liu, B., & Jin, Y. (2012). How audiences seek out crisis information: Exploring the social-mediated crisis communication model. *Journal of Applied Communication Research*, *40*(2), 188–207. https://doi.org/10.1080/00909882.2012.654498

Bargain, O., & Aminjonov, U. (2020). Trust and compliance to public health policies in times of COVID-19. *Journal of Public Economics*, *192*, 104316. https://doi.org/10.1016/j.jpubeco.2020.104316

Blair, R., Morse B., & Tsai, L. (2017). Public health and public trust: Survey evidence from the Ebola virus disease epidemic in Liberia. *Social Science & Medicine*, *172*, 89–97. https://doi.org/10.1016/j.socscimed.2016.11.016

Cardoso, G., Baldi, V., Paisana, M., & Quintanilha (2020). *Pandemia e consumos mediáticos*. OberCom – Observatório de Comunicação.

Cinelli, M., Quattrociocchi, W., Galeazzi, A., Valensise, C. M., Brugnoli, E., Schmidt, A. L., Zola, P., Zollo, F., & Scala, A. (2020). The COVID-19 social media infodemic. *Scientific Reports*, *10*, 16598. https://doi.org/10.1038/s41598-020-73510-5

Cohen, J. (1988). *Statistical power analysis for the behavioral sciences* (2nd ed.). Lawrence Earlbaum.

De Giorgi, E., & Santana-Pereira, J. (2020). The exceptional case of post-Bailout Portugal: A comparative outlook. *South European Society and Politics*, *25*(2), 127–150. https://doi.org/10.1080/13608746.2021.1872152

Devos, T., Spini, D., & Schwartz, S. (2002). Conflicts among human values and trust in institutions. *British Journal of Social Psychology*, *41*(4), 481–494. https://doi.org/10.1348/014466602321149849

Diers-Lawson, A. (2020). *Crisis communication: Managing stakeholder relationship*. Routledge.

Dutta-Bergman, M. J. (2004). Complementarity in consumption of news types across traditional and new media. *Journal of Broadcasting & Electronic Media*, *48*(1), 41–60. https://psycnet.apa.org/doi/10.1207/s15506878jobem4801_3

Earle, T., & Siegrist, M. (2008). Trust, confidence and cooperation model: A framework for understanding the relation between trust and risk perception. *International Journal of Global Environmental Issues*, *8*(1–2), 17–29. https://doi.org/10.1504/IJGENVI.2008.017257

Earle, T. C., Siegrist, M., & Gutscher, H. (2010). Trust in risk management: Uncertainty and scepticism in the public mind. In T. C. Earle, M. Siegrist, & H. Gutscher (Eds.), *Trust, risk perception and the TCC model of cooperation* (pp. 1–49). Routledge. https://doi.org/10.4324/9781849773461

Evanega, S., Lynas, M., Adams, J., Smolenyak, K., & Insights, C.G. (2020). Corona- virus misinformation: Quantifying sources and themes in the COVID-19 'infodemic'. *JMIR Preprints*, *19*(10) [online]. https://allianceforscience.cornell.edu/wp-content/uploads/2020/10/Evanega-et-al-Coronavirus-misinformation-submitted_07_23_20.pdf

Financial Times. (2021). *Portugal suffers surging Covid-19 deaths after mastering first wave*. https://www.ft.com/content/fbeb622e-0a69-4f5c-a6fe-6653a72d2377

Frandsen, F., & Johansen, W. (2020). Public sector communication: Risk and crisis communication. In V. Luoma-aho & M. J. Canel (Eds.), *The handbook of public sector communication* (pp. 229–244). John Wiley & Sons, Inc.

Fraustino, J., Liu, B-F., & Jin, Y. (2017). Social media during disasters: A research synthesis and road map. In Y. Jin & L. Austin (Eds.), *Social media and crisis communication* (pp. 283–295). Routledge.

Fuchs, C. (2020). Everyday life and everyday communication in coronavirus capitalism. *TripleC: Communication, Capitalism & Critique*, *18*(1), 375–399. https://doi.org/10.31269/triplec.v18i1.1167

Gonçalves, M. (2021). Relatos de um "cenário de guerra": Como influenciadores e redes sociais estão a dar voz aos hospitais portugueses. *Jornal Observador*. https://observador.pt/2021/01/18/relatos-de-um-cenario-de-guerra-como-influenciadores-e-redes-sociais-estao-a-dar-voz-aos-hospitais-portugueses/

Gonçalves, G., Piñeiro-Naval, V., & de Sá, S. (2022). Risk communication and disinformation in Portugal: How media consumption affects understanding of Covid health-protective messages. In R. Tench, J. Meng, & A. Moreno (Eds.), *Strategic communication in a global crisis* (pp. 112–131). Routledge. https://doi.org/10.4324/9781003184669-12

Gonçalves, G., Piñeiro-Naval, V., & Toniolo, B. P. (2021). Who do the Portuguese trust? Government communication management in the Covid-19 pandemic. *Comunicação e Sociedade*, *40*, 169–187. https://doi.org/10.17231/comsoc.40(2021).3251

Hair, J. F., Black, W. C., Babin, B. J., & Anderson, R. E. (1999). *Multivariate data analysis*. Pearson Prentice Hall.

Johnson, B. T., Scott-Sheldon, L. A. J., Snyder, L. B., Noar, S. M., & Huedo-Medina, T. B. (2008). Contemporary approaches to meta-analysis in communication research. In A. F. Hayes, M. D. Slater, & L. B. Snyder (Eds.), *The Sage sourcebook of advanced data analysis methods for communication research* (pp. 311–347). Sage.

Kuipers, S., & Welsh, N. H. (2017). Taxonomy of the crisis and disaster literature: Themes and types in 34 years of research. *Risk, Hazards & Crisis in Public Policy*, *8*(4), 272–283. https://doi.org/10.1002/rhc3.12123

Laajalahti, A., Hyvärinen, J., & Vos, M. (2016). Crisis communication competence in co-producing safety with citizen groups. *Social Sciences*, *5*(1), 1–15. https://doi.org/10.3390/socsci5010013

Li, H. O.-Y., Bailey, A., Huynh, D., &, Chan, J. (2020). YouTube as a source of information on COVID-19: A pandemic of misinformation? *BMJ Global Health*, *5*, e002604. http://doi.org/10.1136/bmjgh-2020-002604

Liu, B. F., Fraustino, J. D., & Jin, Y. (2016). Social media use during disasters: How information form and source influence intended behavioral responses. *Communication Research*, *43*(5), 626–646. https://doi.org/10.1177/0093650214565917

Llewellyn, S. (2020). Covid-19: How to be careful with trust and expertise on social media. *BMJ*, *368*, m1160. https://doi.org/10.1136/bmj.m1160

Lopes, F., Santos, C. A., Peixinho, A. T., Magalhães, O. E., & Araújo, R. (2021). COVID-19: Uma pandemia que reconfigura o jornalismo? *Media & Jornalismo*, *21*(39), 57–75. https://doi.org/10.14195/2183-5462_39_3

Lu, X., & Jin, Y. (2020). Information vetting as a key component in social-mediated crisis communication: An exploratory study to examine the initial conceptualization. *Public Relations Review*, *46*(2), 101891. https://doi.org/10.1016/j.pubrev.2020.101891

Lundgren, R. E., & McMakin, A. H. (2013). *Risk communication: A handbook for communicating environmental safety and health risks*. Wiley.

McLean, H., & Ewart, J. (2015). Hindrance or help? A model for the involvement of politicians in communicating with publics during disasters. *International Journal of Mass Emergencies and Disasters*, *33*(2), 228–252. https://doi.org/10.1177/028072701503300205

Meyer, S., Ward, P., Coveney, J., & Rogers, W. (2014) Trust in the health system: An analysis and extension of the social theories of Giddens and Luhmann. *Health Social Review*, *17*(2), 177–186. https://doi.org/10.5172/hesr.451.17.2.177

Moreno, Á., Fuentes-Lara, C., & Navarro, C. (2020). Covid-19 communication management in Spain: Exploring the effect of information-seeking behavior and message reception in public's evaluation. *El profesional de la información*, *29*(4), e290402. https://doi.org/10.3145/epi.2020.jul.02

Olsson, E. K. (2014). Crisis communication in public organisations: Dimensions of crisis communication revisited. *Journal of Contingencies and Crisis Management*, *22*(2), 113–125. https://doi.org/10.1111/1468-5973.12047

Park, S., Boatwright, B., & Johnson-Avery, E. (2019). Information channel preference in health crisis: Exploring the roles of perceived risk, preparedness, knowledge, and intent to follow directives. *Public Relations Review*, *45*(5), 101794. https://doi.org/10.1016/j.pubrev.2019.05.015

Pummerer, L., Böhm, R., Lilleholt, L., Winter, K., Zettler, I., & Sassenberg, K. (2021). Conspiracy theories and their societal effects during the COVID-19 pandemic. *Social Psychological and Personality Science*, *13*(1), 49–59. https://doi.org/10.1177/19485506211000217

Reich, Z., Bentman, M., & Jackman, O. (2011). A crisis communication guide for public organisations. In M. Vos, R. Lund, Z. Reich, & H. Harro-Loi (Eds.), *Developing a crisis communication scorecards: outcomes of an international research project 2008–2011*. University of Jyväskylä. http://www.crisiscommunication.fi/criscomscore/files/download/GUIDE_for_Public_Organisations.pdf

Renn, O., & Levine, D. (1991). Credibility and trust in risk communication. *Communicating Risks to the Public: International Perspectives*, *4*, 175–218.

Robinson, J. P., Shaver, P. R., & Wrightsman, L. S. (1991). Criteria for scale selection and evaluation. In J. P. Robinson, P. R. Shaver, & L. S. Wrightsman (Eds.), *Measures of personality and social psychological attitudes* (pp. 1–16). Academic Press.

Seeger, M. W., Pechta, L., Price, S., Lubell, K. M., Rose, D. A., Sapru, S., Chansky, M. C., & Smith, B. J. (2018). A conceptual model for evaluating emergency risk communication in public health. *Health Security*, *16*(3), 193–203. https://doi.org/10.1089/hs.2018.0020

Seeger, M. W., Sellnow, T. L., &, Ulmer, R. R. (2003). *Communication and organizational crisis*. Praeger.

Sellnow, D. D., Johansson, B., Sellnow, T. L., & Lane, D. R. (2019). Toward a global understanding of the effects of the IDEA model for designing instructional risk and crisis messages: A food contamination experiment in Sweden. *Journal of Contingencies and Crisis Management*, *27*, 102–115. https://doi.org/10.1111/1468-5973.12234

Sellnow, T. L., & Seeger, M. W. (2013). *Theorizing crisis communication*. Wiley.

Siegrist, M., & Cvetkovich, G. (2000). Perception of hazards: The role of social trust and knowledge. *Risk Analysis*, *20*(5), 713–720. https://doi.org/10.1111/0272-4332.205064

Tai, Z., & Sun, T. (2007). Media dependencies in a changing media environment: The case of the 2003 SARS epidemic in China. *New Media & Society*, *9*(6), 987–1009. https://doi.org/10.1177/1461444807082691

Valentini, C., Ihlen, O. & Tench, R. (2022). A question of trust: Exploring trust concepts, experiences and early observations from Europe. In R. Tench, J. Meng & A. Moreno (Eds.), *Strategic Communication in a Global Crisis*. Routledge. https://doi.org/10.4324/9781003184669

WHO. (2011). Report of the Review Committee on the functioning of the international health regulations (2005) in relation to pandemic (H1N1) 2009. World Health Organization. https://apps.who.int/gb/ebwha/pdf_files/WHA64/A64_10-en.pdf

Wukich, C. (2016). Government social media messages across disaster phases. *Journal of Contingencies and Crisis Management*, *24*(4), 230–243. https://doi.org/10.1111/1468-5973.12119

Index

For Product Safety Concerns and Information please contact our EU representative GPSR@taylorandfrancis.com
Taylor & Francis Verlag GmbH, Kaufingerstraße 24, 80331 München, Germany

www.ingramcontent.com/pod-product-compliance
Ingram Content Group UK Ltd.
Pitfield, Milton Keynes, MK11 3LW, UK
UKHW022040061126
477531UK00009B/442

* 9 7 8 1 0 3 2 4 5 0 8 0 3 *